**The Mathematical
Theory of Insurance**

The Mathematical Theory of Insurance

An Annotated Selection of Papers on
Insurance published 1960–1972

Karl Borch

Lexington Books
D.C. Heath and Company
Lexington, Massachusetts
Toronto   London

Library of Congress Cataloging in Publication Data

Borch, Karl Henrik.
  The mathematical theory of insurance.

  Bibliography: p.
  1. Insurance—Mathematics—Addresses, essays,
lectures. I. Title.
HG8781.B68   368'.001'51   73-11670
ISBN 0-669-86942-2

Published simultaneously in Canada.

Printed in the United States of America.

International Standard Book Number: 0-669-86942-2

Library of Congress Catalog Card Number: 73-11670

Contents

Foreword

Karl Borch is a well-known name to all of us who have worked in the theory of the economics of uncertainty. In particular, his papers on reinsurance clearly exhibit the importance of understanding markets for the transfer of uncertainty from one economic agent to another. The reinsurance treaties provide a remarkably clear paradigm for this phenomenon. Dr. Borch quickly grasped the importance of the work that has been done on the economics of uncertainty and the value of the expected-utility hypothesis. He has made direct contributions to economic analysis outside of the field of insurance, but perhaps his most valuable work has been in illuminating the special problems of the field of insurance, for he clearly displays many of the deep issues of uncertainty theory.

We are indeed fortunate to have Dr. Borch's papers, previously published in a variety of scattered sources, now collected in one volume. We can now read the papers we have missed and profit from them in the further development of this field where insurance and classical economics intersect.

Kenneth J. Arrow
Harvard University

Acknowledgments

The author and the publisher, D.C. Heath and Company, wish to thank the following associations and societies for permission to reprint the articles included in this book.

International Actuarial Association, Brussels

Chapter 1: An Attempt to Determine the Optimum Amount of Stop Loss Reinsurance: *Transactions of the XVI International Congress of Actuaries,* (1960), Vol. 1, pp. 597–610.

Chapter 15: Payment of Dividend by Insurance Companies: *Transactions of the 17th International Congress of Actuaries,* (1964), Vol. III, pp. 131–143.

Chapter 19: Risk Management and Company Objectives: *Transactions of the 19th International Congress of Actuaries,* (1972), Vol. II, pp. 613–619.

Chapter 21: The Optimal Portfolio of Assets in an Insurance Company: *Transactions of the 18th International Congress of Actuaries,* (1968), Vol. III, pp. 21–31.

Chapter 22: Insurance and the Theory of Financial Markets: *Transactions of the 19th International Congress of Actuaries* (1972), Vol. III, pp. 193–201

The ASTIN Committee of the International Actuarial Association, London

Chapter 2: The Optimal Reinsurance Treaty: *The ASTIN Bulletin* (1969), Vol. V, pp. 293–297.

Chapter 4: Reciprocal Reinsurance Treaties: *The ASTIN Bulletin* (1960), Vol. I, pp. 170–191.

Chapter 6: The Utility Concept applied to the Theory of Insurance: *The ASTIN Bulletin* (1961), Vol. I, pp. 245–255.

Chapter 12: Recent Developments in Economic Theory and their Application to Insurance: *The ASTIN Bulletin* (1963), Vol. II, pp. 322–341.

Chapter 14: The Economic Theory of Insurance: *The ASTIN Bulletin* (1967), Vol. IV, pp. 252–264.

Chapter 16: Control of a Portfolio of Insurance Contracts: *The ASTIN Bulletin* (1966), Vol. IV, pp. 59–71.

Chapter 17: Dynamic Decision Problems in an Insurance Company: *The ASTIN Bulletin* (1968), Vol. V, pp. 118–131.

Chapter 20: The Rescue of an Insurance Company after Ruin: *The ASTIN Bulletin* (1968), Vol. V, pp. 280–292.

Chapter 23: Application of Game Theory to some Problems in Automobile Insurance: *The ASTIN Bulletin* (1962), Vol. II, pp. 208–221.

**The Editorial Board of the Scandinavian
Actuarial Journal, Stockholm**

Chapter 3: Reciprocal Reinsurance Treaties seen as a Two-Person Co-operative Game: *Skandinavisk Aktuarietidskrift* (1960), pp. 29–58.

Chapter 8: The Objectives of an Insurance Company: *Skandinavisk Aktuarietidskrift* (1962), pp. 162–175.

Chapter 9: The Safety Loading of Reinsurance Premiums: *Skandinavisk Aktuarietidskrift* (1960), pp. 163–184.

Chapter 11: A Contribution to the Theory of Reinsurance Markets: *Skandinavisk Aktuarietidskrift* (1962), pp. 176–189.

**American Risk and Insurance Association, Inc.,
Bloomington, Illinois**

Chapter 5: Some Elements of a Theory of Reinsurance: *The Journal of Insurance,* September 1961, pp. 35–43.

The Society of Actuaries, New York

Chapter 7: Utility Theory: *Transactions of the Society of Actuaries* (1969), Vol. XXI, pp. 343–349.

The Econometric Society, New Haven, Connecticut

Chapter 10: Equilibrium in a Reinsurance Market: *Econometrica,* (1962), pp. 424–444.

Nederlandse Reassurantie Groep N.V., Amsterdam

Chapter 13: Ends and Means in Actuarial Science: *Quarterly Letter from the Algemeene Reinsurance Companies,* Jubilee Number, July 1964, Vol. 2, pp. 28–38.

Royal Statistical Society, London

Chapter 18: The Theory of Risk: *Journal of the Royal Statistical Society,* Series B, Vol. 29, (1967), pp. 432–452.

Preface

This volume contains twenty-three papers published in different journals over the years 1960–1972. The papers have been selected from the author's published work on insurance and related subjects over these years. They deal with many different aspects of insurance, but all the papers are in one way or another based on the application of game theory and decision theory to problems in insurance.

These theories open promising possibilities of formulating insurance problems in a more meaningful and more relevant manner than it was in the traditional framework. These possibilities are generally recognized. It is hard to find a respectable insurance journal that does not from time to time publish papers in which the author argues or demonstrates that some new methods from operations research or economic theory can be successfully applied to problems in insurance. It is really surprising that so far no book on such applications is available in English. The only book on the subject seems to be one by Wolff[1] from 1968. This book has had a considerable influence—at least in Europe—but apparently not so much influence that it has been superseded by a more recent work.

In journals devoted to economic theory, management science, and operations research, one can find many papers in which authors who have developed general methods of analysis look to insurance for application. A good example is a paper by Mossin,[2] which will be discussed in Part II. One of the first contributions was made by Eisner and Strotz.[3]

The author of the papers in this book is an actuary, who discovered relatively late in life the relevance and the fascinations of economic theory. This discovery was in the air, and during the last ten to fifteen years it has been made by many actuaries. Some people may find it convenient to have a collection of these papers bound in one volume. The possible interest of a group of actuaries and insurance specialists cannot alone justify the publication of a book. It is the author's hope that the book will find readers also among economists, and that some economists will discover the fascination of some insurance problems and see their relevance to more general problems in economics.

There are many important aspects of the theory of insurance which are not mentioned in this book. A reader will find little about the classical mathematics of life insurance that—although the field is well worked—still dominates many actuarial journals. He will also find little about the marketing or "selling" of

---

1. K. H. Wolff, *Methoden der Unternehmensforschung im Versicherungswesen,* Springer Verlag, 1968.

2. J. Mossin, "Aspects of Rational Insurance Purchasing," *Journal of Political Economy* (1968): 553–568.

3. R. Eisner and R. Strotz, "Flight Insurance and the Theory of Choice," *Journal of Political Economy* (1961): 355–368.

insurance, a subject that occupies a central place in the insurance literature. There is little theory on this subject, and it should be a challenging task to develop a satisfactory theory of insurance markets.

It is, however, clear that the insurance market in many respects will be different from markets familiar in other parts of economic theory. For many kinds of insurance there must exist a point when demand is completely satisfied. When everything afloat is insured up to its full value, it will clearly be impossible to sell more marine insurance. The same must hold for fire and automobile collision insurance. This does not, of course, mean that the market is stationary. New insurable objects are created all the time, and changes in legislation may at any time create new problems and new markets in all kinds of liability insurance. Still, a saturation point must exist.

The situation may obviously be different in life insurance, which usually contains an element of savings, and which generally implies that the insurance buyer gives up present consumption for the benefits of his heirs. There are no obvious limits to which this postponement of consumption can be pushed, so hard-driving sellers of life insurance may possibly expand the market.

It is often argued that insurance has a low price elasticity, in the sense that an insurance company cannot increase its sales substantially by lowering premiums. This is natural if the market is almost saturated, and if customers are reluctant to change their insurance company. It is, however, also argued that a company can increase its sales more by increasing the commission paid to its agents than by reducing premiums. Both these actions will, of course, imply a reduction of the company's premium receipts per policy. If this argument is correct, we will get a market that essentially will be similar to those we know from classical economic theory. The explaining element will not be the rationality of the consumer, however, but the actions of the middlemen, the insurance salesmen. Similar effects may exist in markets other than the insurance market, and the whole problem should be worthy of more detailed studies.

These remarks inevitably lead to a consideration of the "transaction costs," which are usually assumed away in economic theory. It is evident that the best possible security would be offered if every risk in the world were insured in one single insurance company. This does not happen in practice, presumably because transaction costs would be prohibitive. The really large risks are, however, spread through the international reinsurance market, so that they really are covered by a consortium of all major insurance companies in the world. This indicates that there must be some trade-off between risk and transaction costs. I think this is a central problem in the theory of insurance, and some insight in the problem should enable us to decide if our present system of insurance is optimal or not.

Karl Borch

Part I
The Optimal Form of Reinsurance Contracts

A reinsurance contract is essentially an insurance policy issued by one company—the reinsurer—to another company, usually called the "ceding company," or the "direct underwriter."

The early reinsurance arrangements were almost invariable made on a *proportional* basis. The typical situation was that the direct underwriter had accepted an insurance contract, under which he received a premium P, and undertook to pay a claim represented by a stochastic variable X, with a distribution $F(x) = \Pr(X \leqslant x)$. The direct underwriter would then cede a quota or proportion $(1 - q)$ to the reinsurer. In this transaction the reinsurer would receive an amount $(1 - k)P$ as premium, and he would undertake to pay an amount $(1 - k)x$, if the total claim payable under the contract should amount to x.

The net premium $\bar{P}$ for an insurance contract is the expected value of the claim payment, that is,

$$\bar{P} = E(X) = \int_0^\infty x \, dF(x)$$

The net premium is smaller than the gross premium, and the relation between the two is usually expressed as

$$P = (1 + \lambda)\bar{P}$$

where λ is referred to as the "loading factor." The loading must cover the administrative expenses of the company, and the agent's commission, and it usually contains an element generally referred to as "loading for profit." This is really a "risk premium," but this term is not used in insurance. In a reinsurance contract, λ is usually referred to as "commission." The administrative costs of the reinsurer are usually negligible in comparison to those of the direct underwriter, so the loading may be lower on the reinsurance contract than on the direct contract. A reinsurer will, however, usually demand a higher "loading for profit" than a direct underwriter.

Proportional reinsurance is relatively easy to handle. Few computations are necessary in addition to computing the net premium for the direct contract. Proportional reinsurance is usually done on "original terms." This means that the reinsurer accept the premium charged by the ceding company as adequate, so that he is willing to cover a fixed proportion of the risk, if as compensation he receives the same proportion of the premium. If the ceding company has underrated the risk, it may be unable to obtain proportional reinsurance on original terms.

Nonproportional reinsurance contracts have been known for a long time,

1

but these forms of reinsurance became widely used only after World War II. The oldest and most common form of nonproportional reinsurance is the "excess loss" contract. Under this contract the direct underwriter will pay the whole claim, if it is smaller than a fixed amount M. If the claim should exceed M, the whole excess will be paid by the reinsurer. The net premium, i.e., the expected claim payment by the reinsurer, will be

$$\bar{P}_M = \int_M^\infty (x - M)\, dF(x) \tag{1}$$

This expression may appear simple, and $\bar{P}_M$ is easy to compute if the distribution $F(x)$ is known. For large M the net premium P_M will depend on the extreme tail of the distribution. This is the domain of rare events, and usually past experience provides little information about the shape of the distribution. The computation of the net premium for an excess of loss contract can, therefore, in practice be a formidable problem, or be little more than an informed guess.

Excess loss reinsurance applies to a single insurance contract. The same ideas can be applied to a portfolio of insurance contracts, and is then usually called "stop loss" reinsurance. Such "collective" reinsurance contracts are simple to administrate and correspond better to the needs of the two parties. It is after all the total result, the claim payments under the contracts in the portfolio as a whole, which is important, not the payments under single contracts in the portfolio.

The total amount of claim payments under the contracts in a portfolio will be a stochastic variable x with a distribution $F(x)$. If claim payments under different contracts are stochastically independent, this distribution will be the convolution of all the distributions defined by the contracts in the portfolio. The net premium of the stop loss contract can be computed by an expression of the same form as (1). The problems of estimating the tail of the distribution will, however, be much more difficult for a portfolio than for a single contract.

Several varieties of these reinsurance forms are in current use. There may, for instance, be an upper limit N on the reinsurer's liability, or he may pay only a fraction k, of claims exceeding this amount. The net premium for a reinsurance contract of this kind will be

$$\bar{P} = \int_M^N (x - M)\, dF(x) + k \int_N^\infty (x - N)\, dF(x) \tag{2}$$

The most general reinsurance contract for a portfolio is defined by a function $y(x)$ = amount the reinsurer will pay if claims amount to x. The net premium for this contract will be

$$\bar{P}_y = \int_0^\infty y(x)\, dF(x)$$

Two central problems in nonproportional reinsurance are:

1. Estimate net premiums of the form (1) or (2), from relevant statistics. There is an extensive literature concerning this problem. A representative collection of the earlier papers on the subject can be found in the book by Vajda [1].

2. Determine the best reinsurance arrangement for an insurance company in a given situation. This problem may consist in finding the optimal values of the parameters M, N, and k in (2).

The latter of these problems is taken up in Chapter 1. The purpose of reinsurance is to reduce risk, and risk in insurance has traditionally been measured by the standard deviation or the variance of claim payments. This leads to the mathematical problem of determining the reinsurance contract which will give the greatest reduction in variance, for a given net premium. The solution is, not surprisingly, the stop loss contract. The mathematical proof that I gave is valid under some fairly narrow assumptions. It has been improved and generalized by Kahn and Ohlin in papers referred to in Chapter 2.

In Chapter 2 I argue that the problem I formulated in 1960 is not really relevant, in spite of its mathematical interest. The net premium may be negligible for an insurance against some catastrophic event, and one cannot expect a reinsurer to accept a contract of this kind with a "normal" loading, proportional to the net premium. There are, at least, two parties to any reinsurance arrangement, and a treaty can be called optimal only if all parties consider it as the best possible arrangement. This point was made by Vajda [2], who showed that a proportional contract would give the reinsurer the smallest variance for a fixed net premium. The compromise should then be something between the Stop Loss and the proportional contracts, and this is one of the problems discussed in Part II.

References

1. Vajda, S. (ed.). *Non Proportional Reinsurance* (Leyden, *E.J. Brill,* 1955).
2. Vajda, S. "Minimum Variance Reinsurance," *The ASTIN Bulletin* (1962): 257-260.

1

An Attempt to Determine the Optimum Amount of Stop Loss Reinsurance

1. Introduction

1.1. The purpose of this paper is not to try to lay down a set of golden rules as to how an insurance company should arrange its reinsurance. It will indeed be impossible to establish objective rules of this kind. Whether certain risks should be reinsured or not, is a decision which in the last resort will depend on subjective judgments. The theory of risk has to take these judgments as data, it cannot say whether a certain judgment is correct or not. Armed with the techniques of modern risk theory, actuaries can analyze a reinsurance contract, and state that it means, for instance that the company will forego 25% of its expected profits, in order to reduce the probability of ruin before some future date from 0.01 to 0.001. The theory of risk can help us to present the problem in such a clear-cut manner—which in itself is no mean achievement—but it cannot help us to decide whether the company should or should not accept the contract in question. The decision which has to be taken in a case like this is familiar from other parts of business economics. It consists of a choice between high profits and relatively high risk on one hand, and modest profits and high security on the other. This must be a subjective judgment, no theory can tell us which of the two courses of action is the "best," except in trivial cases. The purpose of this paper is to analyze some of the elements which enter into a decision to accept a reinsurance contract, and to try to determine when a contract can be said to be "better" than another in some absolute or objective sense.

1.2. When a company makes arrangements for reinsurance, it seeks to reduce —possibly to zero—the probability of suffering losses which may jeopardize the position of the company. The company obviously has to pay for the security it obtains in this way, and we can consider the company as a buyer of security on the reinsurance market. How much security the company should buy at the prevailing price will depend on the company's objectives and overall policy, i.e., the subjective judgments referred to in the preceding paragraph. However, here we encounter a difficulty of a different nature. There is no obvious way of measuring the amount of security the company buys. In this paper the *variance* of the expected loss is chosen as a measure of risk. This is an arbitrary measure, and it is in many ways inferior to some other measures, such as the "probability of ruin." It is however a measure which lends itself fairly easily to operational treat-

5

ment. The paper deals almost exclusively with stop loss reinsurance, since the choice of variance as measure of risk makes this form of reinsurance the most efficient one.

2. Stop Loss Reinsurance

2.1. We consider an insurance company which holds a portfolio of ν policies. The probability of a claim x_i on the ith policy is $dF_i(x_i)$. We assume that $x_i \geqslant 0$ and that the distribution functions $F_i(x)$ all have finite mean and variance. We further assume that $x_1, x_2, \ldots, x_\nu$ are statistically independent. The probability that total claims on the whole portfolio amount to x will then be $dF(x)$ where

$$x = x_1 + x_2 + \ldots + x_\nu$$

and where $F(x)$ is the convolution of the distribution functions $F_1, F_2, \ldots, F_\nu$. We will call $F(x)$ the *risk distribution* of the company. It follows from our assumptions that the mean and variance of $F(x)$ are finite.

2.2. We assume that to accept this risk the company has received a net premium, which by definition is

$$\pi = \int_0^\infty x \, dF$$

In general the net premium will carry a positive loading λ so that the total receipts of the company are $\pi + \lambda$. The expected profit on the portfolio is then

$$\pi + \lambda - \int_0^\infty x \, dF = \lambda$$

In the following we will disregard the loading λ. Our purpose is to examine the relative merits of alternative reinsurance arrangements, and these can be assumed to be independent of the profits the company expects to make on its direct underwriting. It appears rational, that one reinsurance contract is considered better than another, regardless of how the direct premium has been loaded, although this may not necessarily be in accordance with current practice. The point will be further discussed in para. 3.6.

2.3. The risk distribution will have a shape as indicated in Figure 1. For simplicity we have taken the origin at $x = 0$, although a claim $x < \pi$ actually corresponds to a profit for the company. The purpose of reinsurance is essentially to change the shape of the risk distribution, so that it becomes more favorable to the company. In general there will be little difficulty in deciding that one risk

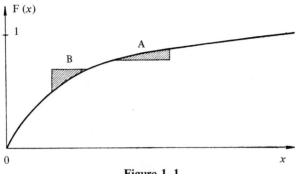

Figure 1-1

distribution is more favorable than another. For instance if $G(x) \geqslant F(x)$ for all x, $G(x)$ is clearly better than $F(x)$. The difficulties discussed in para. 1.2 come in when we want to say how much better one distribution is than another, i.e., how much a company would be justified in paying in order to change its risk distribution from $F(x)$ to $G(x)$.

2.4. Theoretically the risk function can be thrown into any shape by appropriate reinsurance arrangements. It will for instance be possible to move a "block of probability" from the position A to the position B as indicated on the graph. We will study the effect of such a transformation on the mean and variance of $F(x)$.

2.5. Let A and B be two Borel sets of nonnegative numbers, such that every number in B is smaller than or equal to any number in A. Let $\alpha(x)$ and $\beta(x)$ be two nonnegative functions such that

$$\int_A d\alpha(x) = \int_B d\beta(x) = a < 1$$

and

$$\int_{A'} d\alpha(x) \leqslant \int_{A'} dF(x)$$

for any subset A' of A.

We now consider the effect of a reinsurance contract which changes $F(x)$ to $F(x) - \alpha(x) + \beta(x)$. The mean will then change from

$$m_1 = \int_0^\infty x \, dF(x)$$

to

$$m_1' = m_1 - (\textstyle\int_A x\, d\alpha(x) - \int_B x\, d\beta(x))$$

The variance is changed from

$$V = \textstyle\int_0^\infty x^2\, dF(x) - m_1^2$$

to

$$V' = \textstyle\int_0^\infty x^2\, dF(x) - \int_A x^2\, d\alpha(x) + \int_B x^2\, d\beta(x) - {m_1'}^2$$

$$= \textstyle\int_0^\infty x^2\, dF(x) - m_1^2 - \int_A x^2\, d\alpha + \int_B x^2\, d\beta - 2m_1 + c^2$$

where

$$\textstyle\int_A x\, d\alpha(x) - \int_B x\, d\beta(x) = c$$

2.6. If this reinsurance contract is based on the fundamental *Principle of Equivalence*, the reduction of the mean $m_1 - m_1' = c$ will be the net premium which the company has to pay for the reinsurance. We will now take this net premium as given, and seek the reinsurance contract which will give the greatest reduction in the variance. In other words, we seek to maximize $V - V'$, subject to the conditions

$$\textstyle\int_A x\, d\alpha(x) - \int_B x\, d\beta(x) = c$$

$$\textstyle\int_A d\alpha = \int_B d\beta = a$$

where c is a given constant.

By rearranging the terms we obtain

$$V - V' = \textstyle\int_A x^2\, d\alpha - [\int_B x^2\, d\beta - (\int_B x\, d\beta)^2] - (\int_B x\, d\beta)^2 - 2m_1 c + c^2$$

A necessary condition for a maximum is that the term

$$\textstyle\int_B x^2\, d\beta - (\int_B x\, d\beta)^2$$

shall vanish, since this will not restrict the variation of any of the other terms. The condition

$$\textstyle\int_B x^2\, d\beta - (\int_B x\, d\beta)^2 = 0$$

implies that the set B consists of one single point n, which contains the whole probability mass a.

Hence

$\int_B x \, d\beta = an$

Our problem is then reduced to maximize

$\int_A x^2 \, d\alpha - a^2 n^2$

Necessary conditions for a maximum are:

(i) That $\alpha(x)$ everywhere assumes its upper bound $F(x)$.
(ii) That the set A is as extensive as possible, i.e., that it consists of all real numbers greater than n.

Hence

$$\max (V - V') = \int_n^\infty x^2 \, dF(x) - a^2 n^2 - 2m_1 + c^2$$

where n is the unique root of the equation

$$\int_n^\infty x \, dF(x) = c + an$$

2.7. The reinsurance contract we have determined in this manner, is nothing but the familiar *stop loss* cover contract, stipulating that if the loss on the portfolio should exceed n, the excess will be paid by the reinsurer. We can say that this is the "most efficient" form of reinsurance since it gives the greatest reduction in the variance of the portfolio for a given net premium. Whether it also is the cheapest form will depend on the loading. If the loading for all kinds of reinsurance is a fixed proportion of the net premium, stop loss will also be the cheapest form of reinsurance. Should the loading be some function of the variance, for instance, proportional to the standard deviation, it will be a matter of subjective judgment, whether stop loss is better than other forms of reinsurance.

2.8. By reinsurance a company transfers a part of its risks, and cedes a part of the net premium

$$m_1 = \int_0^\infty x \, dF(x)$$

to the reinsurer. By stop loss reinsurance, the company retains

$$P_1 = \int_0^n x \, dF(x) + n \int_n^\infty dF(x) = \int_0^n [1 - F(x)] \, dx$$

and cedes

$$P_2 = \int_n^\infty x \, dF(x) - n \int_n^\infty dF(x) = m_1 - \int_0^n [1 - F(x)] \, dx$$

Of the variance of the original portfolio

$$V = \int_0^\infty x^2 \, dF - (\int_0^\infty x \, dF)^2$$

the company retains

$$V_1 = \int_0^n x^2 \, dF(x) + n^2 \int_n^\infty dF - (\int_0^n x \, dF + n \int_n^\infty dF)^2$$

$$= 2 \int_0^n x \, [1 - F(x)] \, dx - [\int_0^n [1 - F(x)] \, dx]^2$$

and cedes

$$V_2 = \int_n^\infty x^2 \, dF(x) - m_1^2 - n^2 \int_n^\infty dF + (\int_0^n x \, dF + n \int_n^\infty dF)^2$$

$$= V - 2 \int_0^n x \, [1 - F(x)] \, dx + [\int_0^n [1 - F(x)] \, dx]^2$$

The expressions for the two parts of the variance can easily be derived directly by integrating dF from 0 to n and from n to ∞ and adding the mass concentrated in the point n. They follow however immediately from the results in the previous paragraph, since $V_2 = \max(V - V')$.

2.9.   The reinsurer will by the contract assume responsibility for a portfolio where the expected claim is equal to the net premium P_2. However the variance V_r of the portfolio which the reinsurer accepts is smaller than the variance reduction in the portfolio of the ceding ocmpany. We have

$$V_r = \int_n^\infty (x - n)^2 \, dF(x) - P_2^2$$

$$= \int_n^\infty x^2 \, dF + n^2 \int_n^\infty dF - 2n \int_n^\infty x \, dF - (m_1 - \int_0^n [1 - F(x)] \, dx)^2$$

$$= V - 2 \int_0^n x \, [1 - F(x)] \, dx - 2nm_1 + 2(n + m_1) \int_0^n [1 - F(x)] \, dx$$

$$- (\int_0^n [1 - F(x)] \, dx)^2$$

To show that V_r is smaller than V_2 we consider the difference

$$D(n) = V_2 - V_r = 2nm_1 - 2(n + m_1) \int_0^n [1 - F(x)] \, dx + 2(\int_0^n [1 - F(x)] \, dx)$$

or $$D(n) = 2(n - \int_0^n [1 - F(x)] \, dx)(m_1 - \int_0^n [1 - F(x)] \, dx)$$

Since both factors on the right are positive, except at the limits, where $F(n) = 0$ and $F(n) = 1$, D will be positive, except at the two limits, where it will be zero, i.e., $D(o) = D(\infty) = 0$.

2.10. At first it may seem surprising that a certain amount of variance so to speak disappears by reinsurance. The statistical explanation is that the risks in the ceded portfolio are assumed independent of whatever risks the reinsurer might hold, and therefore lead to a smaller total variance when added to this portfolio than when added to the portfolio of the ceding company. The difference D has therefore some of the characteristics of a covariance, and can in fact directly be interpreted as such. It is recognized as good insurance practice to mix as many independent risks as possible in a portfolio, so it does make some sense that the advantage to the ceding company appears greater than the disadvantage of the reinsurer. One should however remember that we reached this result by considering variance reduction as the sole purpose of the reinsurance arrangement. This is certainly not the whole story, since the variance is only one of the many characteristics of a distribution function. In practice the distributions which will occur in connection with stop loss reinsurance can be extremely skew. If we take this into account, for instance, by considering the moments of the third order, we may well find that the disadvantage is definitely on the reinsurer, and that he has to be duly compensated for this by appropriate loading of the premium.

2.11. We found in para. 2.9 that $D(n) > 0$ for all n such that $0 < F(n) < 1$, and that $D(o) = D(\infty) = 0$. Since $D(n)$ is a continuous function of n, it follows that it has a maximum for at least one finite, positive value of n. This value (or values) is determined by

$$\frac{dD}{dn} = 2F(n)\,(m_1 - \int_0^n [1 - F(x)]\,dx)$$

$$\div 2\,[1 - F(n)]\,(n - \int_0^n [1 - F(x)]\,dx) = 0$$

or $n = \int_0^n [1 - F(x)]\,dx + \dfrac{F(n)}{1 - F(n)}(m_1 - \int_0^n [1 - F(x)]\,dx)$

This equation is satisfied for $n = 0$. The equation must have at least one positive root. This root will be unique only if we make assumptions about the risk distribution far more restrictive than those we have made in our previous discussion. We will not discuss the necessary assumptions, but we note that if the risk distribution is symmetrical, i.e., if

$$F(m_1 + x) = 1 - F(m_1 - x) \qquad \text{so that } F(m_1) = \frac{1}{2},$$

m_1 is a root in the equation.
    For this value we obtain

$$D(m_1) = 2\left(m_1 - \int_0^{m_1}[1 - F(x)]\,dx\right)^2 = 2\left(\int_0^{m_1}F(x)\,dx\right)^2$$

Since in the symmetric case the range of the risk distribution is from 0 to $2m_1$, we have

$$\int_0^{m_1}F(x)\,dx = (xF(x))_0^{m_1} - \int_0^{m_1}x\,dF = \int_0^{m_1}(m_1 - x)\,dF$$

$$= \frac{1}{2}\int_0^{2m_1}|x - m_1|\,dF$$

Hence $D(m_1) = \dfrac{1}{2}(\text{mean deviation})^2$

2.12.   As a numerical example we will consider the case where the risk distribution has the simple form

$$F(x) = 1 - e^{-x/a}$$

We have

$$m_1 = a \quad\text{and}\quad V = a^2$$

We find

$$\frac{dD}{dn} = 2e^{-n/a}(-n + 2a - 2ae^{-n/a})$$

The equation

$$\frac{dD}{dn} = 0$$

has the three roots $n = 0$, $n = \infty$, and $n = 1.594a$.

Only the last of these is of interest. For this value of n we have

$$P_1 = a(1 - e^{-n/a}) = 0.797a$$

$$P^2 = ae^{-n/a} = 0.203a$$

$$V_1 = a^2 - 2ane^{-n/a} - a^2e^{-2n/a} = 0.3032a^2$$

$$V_2 = 2an + a^2e^{-2n/a} = 0.6968a^2$$

$$V_r = 2a^2e^{-n/a} - a^2e^{-2n/a} = 0.3648a^2$$

$$D = 2a\,(n - a + ae^{-n/a})\,e^{-n/a} = 0.3320a^2$$

When the risk distribution has this particular shape, almost one-third of the variance "disappears," by an excess of loss ratio of about 160% of the net premium.

3. The Market for Reinsurance

3.1. Let as before V stand for the variance of the portfolio of an insurance company. Let R be the funds the company has in addition to the net premium it received by underwriting the portfolio. R will essentially consist of the loading of the net premium, less underwriting costs, plus free funds the company had before underwriting the portfolio in question. We will assume that the company acts on a set of rules, i.e., that it has a policy which enables it to compare its initial situation (R, V) with another situation (R', V') and decide whether the new situation is better, worse, or equivalent to the original situation. It is then possible to define a "utility function" $U(R, V)$, so that $U(R, V) > U(R', V')$ if (R, V) is preferred to (R', V'). We assume that the purpose of the company's reinsurance operations is to maximize $U(R, V)$.

3.2. We assume further that there exists a market for reinsurance so that:

(i)   Any company can "place" a portfolio with variance V on this market by paying a consideration $P = g(V)$ in addition to the net premium of the portfolio.

(ii) By assuming responsibility for a portfolio with variance V a company can obtain an amount $P = g(V)$ plus the net premium of this portfolio.

The existence of such a market, i.e., of a single-valued, continuous function $g(V)$ cannot be taken for granted. It is known from the theory of equilibrium of exchange that a series of conditions must be fulfilled in order to make sure that the Walras' system of exchange equations shall have a solution which has an economic meaning, i.e., a set of nonnegative prices for all goods which enter the market. It will take us too far to discuss these conditions here. We will therefore assume that a nonnegative function $g(V)$ exists, and that it has a continuous derivative.

3.3. Assume now that the company wants to reduce the variance of its portfolio by an amount V_2. This means that it has to place on the market a portfolio with variance $V_2 - D$. The consideration it has to pay to place this portfolio will be $g(V_2 - D)$. The company will then seek to determine V_2 so that the function

$$U([R - g(V_2 - D)],\, [V - V_2])$$

is maximized.

The value of V_2 which maximizes this function must satisfy the equation

$$\frac{\partial U}{\partial R} g'(V_2 - D) \left(1 - \frac{dD}{dV_2}\right) + \frac{\partial U}{\partial V_2} = 0$$

Whether this equation has a meaningful solution, i.e., a solution V_2 such that $0 \leqslant V_2 \leqslant V$ will depend on the initial values of R and V and on the shape of the functions U and g. It will take us too far to discuss the conditions for a solution here.

We note that the last factor in the first term depends only on n, and on the shape of the distribution function $F(x)$, i.e., on objective elements which must be assumed known to the company.

3.4.   From the expressions in para. 2.8 we obtain

$$\frac{dV_2}{dn} = -2[1 - F(n)] \left(n - \int_0^n [1 - F(x)]\, dx\right)$$

This combined with the expression found in para. 2.11 for dD/dn gives

$$\frac{dD}{dV_2} = 1 - \frac{F(n)\left(m_1 - \int_0^n [1 - F(x)]\, dx\right)}{[1 - F(n)]\left(n - \int_0^n [1 - F(x)]\, dx\right)}$$

or by substituting

$$m_1 - \int_0^n [1 - F(x)]\, dx = \int_n^\infty [1 - F(x)]\, dx$$

$$n - \int_0^n [1 - F(x)]\, dx = \int_0^n F(x)\, dx$$

we obtain

$$1 - \frac{dD}{dV_2} = \frac{F(n)}{\int_0^n F(x)\, dx} \int_n^\infty \frac{1 - F(x)}{1 - F(n)}\, dx$$

It is easy to verify that both factors on the right are monotonically decreasing and that the product decreases from ∞ to 0 when n increases. It follows that when V_2 increases from 0 to V,

$$1 - \frac{dD}{dV_2}$$

will increase monotonically from zero to infinity.

3.5. We will now assume that the company can enter the reinsurance market acting at the same time as ceding company and as reinsurer. In the classical models of equilibrium of markets it is impossible that one agent will act both as seller and buyer of the same commodity at the same time. However in the reinsurance market this is possible, owing to the asymmetric character of the market, which we discussed in para. 2.10. We assume that the company accepts as reinsurer a portfolio with variance V_1, and cedes a portfolio with variance V_2, and wants to choose V_1 and V_2 so that the function

$$U[(R + g\,(V_1) - g\,(V_2 - D)), (V + V_1 - V_2)]$$

is maximized.

The first-order conditions for a maximum are

$$\frac{\partial U}{\partial R}\,g'\,(V_1) + \frac{\partial U}{\partial V} = 0$$

$$\frac{\partial U}{\partial R}\,g'\,(V_2 - D)\left(1 - \frac{dD}{dV_2}\right) + \frac{\partial U}{\partial V} = 0.$$

These conditions lead only to the meaningless solution

$$\frac{\partial U}{\partial R} = \frac{\partial U}{\partial V} = 0$$

unless

$$g'\,(V_1) = g'(V_2 - D)\left(1 - \frac{dD}{dV_2}\right)$$

Hence this equation must be satisfied by the point $(V_1,\ V_2)$ which maximizes U. Unless we make specific assumptions about the shape of the functions U and g, and about the initial values of V and R, we cannot determine the point, nor decide whether it has an economic meaning. There is however one particular case which has some interest, namely the point corresponding to $dD/dV_2 = 0$, i.e., to the maximum value of D. In this case the equation above reduces to

$$g'\,(V_1) = g'\,(V_2 - D)$$

If we assume that $g'\,(V)$ is monotonic increasing (or decreasing) this equation is satisfied only when $V_1 = V_2 - D$. If D_0 stands for the maximum value of D, the value of the utility function in this point will be

$$U\,(R, V - D_0)$$

If we assume that a portfolio with a smaller variance is preferred to one with a larger variance, we have

$$U(R, V) < U(R, V - D_0)$$

From the two very weak assumptions we have made, it follows that an insurance company can always improve upon its initial situation by ceding a part of its portfolio, and accepting in exchange a portfolio from the reinsurance market.

3.6. It does not seem very useful to speculate over the shape of the utility function which the company seeks to maximize. Some reflection will show almost immediately that the motives which guide the reinsurance operations of most companies are too complex to be represented by a function of simple mathematical form. For instance, it may seem tempting to assume that the utility function is a homogeneous function of R and $\sqrt{V}$, i.e., that

$$U(R, V) = U(\gamma R, \gamma \sqrt{V})$$

where γ is an arbitrary positive constant. This assumption means merely that the utility function is invariant under a change of the monetary unit in which accounts are kept. If one further assumes that a portfolio with a smaller variance is always preferred to one with a larger variance, it follows that

$$U(R, V) = W\left(\frac{R}{\sqrt{V}}\right)$$

where W is a monotonically increasing function. However if one tries to choose V_1 and V_2 so that

$$W\left(\frac{R + g(V_1) - g(V_2 - D)}{[V + V_1 - V_2]^{1/2}}\right)$$

is maximized, one sees that there will be an absolute maximum for all values for which the denominator is zero, while the numerator remains positive. If $R > g(V)$ this will happen, for instance, for $V_1 = 0$ and $V_2 = V$. The practical implication is that when a company has accumulated sufficiently large funds, or made a profit on its direct underwriting, its best course of action is to cede its whole portfolio, and quit the insurance business with a clear profit. This may perhaps be said to constitute "rational behavior," but it is certainly not the way in which most insurance companies act, and it will make no sense at all for a mutual company.

It may be more in accordance with current practice to assume that an insurance company seeks to maximize R subject to some condition as $R > 3\sqrt{V}$. This will mean approximately that the company seeks the largest possible premium income, subject to some safety conditions being met. However this cannot be considered as rational in theory, since it will mean that a company always will refuse even a very great reduction in variance, if it leads to a net reduction in its free funds (or premium income).

It is not surprising that it should be difficult to spell out the objectives of a company's reinsurance activity in an operational manner. In practically all other fields of economic activity, one has been able to present the objectives of a firm as that of maximizing a given function, only by making drastic simplifications, simplifications which usually make the models completely unrealistic. However, insurance is probably the only economic activity which is based almost entirely on mathematical and statistical principles, and it may for this reason hold greater possibilities than other activities for formulating rational objectives in an operational form.

Summary

The first part of this paper discusses the subjective elements inherent in any reinsurance. The author emphasizes that actuarial science cannot in any objective manner state how much an insurance company should pay to obtain greater security through reinsurance arrangement.

The second part contains a mathematical proof that a stop loss contract gives a greater reduction in the variance of a portfolio, than any other reinsurance arrangement obtainable against the transfer of a given amount of the net premium. It is also shown that this reduction in the variance of the portfolio of the ceding company is greater than the variance of the portfolio the reinsurer takes over.

The third part introduces a "utility" function for the insurance company. This function contains the two variables

R = the free reserves of the company
V = the variance of the expected claims of the company

The shape of this function is discussed, and some assumptions are made. It is shown that under these very weak assumptions, a company can always improve its position by reinsurance arrangements.

2 The Optimal Reinsurance Treaty

1. Some years ago I discussed optimal reinsurance treaties, without trying to give a precise definition of this term [1]. I suggested that a reinsurance contract could be called "most efficient" if it, for a given net premium, maximized the reduction of the variance in the claim distribution of the ceding company. I proved under fairly restricted conditions that the stop loss contract was most efficient in this respect.

I do not consider this a particularly interesting result. I pointed out at the time that there are two parties to a reinsurance contract, and that an arrangement which is very attractive to one party, may be quite unacceptable to the other.

2. In spite of my own reservations, it seems that this result—which I did not think deserved to be called a theorem—has caused some interest. Kahn [4] has proved that the result is valid under far more general conditions, and recently Ohlin [5] has proved that the result holds for a much more general class of measures of dispersion.

In view of these generalizations it might be useful to state once more, why I think the original result has relatively little interest. In doing so, it is by no means my purpose to reduce the value of the mathematical generalizations of Kahn and Ohlin. Such work has a value in itself, whether the results are immediately useful or not. I merely want to point out that there are other lines of research, which appear more promising, if our purpose is to develop a realistic theory of insurance.

3. To illustrate my point, let us consider an insurance contract, which can lead to the claim payments:

0 with probability 0.99
1 with probability 0.01

Let us next consider a portfolio of 10,000 such contracts, and assume that claim payments under different contracts are stochastically independent.

Expected claim payment under the contracts in the portfolio, i.e., the net premium, is then

$$P = 100$$

The variance of the claim payment is

$$V = 99$$

This is a portfolio which most insurance companies would be glad to have—provided there was a reasonable loading—and it is unlikely that the question of reinsurance should be brought up. It is possible that the portfolio may lead to a total payment of 10,000, but the probability of such a catastrophe is 10^{-20000}, and is almost certain to be ignored.

4. Let us now assume—in spite of the argument above—that our company considers reinsuring a quota of 5% of all contracts in the portfolio. The net premium of this reinsurance cover is obviously

$$P_q = 0.05P = 5$$

The variance of claim payments in the portfolio retained by the company is

$$V_q = (0.95)^2 V = 89$$

Let us next assume that the company considers a stop loss contract at 100, i.e., if claim payments should exceed 100, the excess will be paid by the reinsurer.

It seems fairly safe to represent the claim distribution by a normal distribution with mean = 100 and standard deviation = 10.

With this approximation, the net premium for the reinsurance cover is

$$P_s = \frac{1}{10\sqrt{2\pi}} \int_{100}^{\infty} xe^{-\frac{1}{2}\left(\frac{x-100}{10}\right)^2} dx - \frac{100}{10\sqrt{2\pi}} \int_{100}^{\infty} e^{-\frac{1}{2}\left(\frac{x-100}{10}\right)^2} dx$$

or $P_s = 4$

The variance of the portfolio retained by the company is found to be

$$V_s = \frac{1}{10\sqrt{2\pi}} \int_{0}^{100} x^2 e^{-\frac{1}{2}\left(\frac{x-100}{10}\right)^2} dx + \frac{100^2}{10\sqrt{2\pi}} \int_{100}^{\infty} e^{-\frac{1}{2}\left(\frac{x-100}{10}\right)^2} dx$$

$$- (100 - P_s)^2$$

or $V_s = 34$

5. Our example seems to demonstrate the striking superiority of stop loss reinsurance. It is cheaper, and it gives a far greater reduction of variance than the conventional form of reinsurance. In addition the stop loss contract gives our

company an absolute guarantee—against ruin—provided of course, that the company holds reserves exceeding 100, after the reinsurance premium has been paid.

This seems almost too good to be true, and we should ask ourselves if it is likely that an insurance company ever will have an option of the kind indicated by our example. Do we really expect a reinsurer to offer a stop loss contract and a conventional quota treaty with the same loading on the net premium? If the reinsurer is worried about the variance in the portfolio he accepts, he will prefer to sell the quota contract, and we should expect him to demand a higher compensation for the stop loss contract.

Experience seems to confirm this. The net premium will usually play only a minor part in negotiations over nonproportional reinsurance treaties.

These considerations should remind us that there are two parties to a reinsurance contract, and that these parties have conflicting interests. The *optimal contract* must then appear as a reasonable compromise between these interests. To me the most promising line of research seems to be the study of contracts, which in different ways can be said to be optimal from the point of view of both parties. I discussed this problem first in a paper [2] on reciprocal treaties.

6. The variance has a long tradition as a "measure of risk," but it has also been clear for a long time, that it is not always an adequate measure. To illustrate this, let us consider a reinsurance contract as reinsurers, and assume:

E = expected profit from the contract
V = the variance of profits.

We can then lay down a rule to the effect that for given $E > 0$ we accept the contract if V is not too large. If $V = 0$, the contract is obviously acceptable, since it then offers a certain profit of E.

If V is too large, we reject the contract, i.e., we prefer the certainty of a zero profit to accepting the contract.

Let now the pair (E, V) represent an unacceptable contract, and consider the following contract, which obviously is better than the certainty of a zero profit:

Profit 0 with probability $1 - p$
Profit x with probability p

Expected profit is px, and the variance is $x^2 p (1 - p)$. If we now take

$$p = \frac{E^2}{E^2 + V}$$

$$x = \frac{E^2 + V}{E}$$

our rule will tell us to reject this contract, on which we cannot lose. This is an obvious contradiction.

7. The counter example, which we used above, is evidently artificial. One may well object that such reinsurance contracts do not exist, and hence that there is no need for a rule as to whether they should be accepted or not. Nevertheless, the example should serve as a warning that we cannot always evaluate reinsurance contracts by computing only mean and variance of the claim distribution.

We need a more general rule, and this we find in the utility theory, which I have discussed in another paper [3].

8. It may be thought that the preceding paragraphs dismiss expected values (i.e., net premiums) and variance in a rather high-handed manner. It may, therefore, be useful to recall why these two concepts have played such important parts in actuarial theory:

(i) Net premiums are obviously important when we can appeal to the *law of large numbers*, so that deviations from expected values can be disregarded.
(ii) The variance is a fairly adequate measure of risk, if we only consider probability distributions, which are approximately *symmetrical*. This will be the case if all distributions are approximately normal, which they may be if the law of large numbers and the central limit theorem apply.

These two conditions are not usually fulfilled in reinsurance. The number of contracts, held by a reinsurer, will be small compared to that of a direct underwriter, and the distributions which occur in nonproportional reinsurance, are usually extremely skew. This should indicate that game theory, and the utility theory associated with it, are the proper tools.

References

1. Borch, Karl. "An Attempt to determine the Optimum Amount of Stop Loss Reinsurance," *Transactions of the XVI International Congress of Actuaries,* Vol. 1(1960), pp. 597–610.
2. Borch, Karl. "Reciprocal Reinsurance Treaties," *The ASTIN Bulletin,* Vol. 1 (1961), pp. 170–191.
3. Borch, Karl. "The Utility Concept applied to the Theory of Insurance," *The ASTIN Bulletin,* Vol. 1 (1961), pp. 245–255.

4. Kahn, Paul M. "Some Remarks on a recent Paper by Borch," *The ASTIN Bulletin,* Vol. 1 (1961), pp. 265–272.
5. Ohlin, Jan. "A Generalization of a Result by Borch and Kahn on the Optimal Properties of Stop Loss Reinsurance," *The ASTIN Bulletin,* Vol. 5 (1969), pp. 249–266.

Part II
Reciprocal Reinsurance Arrangements

Insurance literature is generally vague about the objectives of the reinsurance arrangements that most insurance companies make. It is easy to find trivial statements to the effect that the company seeks to reduce risk, without undue reductions in profits. In general, a reduction of risk—no matter how this concept is defined—can only be obtained by sacrificing some expected profits. It therefore seems that an insurance company must have some rule for "trade off" between risk and expected profits, if reinsurance arrangements shall be made in a rational manner. Rules of this kind should apparently play a central part in the theory of reinsurance, and it is surprising that the problem is only exceptionally discussed in the literature.

The explanation of this neglect of an important problem may be that the basic view often has been that an insurance company should reinsure as little as possible. Usually the government will require that an insurance company must satisfy certain "solvency conditions" if it shall be allowed to operate. In theory, if not in practice, these conditions are often formulated as a requirement that the probability that the company shall be ruined, i.e., become insolvent, must be below a certain acceptable level. If a company is unable to satisfy the solvency conditions for some reason, it must reinsure so that the government requirement is met. If only one form of reinsurance cover is available, for instance, proportional reinsurance on "original terms," the company has no choice. If it is possible to satisfy the government conditions by several different reinsurance arrangements, the company will have to find the cheapest solution, a problem that usually is fairly simple.

An insurance company generally wants to retain as much of its portfolio as possible. If it is not obliged to reinsure to satisfy government requirements, a company will not usually give a part of its portfolio away to a reinsurer, unless it gets another, more or less equivalent portfolio in return. Such exchanges of portfolios between two companies are usually referred to as reciprocal reinsurance arrangements. If there is some stochastic independence between the two portfolios, the exchange can clearly be advantageous to both companies, in the sense that they will both be able to reduce their risk, without having to give up any expected profits.

When two companies consider concluding a reciprocal reinsurance contract, an infinity of different possibilities may be open to them, at least if they are prepared to consider unorthodox nonproportional arrangements. It will, therefore, be a formidable problem to determine the contract which both parties can accept as the best possible in the given circumstances. When they try to solve this problem, the managers of the companies cannot get much help from actuarial literature, and they will find few, if any, useful hints in conventional economic theory. The situation of the two companies can most naturally be seen as a game, and it can best be analyzed in the framework of the *Game Theory,* created by von Neumann and Morgenstern. The relevant parts of this theory are often referred to as "bargaining theory," developed almost singlehandedly by Harsanyi [2, 3].

The first problem for each company in a bargaining situation is to decide if one proposed reinsurance arrangement is better than another. To illustrate, let us assume that $F(x)$ is the probability distribution of the profits of one of the companies if no reinsurance arrangements are made. Let $F_1(x)$ and $F_2(x)$ be the profit distributions that the company can obtain by concluding alternative reinsurance contracts. To make a rational decision, the company must have a rule that can tell it which is the best of the distributions $F_1(x)$ and $F_2(x)$, and if any of them is to be preferred to $F(x)$. This rule must be derived from a preference ordering over a set of probability distributions. If this preference ordering is consistent, it can be represented by a utility function $u(x)$ so that $F_1(x)$ is preferred to $F_2(x)$ if and only if

$$\int u(x)\,dF_1(x) > \int u(x)\,dF_2(x) \tag{1}$$

The function $u(x)$ can be interpreted as the "utility of money." Sometimes this interpretation may be useful, but it is not necessary. It is sufficient to take $u(x)$ as an order-preserving operator, which maps a set of probability distributions on the real line and thus provides a simple way of describing a preference ordering.

This is the Bernoulli principle, which was first suggested by Daniel Bernoulli in 1732. Several methematicians, e.g., Laplace, discussed the principle during the following century, and its relevance to insurance seems to have been generally recognized. In 1832 Barrois presented a fairly complete theory of fire insurance, based on Laplace's work on the Bernoulli principle. For reasons that are difficult to explain (see [1]), the principle was almost completely forgotten—by actuaries and economists alike—during the next hundred years.

The creators of game theory, von Neumann and Morgenstern, proved that the principle, which so far had been just a reasonable and enticing hypothesis, could be derived as a theorem from some simple assumptions about the consistency of preference orderings over sets of probability distributions. This proof of (1), today usually referred to as the "expected utility theorem," brought the Bernoulli principle back to the center of the stage.

Chapters 3 to 8 explain how the Bernoulli principle can be applied to insurance problems, and it is argued that the principle is essential in a rational analysis of these problems. Some of the papers have been shortened considerably. The proofs of the theorem which I gave or sketched more than 10 years ago have little interest today, and arguments that seemed new and even startling in actuarial circles at that time appear almost trivial today.

The Bernoulli principle makes it possible for insurance companies to evaluate and compare different reinsurance arrangements. Two companies that consider concluding a reciprocal reinsurance arrangement can use the principle when they negotiate their way to a contract which both parties consider as reasonable. The two companies are in a bargaining situation, and their problem is a familiar one in economic theory. The papers present different solutions to this problem, both in the setting of game theory and in a more classical framework.

Chapter 8 contains a discussion of the possible objectives of an insurance company, and the preference orderings and utility functions implied by these objectives. My present view is that this problem can most naturally be studied in a dynamic setting, and this question is discussed in Part IV. The problem consists in assigning utilities to different profit distributions, i.e., to different probability distributions over "final wealth," to use the current terminology. The utility of final wealth at the end of a period naturally depends on the use that can be made of the wealth in the following period.

Chapters 3 to 8 deal almost exclusively with problems of reinsurance, i.e., with transactions between two insurance companies. In such transactions one can reasonably assume that the rationality assumptions behind the Bernoulli principle hold. In most insurance companies reinsurance decisions are made after extensive calculations by the company's actuary. It is also reasonable to assume that both companies have the same opinion about the probability distributions involved. Reinsurance contracts are based on complete confidence between both parties. If one party has information that may be relevant in the estimation of the probability distributions, it is considered as fraud, or breach of faith, if he does not make this information available to the other party.

Formally, the models can be applied also to direct insurance, i.e., to the transactions between an insurance company and a customer who wants to buy insurance coverage. I do not believe, however, that the assumptions mentioned above will hold for such transactions. There is no reason why the customer should estimate the probabilities of loss in the same way as the company. Further, there are good reasons to assume that the customer does not behave as consistently as the Bernoulli principle requires. To illustrate, we can consider the following example, taken from a paper by Mossin [4].

Assume that a person with initial wealth S is exposed to a risk described by the distribution $F(x)$ Assume further that he can insure against this risk by paying a premium P. If the person's attitude to risk is presented by the utility function $u(x)$, he will take insurance if

$$\int_0^\infty u(S-x)\,dF(x) < u(S-P)$$

Assume now that he can insure a fraction k of the loss by paying a premium kP. He will then consider

$$U(k) = \int_0^\infty u\,(S - kP - (1 - k)x)\,dF\,(x)$$

Differentiating with respect to k, we find

$$U'(k) = \int_0^\infty (x - P)u'\,(S - kP - (1 - k)x)\,dF\,(x)$$

For $k = 1$ we have

$$U'(1) = u'\,(S - P) \int_0^\infty (x - P)\,dF\,(x) < 0$$

provided that $u'\,(S - P) > 0$ and $E\{x\} < P$, i.e., that the premium is greater than the expected loss, as it always will be in practice. This means that a rational person would never take full insurance against a risk. If $U'(k) < 0$ for all $k \in (0, 1)$, the person will not take any insurance at all. If, however, $U'(k) = 0$ for some value of k, a rational person should insure only a fraction of the risk. This is against all observation. If a person takes fire insurance on his house, he takes it for the full value, and not for 80% of the loss. The same holds if he takes insurance to cover his liability as an automobile driver, although he might take a "deductible," which excludes very small claims from the insurance contract.

References

1.   Borch, K. "The Place of Uncertainty in the Theories of the Austrian School," in Hicks and Weber (eds.), *Carl Menger and the Austrian School of Economics* (Oxford: Clarendon Press, 1973), pp. 61–74.
2.   Harsanyi, J. "Bargaining and Conflict Situations in the Light of a New Approach to Game Theory," *The American Economic Review,* 1965, pp. 447–451.
3.   Harsanyi, J. "A General Theory of Rational Behavior in Game Situations," *Econometrica,* 1966, pp. 613–634.
4.   Mossin, J. "Aspects of Rational Insurance Purchasing," *Journal of Political Economy,* 1968, pp. 553–568.

3

Reciprocal Reinsurance Treaties Seen as a Two-Person Cooperative Game

1. Introduction

1.1. In 1930 Professor Cramér wrote: "The object of the theory of risk is to give a mathematical analysis of the random fluctuations in an insurance business, and to discuss the various means of protection against their inconvenient effects ([6], page 7). This definition has obviously been adequate, since Cramér still subscribes to it when 25 years later he makes a comprehensive survey of the subject [7]. However, the mild complaint Cramér made in 1930 that "practical insurance business has hitherto made little or no application of the results offered by the mathematical theory of risk" still has some validity. The very impressive results achieved by the mathematical theory of risk during the last 30 years have certainly found practical applications, but not so many as one would expect, considering that the theory proposes to analyze the very foundations of the insurance business.

1.2. One reason why these theoretical results have found less practical application than their possibilities seem to indicate, may be that the various means an insurance company can use to protect itself against inconvenient effects of random fluctuations will invariably cost money. The risk theory has so far had little to say about how much it is reasonable to pay in order to get rid of a certain amount of inconvenient fluctuations. Since such fluctuations are inherent in the insurance business, they cannot be eliminated, they must somehow be absorbed within the insurance sector of the economy. This means that a part of the insurance sector will have to absorb fluctuations, and demand a compensation from those who are relieved of the inconveience. However, the risk theory has hardly even mentioned the problem of how this compensation should be determined so that it is in some sense "fair" to both parties.

1.3. It is evident that a systematic study of these problems will necessarily lead to a study of the reinsurance market, and the conditions which will bring supply and demand into equilibrium in this market. The present paper does not deal with this general problem. In its scope the paper is confined to an analysis of the simplest conceivable case, that of two insurance companies seeking an arrangement which will protect them both in the best possible way against the inconvenient fluctuations.

2. The Insurance Business

2.1. It is convenient to begin our discussion with a brief and fairly abstract description of the insurance business as such. An insurance contract defines a random variable—the amount of claims which will be made under the contract. Let $F(z)$ be the probability that the claims will not exceed z. In order to accept this contract, an insurance company will demand a *net premium P*, which is given by

$$P = \int_0^\infty z \, dF(z)$$

This is the principle of equivalence, which is the cornerstone of actuarial mathematics. In addition to the net premium, the company will demand a *safety loading L*, so that the total premium it will ask in order to accept the contract will be $P + L$. In this paper we will ignore entirely the loading for administrative expenditure. We will assume that the amounts in question are spent completely for the purpose for which they are collected, and that they do not enter into an analysis of risk situations.

2.2. We assume now that an insurance company has concluded n contracts, and that $F_i(z_i)$ is the probability that the ith contract will lead to an amount of claims not exceeding z_i. We assume that $z_1, \ldots, z_n$ are statistically independent. The company will then have a portfolio for which $F(x)$ is the probability that the total amount of claims will not exceed x, where $F(x)$ is the convolution of

$$F_1(z_1), \ldots, F_n(z_n) \quad \text{and} \quad x = z_1 + z_2 + , \ldots, + z_n$$

It is convenient to have a name for the function $F(x)$, so we will refer to it as the *risk distribution* of the company's portfolio.

2.3. If the company, before it accepted the contracts in question, had funds amounting to R_0, and if L_i is the safety loading on the ith contract, the funds in the hands of the company will amount to

$$R_0 + \sum_{i=1}^n L_i + \int_0^\infty x \, dF(x)$$

With these funds the company has to meet the claims which will be made under the contracts in the portfolio. Since the risk distribution of the portfolio is $F(x)$, the expected value of these claims is $\int_0^\infty x \, dF(x)$. This is the net premium, or the technical reserves. These funds must be present if the company is to be actuarially solvent. However, in the theory of risk the subject of study is the deviations from the expected amount of claims. It is therefore the funds which the company has in excess of the technical reserves, i.e., the "free reserves," which are of importance. If, for the free reserves, we write

$$R = R_0 + \sum_{i=1}^{n} L_i$$

the company's *risk situation* can be characterized by the two elements R and $F(x)$, or by the "point" $(R, F(x))$.

2.4. On this background we can state that the *first task* of the risk theory is to determine the underwriting policy and safety loading of the company so that the resulting risk situation $(R, F(x))$ is the "best possible," or in Cramér's terminology, so that the fluctuations cause as little inconvenience as possible. It is, however, obvious that, owing to the vagaries of the market, the resulting risk situation may be quite different from the one the company aimed at when it laid down its underwriting policy and determined its scale of safety loading.

2.5. This brings us to what we could call the *second task* of the risk theory: to analyze a given risk situation $(R, F(x))$, and see if it is possible to improve it by suitable reinsurance arrangements.

In general a reinsurance arrangement will consist of splitting the random variable x into two components x_1 and x_2, so that $x = x_1 + x_2$, where x_1 is the amount of claims which is paid by the company, and x_2 the amount paid by the reinsurer. Let the joint probability distribution of x_1 and x_2 be

$$dF(x_1, x_2) = f(x_1, x_2) \, dx_1 \, dx_2$$

where obviously

$$F(x) = \int_0^x \int_0^\mu f(u - v, v) \, dv \, du$$

This reinsurance arrangement will change the company's risk distribution from $F(x)$ to

$$F_1(x) = \int_0^x \left(\int_0^\infty f(x_1, x_2) \, dx_2 \right) dx_1$$

By the arrangement the reinsurer will take over a portfolio with a risk distribution

$$F_2(x) = \int_0^x \left(\int_0^\infty f(x_1, x_2) \, dx_1 \right) dx_2$$

2.6. To assume responsibility for this portfolio, the reinsurer will receive the net premium

$$P_2 = \int_0^\infty x \, dF_2(x)$$

In addition to this, the reinsurer will usually demand a consideration or a safety loading Q.

The result of the reinsurance arrangement is then: (i) the risk situation of the company changes from $(R, F(x))$ to $(R - Q, F_1(x))$; (ii) the reinsurer accepts a risk situation $(Q, F_2(x))$.

In this context Q can be interpreted as the price of placing a portfolio with risk distribution $F_2(x)$ on the reinsurance market. If such a market exists, i.e., if it is always possible to place a portfolio at a uniquely determined price, the task of the company will be relatively simple. The task will then consist of choosing, given the price, the retained risk distribution which leads to the most favorable risk situation. In the present paper we shall not examine the conditions under which such a market will exist. Instead we shall study the case of two insurance companies seeking to improve their situations by an exchange of reinsurance, without being bound by any preconceived ideas as to what constitutes a fair bargain.

3. Comparability of Risk Situations

3.1. The problem is to find a rule, which will enable us to compare risk situations of the form $(R, F(x))$ and to state *how much* better one risk situation is than another. This is just the problem which von Neumann and Morgenstern [13] had to solve before they could develop their theory of games. They solved it by showing that the rule they needed could be derived from three axioms which appear very reasonable. We shall follow the same path, although we shall use a simpler formulation of the axioms given by Marschak [10] and generalized by Herstein and Milnor [9].

3.2. Usually we shall find it most convenient to let a risk situation be represented by the pair $(R, F(x))$ since this form explicitly contains the two elements involved: (i) $F(x)$, the probability distribution of the amount of claims; (ii) R, the funds available to meet claims in excess of the expected amount.

It is, however, obvious that a risk situation can be represented by one single probability distribution. If we write $z = R + P - x$ and $G(z) = 1 - F(R + P - z) = 1 - F(x)$, $G(z)$ will be the probability distribution of the company's profits (positive or negative), and we have

$$G(z) = 1 \quad \text{for} \quad R + P \leqslant z$$

3.3. Let **G** be the set of all probability distributions, and let **R** be a binary relation (read: "is at least as good as") on the set **G**.

Axiom 1 (Comparability). *For any two* $G_1(x)$ *and* $G_2(x)$ *in* **G** *at least one of the following holds*

$$G_1(x) \, \mathbf{R} \, G_2(x) \qquad G_2(x) \, \mathbf{R} \, G_1(x)$$

The meaning of the axiom is that when confronted with two risk situations, an insurance company is able to decide that either one is better than the other, or that the two situations are equally good. Since such decisions are taken daily in most insurance companies, the axiom seems quite acceptable.

3.4. If $G_1(x) \, \mathbf{R} \, G_2(x)$ and $G_2(x) \, \mathbf{R} \, G_1(x)$ both hold, and we say that $G_1(x)$, is indifferent to $G_2(x)$, and write $G_1(x) \, \mathbf{I} \, G_2(x)$.
If $G_1(x) \, \mathbf{R} \, G_2(x)$ holds when $G_2(x) \, \mathbf{R} \, G_1(x)$ does not hold, we say that $G_1(x)$ is preferred to $G_2(x)$, and write $G_1(x) \, \mathbf{P} \, G_2(x)$.

Axiom 2 (Transitivity). *If* $G_1(x) \, \mathbf{P} \, G_2(x)$ *and* $G_2(x) \, \mathbf{P} \, G_3(x)$, *then* $G_1(x) \, \mathbf{P} \, G_3(x)$.

The implication of this axiom is that an insurance company is consistent in its preferences. It is well known that persons who must be considered as rational can violate this axiom in their actions. This has been pointed out by several writers, and with particular force by Allais [1]. However, most people will probably agree with Savage [14], who apparently thinks that rational people will correct their statement of preferences if it is pointed out to them that they have violated Axiom 2. This is at least what he did himself when Allais trapped him into stating inconsistent preferences.
If an insurance company bases its decisions on actuarial calculations, this axiom should be a reasonable assumption. If the company's decisions are reached by majority vote, for instance by a board of directors, it is well known that inconsistent preferences may occur. This so-called "voting paradox" has been studied in considerable detail by Arrow [3].

3.5. These two axioms establish a complete ordering on the set **G**. This is sufficient to define a *utility index* $U(G)$ so that

$$U(G_1) > U(G_2) \qquad \text{if and only if } G_1(x) \, \mathbf{P} \, G_2(x)$$

and $\quad U(G_1) = U(G_2) \qquad$ if and only if $G_1(x) \, \mathbf{I} \, G_2(x)$

However, this utility index is to a large extent indeterminate. In fact, if $\varphi(t)$ is an arbitrary increasing function of t, the function $\varphi(U(G))$ can serve as utility index just as well as $U(G)$ itself. The purpose of the following two axioms is to impose further restrictions on the utility index.

3.6. Let $S = \{x \mid P\}$ denote the set of x having the property P.

Axiom 3 (Continuity). *For any $G_1(x)$, $G_2(x)$, and $G_3(x)$ the sets*

$$\{a \mid a\, G_1(x) + (1 - a)G_2(x) \text{ R } G_3(x)\}$$

and $\{a \mid G_3(x) \text{ R } a\, G_1(x) + (1 - a)\, G_2(x)\}$

where a is a real number between 0 and 1, are closed.

The meaning of the axiom is essentially that there are no "singularities" in the preference ordering. In general this is a farreaching assumption. However, when applied to insurance companies, it implies little more than a continuous relationship between the risk and the premium at which it is insured. The axiom rules out the possibility that the company will refuse to insure—at any price— risks where the claim may exceed a certain amount.
An equivalent formulation of the axiom is:

If $\lim\limits_{i \to \infty} a_i = a$

and $a_i\, G_1(x) + (1 - a_i)\, G_2(x) \text{ R } G_3(x)$ for all i

then $a\, G_1(x) + (1 - a)\, G_2(x) \text{ R } G_3(x)$

Axiom 4. *If $G_1(x) \text{ I } G_2(x)$, then for any $G_3(x)$ which is stochastically independent of $G_1(x)$ and $G_2(x)$*

$$(\tfrac{1}{2}G_1(x) + \tfrac{1}{2}G_3(x)) \text{ I } (\tfrac{1}{2}G_2(x) + \tfrac{1}{2}G_3(x))$$

This axiom is the most controversial of the four. Nash [12] admits this, and Allais' devastating attack on the axiomatic approach to utility centers on this axiom. The essence of his criticism is that the axiom is invalid if the degree of "complementarity" between $G_3(x)$ and $G_1(x)$ is different from that between $G_3(x)$ and $G_2(x)$. The assumption of stochastical independence should, however, meet most of his objections.

3.7. The particular form given to Axiom 4 is a mathematical nicety. Herstein and Milnor use these four axioms to prove as a theorem the stronger Axiom 4a, which is equivalent to the axiom used by von Neumann and Morgen- stern and by Marschak.

Axiom 4a. *If $G_1(x) \, I \, G_2(x)$, then*

$$(aG_1(x) + (1-a) G_3(x)) \, I \, (aG_2(x) + (1-a) G_3(x))$$

for any $G_3(x)$ and for any a between 0 and 1.

3.8. Herstein and Milnor define the utility of $G(x)$, $u(G)$ by the relation

$$G(x) \, I \, (u(G) G_1(x) + (1 - u(G)) G_2(x))$$

and prove that the function $u(G)$ is unique, and that

$$u(G_1) > u(G_2) \quad \text{if and only if } G_1(x) \, P \, G_2(x)$$

It is then easily established that

$$u(aG_1 + (1-a) G_2) = au(G_1) + (1-a)u(G_2)$$

3.9. Let $\epsilon(x)$ be a distribution function such that $\epsilon(x) = 0$ for $x < 0$ and $\epsilon(x) = 1$ for $x \geq 0$. $\epsilon(x)$ clearly belongs to the set **G**, and it follows directly from the axioms that there exists a nonempty subset $\mathbf{G}_1$ of **G**, consisting of probability distributions $G_1(x)$ such that

$$G_1(x) \, I \, \epsilon(x)$$

If we write $u(\epsilon(x - R)) = u(R)$, $u(R)$ will be the utility the insurance company attaches to a *certain* profit R. The function $u(R)$ can thus be interpreted as the "utility of money" although in a sense different to the one given to this term in classical economics.

3.10. For any $G(x)$ there will exist a number R such that $G(x) \, I \, \epsilon(x - R)$ and $u(G) = u(R)$. If we substitute $u(G_1) = u(R_1)$ and $u(G_2) = u(R_2)$ in the expression at the end of para. 3.8, we obtain

$$u(a\epsilon(x - R_1) + (1 - a)\epsilon(x - R_2)) = au(R_1) + (1 - a)a(R_2)$$

Let us for the sake of simplicity assume that $R_1 < R_2$ and let $A(x)$ be a probability distribution such that $A(x) = 0$ for $x < R_1$, $A(x) = a$ for $R_1 < x < R_2$ and $A(x) = 1$ for $R_2 \leq x$. It follows that

$$A(x) = a\epsilon(x - R_1) + (1 - a)\epsilon(x - R_2)$$

so that $u(A(x)) = au(R_1) + (1 - a)u(R_2)$

or $u(A(x)) = \int_{-\infty}^{+\infty} u(x)\, dA(x)$

Since $A(x)$ belongs to the set **G**, it follows that by repeated use of this argument, we obtain for any $G(x)$ in **G**

$$u(G(x)) = \int_{-\infty}^{+\infty} u(x)\, dG(x)$$

Hence the utility of any risk situation can be expressed as a weighed average of the utility of money.

3.11.   It is useful to pause here, and emphasize that the concept "utility of money" has been brought into our calculations in a purely formal manner. One should be careful not to read into the concept all the connotations of the classical economists. The position is simply this. If an insurance company has a preference ordering of risk situations which satisfies our axioms, there exists a uniquely defined function $u(x)$ which we have called the "utility of money." This function, and the preference ordering are equivalent. If we want to study the attitude of the company to various risk situations, it amounts to the same whether we study the preference ordering, or the shape of the function $u(x)$.

3.12.   Before we proceed we need, however, a last, and rather trivial axiom.

Axiom 5. $u(R_1) > u(R_2)$ *if and only if* $R_1 > R_2$.

The meaning is that a larger profit is preferred to a smaller one. It should not be necessary to present any explicit justification for this assumption.

3.13.   If an insurance company is in a risk situation characterized by the distribution function $G_0(x)$, it can change this situation by reinsurance arrangements. Let G_1 be the set of risk situations which the company can reach by appropriate reinsurance arrangements, and let $G_1(x)$ be an element of this set. In accordance with the terminology of the decision theory, we will say that the company acts *rationally* if it selects the reinsurance arrangement which results in a situation $G_1(x)$ which is preferred to any other member of G_1. An equivalent statement is that the company acts rationally if it selects the reinsurance arrangement which maximizes $u(G_1(x))$.

4. The Nature of the Preference Ordering

4.1.   As pointed out in a previous paper [5], it does not seem very useful to engage in direct speculations over the shape of the utility functions. In the following, we will write $U(R, F(x))$ for the utility function of a risk situation

$(R, F(x))$ and refer to it as the utility index, to distinguish it from the utility function of money $u(x)$. One can certainly establish some properties which it is reasonable to ascribe to these functions. For instance $u(x)$ must be an increasing function, probably concave toward the x axis. Similarly $U(R, F(x))$ can be assumed to increase with R, and will probably decrease if the variance or some other measure of the dispersion of $F(x)$ increases. However, it seems difficult by a purely speculative approach to make the functions sufficiently determinate to enable us to reach results which may be useful in practice.

4.2. As an alternative approach, we will start with the fundamental equation from para. 3.10:

$$U(R, F(x)) = \int_0^\infty u(R + P - x)\, dF(x)$$

and approximate $u(x)$ by some mathematically simple functions, and see if the resulting $U(R, F(x))$ appears plausible. We will begin by considering:

Case 1. $u(x) = c =$ constant. In practice this will mean that "money doesn't matter." We obtain

$$U(R, F) = c \int_0^\infty dF(x) = c$$

In this case all risk situations are equivalent, as could be expected.

Case 2. $u(x) = c$ for $x \geqslant 0$ and $u(x) = 0$ for $x < 0$, which gives

$$U(R, F) = c \int_0^{R+P} dF = cF(R + P)$$

$F(R + P)$ is the probability that the total amount of claims shall not exceed the funds of the company. This is clearly the complementary probability of Lundberg's probability of ruin at the time when the amount of "risk premium" received by the company reaches P.

We see that in this case all risk situations having the same probability of ruin are equivalent. This is hardly realistic, unless one is willing to assume that insurance companies are so preoccupied with the probability of ruin that they ignore everything else, including expected profits.

Case 3. $u(x) = ax + b$. We find

$$U(R, F) = a\int_0^\infty (R + P - x)\, dF + b = aR + b$$

In this case all risk situations having the same expected profits are equivalent. This may not be entirely unrealistic, but it clearly obviates the need for a theory of *risk.* It is interesting to note that the assumption made in this case is that the utility of money is linear, and that it implies that rational behavior is to maximize expected profits. This is in good agreement with classical economic theory.

Case 4. $u(x) = ax + b$ for $x \geqslant 0$ and $u(x) = 0$ for $x < 0$. We obtain

$$U(R, F) = a \int_0^{R+P} (R + P - x)\, dF(x) + bF(R + P)$$

or since $P = \int_0^\infty x\, dF$

$$U(R,F) = a\left(R + \int_{R+P}^\infty (x - (R + P))\, dF(x)\right) + bF(R + P)$$

The last term on the right is a constant, multiplied by the company's "probability of survival" which also occurred in Case 2. The bracket in the first term contains the company's free reserves plus the net premium of a stop loss reinsurance which will just prevent the company from being ruined. It may be hard to justify this utility index on intuitive grounds, but it has a shape which appears plausible.

Case 5. $u(x) = ax^2 + bx + c$, which leads to

$$U(R, F) = a \int_0^\infty (R + P - x)^2\, dF + b \int_0^\infty (R + P - x)\, dF + c$$

or $aR^2 + bR + c + a \int_0^\infty (x - P)^2\, dF$

However, as $V = \int_0^\infty (x - P)^2\, dF$

is the variance of the risk distribution, we have

$$U(R, F) = aR^2 + bR + c + aV$$

There is obviously no loss of generality if we put $c = 0$, and $a = -1$, since this only means fixing the origin and the unit of measurement of the utility index. We can then write

$$U(R, F) = R(b - R) - V$$

This formula is acceptable only for $2R < b$, unless one is prepared to assume that very large profits are so inconvenient, that they are associated with disutility. Subject to the condition just mentioned, the shape of this utility index appears very plausible, and we will study it in some detail in the following.

5. The Case of Quadratic Utility of Money

5.1. We will study the particular case where the utility index is given by

$$U(R, F) = R(b - R) - V,$$

i.e., where the utility index depends only on the free reserves and on the variance of the risk distribution. Most of the results we shall obtain in the following will hold in the slightly more general case, where the utility index is given by a function $U(R, V)$, satisfying the conditions

$$\frac{\partial U(R, V)}{\partial R} > 0 \quad \text{and} \quad \frac{\partial U(R, V)}{\partial V} < 0$$

These assumptions—although not explicitly stated—seem to be behind most of the classical work on the "individual theory of risk." The results we obtain should therefore be acceptable also to those who may have objections to the assumption that the utility index has the special form $U(R, V) = R(b - R) - V$.

5.2. We now consider two insurance companies: company 1, which is in the risk situation $(R_1 F_0(x))$, and company 2, which is in the risk situation $(R_2 G_0(y))$, where x and y are statistically independent. We assume that the two companies enter into negotiations with the view of improving their risk situations. The outcome of these negotiations will be an agreement that company 1 shall cede to company 2: (i) a portfolio with the risk distribution $F_2(x)$, (ii) the corresponding net premium $P_1 = \int_0^\infty xd\,F_2(x)$, and (iii) an amount $\hat{Q}_1$ of its free reserves, and that company 2 in the same way shall pass on to company 1 the elements

$$G_2(y) \quad P_2 = \int_0^\infty y\, dG_2(y) \quad \text{and} \quad Q_2$$

The net premium does not enter into the utility index, so it can be ignored in the following. Since obviously only the net transfer of free reserves will matter, it is sufficient to study $Q = Q_1 - Q_2$.

5.3. The result of this agreement is the following changes in the risk situations. For company 1, from $(R_1, F_0(x))$ to $(R_1 - Q, F(x))$; for company 2, from $(R_2, G_0(y))$ to $(R_2 + Q, G(y))$.
   Let $F_1(x)$ and $G_1(y)$ be the risk distributions of the parts of the initial portfolios which each company retains. The relationships between $F_0(x), F_1(x)$, and $F_2(x)$ and between $G_0(y), G_1(y)$, and $G_2(y)$ are given in para. 2.5.

Since x and y are statistically independent, we have for the risk distributions resulting from the agreement:

$$F(x) = \int_0^x F_1(x - t)\, dG_2(t)$$

and $\ G(y) = \int_0^y G_1(y - t)\, dF_2(t)$

5.4.   Let var F_0, var F_1, etc., stand for the variance of the distributions $F_0(x)$, $F_1(x)$, etc., and let cov $F_1 F_2$ stand for the covariance of the distributions $F_1(x)$ and $F_2(x)$, and similarly for $G_1(y)$ and $G_2(y)$. We then have

$$\text{var } F_0 = \text{var } F_1 + \text{var } F_2 + 2 \text{ cov } F_1 F_2$$

$$\text{var } G_0 = \text{var } G_1 + \text{var } G_2 + 2 \text{ cov } G_1 G_2$$

and $\text{var } F = \text{var } F_1 + \text{var } G_2$

$$\text{var } G = \text{var } F_2 + \text{var } G_1$$

From this we obtain

$$\text{var } F = \text{var } F_1 + \text{var } G_0 - \text{var } G_1 - 2 \text{ cov } G_1 G_2$$

$$\text{var } G = \text{var } G_1 + \text{var } F_0 - \text{var } F_1 - 2 \text{ cov } F_1 F_2$$

The result of the agreement will be the following changes in the utility index: company 1, from $U(R_1, \text{var } F_0)$ to $U(R_1 - Q, \text{var } F)$; company 2, from $U(R_2, \text{var } G_0)$ to $U(R_1 + Q, \text{var } G)$.
There is no need to assume that the two companies have the same utility index. However, to indicate that the two indices may be different in every formula, will lead to an unnecessarily cumbersome system of notation.

5.5.   The purpose of the negotiations between the companies is then to agree on a number Q and on a way of dividing the two initial portfolios. During the negotiations company 1 will seek an agreement which leads to the greatest possible value of $U(R_1 - Q, \text{var } F)$. Company 2 will similarly seek to maximize $U(R_1 + Q, \text{var } G)$.
The situation the two companies are facing is well known in economics, and is usually referred to as a "bargaining situation." In the theory of games, the situation is known as a "two-person cooperative game."
The mathematical nature of the problem imposes the following two restrictions:

(i) $-R_2 \leqslant Q \leqslant R_1$

(ii) If $P(\xi_1 \leqslant x) = F_1(x)$ and $P(\xi_2 \leqslant x) = F_2(x)$

then $P(\xi_1 + \xi_2 \leqslant x) = F_0(x)$

and if $P(\eta_1 \leqslant y) = G_1(y)$ and $P(\eta_2 \leqslant y) = G_2(y)$

then $P(\eta_1 + \eta_2 \leqslant y) = G_0(y)$

We further assume that the two companies act rationally, and that they have agreed to cooperate. This means: (i) No company will accept an agreement which gives it a lower utility index than it had in the initial situation; (ii) in considering the various possible agreements the companies will rule out any agreement which is such that there exists another agreement which will give a higher utility index to *both* companies.

5.6.   In most problems in game theory the players' knowledge of the opponent's resources and motives is of fundamental importance. The question does not seem to be particularly important in bargaining between insurance companies. In negotiations over reciprocal reinsurance treaties one must assume that both companies have full knowledge of their own and their opponent's free reserves and risk distribution. It is conceivable that in such negotiations an insurance company could conceal its real objectives, i.e., the shape of the utility index it seeks to maximize. In most games it will be an advantage to do this. However, in the special case we consider it is difficult to think of any reason why insurance companies should have different utility indices. Different utility indices will in fact mean that the two companies in some sense attach different values to an increase in profits from 1 million to 2 millions. In a more general case the point may be relevant. If a company, for instance, for prestige reasons, wants a high premium income, it may be an advantage to give the opponent the impression that it is interested exclusively in maximizing a utility index of the form we are considering.

5.7.   The first hurdle our two companies have to overcome is to agree on the form of reinsurance they shall use. Both companies want to reduce the variance of their portfolio. From the expressions in para. 5.4 it is seen that the variance of both companies can be reduced by increasing the covariances terms cov $F_1 F_2$ and cov $G_1 G_2$. These terms reach their maximum values if there is perfect correlation between the part of any claim paid by the company, and the part paid by the reinsurer, i.e., if of an arbitrary claim x, an amount kx is paid by the reinsurer, and the remaining $(1 - k)x$ by the company. However, a reinsurance arrangement to this effect is nothing but the familiar *quota share* treaty, whereby the reinsurer assumes responsibility for $100k\%$ of any claim made against the company. In other words the quota share treaty is superior to any other form of reinsurance, because it gives both companies the smallest possible variance.

5.8. When there is perfect correlation, we have

$$\text{cov } F_1 F_2 = (\text{var } F_1 \text{ var } F_2)^{1/2}$$

$$\text{cov } G_1 G_2 = (\text{var } G_1 \text{ var } G_2)^{1/2}$$

Assume now that the companies have agreed on two quota share treaties, according to which company 1 cedes a proportion of $100k_1\%$ of each risk to company 2, and receives in return $100k_2\%$ of each risk in the initial portfolio of company 2. This gives

$$\text{var } F_1 = (1 - k_1)^2 \text{ var } F_0 \qquad \text{var } F_2 = k_1^2 \text{ var } F_0$$

$$\text{var } G_1 = (1 - k_2)^2 \text{ var } G_0 \qquad \text{var } G_2 = k_2^2 \text{ var } G_1$$

and $\text{cov } F_1 F_2 = k_1 (1 - k_1) \text{ var } F_0$

$$\text{cov } G_1 G_2 = k_2 (1 - k_2) \text{ var } G_0$$

Inserting this in the expressions of para. 5.4, we obtain

$$\text{var } F = (1 - k_1)^2 \text{ var } F_0 + k_2^2 \text{ var } G_0$$

or, if we introduce special symbols for the initial variances $V_1 = \text{var } F_0$ and $V_2 = \text{var } G_0$ we obtain

$$\text{var } F = (1 - k_1)^2 V_1 + k_2^2 V_2$$

and $\text{var } G = k_1^2 V_1 + (1 - k_2)^2 V_2$

5.9. When the form of the reinsurance treaty is settled, the negotiations between the companies will be considerably simplified. The companies will now have to agree on three numbers (Q, k_1, k_2). When agreement is reached, the utility indices of the companies will change as follows: for company 1, from

$$U(R_1, V_1) \qquad \text{to} \qquad U(R_1 - Q, (1 - k_1)^2 V_1 + k_2^2 V_1)$$

and from company 2 from

$$U(R_2, V_2) \quad \text{to} \quad U(R_2 + Q, k_1{}^2 V_1 + (1 - k_2)^2 V_2)$$

The restriction imposed by the nature of the problem is that the point (Q, k_1, k_2) must be in the set defined by $-R_2 \leqslant Q \leqslant R_1, 0 \leqslant k_1 \leqslant 1, 0 \leqslant k_2 \leqslant 1$. It is fairly easy to see that the point defined by the subset $k_1 + k_2 = 1$ constitutes a Pareto optimum, i.e., for any point not belonging to this subset, it is possible to increase the utility indices of *both* companies by moving to a point in the Pareto optimum.

5.10. To prove this assertion rigorously, consider the point (u, v) in a $k_1 k_2$ plane corresponding to an arbitrary value of Q. We introduce new variables k and t so that

$$u = k + \frac{t}{V_1} \quad \text{and} \quad v = (1 - k) + \frac{t}{V_2}$$

and substitute these in the expression for var F. We obtain:

$$\text{var } F = (1 - u)^2 V_1 + v^2 V_2$$

$$= \left(1 - k - \frac{t}{V_1}\right)^2 V_1 + \left(1 - k + \frac{t}{V_2}\right)^2 V_2$$

$$= (1 - k)^2 V_1 + (1 - k)^2 V_2 + \frac{t^2}{V_1} + \frac{t^2}{V_2}$$

If $t \neq 0$, i.e., if the point (u, v) is not in the set $k_1 + k_2 = 1$, the point $(k, 1 - k)$ will give a smaller value of var F than the point (u, v). It is easy to prove that the same will hold for var G.

5.11. It may be useful to pause for a moment to consider the implications of this result. It will be directly irrational of the two companies to agree on an exchange of a pair of quotas which do not add up to unity. Both companies can reduce their variance, and hence increase their utility, by choosing a pair of quotas which satisfy that condition. The only assumption we have made in order to reach this result, is that both companies want to reduce the variance of their portfolios, if this can be done without extra cost, i.e., without paying out any part of their free reserves.

5.12. The bargaining problem of the companies has now been reduced to agreeing on a point (Q, k) in a two-dimensional set. The utility indices which the companies seek to maximize have been simplified to:

Company 1: $U(R_1 - Q, (1 - k)^2(V_1 + V_2))$

Company 2: $U(R_2 + Q, k^2(V_1 + V_2))$

where k is the quota ceded by company 1.

It is not possible to obtain a more determinate solution to the problem without making further assumptions about the shape of the utility index. We will therefore from now on assume that the index has the form given in para. 5.1, i.e., that

$$U(R, V) = R(b - R) - V$$

This means that in the bargaining over the choice of the point (Q, k), the functions which the companies seek to maximize are:

Company 1: $(R_1 - Q)(b - R_1 + Q) - (1 - k)^2(V_1 + V_2)$

Company 2: $(R_2 + Q)(b - R_2 - Q) - k^2(V_1 + V_2)$

5.13. We can show that in this case there is a Pareto optimum given by $Q = -(b - R_1 - R_2)k + \frac{1}{2}b - R_2$. The formal proof follows the same lines as that in para. 5.10. We consider an arbitrary point (u, v) in the Qk plane, and write

$$u = Q' + t$$

$$v = k' + t\frac{b - R_1 - R_2}{V_1 + V_2}$$

where the point (Q', k') belongs to the Pareto optimum. We can then show that (u, v) gives a smaller value of both utility indices than (Q', k').

5.14. The utility indices in the Pareto optimum are as follows:

(i)   Expressed by k:

Company 1: $\frac{1}{4}b^2 - (1 - k)^2[(b - R_1 - R_2)^2 + V_1 + V_2]$

Company 2: $\frac{1}{4}b^2 - k^2[(b - R_1 - R_2)^2 + V_1 + V_2]$

(ii) Expressed by Q:

Company 1: $(R_1 - Q)(b - R_1 + Q) - \dfrac{(\frac{1}{2}b - R_1 + Q)^2}{(b - R_1 - R_2)^2}(V_1 + V_2)$

Company 2: $(R_2 + Q)(b - R_2 - Q) - \dfrac{(\frac{1}{2}b - R_2 - Q)^2}{(b - R_1 - R_2)^2}(V_1 + V_2)$

In principle k can take any value between 0 and 1, and Q any value between $-R_2$ and R_1. However, if we assume that neither company will conclude an agreement which leaves it worse off than it was in the initial situation, we obtain narrower limits. From the first pair of the expressions above, we obtain

$$\tfrac{1}{4}b^2 - (1 - k)^2[(b - R_1 - R_2)^2 + V_1 + V_2] \geqslant R_1(b - R_1) - V_1$$

$$\tfrac{1}{4}b^2 - k^2[(b - R_1 - R_2)^2 + V_1 + V_2] \geqslant R_2(b - R_2) - V_2$$

or $(1 - k)^2 \leqslant \dfrac{(\frac{1}{2}b - R_1)^2 + V_1}{[(\frac{1}{2}b - R_1) + (\frac{1}{2}b - R_2)]^2 + V_1 + V_2} = A^2$

$k^2 \leqslant \dfrac{(\frac{1}{2}b - R_2)^2 + V_2}{[(\frac{1}{2}b - R_1) + (\frac{1}{2}b - R_2)]^2 + V_1 + V_2} = B^2$

from which we obtain $1 - A \leqslant k \leqslant B$. It is easy to see that $(A + B)^2 > 1$, so that $B > 1 - A$, i.e., that the inequalities are not empty. The corresponding inequality for Q is

$$\tfrac{1}{2}b - R_2 - (b - R_1 - R_2)B \leqslant Q \leqslant \tfrac{1}{2}b + R_1 + (b - R_1 - R_2)A$$

5.15.   The meaning of these results is that if the two companies act rationally, they will agree on a point which belongs to the Pareto optimum given in para. 5.13, and which lies in the interval defined by the inequalities in para. 5.14. To agree on a point outside the Pareto optimum will clearly be irrational, since *both* companies can get a higher utility index by switching to a point in the Pareto optimum. However, in the Pareto optimum the interests of the two companies are directly opposed, in the sense that one company can only increase its utility index by reducing the utility index of the other company. For instance, if the companies agree on $k = 1 - A$, the utility index of company 1 will remain the same as if it was in the initial situation, and company 2 will reap the whole gain of the reinsurance arrangements. If the agreement is $k = B$, the roles of the companies will be reversed.

5.16.　Such conflict situations have been discussed frequently in economic theory, and it is accepted that one cannot arrive at a more determinate solution without making *additional assumptions* about the bargaining skill, or some other characteristics of the participants. However, there does not seem to be any such assumptions which naturally suggest themselves to supplement our five axioms. This is the view of von Neumann and Morgenstern, who conclude that the whole interval must be considered as the solution unless one is prepared to make assumptions about the "negotiating, bargaining, higgling, contracting and re-contracting" which may have preceded the agreement concluded [13, page 557].

The purpose of these additional assumptions can be simply to describe or explain how the two parties to the bargain reach an agreement. Two assumptions which serve this limited purpose are discussed in paras. 5.19 and 5.20.

One can, however, be more ambitious and seek assumptions of a normative kind. This has been done by Nash and Zeuthen, who claim that the determinate solution they reach *should* be accepted as an adequate solution by rational bargainers, who will realize that if the opponent also acts rationally, they cannot do any better for themselves by resorting to threats, bluff, and similar devices.

5.17.　Nash [11, 12] has proposed a set of axioms which leads to a determinate solution in the general case. His axioms are to a large extent the same as those we used in Section 4. The *additional assumption* made by Nash is that in a symmetric game the two parties will agree to split the gain equally. Since the utility function is determined only up to a linear transformation, a general game can be made symmetric by a change of origin and unit of measurement. From this assumption Nash shows that the solution is the point where the product of the utilities (measured from the initial utility as origin) of the two parties attains its maximum.

In para. 5.14 we found for the utility of company 1,

$$\tfrac{1}{4}b^2 - (1 - k)^2 [(b - R_1 - R_2)^2 + V_1 + V_2]$$

If we write $U(1 - k)$ for this expression, the utility of the company in the initial situation is $U(A)$, where $1 - A$ is the lower limit of k. Similarly the utility of company 2 can be written $U(k)$, with the initial value $U(B)$, where B is the upper limit of k. The Nash solution is then the value of k which maximizes the product

$$(U(1 - k) - U(A))(U(k) - U(B))$$

or, what amounts to the same, the value which maximizes

$$((1 - k)^2 - A^2)(k^2 - B)$$

Differentiation shows that the solution is a root of the equation

$$k(A^2 - (1 - k)^2) = (1 - k)(B^2 - k^2)$$

When k increases from $1 - A$ to B, the left-hand term will increase uniformly from 0 to $B(A^2 - (1 - B)^2)$, and the right-hand term will decrease uniformly from $A(B^2 - (1 - A)^2)$ to 0. Hence the equation has only one root between $1 - A$ and B, so that the Nash solution is unique.

5.18.   The same result could have been derived directly by differentiating the product of the expressions in para. 5.9 with respect to Q, k_1 and k_2. It is implicit in Nash's axioms that the solution must lie in the successive Pareto optima which we found.

Nash's solution of the bargaining problem is essentially an elegant mathematical derivation of the solution from a few simple, and apparently very acceptable axioms. Harsanyi [8] has, however, shown that Nash's solution is identical with a solution offered by Zeuthen [17] more than 20 years earlier. Zeuthen reaches his result after an analysis of how the actual bargaining takes place. His main argument is as follows.

Suppose that company 1 insists on an agreement on k' which will give it a utility of $U(1 - k')$ and company 2 a utility of $U(k')$, and that company 2 insists on k'', which will give the companies utilities of $U(1 - k'')$ and $U(k'')$ respectively. It is then reasonable that company 1 should make a concession if

$$\frac{U(1 - k') - U(1 - k'')}{U(1 - k') - U(A)} < \frac{U(k'') - U(k')}{U(k'') - U(B)}$$

The idea is that in this case company 1 will lose less than company 2 by making a concession. If the concession is sufficiently great, the inequality will be reversed, and it will be up to company 2 to make a concession. It is easy to see that this will lead to the same solution as the one following from the axioms of Nash.

5.19.   In practice most bargaining problems seem to find a determinate solution because there are some conventions or preconceived ideas as to what will constitute a "fair" bargain. In our case this means that before entering the negotiations, the companies have definite ideas as to what is a "fair price" for reinsurance coverage. For instance, the two companies can agree in advance that only net premiums shall be paid for the coverage. This means $Q = 0$, and will give a determinate solution, but it may happen that $Q = 0$ is not included in the interval given at the end of para. 5.14. In this case the principle that only net premiums shall be paid will lead to a nonoptimal solution.

The principle $Q = 0$ is really inconsistent with the particular utility function we are studying, since it implies that the only aim of the companies is to reduce their variance as much as possible. The appropriate utility function should then be a decreasing function of V alone. That the aim of reinsurance arrangements is to reduce the variance, and at the same time retain as much as possible of the net premium is assumed, more or less explicitly, by many writers, for instance, by Thepaut [15]. This principle, as shown in [5], leads to a stop loss treaty as the most efficient form of reinsurance.

5.20. Several authors have suggested that the correct loading of reinsurance premiums should be proportional to the standard deviation. As early as in 1936 Wold [16] mentions this as a "natural rule." Ammeter [2] in 1955 states that in his opinion "there are definite reasons to make the loading proportionate to the standard deviation."

The principle means in our terminology that

$$Q_1 = \alpha k_1 \sqrt{V_1} \quad \text{and} \quad Q_2 = \alpha k_2 \sqrt{V_2}$$

where α is constant. We find

$$Q = \alpha(k_1 \sqrt{V_1} - k_2 \sqrt{V_2})$$

or $\quad Q = \alpha(k \sqrt{V_1} - (1 - k) \sqrt{V_2}$

which, when substituted in the Pareto condition

$$Q = -(b - R_1 - R_1)k + \tfrac{1}{2}b - R_2$$

gives the determinate solution

$$k = \frac{\tfrac{1}{2}b - R_2 - \sqrt{V_2}}{\alpha(\sqrt{V_1} + \sqrt{V_2}) + (b - R_1 - R_2)}$$

which can be nonoptimal for certain values of α. Ammeter does not explain his "definite reasons" in any detail. However, if spelt out in our terminology these reasons would certainly appear to be that he assumes a utility function different from the one we have used in this chapter.

6. A Numerical Example

6.1. It may be useful to illustrate the results above by means of a simple numerical example. Let

$$R_1 = 1 \quad V_1 = 1 \quad R_2 = 2 \quad V_2 = 4$$

Table 3-1
Optimal solution: Value of the utility index[a]

		Utility index	
k	Q	Company 1	Company 2
0.400	-0.200	3.960	6.760
0.402	-0.207	4.000	6.733
0.450	-0.350	4.765	6.165
0.500	-0.500	5.500	5.500
0.550	-0.650	6.165	4.765
0.598	-0.793	6.733	4.000
0.600	-0.800	6.760	3.960

[a]The Nash solution is given by $k = 0.5$.

According to the classical theory of risk, these two companies are in equivalent situations, since they both have free reserves equal to the standard deviation of the risk distribution.

Further let $b = 6$. This is an arbitrary choice, for which we offer no particular justification. We note, however, that in general $b = 2(R_1 + R_2)$ means that the utility index reaches its highest possible value only if one company acquires all the free reserves of the other.

6.2. For the initial values of the utility index we have

Company 1: $R_1(b - R_1) - V_1 = 4$

Company 2: $R_2(b - R_1) - V_2 = 4$

The pareto optimum is given by $Q = -3k + 1$. The solution is given by the intervals

$$0.402 \leqslant k \leqslant 0.598$$

$$-0.793 \leqslant Q \leqslant -0.207$$

The utility indices (expressed by k) after the agreement has been reached are:

Company 1: $9 - 14(1 - k)^2$

Company 2: $9 - 14k^2$

The value of these indices for some values of k are given in Table 3-1.

6.3. As an example of a nonoptimal solution, we will consider the case where the two companies at the outset of their negotiations agree that it is "fair"

Table 3-2
Nonoptimal solution: Value of the utility index

k	Utility index	
	Company 1	Company 2
0.50	3.750	6.750
0.55	3.983	6.487
0.60	4.200	6.200
0.65	4.387	5.887
0.70	4.550	5.550
0.75	4.683	5.183
0.80	4.800	4.800
0.85	4.883	4.383
0.90	4.950	3.950

that only the net premium should be paid for placing the reinsurance, i.e., $Q = 0$. We assume that the two companies realize that the Pareto optimum consists of quotas which add up to unity, and that they agree that company 1 shall cede a quota k, and in return receive a quota $1 - k$ from company 2. The utility indices will be

Company 1: $\quad R_1(b - R_1) - (1 - k)^2 (V_1 + V_2) = 5 - 5(1 - k)^2$

Company 2: $\quad R_2(b - R_2) - k^2(V_1 + V_2) = 8 - 5k^2$

Table 3-2 gives the value of these indices for some selected values of k. It is easy to show that, unless $0.553 \leqslant k \leqslant 0.894$, one of the companies will be worse off than it was in the initial situation.

6.4. As another example of a nonoptimal solution we will consider the case where $Q = 0$, and where the quotas do not add up to unity. Let k_1 be the quota ceded by company 1 to company 2, and let k_2 be the quota ceded by company 2 to company 1. The utility indices will be

Company 1: $\quad R_1(b - R_1) - (1 - k_1)^2 V_1 - k_2^2 V_2 = 5 - (1 - k_1)^2 - 4k_2^2$

Company 2: $\quad R_2(b - R_2) - k_1^2 V_1 - (1 - k_2)^2 V_2 = 8 - k_1^2 - 4(1 - k_2)^2$

Table 3-3 gives the utility indices for some selected values of k_1 and k_2.

6.5. The three tables illustrate very well the "loss of utility" by concluding an agreement represented by a point (Q, k_1, k_2) which is not in the Pareto optimum. This is best seen by comparing the cases where the gain in utility is the same for both companies. We find

Table 3-3
Nonoptimal solution: Value of the utility index

		Utility index	
k_1	k_2	Company 1	Company 2
0.1	0.1	4.15	4.75
0.1	0.2	4.03	5.43
0.1	0.3	3.83	6.03
0.2	0.1	4.32	4.72
0.2	5.2	4.20	5.40
0.2	0.3	4.00	6.00
0.3	0.1	4.43	4.67
0.3	0.2	4.35	5.35
0.3	0.3	4.15	5.95
0.4	0.1	4.60	4.60

(i)   For the optimal point (the Nash solution), (-0.5, 0.5, 0.5)) in Table 3-1, utility index 5.5
(ii) For the nonoptimal point, (0, 0.8, 0.2) in Table 3-2, utility index 4.8
(iii) For the nonoptimal point (0, 0.4, 0.1) in Table 3-3, utility index 4.6

In the initial situation, i.e., in the point (0, 0, 0) the utility index is 4.0.

The significance of an increase in the utility index may not be immediately clear, particularly since the utility index itself is determined only up to a linear transformation. To get an interpretation with more of an intuitive appeal, we note that the utility index can be increased by adding to the free reserves of the company, without making any reinsurance arrangements. This means that the increase in utility resulting from a gift to the company of a certain sum of money must be the same as the increase resulting from the reinsurance arrangement. Mathematically this means that if a reinsurance arrangement changes the utility index from $U(R, V)$ to $U(R', V')$, there exists a number S such that

$$U(R + S, V) = U(R', V')$$

S is the "gift" which measures the gain in utility by the reinsurance arrangement. For company 1 we find that a utility index of 5.5 corresponds to an increase of 42% in the free reserves, a utility index of 4.8 corresponds to an increase of 21%, and a utility index of 4.6 to an increase of 10%.

6.6.   We have made a number of—possibly doubtful—assumptions to reach this result, so one should be careful not to draw any sweeping conclusions. However, one may be warranted in stating that a careful analysis of the *objectives* of a company's reinsurance policy may be an investment which might pay a handsome dividend. Only if the objectives are clear can a company be certain that it does not pay too much for the security it obtains by reinsurance.

References

1. Allais, M. Le comportement de l'homme rationnel devant le risque: Critique des postulates et axiomes de l'école américaine. *Econometrica* (1953): 503–546.
2. Ammeter, H. The calculation of premium rates for excess of loss and stop loss reinsurance treaties. Pp. 79–110 in *Non-proportional Reinsurance,* ed. by S. Vajda (Brussels 1955).
3. Arrow, K. *Social Choice and Individual Values,* Cowles Commission Monograph No. 12, Chicago 1951.
4. Bernoulli, D. Exposition of a New Theory on the Measurement of Risk, *Econometrica* (1954): 23–46. (Translation of "Specimen Theoriae Novae de Mensura Sortis," St. Petersburg, 1738).
5. Borch, K. An attempt to determine the optimum amount of stop loss reinsurance. Proceedings of the XVIth International Congress of Actuaries, Vol. I, 597–610, Brussels 1960.
6. Cramér, Harald. "On the Mathematical Theory of Risk," *Skandia Jubilee Volume* (Stockholm, 1930): 7–84.
7. Cramér, Harald. "Collective Risk Theory," *Skandia Jubilee Volume* (1955).
8. Harsanyi, J. C. "Approaches to the Bargaining Problem Before and After the Theory of Games," *Econometrica* (1956): 144–157.
9. Herstein, I. N. and Milnor, J. "An Axiomatic Approach to Measurable Utility," *Econometrica* (1953): 291–297.
10. Marschak, J. Rational Behaviour, Uncertain Prospects, and Measurable Utility, *Econometrica* (1950): 111–141.
11. Nash, J. F. "The Bargaining Problem," *Econometrica* (1950): 155–162.
12. ——. "Two Person Co-operative Games," *Econometrica* (1953): 128–140.
13. Neumann, J. von and Morgenstern, O. *Theory of Games and Economic Behaviour,* 2nd edition (Princeton University Press, 1947).
14. Savage, L. *The Foundation of Statistics* (New York: John Wiley & Sons, 1954).
15. Thepaut, A. Le traité d'excédent de coût moyen relatif (ECOMOR), *Bull. Inst. Actu. Franç.* (1950): 273–344.
16. Wold, H. *Landsbygdens Brandförsäkringsbolags Maximaler och Återförsäkring* (Stockholm, 1936).
17. Zeuthen, F. *Problems of Monopoly and Economic Warfare* (London, 1930).

4 Reciprocal Reinsurance Treaties

I. Introduction

1.1. In this paper we shall study the situation of two insurance companies which are negotiating with the view of concluding a reciprocal reinsurance treaty. We assume that the two companies are under no compulsion to reach an agreement. This means that if the companies conclude a treaty, the treaty must be such that *both* companies consider themselves better off than without any treaty. We further assume that no third company can break into the negotiations. This means that the two companies either have to come to terms, or be without any reinsurance.

1.2. How the two parties reach an agreement in a situation like this, is one of the classical problems of theoretical economics. It is usually referred to as the "bargaining problem." The problem appears very simple, but this is a deception. It has proved extremely difficult to formulate generally acceptable assumptions which give the problem a determinate solution. The "theory of games," developed by von Neumann and Morgenstern [10], does not give a determinate solution, but it has greatly increased our understanding of such problems, and the present paper will draw heavily on that theory.

1.3. The situation which we propose to study, is very simple, may be too simple to have any bearing on reinsurance negotiations in real life. If there exists a reinsurance market, which also is a *perfect market* in the sense given to this term in economic theory, bartering between two companies does not make any sense. They could both do equally well or better by dealing in the market at the market price.

To illustrate the point, let us consider two suburban housewives who go downtown for shopping. If they both do their shopping according to a well-prepared list at a perfect supermarket, neither of them will gain anything by swapping the goods they have bought, after they get home to their suburb. However, if the two housewives go bargain-hunting at a sale, they may both gain considerably by a friendly private barter after their return to peaceful suburban surroundings.

It seems likely that the reinsurance market is more similar to the bargain counter than to the well-ordered supermarket, where everything is available at a

53

fixed price. If this is so, there will be scope for reciprocal treaties, also between companies which have made full use of their possibilities of dealing in the market.

1.4. Even if the model we propose to study is too simple to have any practical value, it may still be of interest to analyze it in some detail. Only if we gain a full understanding of the simplest possible case, that of the two companies, can we hope to tackle the more complicated cases with some success.

2. The Model

2.1. We assume that company 1 has a portfolio of insurance contracts such that $F_1(x_1)$ is the probability that the total amount of claims made under these contracts shall not exceed x_1. We shall call $F_1(x_1)$ the *risk distribution* of company 1. We assume further that the company holds funds amounting to S_1 which are available to pay claims. The two elements $F_1(x_1)$ and S_1 determine what we shall call the *risk situation* of the company.

The company will be solvent in the ordinary actuarial sense if

$$\int_0^\infty x_1 \, dF_1(x_1) \leqslant S_1$$

Similarly we assume that company 2 has a risk distribution $F_2(x_2)$ and funds S_2. We assume that the random variables x_1 and x_2 are statistically independent.

2.2. The companies have no control over the random variables x_1 and x_2. If claims amounting to x_1 and x_2 occur, the companies have to meet these claims. Unless they agree otherwise, company 1 will pay the amount x_1 and and company 2 x_2. However, the companies are completely free to agree on any other way of dividing the total amount of claims $x_1 + x_2$ between themselves. The companies can for instance agree that company 1 shall pay an amount $y(x_1, x_2)$ if claims amounting to x_1 and x_2 occur in the two portfolios. Company 2 will then have to pay the remainder, i.e., $x_1 + x_2 - y(x_1, x_2)$.

Hence any real-valued function $y(x_1, x_2)$ defined for all positive values of x_1 and x_2 will represent a possible agreement between the two companies, i.e., a reciprocal reinsurance treaty.

2.3. The function $y(x_1, x_2)$ depends only on the total amounts of claims x_1 and x_2. Hence a function of this kind can only represent a treaty which is truly *collective* in the sense that the reinsurer's liability depends only on the total amount of claims. Whether this amount has arisen as a result of one big claim or a large number of small ones, is irrelevant. Many, if not most, of the treaties we meet in practice are not collective in this sense.

It would not be difficult to generalize our model so that such noncollective treaties can be included. However, this would necessitate considering separately each contract in the portfolio and would certainly lead to very cumbersome formulas. It seems preferable at the present stage to avoid such arithmetical complications and confine our study to collective treaties.

2.4.   It may be desirable to give a few examples which will illustrate the kind of treaties which can be represented by a function $y (x_1, x_2)$.

(i) *No treaty.*   If the companies do not conclude any agreement, it is obvious that

$$y (x_1, x_2) = x_1$$

(ii) *Stop loss cover.*   It is agreed that if claims against company 1 exceed N, the excess shall be paid by company 2. This treaty gives

$$y (x_1, x_2) = x_1 + P \quad \text{for } x_1 \leqslant N$$

$$= N + P \quad \text{for } N < x_1$$

where P is the premium company 1 pays for the cover.

If we want to take into consideration the possibility that company 2 may be unable to meet its commitments, we get a more complicated function. If other claims against company 2 have priority over claims under the treaty, we obtain

$$y (x_1, x_2) = x_1 + P \qquad \text{for } x_1 \leqslant N \text{ for all } x_2$$

$$= N + P \qquad \text{for } N < x_1 \text{ and } x_2 < S_2 + P + N - x_1$$

$$= x_1 + x_2 - S_2 \qquad \text{for } N < x_1 \text{ and } S_2 + P + N - x_1$$

$$< x_2 < S_2 + P$$

$$= x_1 + P \qquad \text{for } N < x_1 \text{ and } S_2 + P < x_2$$

In practice it is not usual to consider the possibility that the reinsurer shall become insolvent, but in our artificial two-company world such considerations may be important. Nevertheless, we will ignore them in the following.

(iii) *Quota share treaty.*   Company 1 agrees to cede a quota k of each risk in its portfolio, against a commission α. This is expressed by

$$y (x_1, x_2) = (1 - k)x_1 + kP_1 - \alpha k P_1$$

where P_1 is the premium of the total portfolio of company 1.

(iv) *Quota Share with sliding scale commission.*   Let the commission be:

$$\alpha_1 \qquad\qquad \text{for } \frac{x_1}{P_1} < r_1$$

$$\alpha_2 \qquad\qquad \text{for } \frac{x_1}{P_1} > r_2$$

$$\frac{\alpha_1 (r_2 - x_1/P_1) + \alpha_2 (x_1/P_1 - r_1)}{r_2 - r_1} \quad \text{for } r_1 \leqslant \frac{x_1}{P_1} \leqslant r_2$$

Inserting this in the expression in the previous example, we find

$$y(x_1, x_2) = (1 - k)x_1 + (1 - \alpha_1)kP_1 \qquad \text{for } \frac{x_1}{P_1} < r_1$$

$$= (1 - k)x_1 + (1 - \alpha_2)kP_1 \qquad \text{for } \frac{x_1}{P_1} > r_2$$

For $r_1 \leqslant x_1/P_1 \leqslant r_2$ we have:

$$y(x_1, x_2) = (1 - k)x_1 + \left(1 - \frac{\alpha_1(r_2 - x_1/P_1) + \alpha_2(x_1/P_1 - r_1)}{r_2 - r_1}\right)kP_1$$

$$= \left(1 - k + k\frac{\alpha_1 - \alpha_2}{r_2 - r_1}\right)x_1 + kP_1 - \frac{r_2\alpha_1 - r_1\alpha_2}{r_2 - r_1} kP_1$$

In practice we frequently find treaties where $\alpha_1 + r_1 = \alpha_2 + r_2$. Golding [8] gives an example where $r_1 = 0.46, r_2 = 0.65$, and $\alpha_1 + r_1 = \alpha_2 + r_2$ is approximately 0.975. In this case we will have

$$y(x_1, x_2) = x_1 + 0.025 \, kP_1 \qquad \text{for } 0.46 < \frac{x_1}{P_1} < 0.65$$

Benktander [2] has with some justification called a treaty of this kind an "Imperfect Nonsense Treaty," perfection being achieved as $r_1 \to 0$ and $r_2 \to \infty$.

2.5. We now assume that the two companies open negotiations with the purpose of improving their risk situations. The outcome of these negotiations will be a reciprocal treaty, which we assume can be represented by a function $y(x_1, x_2)$. However, the purpose stated has no meaning, unless the companies have some *scale of value* which will enable them to decide whether one risk situation is better than another.

It seems almost self-evident that an insurance company must have such a scale of value in order to be able to decide in a rational manner whether it shall accept or reject any contract which is offered. If we assume that this scale is *complete,* in the sense that it can be applied in any situation, without ever leading to inconsistencies and discontinuities, this will have farreaching implications. The precise formulation of these assumptions and their consequences have been discussed in some detail in a previous paper [5] and will not be repeated here.

2.6.   If an insurance company states that S is the lowest price at which it will accept responsibility for a portfolio with risk distribution $F(x)$, the company must somehow consider that the advantage of receiving the amount S with certainty just balances the disadvantage of assuming liability for the claims which may occur in the portfolio. This equivalence between a payment made with certainty and a payment which is a random variable, is the basis for all insurance contracts.

Assume now that $u(x)$ is the value or *utility* the company attaches to the prospect of receiving an amount x with certainty. From the assumptions mentioned in the preceding paragraph it then follows that the company will attach a utility $U(S, F(x))$ to a risk situation with elements S and $F(x)$, where

$$U(S, F(x)) = \int_0^\infty u(S - x)\, dF(x)$$

This is the farreaching implication referred to. It should be noted that $u(x)$, and hence $U(S, F(x))$ are determined only up to a linear transformation. The function $u(x)$ is usually referred to as the *utility of money* to the company. This function should be interpreted as a rule for computing certain payment which is equivalent to a risk situation. We will assume that $u(x)$ is a nondecreasing differentiable function of x.

2.7.   The purpose of the negotiation between the companies can now be stated in a more precise manner. Let $u_1(x)$ be the utility of money to company 1. The company's utility in the initial situation is then

$$U_1(0) = \int_0^\infty u_1(S_1 - x_1)\, dF_1(x_1)$$

The reinsurance treaty defined by $y(x_1, x_2)$ will change the company's utility to:

$$U_1(y) = \int_0^\infty \int_0^\infty u_1(S_1 - y(x_1, x_2))\, dF_1(x_1)\, dF_2(x_2)$$

[It may be more consistent if we write $U_1(x_1)$ for the utility in the initial situation, but we shall prefer $U_1(0)$].

In the negotiations company 1 will try to secure agreement on a function

$y\,(x_1, x_2)$ which gives $U_1\,(y)$ the highest possible value. If $u_2\,(x)$ is the utility of money to company 2, this company has an initial utility of

$$U_2\,(0) = \int_0^\infty u_2\,(S_2 - x_2)\,dF_2(x_2)$$

The treaty defined by $y\,(x_1, x_2)$ will change this utility to

$$U_2\,(y) = \int_0^\infty \int_0^\infty u_2\,(S_2 - x_1 - x_2 + y\,(x_1, x_2))\,dF_1(x_1)\,dF_2(x_2)$$

In the negotiations company 2 will try to obtain the greatest possible value of $U_2\,(y)$. Since $u_1\,(x)$ and $u_2\,(x)$ are nondecreasing functions, it is clear that the two companies are pursuing objectives which are directly opposed and that they will have to reach a compromise. The outcome of the negotiations will be a function $y\,(x_1, x_2)$ which is optimal in the sense that both parties consider that it represents the best treaty they could obtain in the given situation.

3. The Optimal Treaty

3.1.   In order to determine the optimal treaty, we must make some assumptions as to the manner in which the negotiations are conducted. We assume that the companies act *rationally* and that they *cooperate*. This implies that they will not agree on a function $\bar{y}\,(x_1, x_2)$ if there exists another function $y\,(x_1, x_2)$ such that

$$U_1\,(\bar{y}) \leqslant U_1\,(y) \quad \text{and} \quad U_2\,(\bar{y}) \leqslant U_2\,(y)$$

where both equality signs cannot hold simulatneously.

$\bar{y}\,(x_1, x_2)$ is clearly inferior to $y\,(x_1, x_2)$, since the latter function gives a higher utility to at least one of the companies. We say that $\bar{y}\,(x_1, x_2)$ is *dominated* by $y\,(x_1, x_2)$. The set of functions $y\,(x_1, x_2)$ which are not dominated is referred to as the *Pareto optimal* set.

It follows from our assumptions of rationality that neither company will agree to a function $y\,(x_1, x_2)$ if it gives a lower utility than the company has in the initial situation. The company will be better off by refusing to conclude a treaty.

From our assumptions it follows that the optimal treaty is represented by a function $y\,(x_1, x_2)$ with the following properties:

(i)   It belongs to the Pareto optimal set.
(ii) It satisfies the conditions:

$$U_1\,(0) \leqslant U_1\,(y) \quad \text{and} \quad U_2\,(0) \leqslant U_2\,(y)$$

3.2. These conditions will in general define a set of functions, and not a unique optimal function. To get a determinate solution to our problem we must make additional assumptions. This can be done in several ways. The most general and most attractive is probably the set of axioms proposed by Nash [9].

The basic assumptions made by Nash is that in a completely symmetric situation two rational bargainers will agree to maximize the joint gain, and then divide it equally between themselves. Applied to our particular case, this means that the two companies will agree upon the function $y(x_1, x_2)$ which maximizes the product:

$$\left\{U_1\left(y(x_1, x_2)\right) - U_1(0)\right\}\left\{U_2\left(y(x_1, x_2)\right) - U_2(0)\right\}$$

This function will be referred to as the Nash solution to our problem.

3.3. We will now determine the Pareto optimal set. We assume that $y(x_1, x_2)$ belongs to this set, and we consider the function

$$\bar{y}(x_1, x_2) = y(x_1, x_2) + \epsilon(x_1, x_2)$$

where $\epsilon(x_1, x_2)$ is an arbitrary function of small absolute value.

The assumptions that $y(x_1, x_2)$ is Pareto optimal implies that the two inequalities

$$\Delta U_1 = U_1(\bar{y}) - U_1(y) > 0$$
$$\Delta U_2 = U_2(\bar{y}) - U_2(y) > 0$$

cannot hold simultaneously for any $\epsilon(x_1, x_0)$

We have for company 1

$$\Delta U_1 = \int_0^\infty \int_0^\infty \left\{u_1(S_1 - y - \epsilon) - u_1(S_1 - y)\right\} dF_1(x_1) dF_2(x_2)$$

Since $\epsilon(x_1, x_2)$ is small in absolute value, we can write

$$u_1(S_1 - y - \epsilon) - u_1(S_1 - y) = -u_1'(S_1 - y)\epsilon(x_1, x_2)$$

hence

$$\Delta U_1 = -\int_0^\infty \int_0^\infty u_1'(S_1 - y)\epsilon(x_1, x_2) dF_1(x_1) dF_2(x_2)$$

For company 2 we find

$$\Delta U_2 = \int_0^\infty \int_0^\infty u_2'(S_2 - x_1 - x_2 + y)\epsilon(x_1, x_2) dF_1(x_1) dF_2(x_2)$$

Both ΔU_1 and ΔU_2 will change sign with $\epsilon\,(x_1, x_2)$. Hence to make certain that the inequalities

$$\Delta U_1 > 0 \quad \text{and} \quad \Delta U_2 > 0$$

are not both satisfied for any $\epsilon\,(x_1, x_0)$ we must require that

$$\Delta U_1\,\Delta U_2 \leqslant 0 \quad \text{for all } \epsilon\,(x_1, x_2)$$

A *sufficient* condition is that

$$u_2'\,(S_2 - x_1 - x_2 + y) = k u_1'\,(S_1 - y)$$

where k is a positive constant.

If this condition is satisfied, we have

$$\Delta U_1\,\Delta U_2 = -k\left\{\int_0^\infty \int_0^\infty u_1'\,(S_1 - y)\epsilon(x_1, x_2)\,dF_1\,(x_1)\,dF_2\,(x_2)\right\}^2$$

3.4. To prove that the condition also is necessary, we put

$$u_2'\,(S_2 - x_1 - x_2 + y) = k\left\{u_1'\,(S_1 - y) + v\,(x_1, x_2)\right\}$$

where $v\,(x_1, x_2) = 0$ except over a set A.

We can then show that unless

$$\int_A dF_1\,(x_1)\,dF_2(x_2) = 0$$

it will be possible to find a function $\epsilon\,(x_1, x_2)$ such that

$$\Delta U_1\,\Delta U_2 > 0$$

This proves the statement.

3.5. We have thus found that the Pareto optimal set consists of the functions $y\,(x_1, x_2)$ which satisfy the condition

$$u_2'\,(S_2 - x_1 - x_2 + y) = k u_1'\,(S_1 - y)$$

We have previously assumed that $u_1\,(x)$ and $u_2\,(x)$ are nondecreasing functions. If further we assume that $u_1'\,(x)$ and $u_2'\,(x)$ are monotonic decreasing functions (decreasing marginal utility of money), there will correspond at most one function $y(x_1, x_2)$ to any value of k. Hence the purpose of the negotiations between the companies is to agree on one value of k. It is easy to see that y will increase with k. Hence the smaller k is, the more favorable will the treaty be to company 1. Company 2 on the other hand will try to obtain agreement on the largest possible value of k.

We note that y does not depend on x_1 and x_2 separately, but only on their sum $x_1 + x_2 = z$, so that the treaty can be defined by a function $y(z, k)$.

The Nash solution to our problem will then be the value of k which maximizes

$$\left\{ U_1(y(z, k)) - U_1(0) \right\} \left\{ U_2(y(z, k)) - U_2(0) \right\}$$

3.6. It is remarkable that $y(z, k)$ depends only on the utility functions $u_1(x)$ and $u_2(x)$ and not on the risk distributions $F_1(x)$ and $F_2(x)$. This means that the type of reinsurance treaty which is optimal to two companies, depends only on the objectives which the companies pursue, or if one prefers another formulation, on the attitude to risk which determines these objectives. The composition of the portfolios, as expressed by the risk distributions, enters into the play only when it comes to selecting a particular value of k.

3.7. The preceding paragraphs should make it clear that a prerequisite to a rational theory of reinsurance is an *operational* statement of the objectives which the companies pursue. By "operational" is meant that the objectives are reduced to that of maximizing a mathematical expression.

Very little is known about these objectives. The few "statements of policy" which one finds from time to time are usually too incomplete to make an operational formulation possible. In some cases one may suspect that a statement of objectives, if completed, would prove inconsistent. It does therefore not seem to be a very promising approach to collect statements of policy and try to derive from them the properties of the functions which insurance companies try to maximize in their dealings on the reinsurance market.

Another approach would be from the normative point of view. From some general considerations one could probably lay down a set of rules as to what objectives an insurance company *ought to* pursue in its reinsurance policy. From these rules one could then derive the characteristics of the function which the company should seek to maximize.

However, before taking up any of these lines of thought, it is useful to gain some knowledge about the nature of the relations between the utility function and the optimal treaty. We will therefore in the following section study a few particular cases. We will select some mathematically simple and economically acceptable functions to represent the utility of money and find the form of treaty which in each case is optimal.

4. Some Special Cases

4.1. The simplest possible case appears to be that of both companies having a linear utility of money, so we are led to consider:

Example 1. $u_1(x) = a_1 x + b_1$ and $u_2(x) = a_2 x + b_2$.

It is easy to see that in this case the sole objective of the companies is to maximize expected profits. This means that the companies will not take into consideration the possibility of losses which may occur owing to deviations from the expected value of the amount of claims. It is intuitively clear that in this case there is no reason for an exchange of risks between the two companies. This is also brought out by the condition found in para. 3.5:

$$u_2'(S_2 - z + y) = k u_1'(S_1 - y)$$

which in this case is reduced to

$$a_2 = a_1 k$$

Since the utility function is determined only up to a linear transformation, the coefficients a_1 and a_2 have no significance, so that the condition can determine neither a value k, nor a function $y(x_1, x_2)$.

4.2. As the first nontrivial case we will consider:

Example 2. $u_1(x) = -x^2 + ax$

$$u_2(x) = x$$

The utility function $u_1(x) = -x^2 + ax$ has been studied in some detail in a previous paper [5]. It has an acceptable shape for $x < \frac{1}{2}a$. For $x > \frac{1}{2}a$ utility will decrease with increasing x, and this seems unreasonable. If no claims occur, the company's funds S_1 will become a clear profit. The utility function ought to be such that this result appears as the best possible outcome of the company's underwriting, i.e., we should have $2S_1 < a$.

To rule out any distortions due to decreasing utility of money, we will assume that $2(S_1 + S_2) < a$.

It is clear that the greater a is, the greater is the weight the company attaches to expected profits as compared to the weight given to possible losses.

The function $y(z, k)$ is determined by the relation

$$u_2'(S_2 - z + y) = k u_1'(S_1 - y)$$

In this example it is convenient to write $1/k$ instead of k, so that the relation becomes

$$k = -2 (S_1 - y) + a$$

which gives

$$y (z, k) = S_1 - \tfrac{1}{2}(a - k)$$

We see that $y (z, k)$, i.e., the amount which company 1 shall pay, does not depend on x_1 and x_2. Hence the optimal treaty is that company 2 shall take over liability for the whole portfolio of company 1, against a compensation of $S_1 - \tfrac{1}{2}(a - k)$.

It is not difficult to see that this must be the outcome of the negotiations between the two companies. In this example company 2 is not worried about risk of loss. It will accept any insurance contract as long as the premium it receives is just greater than the expected amount of claims. However, in its negotiations with company 1, company 2 obviously tries to obtain a compensation greater than this minimum premium. Company 1 on the other hand has a certain risk aversion. This means that it is willing to part with its whole portfolio, if it can retain a sufficiently large part of its funds. It will therefore try to pass on its total liability to company 2, against the lowest possible payment.

4.3. Since this example is very simple, it is useful to analyze it in some further detail. This will illustrate a number of points which it will be difficult to bring out clearly in the more complicated examples which will be considered later.

For the initial utilities we have:

Company 1: $U_1 (0) = \int_0^\infty \left\{ - (S_1 - x)^2 + a (S_1 - x) \right\} dF(x)$

or $U_1 (0) = -(S_1 - P_1)^2 + a (S_1 - P_1) - V_1$

where $P_1 = \int_0^\infty x \, dF_1 (x)$—the mean of the risk distribution—can be interpreted as the net premium of the company's portfolio, and where

$$V_1 = \int_0^\infty (x - P_1)^2 \, dF_1(x)$$

is the variance of the risk distribution.

Company 2: $U_2 (0) = \int_0^\infty (S_2 - x) \, dF_2 (x) = S_2 - P_2$

After the conclusion of the treaty, the utilities will be:

Company 1: $U_1(y) = -(\frac{1}{2}(a-k))^2 + a(\frac{1}{2}(a-k))$

or $U_1(y) = \frac{1}{4}(a^2 - k^2)$

Company 2: $U_2(y) = S_1 + S_2 - (P_1 + P_2) - \frac{1}{2}(a-k)$

It is easily verified that

$$U_1(y) > U_1(0) \text{ for } k < \sqrt{(a - 2(S_1 - P_1))^2 + 4V_1}$$

and $U_2(y) > U_2(0)$ for $k > a - 2(S_1 - P_1)$

Hence both companies will increase their utility if they agree on a value of k which satisfies the condition

$$a - 2(S_1 - P_1) < k < \sqrt{(a - 2(S_1 - P_1))^2 + 4V_1}$$

4.4. From our general assumptions of rationality and cooperation we can only deduce that the companies will agree on some value of k in this interval. In order to determine which value they will agree upon, we must, as mentioned in para. 3.2, introduce some additional assumptions.

According to the assumptions made by Nash, the companies will agree on the value of k which maximizes the product:

$$\{U_1(y) - U_1(0)\}\{U_2(y) - U_2(0)\}$$

which in this particular case becomes

$$\{S_1 - P_1 - \frac{1}{2}(a-k)\}\{\frac{1}{4}(a^2 - k^2) + (S_1 - P_1)^2 - a(S_1 - P_1) + V_1\}$$

This value is found to be

$$k = \frac{2}{3}\sqrt{(a - 2(S_1 - P_1))^2 + 4V_1} + \frac{1}{3}(a - 2(S_1 - P_1))$$

which is the Nash solution to the problem.

We note that as V_1 increases, k will increase, and hence the treaty will become more and more favorable to company 2. This illustrates one of the essential points in a bargaining situation. The greater V_1 is, the more anxious will company 1 be to obtain some reinsurance cover. Company 2, knowing this, will take advantage of the situation and exact a higher price.

It is also easy to show that the amount which company 1 pays, i.e., $S_1 - \frac{1}{2}(a-k)$ will decrease with increasing a, if k is determined as the Nash solution. This means that the less company 1 is concerned over the possibilities of loss, the better is the bargain it can make with company 2.

4.5. *Example 3.* $u_1(x) = -x^2 + a_1 x$

$$u_2(x) = -x^2 + a_2 x$$

The function $y(z, k)$ is determined by

$$-2(S_2 - z + y) + a_2 = k(-2(S_1 - y) + a_1)$$

which gives

$$y(z, k) = \frac{1}{1+k} z + \frac{k}{1+k} S_1 - \frac{1}{1+k} S_2 + \frac{a_2 - a_1 k}{2(1+k)}$$

By some rearrangement this can be written

$$y(x_1, x_2) = \frac{1}{1+k} (x_1 + x_2) + \frac{k}{1+k} P_1 - \frac{1}{1+k} P_2 +$$

$$+ \frac{2(S_1 - P_1) - 2k(S_2 - P_2) + a_2 - a_1 k}{2(1+k)}$$

It is easy to see that in this case the optimal treaty is an *exchange of quota shares*.

Company cedes a quota $k/(1+k)$ of its premium to company 2. If a claim x_1 occurs in the portfolio of company 1, this company will pay only the retained quota $1 - k/(1+k) = 1/(1+k)$.

Similarly company 2 cedes a quota $1/(1+k)$ of its premium P_2, and company 1 pays the amount $1/(1+k)/x_2$ if a claim amounting to x_2 occurs in the portfolio of company 2.

It is worth noting that the quotas ceded add up to unity.

4.6. *Example 4.* $u_1(x) = x^{1/3}$

$$u_2(x) = -x^2 + ax$$

The function $u_1(x) = x^{1/3}$ appears fairly acceptable as the utility function of an insurance company. For large positive values of x the function increases very slowly, and this seems quite plausible for a company which is not primarily concerned with making large profits. The rapid fall in utility as x decreases toward and through zero also seems acceptable. The function's behavior for large negative values of x is not so satisfactory, although it may be possible to provide some justification.

The function $y(z, k)$ is determined by

$$- 2 (S_2 - z + y) + a = \frac{k}{3} (S_1 - y)^{-2/3}$$

This is an equation of the fifth degree in y. To discuss its roots, we solve with respect to z and find:

$$z = y - \tfrac{1}{2}a + S_2 + \frac{k}{6} (S_1 - y)^{-2/3}$$

From this expression we see that:

(i)   As y increases from $-\infty$ to S_1, z will increase from $-\infty$ to $+\infty$.
(ii) As y increases from S_1 to $+\infty$, z will decrease from $+\infty$ to a certain mini-mum, and then increase to $+\infty$.

Hence to a given value of z there may correspond three values of y. However, two of these values will be greater than S_1, and this obviously has no meaning. $y (z, k) > S_1$ for all z and k means that company 1 accepts ruin in advance by agreeing to pay out more than the total of its funds, regardless of what the claims may amount to. However, there exists, for any positive z a unique function $y (z, k) \leqslant S_1$ which represents the Pareto optimal treaties.

It is clear that this set of treaties will give company 1 an assurance against ruin, since regardless of what the claims are, company 1 will never be called upon to pay more than S_1. The optimal treaty is thus very similar to a familiar *stop loss cover*.

4.7. *Example 5.* $u_1 (x) = \log x$

$$u_2 (x) = - x^2 + ax$$

$\log x$ is the utility function first proposed by Daniel Bernoulli. The function is not particularly suitable for our purpose, so we will study it owing to its histor-ical interest, and also because it may be useful as a limiting case of more accept-able functions.

The function $y (z, k)$ is given by

$$- 2 (S_2 - z + y) + a = \frac{k}{S_1 - y}$$

from which we obtain

$$y = \tfrac{1}{4}(a + 2S_1 - 2S_2 + 2z \pm \sqrt{(a - 2S_1 - 2S_2 + 2z)^2 + 8k}$$

If we take the square root with positive sign, we get

$$y\,(z,\,k) > \tfrac{1}{2}a - S_2 \qquad \text{for all } k$$

This means that we for all z and k will have $S_1 < y(z,\,k)$, since we have assumed in para. 4.2 that $2(S_1 + S_2) < a$. Hence we discard this case as meaningless, as we did it in the preceding example. Taking the negative sign of the square root, we get as the unique solution a function

$$y\,(z,\,k) < S_1 \qquad \text{for all } z \text{ and } k.$$

Hence the optimal treaty is also in this case a kind of stop loss cover.

4.8. It is interesting to compare the two last examples. It is clear that company 1 is in a much stronger bargaining position in Example 4 than in Example 5. In the former example the company is able to face the disagreeable prospect of ruin with some equanimity. It should therefore be able to make a favorable deal with company 2.

In example 5 the company considers its risk situation as infinitely bad if there is a probability of ruin different from zero, and the company is willing to pay any finite amount to get out of this situation. One is tempted to say that a company with this attitude to risk has nothing to do in the insurance business. Company 2 will obviously take advantage of this situation and drive a hard bargain. Since the initial utility of company 1 is $-\infty$, the case is messy and difficult to analyze in a neat manner, for instance, we can not apply Nash's methods without modifications. However, it is easy to see that almost any reasonable assumptions will lead to a treaty whereby Company 2 takes over the whole portfolio and all the funds of company 1.

4.9. It is also interesting to compare Example 2 and Example 5, since in both cases the optimal solution was that company 1 should hand its whole portfolio over to company 2. However, in Example 2 company 1 did not feel compelled to get rid of its portfolio. On the contrary it may be more to the point to say that company 1 takes advantage of the lighthearted attitude to risk of company 2, and gets rid of its liability on favorable terms. Company 1 may, for instance, be able to keep as profits a part of the safety loading in the premium it charged on its direct underwriting.

4.10. All the examples discussed above have given optimal treaties which in important aspects differ from the reinsurance arrangements we know from practice. However, these treaties are optimal only in our two-company model, and only under the assumptions which we have made. Before even thinking of applying our results in practice, we must examine the model critically. This is done in the following section.

5. Limitations of the Model

5.1.   The most obvious limitation is that our model only deals with the negotiations between *two companies*. This point has already been discussed in para. 1.3. It is well known from the theory of games that the situation will change radically if a third company enters into the negotiations. This is brought out clearly in Example 5. Here company 1 considers itself in desperate need of reinsurance, and company 2 takes advantage of this to acquire all the funds of company 1. If, however, a company 3 should make a competing offer, which would enable company 1 to retain a part of its funds, this offer will obviously be preferred to the harsh terms dictated by company 2. This may again induce company 2 to make a better offer. If there is no "collusion" between companies 2 and 3, the problem will have a solution. In general the solution will be a treaty such that any treaty more favorable to company 1 would give at least one of the companies 2 and 3 a lower utility than they have in the initial solution.

However, if companies 2 and 3 should agree to join in exercising pressure on company 1, this company would have to part with all its funds. The two other companies would then have to bargain on how they should divide between themselves the proceeds of their collusion.

Neither the theory of games, nor other theories of oligopoly are at the present time able to deal with the problem of collusion in a fully satisfactory manner. It therefore seems extremely difficult to extend the model to include more than two companies, except in the case of perfect competition or no collusion. This problem is the subject of a paper [6].

5.2.   As mentioned in para. 2.4 our model does not take into consideration the possibility that the *reinsurer may be ruined*. In Examples 4 and 5 in Section 4 we found optimal treaties which implied that company 1 should pay more than its total funds to company 2. These treaties appeared as optimal because they would be extremely favorable to company 2 if they could be carried out. In the two examples mentioned we were able to reject these treaties. However, the same factor has obviously had some influence also in the other examples and may have distorted the results.

We do not propose to study this difficulty any further, since it is almost entirely of our making. It has been brought into the model by our drastic simplifications, and is likely to disappear in a more general and a more realistic model.

5.3.   The model we have studied appears to be *completely static*. The risk distribution $F(x)$ was presented as the probability that the portfolio in hand on a certain day should lead to an amount of claims not exceeding x by the time when all contracts in the portfolio have expired. If one can assume that new business comes in at a rate which will keep the company's risk distribution fairly constant over a certain period of time, the model may have some practical applicability, although certainly of a very limited scope.

However, there should be no principal difficulty involved in replacing the risk distribution $F(x)$ by a stochastic process and develop a more general theory. This would leave a major part of our formulas virtually unchanged, while the text would have to be reworded, and considerably more care would be required in the mathematical proofs. We have not attempted such a generalization in the present paper, since this inevitably would have focused attention on purely mathematical problems, which really are of secondary importance. The essential elements are the companies' evaluation of risk situations, and the ways in which companies can improve their risk situation through reinsurance arrangements, and these elements can best be understood by a detailed analysis of a simple and manageable model.

5.4.   Our model assumes that *both risk distributions are given,* or rather that both companies consider them as given. Behind this there must be some assumption that the two companies agree on the evaluation of every probability which enters into either portfolio. It was this assumption which in para. 3.5 led to optimal treaties implying that the companies should pool their portfolios, and then seek an agreement as to how the total amount of claims occurring in the joint portfolio should be divided between the companies.

If now one company proposes to put into the pool a contract according to which a claim x may occur with a probability p, the other company may suspect that the probability is underestimated. This company can either refuse to let the contract enter the pool, or it can demand that the first company as a proof of good faith shall retain a part of this contract on its own account, and only let the remainder go into the pool. We shall not elaborate this point. It is evident that considerations such as those above will lead to treaties of a more familiar kind, based on reinsurance of excedents.

5.5.   The assumptions, referred to in para. 2.6, which make it possible to represent a scale of values for risk situations by a real valued utility function, are usually referred to as the *Bernoulli hypothesis.* The hypothesis has been severely criticized by some authors such as Allais [1]. However, most authors seem to accept it as a normative rule for decision making under uncertainty. It has been shown by Chipman [7] that under weaker assumptions utility can be represented by a vector in a "lexicographical" ordering. We will not here explore the possibilities offered by Chipman's approach, although his utility concept seems very suitable for analyzing some statements of objectives made by insurance companies.

5.6.   In our model the only purpose of reinsurance is to improve the risk situation of the company. In practice there are a number of other factors which must be taken into account. For instance to a small company the contact with a large reinsurance company may be very valuable in itself. The reinsurer will be able to provide the company with useful advice and information from his world-wide connections and experience. On the other hand, a reciprocal treaty may have some inherent disadvantages to two companies which compete against each other, since the treaty necessitates making available a considerable amount of information to the competitor.

These factors are closely related to what authors on the theory of games refer to as "the pleasure derived from the game" and "the cost of playing the game." They are usually dismissed as being only of secondary importance, and do not seem to have been studied very much. We will not at the present study these factors, although they may justify some reinsurance treaties which appear irrational according to a simplified theory.

6. Conclusion

6.1.   The concept of utility has played a rather obscure part in economics and statistics since it was first introudced by Daniel Bernoulli [3] more than 220 years ago. The concept enjoyed a comparatively brief period of respectability when the Austrian School made marginal utility the very cornerstone of economic theory. The recent popularity of utility is due to von Neumann and Morgenstern [10] who made measurable utility an essential part of their "Theory of Games." Owing to the vast range of problems to which this theory can be applied, utility has become an apparently indispensable element in rational decision making, scientific management, and other disciplines closely related to the problems of reinsurance.

6.2.   Nolfi seems to have been the first to apply the modern utility concept to problems in insurance mathematics. In his first application [11] he studies the utility function of an insured person. In a later paper [12] he studies the utility function which an insurance company should maximize when deciding what safety loading to include in its premiums. This function weighs the loss which may occur if the loading is too small, against the possible inconveniences of a too heavy loading. This latter problem has also been discussed by Bierlein [4].

6.3.   The utility functions used by these authors seem plausible, and lead to reasonable results. One could, however, think of other functions which seem equally acceptable, but which will lead to very different, although still reasonable results.

The same applies to the utility functions studied in the present paper. Few of the functions discussed in the examples are so obviously unreasonable that they can be rejected outright. However, the various functions lead to very different optimal treaties. We have no means of saying which of these solutions are right or wrong, in general, or for particular types of insurance companies.

6.4. The inescapable conclusion seems to be that we know far too little about the objectives which insurance companies pursue, or ought to pursue in their reinsurance policy. However, unless these objectives can be spelt out in an operational manner, it is difficult to deny that the whole theory of risk and reinsurance hangs in the air. It is also difficult to see how one can avoid some concept of utility in order to build a firm foundation under this theory.

References

1. Allais, M. "Le Comportement de l'Homme Rationnel devant le Risque: Critique des Postulats et Axiomes de l'Ecole Americaine," *Econometrica*, vol. 23, pp. 503–546.
2. Benktander, G. Contribution to the discussion. *Transactions of the XVI International Congress of Actuaries*, Vol. 3.
3. Bernoulli, D. "Specimen Theoriae Novae de Mensura Sortis," St. Petersburg 1738. English translation *Econometrica*, vol. 22, pp. 23–36.
4. Bierlein, D. "Spieltheoretische Modelle für Entscheidungssituationen des Versicherers," *Blätter der Deutschen Gesellschaft für Versicherungs-Mathematik*, vol. III, pp. 461–469.
5. Borch, K. "Reciprocal Reinsurance Treaties seen as a Two-Person Co-operative Game," *Skandinavisk Aktuarietidskrift*, 1960, pp. 29–58.
6. Borch, K. "Equilibrium in a Reinsurance Market," *Econometrica*, vol. 30, pp. 424–444.
7. Chipman, J. S. "The Foundations of Utility," *Econometrica*, vol. 28, pp. 193–224.
8. Golding, C. E. *The Law and Practice of Reinsurance* (London: Buckley Press, 1954).
9. Nash, J. F. "The Bargaining Problem," *Econometrica*, vol. 18, pp. 155–162.
10. Neumann, J. von and O. Morgenstern. *Theory of Games and Economic Behavior* (Princeton, 1944).
11. Nolfi, P.: "Zur mathematischen Darstellung des Nutzens in der Versicherung," *Mitteilungen der Vereinigung schweizerischer Versicherungsmathematiker*, vol. 55, pp. 395–407.
12. Nolfi, P.: "Die Berücksichtigung der Sterblichkeitsverbesserung in der Rentenversicherung nach der Optimalmethode der Spieltheorie," *Mitteilungen der Vereinigung schweizerischer Versicherungsmathematiker*, vol. 59, pp. 29–48.

5 Some Elements of a Theory of Reinsurance

This paper will attempt to show that the so-called mathematical theory of risk is inadequate for proper analysis of the reinsurance problems which insurance companies have to deal with in practice. It will indicate how a more complete and possibly more useful theory can be developed by bringing in some elements of modern decision theory.

The theory of risk, which has been the pride of actuarial mathematics for almost a century, looks very impressive. In developing this theory, actuaries have overcome formidable mathematical problems and they have made important contributions to theoretical statistics. These byproducts are probably of greater value than the theory itself, which has found few applications in practice. Most of the insurance world seems, with some justification, to consider the theory of risk as a harmless hobby cultivated by actuaries in Continental Europe and particularly in Scandinavian countries. In a review article in a recent number of this *Journal*, Houston [6] concludes that the contemporary theory of risk, in spite of its many attractions, can hardly be considered as "practical."

The purpose of developing a theory of risk was to obtain a scientific basis for determining the correct safety-loading of premiums and the optimum amount of self-retention in life insurance, two eminently practical problems. In this paper, the question of safety-loading will not be discussed. A full analysis of this problem will require some assumptions about the demand for insurance and its price elasticity. This in itself is a very difficult subject which cannot be taken up here without being diverted from the main purpose of this paper.

When an insurance company reinsures a part of its portfolio, it buys security and pays for it. The company will forego a part of its expected profits in order to reduce the possibility of inconvenient losses. The management of the company has to weigh expected profit against possible loss. To reach the right decision in such situations is the main problem in reinsurance, and on this point the theory of risk is of little help.

The Present Theory of Risk

A practical example from a paper by Hultman [7] will illustrate the problem. Examining the records of the Swedish life insurance company THULE over the years 1929–1931, Hultman found that the *probability of ruin* for the company would be 0.387 if the company had made no arrangements for reinsurance. Usually it is extremely difficult to calculate this probability of ruin, which plays a leading part in the modern, so-called "collective" theory of risk, and Hultman's figure is an approximation, deliberately overestimated to be on the "safe side."

Hultman found that the average amount under risk on the insurance contracts in the company's portfolio was M = Swedish Kronor 4061. Hultman investigated what the probability of ruin would be under various reinsurance arrangements. Some of his results are given in Table 5–1.

Hultman and most other writers on the theory of risk, conclude their papers with a table of this kind. However, in spite of all the elegant mathematics which usually is displayed to calculate the probability of ruin, this is a rather sterile result. It is hard to imagine how a board of directors will use such a table when deciding what should be the maximum retention of their company. It is only in Finland that results of this kind seem to have found any important applications in practice. The Finnish Law of Insurance Companies of 1952 (§ 46) obliges the companies to keep an "adjustment reserve" calculated by the methods of the theory of risk.

In practice this means that the Government Inspector can order an insurance company to maintain adjustment reserves which are sufficient to keep the probability of ruin below a certain acceptable figure. So far no hard and fast rules have been laid down as to what ruin probability the Government Inspector will consider permissible for various types of companies. The principal reason appears to be that the probability can only be calculated approximately, and usually one knows little about how close the approximation may be. Another reason is that the practical significance of the probability of ruin is hard to grasp. By definition, the probability of ruin is the probability that the company shall be insolvent at least once, some time in the future, if there are changes neither in premium income nor in the basic probabilities underlying the claims, a very drastic *ceteris paribus* assumption.

In the example used by Hultman, the total amount of risk premium received by the company is Kronor 3 million. He assumes the safety-loading to be

Table 5–1

Maximum retention on one life	Probability of ruin
2M	0.000 051
3M	0.000 21
5M	0.001 61
10M	0.011 8
20M	0.048 5
50M	0.190
80M	0.350
∞	0.387

10%, so that the expected profit will be Kronor 300,000 if the company retains all risks for its own account. If the company reinsures a part of the larger risks, it is obvious that a part of expected profits will have to be passed on to the re-insurer, and Hultman assumes that the reinsurer requires a safety-loading of 15%. On the basis of these assumptions, Table 5-2 has been constructed as perhaps having a bearing on the real problem of reinsurance as it appears to a board of directors. This table illustrates how the management of an insurance company has to weigh expected profits against risk, measured by the probability of ruin, and decide on a maximum retention. Decisions of this kind have to be taken by managers in any kind of business, although they will hardly ever appear as clear cut as in the case of an insurance company.

Table 5-2 brings out the fact that the model considered in the theory of risk is very simple and quite arbitrary. The theory assumes that management considers only two *decision parameters,* the probability of ruin, and another which usually is left unspecified, although tacitly assumed to be expected profits.

A More General Theory

It is easy to generalize the model described in the preceding paragraphs. Any portfolio of insurance contracts will define a probability distribution $F(x)$, where $F(x)$ is the probability that the total profits on the portfolio shall not exceed x. The function $F(x)$ can be determined in two ways:

(i) As in the classical theory of risk, by building up $F(x)$ from the probability distributions defined by the individual contracts in the portfolio. (See Cramer [3].)

(ii) As in the collective theory of risk, by estimating the probability that a claim shall occur in a unit interval of time, and by determining the probability distribution of the size of the claims which occur. (See Cramer [4].)

For practical purposes, the latter method is obviously the easiest to apply. The

Table 5-2

Maximum retention	Expected profits	Probability of ruin
8 000	114 000	0.000 051
12 000	150 000	0.000 21
20 000	184 800	0.001 61
40 000	225 000	0.011 8
80 000	258 000	0.048 5
200 000	266 000	0.190
320 000	290 000	0.350
∞	300 000	0.387

data required can be obtained without difficulty from the records kept by any insurance company.

The two decision parameters of Table 5-2 are easily expressed by $F(x)$:

$$\text{Expected profits} = \int_{-\infty}^{+\infty} x \, dF(x)$$

$$\text{Probability of ruin} = \int_{-\infty}^{-S} dF(x)$$

where S is the total assets of the company. If profits are smaller than $-S$, the company will obviously be ruined.[1]

Assume now that a company considers a proposed reinsurance arrangement which will change the probability distribution of its portfolio from $F(x)$ to $G(x)$. It is obvious that the company will accept this arrangement only if in some way $G(x)$ is considered as "better" than $F(x)$. To select the best among a number of possible reinsurance arrangements is therefore the same problem as that of selecting the best in a set of probability distributions. The basic assumption of the theory of risk so far has been that when selecting the best probability distribution, it is sufficient to consider only the two parameters referred to above, and that all other properties of the probability distribution can be ignored. This assumption can, at best, be only a first approximation to a realistic analysis of reinsurance problems.

To give some meaning to the term "the best probability distribution," it is necessary to assume that an insurance company has some rule or standard which enables it to rank probability distributions according to their "goodness." In principle it is sufficient to assume that the set of all probability distributions is *completely ordered* with regard to the company's preference. This assumption implies the following:

(i)   When confronted with two probability distributions $F(x)$ and $G(x)$, the company is able to decide either that one of the distributions is better than the other, or that the two distributions are equally good.

(ii) If a company considers $F(x)$ as better than $G(x)$, and $G(x)$ as better than $H(x)$, it will also consider $F(x)$ as better than $H(x)$.

It seems almost self-evident that these assumptions must hold for any rationally managed insurance company. Now let $U(F(x))$ be a function defined for any probability distribution, such that

$$U(F(x)) < U(G(x))$$

if, and only if $G(x)$ is better than $F(x)$. $U(F(x))$ will be referred to as the *utility* of $F(x)$.

---

1. The ruin probability in Hultman's table is defined in a different way. It is however not necessary to discuss the point for the purpose of this paper.

Consider now the degenerate probability distribution $\epsilon(x - R)$ defined by

$$\epsilon(x - R) = 0 \quad \text{for } x < R$$

$$\epsilon(x - R) = 1 \quad \text{for } x \geqslant R$$

The utility of this distribution, $U(\epsilon(x - R))$ will then be the utility attached to the certainty of a profit R, and it is convenient to write $U(\epsilon(x - R)) = u(R)$.

If in addition to the assumptions made in the preceding paragraph, an assumption of continuity is also made, it follows that $u(R)$ is determined up to a linear transformation, and that

$$U(F(x)) = \int_{-\infty}^{+\infty} u(x) \, dF(x)$$

This result is usually referred to as the Bernoullian hypothesis. It gives the utility of a probability distribution expressed by the utility of events which are certain, or colloquially it states that the utility of a lottery ticket equals the weighed sum of the utilities of the prizes, and that the weights are the probabilities of gaining the various prizes. The assumptions leading to this result can be given in different forms. The most elegant derivation of the result is probably the one given by Herstein and Milnor [5].

The function $u(x)$ is usually referred to as the *utility of money*. It should be seen as an operator establishing an ordering over the set of all possible probability distributions, unless one is prepared to attach a meaning to statements such as: A profit of 2 million dollars is 10% bettern than a profit of 1 million dollars.

At this stage it is convenient to make a slight change of notation:

Let $F(x)$ stand for the probability that the amount of *claims paid* under the contracts in the portfolio shall not exceed x. In order to assume responsibility for this portfolio, the company has received a net premium

$$P = \int_0^\infty x \, dF(x).$$

In addition to the funds P, which the company must have in order to be solvent, it is assumed that the company has funds amounting to R. R will be referred to as the company's "free reserves."

The *risk situation* of the company is then completely determined by the following three elements:

(i)   Its underwriting responsibility, represented by the function $F(x)$, referred to as the *risk distribution*.
(ii) Its technical reserves P.
(iii) Its free reserves R.

The utility which the company attaches to this situation will be

$$\int_0^\infty u(R + P - x)\, dF(x)$$

Assume now that the company makes a reinsurance arrangement such that if a claim amounting to x occurs, the company will itself only pay the amount $y(x)$. The difference $x - y(x)$ will be paid by the reinsurer. It is easy to see that this arrangement will change the utility of the company to

$$\int_0^\infty u(R + P - y(x))\, dF(x)$$

$y(0)$, the amount to be paid if no claim occurs, can obviously be interpreted as the *price* which the company pays for reinsurance coverage. If there exists a reinsurance market where a company can obtain any kind of reinsurance coverage at a uniquely determined price, the company's problem would be to maximize its utility in the same way as consumers do in classical economic theory. However, it is by no means obvious that such a market exists, and this general problem will not be tackled in all its complexity. Instead, the simplest possible case will be analyzed in detail, that of two companies which seek to negotiate an agreement for exchange of risks, to the benefit of both parties. In insurance terminology, this is the case of two companies which negotiate a reciprocal reinsurance treaty. In the "Theory of Games" [9], the situation is referred to as a "two-person cooperative game."

Now let the risk situation of company 1 be determined by the elements

$$F_1(x_1), \quad R_1, \quad \text{and } P_1$$

where $P_1 = \int_0^\infty x_1\, dF_1(x_1)$

Assume further that the utility which the company attaches to an amount x of money is $u_1(x)$.

For company 2 we have in the same way:

$$F_2(x_2), R_2, P_2, \text{ and } u_2(x)$$

Assume that x_1 and x_2 are stochastically independent. The purpose of the negotiations between the two companies is to agree on a function $y(x_1, x_2)$. If the claims occurring in the two portfolios amount to x_1 and x_2, respectively, company 1 will pay the amount $y(x_1, x_2)$, and company 2 the remainder of the claims, i.e., $x_1 + x_2 - y(x_1, x_2)$.

It is clear that company 1 will seek agreement on a function $y(x_1, x_2)$ which makes the expression

$$\int_0^\infty \int_0^\infty u_1(R_1 + P_1 - y(x_1, x_2)) \, dF_1(x_1) \, dF_2(x_2) = U_1(y)$$

as great as possible. On the other hand, company 2 will seek to maximize the expression

$$\int_0^\infty \int_0^\infty u_2(R_2 + P_2 - x_1 - x_2 + y(x_1, x_2)) \, dF_1(x) \, dF_2(x) = U_2(y)$$

It is evident that the interest of the two companies, to some extent, are opposed, and that they will have to negotiate their way to a compromise. If the two companies proceed in a rational manner, their first step will be to discard all functions which can be considered as *nonefficient* solutions to their problem. It can be said that a function $\bar{y}(x_1, x_2)$ is nonefficient if there exists another function $y(x_1, x_2)$ which gives both companies a higher utility. If no such function exists, it can be concluded that $\bar{y}(x_1, x_2)$ is an efficient solution to the bargaining problem.

It has been shown in a previous paper [2] that a necessary and sufficient condition that $y(x_1, x_2)$ is an efficient solution, is that it satisfies the condition

$$u_1'(R_1 + P_1 - y(x_1, x_2)) = k u_2'(R_2 + P_2 - x_1 - x_2 + y(x_1, x_2))$$

where k is a positive constant. This general equation will not be discussed. Instead, the principles will be illustrated by analysis of a special case.

A Special Case

Let it be assumed that the utility of money to the two companies is given by

$$u_1(x) = -a_1 x^2 + x$$

$$u_2(x) = -a_2 x^2 + x$$

Utility functions of this form have been studied in a previous paper [1], and they seem to give satisfactory results.

In this case the condition for an efficient solution becomes

$$2a_1(R_1 + P_1 - y(x_1, x_2)) - 1 = 2a_2 k(R_2 + P_2 - x_1 - x_2 + y(x_1, x_2)) - k$$

which gives

$$y(x_1, x_2) = \frac{2a_1(R_1 + P_1) - 2a_2 k(R_2 + P_2) + 2a_2 k(x_1 + x_2) + k - 1}{2(a_1 + a_2 k)}$$

$$= \frac{a_2 k}{a_1 + a_2 k}(x_1 + x_2) + \frac{a_1}{a_1 + a_2 k}P_1 - \frac{a_2 k}{a_1 + a_2 k}P_2$$

$$+ \frac{2a_1 R_1 - 2a_2 k R_2 + k - 1}{2(a_1 + a_2 k)}$$

To simplify this expression the following symbols are introduced:

$$h = \frac{a_1}{a_1 + a_2 k'} \qquad 1 - h = \frac{a_2 k}{a_1 + a_2 k}$$

$$Q = \frac{2a_1 R_1 - 2a_2 k R_2 + k - 1}{2(a_1 + a_2 k)} = (1 - h)\left(\frac{1}{2a_2} - R_2\right) - h\left(\frac{1}{2a_1} - R_1\right)$$

One can then write

$$y(x_1, x_2) = (1 - h)(x_1 + x_2) + h P_1 - (1 - h) P_2 + Q$$

It is easy to see that the reciprocal reinsurance treaty defined by this function is an exchange of quota shares, where the quotas which are ceded add up to unity. Company 1 cedes to company 2 a quota of $100h\%$ of its net premium P_1. If claims amounting to x_1 occur in the portfolio of company 1, a corresponding quota will be paid by company 2. Company 1 itself will pay only the remainder $(1 - h)x_1$. In the same way, company 2 will cede a quota of $100(1 - h)\%$ to company 1. The last term Q, which may be a positive or negative, represents a net transfer of free reserves from company 1 to company 2.

When the utility function has the special form introduced in the first paragraph of this section, the initial utility of company 1 is:

$$U_1(0) = \int_0^\infty u_1(R_1 + P_1 - x_1)\, dF_1(x_1) = \int_0^\infty [-a_1(R_1 + P_1 - x_1)^2$$

$$+ (R_1 + P_1 - x_1)]\, dF_1(x_1) = -a_1 \int_0^\infty [R_1^2 + 2R_1(P_1 - x_1)$$

$$+ P_1 - x_1)^2]\, dF_1(x_1) + \int_0^\infty (R_1 + P_1 - x_1)\, dF_1(x_1)$$

$$= -a_1 R_1^2 - a_1 \int_0^\infty (P_1 - x_1)^2\, dF_1(x_1) + R_1$$

which by some rearrangement can be written

$$U_1(0) = \frac{1}{4a_1} - a_1\left(\frac{1}{2a_1} - R_1\right)^2 - a_1 V_1$$

where $V_1 = \int_0^\infty (x - P_1)^2 \, dF_1(x)$

is the variance of the company's risk distribution. It is easy to verify that the re-insurance treaty defined by $y(x_1, x_2)$ will give the company a utility:

$$U_1(y) = \frac{1}{4a_1} - a_1(1 - h)^2 \left[\left(\frac{1}{2a_1} + \frac{1}{2a_2} - R_1 - R_2 \right)^2 + V_1 + V_2 \right]$$

For company 2, the same procedure shows

$$U_2(0) = \frac{1}{4a_2} - a_2 \left(\frac{1}{2a_2} - R_2 \right)^2 - a_2 V_2$$

and $U_2(y) = \frac{1}{4a_2} - a_2 h^2 \left[\left(\frac{1}{2a_1} + \frac{1}{2a_2} - R_1 - R_2 \right)^2 + V_1 + V_2 \right]$

The subject of the negotiations between the companies is reduced to reaching agreement on a value of h. It is evident that company 1 will try to get agreement on the largest possible value of $h \leq 1$, and that company 2 will hold out for a value of h as small as possible.

If the companies act rationally, neither of them will accept a treaty which gives a lower utility than the company has in the initial situation, i.e., before any treaty is concluded. Hence we must have

$$U_1(0) \leq U_1(y)$$

$$U_2(0) \leq U_2(y)$$

These inequalities will define an interval for the values of h which are acceptable to both companies. However, which value of h within the interval, which the companies finally will agree upon cannot be determined without making some assumptions about the manner in which the negotiations are carried out.

Nash [8] has given an elegant proof that under some general and very acceptable assumptions rational bargainers will agree upon the value of h which maximizes the product

$$[U_1(y) - U_1(0)] \ [U_2(y) - U_2(0)]$$

This solution will not be discussed further. Its meaning will become clear in the following paragraphs.

It may be useful to discuss a simple numerical example to illustrate the results.

Let $R_1 = 1, R_2 = 3$ and $V_1 = 1, V_2 = 3$. Assume that the two companies have the same attitude to risk, and let

$$a_1 = a_2 = {}^1\!/_8$$

It is evident that company 2 is considerably better off than company 1. If the initial utilities are calculated by the formulae given earlier, they are found to be $^3\!/_4$ and $^3\!/_2$. To avoid unnecessary fractions, multiply all utilities by 8, (a change of unit measurement) so that the situation can be written

$$U_1(0) = 6 \quad \text{and} \quad U_2(0) = 12$$

If the companies conclude an efficient reinsurance treaty, the utilities bill become

$$U_1(y) = 16 - 20(1 - h)^2$$

$$U_2(y) = 16 - 20h^2$$

where h must lie in the interval

$$0.29 \leqslant h \leqslant 0.49$$

We find further $Q = 1 - 4h$.

The Nash solution is the value of h which maximizes the product

$$[10 - 20(1 - h)^2]\,[4 - 20h^2]$$

This value will be determined by a third-degree equation which has only one root between 0 and 1. This root is found to be approximately $h = {}^3\!/_8$. The corresponding transfer of free reserves is $Q = -0.5$.

Assume now that the two companies have realized that the efficient arrangement is to exchange quota shares which add up to unity. This really means that the companies pool their portfolios and divide claims against the pool between themselves, in a fixed proportion, and it is fairly easy to realize that this arrangement will give the best spread of risk. It is not so obvious how Q, the transfer of free reserves should be determined. For this purpose, simply assume that the companies make some arrangement. They can for instance agree that only net premiums should be paid for reinsurance cover, i.e., that $Q = 0$, or they can agree to calculate Q by adding a proportional loading to the net premiums ceded.

Table 5-3 gives the utilities of the two companies for some selected values of h and Q. The upper figure in each box gives the utility of company 1 and the lower figure the utility of company 2. The figures representing efficient solutions

Table 5–3
Utilities of the Two Companies by Various
Reinsurance Arrangements

h/Q	-1.0	-0.75	-0.5	-0.25	0	+0.25
$\frac{1}{8}$	8.96	7.90	6.71	5.39	3.96	2.40
	11.94	12.88	13.69	14.40	14.96	15.90
$\frac{1}{4}$	9.75	8.69	7.50	6.18	*4.75*	3.19
	11.75	12.69	13.50	14.19	*14.75*	15.69
$\frac{3}{8}$	10.44	9.38	*8.19*	6.87	5.44	3.88
	11.44	12.38	*13.19*	13.88	14.44	15.38
$\frac{1}{2}$	*11.00*	9.94	8.75	7.43	6.00	4.44
	11.00	11.96	12.75	13.44	14.00	14.94
$\frac{5}{8}$	11.44	10.38	9.19	7.87	6.44	4.88
	10.44	11.38	12.19	12.88	13.44	14.38
$\frac{3}{4}$	11.75	10.69	9.50	8.18	6.75	5.19
	9.75	10.69	11.50	12.19	12.75	13.69
$\frac{7}{8}$	11.94	10.88	9.69	8.37	6.94	5.38
	8.96	9.90	10.71	11.40	11.96	12.90

are set in italics. The Nash solution, corresponding to $h = \frac{3}{8}$ and $Q = -0.5$ gives utilities 8.19 and 13.19. It clearly represents a deal which two rational bargainers might settle for.

This table shows a whole range of possible agreements. However, only the agreements corresponding to the figures within the contour will have practical interest, since they alone will give *both* companies a higher utility than they have in the initial situation. The table brings out clearly that some preconceived idea, for instance that only net premiums should be paid to the reinsurer, can lead to nonefficient solutions. The column corresponding to $Q = 0$ is clearly nonefficient, since the columns to its left contain pairs which give both companies higher utility.

It has been assumed that each company has full knowledge of its own risk situation, as well as of the other party's. This is a reasonable assumption. It is not usual in reinsurance negotiations to hide information from the other party. There may be uncertainty about how one should evaluate some of the probabilities which enter into the risk distributions. However, it is still reasonable to assume that, having considered all the available information, the two companies arrive at the same evaluation of these probabilities.

It has also been assumed that both companies know the shape of the utility function which the other party seeks to maximize. This may be a dangerous assumption. There is nothing to prevent a company, during some reinsurance negotiation, from hiding its real motives from the opponent, and this may bring substantial advantages. This can be illustrated by an example.

If the utility function has the form $-ax^2 + x$, it is clear that the smaller a is, the less worried will the company be about risk. In the limiting case $a = 0$, the company will not be concerned with risk at all. Its sole objective will be to maximize expected profits.

Assume now that in reality the two companies' attitude to risk is such that $a_1 = a_2 = \frac{1}{8}$ as in our example, but that company 1 is able to give the impression that in its utility function $a_1 = \frac{1}{6}$. This means essentially that company 1 pretends to be more worried over risk than it really is, and exacts a higher compensation for the reinsurance cover it gives to company 2. If the bluff succeeds, and if the two companies, through some rational bargaining procedure, arrive at a Nash solution as a best possible deal, this will be the solution corresponding to $a_1 = \frac{1}{6}$ and $a_2 = \frac{1}{8}$. From the general formulas already given, the solution is found to be approximately

$$h = 0.5 \quad \text{and} \quad Q = -0.5$$

Table 5–3 shows that this solution will give company 1 a higher utility than $h = \frac{3}{8}$ and $Q = -0.5$, the solution corresponding to the true situation $a_1 = a_2 = \frac{1}{8}$. In other words, company 1 had made a gain at the expense of company 2, by hiding its real objectives.

This problem does not need to be discussed in more detail. It is obvious that possibilities of deceiving the opponent exist in most bargaining situations in real life, and a realistic theory of reinsurance should take account of such possibilities.

Conclusion

One who studies the theory of risk, inevitably becomes impressed by the brilliant mathematical analysis so many actuaries have produced in order to calculate the probability of ruin. However, one is also a little surprised that they hardly ever take time to explain why and how this probability is relevant to the decisions which are made by the management in an insurance company. This trivial question is pushed aside for the fascination of mathematical display.

A paper by Tauber [10] at the Sixth International Congress of Actuaries is typical in this respect. Tauber presented his paper in Vienna in 1909 when the Austrian school of economics had its heyday. It was therefore natural that he should begin with some introductory words to the effect that a reinsurance contract is a purchase of security, and that security like all other commodities must have its price. This price must be determined by supply and demand, i.e., by cost and utility. If Tauber had followed up this idea, the "theory of games and economic behavior" might have begun in Vienna in 1909 and not at Princeton in 1944. However, he dropped the subject, and after his two-page introduction, Tauber presents 60 pages of mathematics which has no bearing on the general problem which he formulated in a surprisingly modern manner.

The mathematical tools which Tauber needed to solve his problems have since been developed outside the insurance world. The purpose of this paper has been to show that these tools can be applied to the problems of reinsurance, and that they may help in gaining a deeper understanding of the mechanism of reinsurance markets.

References

1. Borch, K. "Reciprocal Reinsurance Treaties seen as a Two-Person Cooperative Game," *Skandinavisk Aktuarietidsskrift* (1960): 29–58.
2. Borch, K. "Reciprocal Reinsurance Treaties," *The ASTIN Bulletin*, vol. 1, pp. 170–191.
3. Cramer, H. "On the Mathematical Theory of Risk," *Skandia Jubilee Volume* (1930): 7–84.
4. Cramer, H. "Collective Risk Theory," *Skandia Jubilee Volume* (1955).
5. Herstein, I. N. and J. Milnor. "An Axiomate Approach to Measurable Utility," *Econometrica* (1953): 291–297.
6. Houston, D. B. "Risk Theory," *The Journal of Insurance*, vol. 27, no. 1, pp. 77–82.
7. Hultman, K. "Einige Numerische Untersuchungen auf Grund der kollektiven Risikotheorie," *Skandinavisk Aktuarietidsskrift* (1942): 84–119 and 169–199.
8. Nash, J. "The Bargaining Problem," *Econometrica* (1950): 155–162.
9. Neumann, J. von and O. Morgenstern. *Theory of Games and Economic Behavior* (Princeton, 1944).
10. Tauber, A. "Über Risiko und Sicherheitszuschlag," *Report of the Sixth International Congress of Actuaries*, pp. 781–842, Vienna, 1909.

6

The Utility Concept Applied to the Theory of Insurance

1. Introduction

1.1. In some recent papers [1, 2, 3] about reinsurance problems I have made extensive use of utility concepts. It has been shown that if a company follows well-defined objectives in its reinsurance policy, these objectives can be represented by a utility function which the company seeks to maximize. This formulation of the problem will in general make it possible to determine a unique reinsurance arrangement which is optimal when the company's objectives and external situation are given.

1.2. More than 50 years ago Guldberg [4] wrote (about the probability of ruin): "Wie hoch diese Wahrscheinlichkeit gegriffen werden soll, muss dem subjektiven Ermessen oder von Aussen kommenden Bedingungen überlassen bleiben." This is the traditional approach to reinsurance problems. It does obviously not lead to a determinate solution. Most authors taking this approach conclude their studies by giving a mathematical relation between some measure of "stability," such as the probability of ruin, and some parameter, for instance maximum retention, to which the company can give any value within a certain range. Such studies do usually not state which particular value the company should select for this parameter, i.e., what degree of stability it should settle for. This question is apparently considered as being outside the field of actuarial mathematics.

1.3. The traditional approach implies that the actuary should play a rather modest part in the management of his company. He should provide facts and figures for the use of his superiors, who would make the final decisions on behalf of the company. How these decisions were reached should in principle be no concern of the actuary. This may have been correct in theory 50 years ago, when the famous "hunch" of the born manager was the best available guide for top-level decisions in business. However, the last decades have seen the development of mathematical theories for decision making under uncertainty, and in the light of these theories it appears that the actuary should take a broader view of his duties.

1.4. These mathematical theories can obviously not eliminate the subjective element referred to by Guldberg. However, if one assumes that there is, or at least that there should be some consistency in the various subjective judgments made by an insurance company, fairly extensive mathematical treatment becomes possible. To introduce a utility function which the company seeks to maximize, means only that such consistency requirements are put into mathematical form.

2. The Theory of Risk

2.1.   To illustrate our point, we shall begin by studying a very simple model. We shall consider an insurance company which holds a portfolio of insurance contracts, all of which will expire before the end of a certain period. We assume that the premium for all contracts has been paid to the company in advance.

The *risk situation* of the company is then determined by the following two elements:

(i) $F(x)$ = the probability that the total amount of claims being made under the contracts in the portfolio shall not exceed x.
(ii) S = the funds which the company holds, and which it can draw upon to pay claims.

At the end of the period the company will hold the amount $y = S - x$, where y is a variate with the probability distribution $G(y) = 1 - F(S - y)$ where $-\infty \leqslant y \leqslant S$. It is convenient to refer to $G(y)$ as the *profit distribution* associated with the risk situation $(S, F(x))$.

2.2.   In this simple model we can assume that the only thing which matters to the company, is the situation when all contracts have expired. This means that the contract period must be so short that we can ignore the interest earned by the premiums paid in advance into the company's funds. In this case all relevant properties of the risk situation are contained in the profit distribution.

In the classical theory of risk attention is focused on the probability that profits shall be negative at the end of the period, i.e., that the company shall be ruined. This probability is obviously given by

$$\int_S^\infty dF(x) = p(S, F) = 1 - F(S)$$

2.3.   The classical theory seems to assume, usually tacitly, that a company should reinsure as little as possible. The reasoning behind this appears to be that reinsurance invariably means a reduction of expected profit. Taking this as a starting point, we can formulate the objectives of the classical theory in an operational manner as follows.

If there are n possible reinsurance arrangements, which will change the risk situation of the company from the initial $(S, F(x))$ to $(S_1, F_1(x)), \ldots ,$ $(S_n, F_n(x))$, the company should select the arrangement i which maximizes expected profit

$$S_i - \int_0^\infty x \, dF_i(x)$$

subject to the condition

$$p(S_i, F_i) \leq \alpha$$

where α is the probability which Guldberg considered had to be given from outside.

2.4.   This formulation leads to the familiar mathematical problem of maximizing a given function when the solution is restrained by an inequality. When α is given, the solution of the problem is straight forward, although the computation involved can present considerable difficulties.

It is, however, evident that this formulation of the reinsurance problem is not very satisfactory. We have taken into account only *two* properties of the profit distribution, namely its mean, and the part to the left of the origin. It seems unreasonable to assume that an insurance company is completely disinterested in any other property of this distribution, so it is desirable to develop a more general theory. For such a theory it appears that a utility concept, or something equivalent is indispensable.

2.5.   The modern, so-called "collective" theory of risk considers a more general model than the one we have discussed. However, the generalization is not along the lines indicated in the preceding paragraph. This theory drops the assumption we made in para. 2.1 that all premiums have been paid in advance. Instead it is assumed that premiums are paid continuously into the company's funds. This will in general make it necessary to take into account the probability of ruin *within* the period considered. It is well known that this leads to a family of ruin probabilities, far more complicated than the simple $p(S, F)$ which we have introduced above. Whether this generalization is worth the heavy mathematics involved is an open question. Personally I think it of more interest to generalize the classical model to take into account *all* properties of the profit distribution.

3. Measurable Utility

3.1.   The utility concept was the very cornerstone of the economic theory developed in the last decades of the nineteenth century. However, many economists found it difficult to accept this concept which was impossible to measure, and difficult even to define in a precise manner. It was therefore considered as a major advance when Pareto showed that one could do without utility, and derive all the results of classical economics from the theory of indifference curves.

However, classical theory was not very successful when it came to analyzing the uncertainty element in economics. When the first real breakthrough was made in this field by von Neumann and Morgenstern [6], it appeared that utility was indispensable after all.

3.2. The authors of "Theory of Games" showed that utility could be defined in a rigorous manner, and that this utility concept was "measurable" in the sense that it was determined up to a linear transformation. They derived this result from a few axioms which essentially are topological in nature. The necessary axioms have later been given in several different forms, in order to make the basic assumptions clearer and more acceptable. However, the way to a desired theorem will in general become longer and more complicated when one takes simpler and more basic axioms as starting point. The reformulation of the axioms has therefore not encouraged many economists—or actuaries—to make full use of the possibilities of mathematical manipulations which are open, once utility is assumed measurable.

3.3. The few economists who have tried to apply this utility concept to "practical" problems, have approached their task with extreme suspicion. They usually have, like for instance Markowitz [5], gone through the axioms, one by one, in order to satisfy themselves that the axioms can be justified in the particular economic situation which they want to study. I have taken this approach myself in a previous paper [3]. However, such an elaborate procedure can usually be avoided. All economic analysis is based on a number of assumptions, and in most cases we will find that these assumptions either imply, or are closely related to the axioms which lead to measurable utility.

3.4. In insurance a basic assumption is that there will always exist a unique amount of money which is the lowest premium at which a company will undertake to pay a claim with a known probability distribution. This assumption establishes an equivalence between certain and uncertain events. The crucial, and most debated point in the utility theory of von Neumann and Morgenstern is the existence of an equivalence of this kind. Once it is taken for granted, as it seems natural to do in insurance, the measurable utility follows as an almost trivial consequence.

3.5. The basic assumption referred to can be formulated as: *Axiom* 1. An insurance company has a complete preference ordering over the set of all probability distributions so that:

(i)   To any probability distribution $F(x)$ there corresponds one, and only one number R, so that the two probability distributions $F(x)$ and $\epsilon(x - R)$ are equivalent.

(ii) $\epsilon(x - R_1)$ is preferred to $\epsilon(x - R_2)$ if, and only if $R_1 > R_2$.

Here $\epsilon(x)$ is the degenerate probability distribution defined by

$$\epsilon(x) = 0 \quad \text{for } x < 0$$

$$\epsilon(x) = 1 \quad \text{for } 0 \leqslant x$$

To each probability distribution $F(x)$ we can now associate a utility indicator, i.e., a number $U(F(x))$, such that:

(i) $U(F(x)) = U(G(x))$ if $F(x)$ and $G(x)$ are equivalent.

(ii) $U(F(x)) > U(G(x))$ if $F(x)$ is preferred to $G(x)$.

3.6.   The utility indicator $U(F(x))$ is indeterminate in the sense that $\varphi(U)$, where $\varphi(y)$ is an arbitrary increasing function of y, can serve as utility indicator for the preference ordering. To get a more determinate indicator, one must make some assumptions that the company is "rational" or "consistent" in its preferences. We will express this as:

Axiom 2. If the probability distributions $F_1(x)$ and $F_2(x)$ are equivalent, the probability distributions $\alpha F_1(x) + (1 - \alpha) G(x)$ and $\alpha F_2(x) + (1 - \alpha) G(x)$ will also be equivalent.

Here $G(x)$ is an arbitrary probability distribution, and α is a real number $0 \leqslant \alpha \leqslant 1$.

3.7.   From Axiom 2 it follows that

$$U(\alpha F_1(x) + (1 - \alpha) G(x)) = U(\alpha F_2(x) + (1 - \alpha) G(x))$$

or if we take $G(x) = F_2(x)$

$$U(\alpha F_1(x) + (1 - \alpha) F_2(x)) = U(F_2(x))$$

Since the left-hand side must be independent of α, it follows that the utility indicator must be of the form

$$U(\alpha F_1(x) + (1 - \alpha) F_2(x)) = \alpha U(F_1(x)) + (1 - \alpha) U(F_2(x))$$

For an arbitrary probability distribution we can write

$$F(x) = \int_{-\infty}^{+\infty} \epsilon(x-y)\, dF(y)$$

Hence we have in general

$$U(F(x)) = \int_{-\infty}^{+\infty} U(\epsilon(x-y))\, dF(y)$$

This is the Bernoullian hypothesis, which gives the utility of a probability distribution (or a risk situation) as a weighed sum of the utilities attached to degenerate distributions, i.e., certain events.

3.8. It is convenient to write

$$u(y) = U(\epsilon(x-y))$$

$u(y)$ is then the utility attached to an amount of money y, payable with probability 1, i.e., $u(y)$ can be interpreted as the "utility of money," which plays an important part in classical economic theory.
We can then write

$$U(F(x)) = \int_{-\infty}^{+\infty} u(x)\, dF(x)$$

It is easily verified that the preference ordering determines $u(x)$ only up to a linear transformation, i.e., $u(x)$ and $Au(x) + B$, where A and B are constants, will represent the same preference ordering.

3.9. The "utility of money" can best be considered as an *operator* which establishes an ordering over the set of profit distributions. To give it a more direct interpretation implies that we attach a meaning to statements such as: "An increase in profits from $0.5 million to $1 million is 50% better than an increase from $2 millions to $3 millions." This is not an attractive starting point for a rational theory of insurance, although something of this nature obviously is implied in the two axioms.

4. Application to Reinsurance

4.1. We will now consider an insurance company which has a preference ordering over the set of all profit distributions. We will assume that this preference ordering satisfies the two axioms in Section 3, and that it can be represented by a "utility of money" $u(x)$.

The utility which the company attaches to the risk situation $(S, F(x))$ is then given by

$$U(S, F(x)) = \int_0^\infty u(S - x)\, dF(x)$$

The reinsurance problem formulated in para. 2.3 can now be generalized to that of maximizing this expression over the set of risk situations which the company can reach by reinsurance arrangements. This procedure will obviously take into account all properties of $F(x)$ as we required in para. 2.5.

4.2. The previous papers [1], [2], and [3] already referred to, contain several examples of such maximizing problems. We shall therefore in the present paper only consider one simple example.

We assume that a company in the risk situation $(S, F(x))$ wants to reinsure a quota k of its portfolio. For this reinsurance cover the company has to pay the net premium kP of the ceded quota, plus a loading λkP.

The optimal quota will then evidently be the value of k which maximizes the expression

$$\int_0^\infty u(S - (1 + \lambda)kP - (1 - k)x)\, dF(x)$$

where P is the net premium of the whole portfolio, i.e.,

$$P = \int_0^\infty x\, dF(x)$$

It is obvious that this maximizing problem can be solved when $F(x)$ and $u(x)$ are given.

4.3. We will now assume that

$$F(x) = 1 - e^{-x}$$

and

$$u(x) = -ax^2 + x + b$$

This form of $u(x)$ has been studied in some detail in previous papers. It seems to give acceptable results, provided that a is positive, and so small that $u(x)$ is increasing over the whole range considered, i.e., $2aS < 1$. a can obviously be taken as a measure of the company's "risk aversion." If $a = 0$, the company will be indifferent to risk. The utility attached to any risk situation will then be proportional to expected profit.

It is easy to verify that the value of k which maximizes the company's utility, is given by

$$k = \frac{2a\,(1 - \lambda) - \lambda\,(1 - 2aS)}{2a\,(1 + \lambda^2)}$$

4.4. To give a numerical illustration, we will take

$a = \frac{1}{3}$ $b = 0.135$

$S = 1.2$ $\lambda = 0.1$

We find that in this case the company's utility is maximized for $k = 0.86$. The table below gives the utility for different values of k. That utility is zero in the initial situation, i.e., for $k = 0$, has of course no significance, since the origin and the unit of measurement for the utility scale can be chosen arbitrarily. The last two columns of the table give expected profit and the probability of ruin, i.e., the probability that the company shall be insolvent at the end of the period considered.

5. Conclusion

5.1. The example in Section 4 shows that it is relatively simple to determine the optimal reinsurance arrangement if we assume that the utility of money to an insurance company can be represented by a continuous, increasing function. However, the existence of such a function follows from the innocent looking axioms in Section 3, and it seems difficult to argue that well managed insurance companies should violate these axioms.

Table 6-1
Quota Share Reinsurance

k	Utility	Expected profit	Probability of ruin
0	0	0.20	0.3012
0.1	0.056	0.19	0.2982
0.2	0.101	0.18	0.2923
0.3	0.142	0.17	0.2865
0.4	0.174	0.16	0.2808
0.5	0.195	0.15	0.2725
0.6	0.216	0.14	0.2645
0.7	0.230	0.13	0.2393
0.8	0.237	0.12	0.2019
0.86	0.240	0.115	0.1791
0.9	0.238	0.11	0.1225
1.0	0.231	0.10	0

THE UTILITY CONCEPT APPLIED TO THE THEORY OF INSURANCE   95

5.2. The validity of the axioms leading to the Bernoullian theorem has been questioned by several authors, on different grounds. The most important criticism has been directed against the substitution principle implicit in the axioms. It is easy to show by examples that this principle does not seem to be generally applicable. It is doubtful, to say the least, that there exist certain public honors (or disgrace) which are equivalent to a fifty-fifty chance of either being hanged or receiving $1 million. One of Walter Scott's heros ("Waverly") is willing to make a toss for a coronet or a coffin, but we cannot assume, as the axioms imply, that any person would be willing to play such a game if the probabilities were suitably adjusted. It seems, however, that this general criticism does not concern the applicability of the Bernoullian hypothesis to insurance where the only events considered are payment of different amounts of money.

5.3. Another group of critics has contested the relevance of probabilities to economic decisions made under uncertainty. The most eloquent member of this group is probably Shackle [7]. Shackle maintains that a businessman will not consider all possible outcomes which may follow a decision he is about to make. Instead he will pay attention only to two *focal values.* These values are the worst and the best outcome which the businessman considers so likely that they must be taken into account. Other outcomes which are "out of focus," are ignored.

It seems almost preposterous to maintain that companies ignore probabilities when they take decisions concerning reinsurance. It should, however, be noted that Shackle does not consider his theory as *normative* in the sense that it states how rational businessmen *should* take decisions. All he claims is that his theory describes, or explains how businessmen actually reach their decisions. This might apply to insurance companies, since as we have seen, the theory of reinsurance has almost exclusively considered the two "focal values," ruin and expected profit.

5.4. Shackle's views are well expressed by Giraudoux's Belle Hélène ("La guerre de Troie n'aura pas lieu"):

Hélène: Ne me brusquez pas. Je choisis les événements comme je choisis les objects et les hommes. Je choisis ceux qui ne sont pas pour moi des ombres. Je choisis ceux que je vois.

Hector: Voici ta concurrante, Cassandre. Celle-là aussi lit l'avenir.

Hélène: Je ne lis pas l'avenir. Mais dans cet avenir, je vois des scènes colorées, d'autres ternes. Jusqu'ici ce sont toujours les scènes colorées qui ont eu lieu.

If Cassandra should look for a job, any insurance company could profitably employ her. As she presumably is not available, companies seem to have engaged, as a substitute, la belle Hélène, who can only see the dreadful possibility of ruin and the rosy situation where everything goes according to mathematical expectation. She may have her attractions, but one may ask if she is the right person to take charge of the reinsurance arrangements.

References

1. Borch, Karl. "An Attempt to Determine the Optimum Amount of Stop Loss Reinsurance," *Transactions of the XVIth International Congress of Actuaries,* vol. 2, pp. 597–610.
2. Borch, Karl. "Reciprocal Reinsurance Treaties," *The Astin Bulletin,* vol. 1, pp. 170–191.
3. Borch, Karl. "Reciprocal Reinsurance Treaties seen as a Two-Person Co-operative Game," *Skandinavisk Aktuariettdskrift,* 1960, pp. 29–58.
4. Guldberg, Alf. "Zur Theorie des Risikos," *Reports of the Sixth International Congress of Actuaries,* vol. 1, pp. 753-764.
5. Markowitz, Harry. *Portfolio Selection,* John Wiley & Sons, 1959.
6. Neumann, J. von and O. Morgenstern. *Theory of Games and Economic Behavior* (Princeton, 1944).
7. Shackle, G. L. S. *Expectation in Economics* (Cambridge, 1949).

7 Utility Theory

In this presentation I shall argue that the real difficulty in many decision problems is to spell out what we want to achieve. This may sound surprising and possibly disappointing. The typical decision maker in insurance is usually thought of as a company president or a high-level executive, who may seek the advice of experts. This decision maker will probably be taken aback if his experts tell him that he must make up his mind before they can set to work and give their advice. Experts do not, of course, behave in this way. They will usually admit that their task is to "sort out" the problem, leaving the decision to the judgment of the decision maker.

This division of labor may seem natural, but it may not always be very efficient. As an illustration, let us assume that a reinsurance company has to choose one of the following two contracts:

Contract 1 will give a loss of $10 million with probability p or a profit of $600,000 with probability $1 - p$.

Contract 2 will give a loss of $4 million with probability p or a profit of $200,000 with probability $1 - p$.

In this situation the task of an expert is to estimate the probability p and possibly add some measure of the "credibility" attached to this estimate. He may, however, waste his time if the company's president has decided that he will not risk a loss of $10 million on a single contract, unless, of course, p is virtually zero. If the expert had known this from the outset, he could have used a very coarse estimator for the probability.

The example we have presented shows that the outcome of a decision in insurance cannot be described or "predicted" as a certain profit or loss. The best that we can do is to specify a probability distribution over the possible outcomes. If we can appeal to the law of large numbers, it may be possible for practical purposes to ignore the shape of the probability distribution and consider only its first moment, that is, the expected profit or loss. The classical actuarial mathematics rests on the law of large numbers. When this law does not apply, we will need a different mathematical apparatus, an apparatus which actuaries for more than a century have referred to as the "theory of risk."

The Utility Concept

From the observations in the preceding paragraph it follows that the typical decision problem in insurance consists in selecting the best probability distribution from an available set. In order to make decisions of this kind, we must have a rule which tells us when one probability distribution—over a range of profits—is better than another. A rule of this kind must necessarily be of a subjective nature. The rule will represent an "attitude to risk," and there is clearly no objective rule which can tell us which attitude is the right one to take.

A rule for choosing among probability distributions can be described in different ways. If, however, the rule is consistent in the precise sense of von Neumann and Morgenstern [8], it is possible to describe the rule by specifying a *utility function, u(x),* such that

$$\int u(x)\, dF(x) > \int u(x)\, dG(x)$$

if, and only if, the distribution $F(x)$ is considered better than $G(x)$.

The consideratons above indicate that a general theory of insurance must, or at least could, be based on the utility concept. This has in fact been recognized for a long time. Almost 140 years ago Barrois [1] constructed a very complete theory of fire insurance, based on the particular utility function, $u(x) = \log x,$ originally used by Bernoulli [2]. It must, however, be admitted that the present popularity of the utility concept in insurance literature is due to the result by von Neumann and Morgenstern mentioned above rather than to the half-forgotten studies of nineteenth century actuaries.

The utility concept may be considered indispensable in theoretical work on insurance, but it does not seem to have found many applications to insurance practice. One explanation of this apparent paradox may be that presidents and executives of insurance companies find it difficult to specify the utility function which represents their preference-ordering over the set of attainable profit distributions. This is a real problem which we shall discuss in some detail in the following section. Another explanation may be that we have oversimplified the problem. Any decision problem in an insurance company certainly involves a choice among probability distributions, but it is not certain that these decisions or choices can be studied in isolation. In simple terms, any decision may depend on the whole situation of the company, and this situation may again depend on the choices which are expected to be available in the future. If some dependence of this kind is important in real life, we must dismiss the simple static decision problem as irrelevant and develop a dynamic theory. Some ways of doing this have been discussed in other papers [3, 4].

A Simple Example

To construct a simple example, let us assume that the utility function is a polynomial of second degree. The expected utility will then be a linear function of the two first moments of the probability distribution. This means that, when evaluating a profit distribution, the decision maker will consider only expected profits and the variance of profits. As a first approximation this decision rule may seem reasonably acceptable, and it is the basis of much of the earlier work on the theory of risk. A brief historical sketch and a number of references are given in another paper [3]. The rule has become very popular during the last decade, through the work of Markowitz [6], Tobin [7], and others. It is well known that the rule can lead to contradictions [5], but we shall not elaborate this point, since we are using the rule only to illustrate some more basic problems.

Let us now consider the following insurance contract:

Premium: $110
Possible claim payments:
$10,000 with probability 0.01
    0   with probability 0.99

This contract will given an expected profit E = $10, and the standard deviation of the profit is approximately S = $1,000. If an insurance company sells n contracts of this kind, it will obtain a portfolio with

Expected profit $= nE$,
Standard deviation $= \sqrt{n}\, S$.

In the following we shall ignore administrative costs. We can safely do this by assuming that they are covered by a suitable loading of the premium. We shall, however, assume that it will cost the company $500,000 to bring this contract to the market, that is, to make it available to the public. The problem of the company is then to decide whether this contract should be launched on the market or not. It is obvious that this decision must depend on the number of contracts which the company expects to sell. To facilitate the decision, the company can prepare a table like the one following:

From the table we see that the company can be expected to "break even" if it can sell at least 50,000 contracts. It is, however, likely that the company will

Table 7-1

n (Number of Contracts Sold)	nE (Expected Profit)	$\sqrt{n}S$ (Standard Deviation of Profit)
0	-$ 500,000	$ 0
10,000	- 400,000	100,000
40,000	- 100,000	200,000
50,000	0	225,000
90,000	400,000	300,000
100,000	500,000	315,000
120,000	700,000	345,000
160,000	1,100,000	400,000

want to do better than just break even, if it decides to take the risk involved in launching the new contract. The risk is represented by the standard deviation, and it is easy to see that substantial losses can occur.

After gazing at this table for some time, the decision maker may decide that it is worthwhile to launch the new contract if sales will exceed 120,000. He may justify this decision by noting that the profit distribution must be approximately normal. Expected profit is more than twice the standard deviation, so that the operation is virtually certain to be profitable.

The decision that we have suggested does, in a sense, imply that the buck is passed on to the marketing department of the company. It is, however, obvious that market research can never predict sales with certainty. At best the outcome of such research can be a probability distribution over a set of possible sales. Let this distribution be $g(n)$, the probability that n contracts will be sold. We then have

$$\sum_{n=0}^{\infty} g(n) = 1$$

If the market research indicates that $g(n) = 0$ for $n < 120{,}000$, the marketing department can guarantee that sales will exceed 120,000 and it can then recommend that the new contract be launched. Normally a marketing department does not make statements in this form. A more likely statement would be

$$\sum_{n=0}^{120{,}000} g(n) < 0.05$$

This means that there is a probability of 0.95 that sales will exceed the level of 120,000, which the decision maker considered as a minimum after having studied the above table. The decision maker may then decide to launch the new contract.

There are reasons to believe that some decisions in insurance companies actually are made in a manner similar to the one we have indicated. This decision procedure has, however, some unsatisfactory aspects. There is, for instance, no obvious reason why uncertainty due to "sampling fluctuations," as expressed in the table, shall be treated in a manner different from that of the uncertainty about market reaction—represented by the distribution $g(n)$.

To study this question, it is convenient to express our argument in a slightly more general form. Let $F(x)$ be the cumulative probability distribution of profits from one single insurance contract with expectation E and standard deviation S. Profits from a portfolio of n such contracts will then have the probability distribution $F^{(n)}(x)$, which can be computed as the nth convolution of $F(x)$ with itself. If $g(n)$ is the probability that n contracts are sold, the distribution of profits from the resulting portfolio is

$$H(x) = \sum_{n=0}^{\infty} F^{(n)}(x)g(n)$$

If $\lambda(t)$ is the characteristic function of $F(x)$, the characteristic function of $H(x)$ is

$$\gamma(t) = \sum_{n=0}^{\infty} [\lambda(t)]^n g(n)$$

Differentiating twice and setting $t = 0$, we obtain

$$\gamma'(0) = \lambda'(0) \sum_{n=0}^{\infty} ng(n)$$

$$\gamma''(0) = [\lambda'(0)]^2 \sum_{n=0}^{\infty} n(n-1)g(n) + \lambda''(0) \sum_{n=0}^{\infty} ng(n)$$

Since $\lambda'(0) = E$ and $\lambda''(0) = S^2 + E^2$, we have for the portfolio:

Expected profit: NE
Standard deviation: $(NS^2 + E^2 T^2)^{1/2}$

where N and T are, respectively, mean and standard deviation of $g(n)$.

Through these manipulations we have reduced our problem, so that it now consists in simply deciding if the pair $[NE, (NS^2 + E^2 T^2)^{1/2}]$ is acceptable or not; that is, if it is better than the pair $(0, 0)$.

It appears that a decision of this kind is often considered very difficult in practice. It seems at least that many executives are reluctant to make the decision, without asking for "more information." Such information will usually consist of further studies, which conceivably may reduce the standard deviation and which are certain to cost money, hence reduce expected profits. Before asking for additional information of this kind, one should at least be sure that it really will make the decision easier.

In real life an insurance cmpany may have to choose among many different actions, each leading to specific profit distributions, represented by pairs $(E_1, S_1), (E_2, S_2), \ldots$. The decision maker may find it difficult to pick the best pair from this set, and his easy way out is to ask that the whole set be recalculated. This means, however, only that the difficulties are postponed. Sooner or later the decision maker must formulate some rule as to when one *ES*-pair is better than another.

Generalizations

In our example we have assumed that only the two first moments of the profit distribution were considered by the decison maker. This implied that a preference-ordering over a set of probability distributions could be represented by an ordering over a set of *ES*-pairs.

The assumption is obviously unrealistic, but it served to illustrate our main point. This point stands out even more clearly when we try to generalize the model. If the decision maker feels that other properties of the profit distribution should be taken into account, he will probably find it difficult to explain exactly how these properties (skewness, "tails," etc.) affect the decision. The real problem is, of course, to specify the utility function which represents the decision maker's preference-ordering over a set of probability distributions.

In real life the problem is even more difficult, as we cannot usually ignore the *time element.* At a given point of time, the future profits of an insurance company can only be described by a stochastic process: $x_1, x_2, \ldots, x_t, \ldots$. The decisions made by the management will influence this process, and the problem is to steer the process so that it developes in the most desirable way. In order to solve this problem, the company's management must have a preference-ordering set of stochastic processes. An ordering of this kind cannot be represented by a simple utility function.

References

1.   Barrois, T. *Essai sur l'application du calcul des probabilités aux assurances contre l'incendie* (Lille: Daniel, 1834).
2.   Bernoulli, D. "Exposition of a New Theory on the Measurement of Risk," *Econometrica,* 1954, pp. 23–46 (translation of a paper in Latin, published in St. Petersburg in 1738).
3.   Borch, K. "The Theory of Risk," *Journal of the Royal Statistical Society,* Series B, 1967, pp. 432–67.
4.   ——. "Dynamic Decision Problems in an Insurance Company," *ASTIN Bulletin,* 1968, pp. 118–31.
5.   ——. "A Note on Uncertainty and Indifference Curves," *Review of Economic Studies,* 1969, pp. 1–4.
6.   Markowitz, H. *Portfolio Selection* (New York: Wiley, 1959).

7. Tobin, J. "Liquidity Preference as Behavior towards Risk," *Review of Economic Studies,* 1958, pp. 65–86.

8. von Neumann, J., and Morgenstern, O. *Theory of Games and Economic Behavior,* 2d ed. (Princeton, N.J.: Princeton University Press, 1947).

8

The Objectives of an Insurance Company

1. Introduction

1.1. In some previous papers [2] and [3] it has been pointed out that the objectives pursued by an insurance company can be formulated so that they consist of maximizing a mathematical function. Such a formulation appears indeed essential for a rational theory of insurance. The function to be maximized is usually referred to as the *utility* function, a name which has an old standing in economic theory. Recently the term *objective function* seems to have gained considerable popularity. This is probably the more appropriate of the two terms, but in this paper we shall stick to the older word of "utility."

1.2. A utility concept applied to insurance companies must refer to what usually is called the *risk situation* of the company. In the simplest possible case a risk situation is completely determined by the following two elements:

(i) $F(x)$ = the probability that claims made under the insurance contracts in the company's portfolio shall not exceed x
(ii) S = the funds available to the company for paying claims

This model is valid only if we assume that the premiums for all contracts in the portfolio are paid in advance, and that the contract periods are so short that it does not matter at which time within the period claims become payable. It is possible to relax these assumptions without running into fundamental difficulties. We shall, however, not attempt to do this in the present paper, since the gain in generality will not be worth the cumbersome arithmetics involved.

1.3. We can now assume that the utility which an insurance company assigns to a risk situation $(S, F(x))$ is given by a functional $U(S, F(x))$. If the company shall be consistent in the way it assigns utility over the set of all risk situations we must have

$$U(S, F(x)) = \int_0^\infty u(S - x)\, dF(x)$$

where

$$u(S) = U(S, \epsilon(x))$$

105

i.e., $u(S)$ is the utility assigned to the "degenerate" risk situation where the company's funds are S, and the probability is one that claims shall be zero. It is convenient to refer to this function as the *utility of money*.

The formula above is usually referred to as *Bernoulli's hypothesis*. Von Neumann and Morgenstern [5] proved the hypothesis as a theorem derived from a few simple assumptions, which essentially imply consistent behavior in assigning utility to risk situations. The validity of these assumptions for insurance companies has been discussed in some detail in a previous paper [3].

1.4. With the concepts introduced above, the objective of the company will be to reach the risk situation which has the highest possible utility. *Rational behavior* by the company means that in any decision which has to be taken, the company will choose the decision which gives the highest utility.

However, the results are not of much use unless we know something about the form of the utility function which the company seeks to maximize. In the following we shall study this question in some detail.

2. The Form of the Utility Function

2.1. The natural approach to our problem would be to observe the decisions actually made by insurance companies and assume that these decisions are the outcome of a coherent policy, i.e., of a systematic pursuit of well-defined objectives. From these observations we could then infer something about the policy—if any—which lies behind the decisions.

2.2. The two most important kinds of decisions which we could study in this context, appear to be:

(i)   How an insurance company determines the premiums which are offered to the public, and the amounts which should be spent to promote the sale of the company's policies. It is obvious that lower premiums and higher costs per policy written will reduce the utility of the company, unless they result in an increased volume of business. This means that we cannot infer anything about the company's objectives from such decisions, unless we make assumptions about how the company expects that volume of business will respond to lower premiums and increased sales effort. At the present stage of our knowledge, any assumptions in this field will be mere conjectures.

(ii) The company's reinsurance decisions, which should give a direct reflection of the utility which the company assigns to the various risk situations which can be reached by suitable reinsurance arrangements. However, insurance companies are usually very secretive about their reinsurance arrangements, and it does not at present appear possible to make a study based on proper statistical data.

A third group which might be studied are the investment decisions of the companies. When investing its funds, the company must balance expected return against risk of loss, just as it does in its reinsurance decisions. However, investment decisions do not enter into our model owing to the simplifying assumptions we made in para. 1.2.

2.3.   In the following we shall discuss the inference one can make about the objectives of an insurance company from its reinsurance decisions, under assumptions which *a priori* appear plausible, and which lead to results which to not appear utterly unreasonable in the light of our experience. A more precise study does not seem possible at the present state of our knowledge.

It is worth adding that there are strong theoretical reasons why companies should keep their reinsurance decisions secret. It has been shown in a previous paper [4] that in a reinsurance market there exists no price which can both lead to a Pareto optimal situation, and balance supply and demand. This means that a reinsurance market is essentially an *n-person game* [5] , where the outcome is not completely determined by assumptions of rational behavior. What actually determines the outcome in *n*-person games is still an open question. It seems, however, that under most assumptions it will be to the advantage of a player to conceal from the others his real objective and the strategy which he uses in his endeavor to reach this objective.

2.4.   The focal point in the theory of risk and reinsurance has for almost a century been the *probability of ruin*. It has been assumed that at least a partial objective of an insurance company is to make certain that the probability of ruin does not exceed a given number, say α. The theory is usually very vague, or completely silent about how the number α should be determined. The model seems to make most sense if a value of α is imposed from outside, for instance, by a government inspector.

To illustrate the point, let us assume that a company which is in the risk situation $(S, F(x))$ can reach any of the following risk situations $(R_1, G_1(x), \ldots,$ $(R_n, G_n(x))$ by reinsurance arrangements. The classical condition then implies that an arrangement leading to the risk situation $(R_i, G_i(x))$ is permissible only if

$$\int_{R_i}^{\infty} dG_i(x) < \alpha$$

It is obvious that a given value of α does not determine the objective completely, if this inequality is satisfied for more than one i. In order to determine which arrangement the company will choose, we must be able to assign utilities to all permissible risk situations.

It is equally obvious that an objective consisting of making the ruin probability as small as possible has little meaning, since this implies that the company really wants to quit the insurance business all together, i.e., the objective is to reach a risk situation of the type $(R, \epsilon(x))$.

2.5. In the classical theory of reinsurance, based on the ruin probability, it seems generally to be assumed that a company should not reinsure if the initial risk situation is permissible, i.e., if

$$\int_s^\infty dF(x) < \alpha$$

The reason for this assumption seems to be that reinsurance will reduce expected profits, i.e.,

$$S - \int_0^\infty x \, dF(x) > R_i - \int_0^\infty x \, dG_i(x)$$

because reinsurance premiums paid for any kind of cover will be higher than the net premium. Hence the objective appears to be to maximize expected profits, subject to the condition that the ruin probability is smaller than the given number α.

2.6. The objective found in the previous paragraph makes some sense if α is imposed from outside, and if some companies have a ruin probability higher than α in the initial situation. These companies can then make reinsurance arrangements which will bring their ruin probability down to the required level. These arrangements will imply that the companies considered pass some of their expected profits on to the other companies.

If all companies in the initial situation have a ruin probability lower than α, no reinsurance will take place. The total expected profits of all companies in the market cannot be increased by reshuffling risks through reinsurance arrangements. It will usually be possible to reduce the ruin probability for all companies by reinsurance arrangements. However, under our assumption the companies will not be interested in reducing the ruin probability below α.

During the years when the early theory of risk was developed, insurance companies may actually have pursued the objective we have discussed in this paragraph. However, they do not do so today. The present popularity of reciprocal reinsurance treaties is sufficient evidence. We can probably see this development of reciprocity as a sophistication of the objectives of insurance companies.

2.7. The considerations in the preceding paragraph seem to suggest that companies in some way balance an increase in the probability of ruin against increases in expected profit. This means that the companies will seek to maximize a utility function of two variables

$$U(p, m) = U(S, F(x))$$

where

$$p = \text{ruin probability} = \int_s^\infty dF(x)$$

m = expected profits = $S - \int_0^\infty x \, dF(x)$

If this assumption shall be acceptable, we must have

$$\frac{\partial U}{\partial p} \leqslant 0 \quad \text{and} \quad \frac{\partial U}{\partial m} \geqslant 0$$

It is obvious that this utility function is inconsistent with the Bernoulli hypothesis which we introduced in para. 1.3, and we shall show that it leads to a contradiction.

For $p > 0$ and a positive m, there will exist an $m_0 > 0$ so that

$$U(p, m) = U(0, m_0)$$

This will hold if there exists an amount of cash m_0 against which the company is willing to part with all its assets and liabilities.

Here we must have $m > m_0$. If $m = m_0$, utility will be independent of the ruin probability, which is against our assumption. $m < m_0$ must also be ruled out.

We now let m decrease to zero. During this process m_0 will necessarily become negative. However, a risk situation with negative expected profits cannot have a ruin probability equal to zero. Hence the objective we have studied contains a contradiction.

2.8. It is natural to assume that the objectives of an insurance company in some way can be derived from the personal objectives of those who control the company. For a joint stock company the persons in ultimate control should be the stockholders. Theoretically their attitude to risk should determine the objectives of the company, subject of course to any safety measures which may be imposed from outside. However, it is probably not quite realistic to assume that the objectives of the company are determined as a compromise between the different investment objectives of the stockholders. A stockholder does not generally have to compromise. If he thinks that the company's policy is too risky or too conservative, he can sell his stock, and buy other securities more suitable to his investment objectives.

It may be more realistic to assume that the objectives to be pursued by an insurance company are laid down almost accidentally, and that the company eventually ends up with having stockholders who unanimously approve of these objectives.

In real life it is likely that both the elements we have mentioned play their part. Since we know next to nothing about their relative importance, it will be mere conjecture to make assumptions about how they together determine the objectives of the company. A complete discussion of the problem will in any case be impossible without making assumptions about the alternative investments available to dissatisfied stockholders.

2.9. Many of the arguments in the preceding paragraph apply with equal force to mutual insurance companies. However, it seems that there is some justification for assuming that the objective of a mutual company is established as a compromise between the objectives of the members. A member who is dissatisfied can of course quit, but the managers of the company may be willing to do more to accommodate him, than they would for a stockholder who wants to sell his stock. We shall therefore in the following study the possible objectives of a mutual insurance company in some detail.

3. The Objectives of a Mutual Insurance Company

3.1. We will consider n persons who all have the same attitude to risk. We will assume in para. 1.3 that this attitude to risk is determined by a utility of money represented by a function $u(x)$. We assume further

(i)   Person i has assets worth S_i $(i = 1, 2, \ldots, n)$.
(ii)   Each person is exposed to a risk which will cause a loss x, where x is a random variable with probability distribution $F(x)$.

3.2. Under the Bernoulli hypothesis, person i will attach the utility

$$U_i(1) = \int_0^\infty u(S_i - x)\, dF(x)$$

to this initial situation.

We assume now that the individuals form a mutual insurance company in order to increase their utilities.

If the loss suffered by any person is stochastically independent of the losses suffered by the others, the total loss of the group will be a random variable with a probability distribution $G(z)$ which is the nth convolution of $F(x)$ with itself.

If each person contributes an amount $(1/n)z$ to cover the losses suffered by the group, the utility of individual i will be

$$U_i(n) = \int_0^\infty u\left(S_i - \frac{z}{n}\right) dG(z)$$

It is obvious that individual i will not join the mutual company unless

$$U_i(1) \leqslant U_i(n)$$

3.3. Assume now that the persons consider the possibility of increasing their utility still further by a reinsurance arrangement for their company.

For the sake of simplicity we will assume that they only consider a quota share treaty, according to which the company will cede a quota of $100k\%$ to a reinsurer. We assume that the reinsurer offers this kind of coverage against the net premium + a loading of $100\lambda\%$.

Person i will then obviously want the company to cede the quota k which will maximize

$$U_i(n, k) = \int_0^\infty u\left(S_i - (1 - k)\frac{z}{n} - k(1 + \lambda)\frac{Q}{n}\right)dG(z)$$

$$= \int_0^\infty u(A_i - Bz)\,dG(z) = \int_0^\infty u(y)\,dG(z)$$

where

$$Q = \int_0^\infty z\,dG(z)$$

is the net premium.

3.4. The first-order condition for a maximum is

$$\frac{dU_i(k)}{dk} = \int_0^\infty u'(A_i - Bz)\left\{\frac{dA_i}{dk} - z\frac{dB}{dk}\right\}dG(z) = 0$$

or $(1 + \lambda)P\int_0^\infty u'(y)\,dG(z) = \int_0^\infty zu'(y)\,dG(z)$

In general this equation will determine a unique value of k which will maximize the utility of person i.

In order to illustrate the nature of the solution, we shall assume that

$$u(x) = -\tfrac{1}{2}ax^2 + x$$

This utility function has been studied in some previous papers [2, 4], and it seems to give reasonable results, provided that a is sufficiently small.

3.5. We find that without any insurance, the utility of person i is:

$$U_i(1) = \int_0^\infty \left(-\frac{a}{2}(S_i - x)^2 + (S_i - x)\right)dF(x)$$

or $U_i(1) = \frac{1}{2a} - \frac{a}{2}\left(V + \left(\frac{1}{a} - S_i + P\right)^2\right)$

where

$$V = \int_0^\infty (x - P)^2 \, dF(x)$$

and $P = \int_0^\infty x \, dF(x)$

Insurance in the mutual company will lead to the utility

$$U_i(n) = U_i(n, 0) = \frac{1}{2a} - \frac{a}{2}\left(\frac{V}{n} + \left(\frac{1}{a} - S_i + P\right)^2\right)$$

and reinsurance of a quota k will give

$$U_i(n, k) = \frac{1}{2a} - \frac{a}{2}\left\{(1 - k)^2 \, \frac{V}{n} + \left(\frac{1}{a} - S_i + (1 + k\lambda) P\right)^2\right\}$$

We see that the insurance gives the gain in utility

$$U_i(n) - U_i(0) = \tfrac{1}{2}aV\left(1 - \frac{1}{n}\right)$$

The gain will of course increase with increasing n, but it is independent of the initial assets S_i.

If the mutual company reinsures a quota k, there will be a further gain

$$U_i(n, k) - U_i(n, 0) = \frac{aV}{2n}(2k - k^2) + \frac{ak\lambda Q}{2}\left(2\left(\frac{1}{a} - S_i + P\right) - k\lambda P\right)$$

which clearly can be both positive and negative, depending on the value of S_i.

3.6. To study the problem further we shall choose convenient numerical values for the parameters. We assume:

(i)   That $a = 0.1$, and we add a constant to the utility function so that it be-
      comes $u(x) - 0.05x^2 + x + 6$
(ii) That each person is exposed to risk of a loss 100 with probability 0.01,
      which gives

      $V = 99$ and $P = 1$

(iii) That the amount of money owned by the various persons S_i, lies in the
      range 0 to 10

(iv) That $n = 20$ and $\lambda = 0.2$

Table 8–1 gives the initial utility and the utility reached by forming a mutual company, for some selected values of S_i.

We see that the table brings out the result of para. 3.5 that the gain of utility is independent of the person's funds S_i.

3.7. From the formula in para. 3.5 it follows that it may be possible to increase the utility, at least for some of the persons, if the mutual company reinsures a quota k. It is easy to establish that the value of k which maximizes the utility of a person with assets S_i, is given by

$$k = 0.59 + 0.04\, S_i$$

In Table 8–2 we have calculated the utility of our persons for various values of k.

3.8. Comparing Tables 8–1 and 8–2, we see that the utility of all persons will increase by a reinsurance arrangement. However, they will have different views as to what is the best reinsurance treaty. In general those with large funds will prefer that the mutual company should reinsure a high quota. This makes good sense, since these persons who are in a relatively comfortable situation, naturally dislike being called upon to pay large amounts to cover possible losses of their mutual company. Those who have small funds to start with, are more ready to run a risk.

If the members decide by vote what quota their company should reinsure, the company's objectives will be to maximize the utility of its "average" member, a reasonable, although hardly unexpected result.

Table 8–1
Utilities of a Person with Funds S_i Before and After Insurance

S_i	Without Insurance	With Insurance
0	0.0	4.70
1	1.05	5.75
2	2.00	6.70
3	2.85	7.55
4	3.60	8.30
5	4.25	8.95
6	4.80	9.50
7	5.25	9.95
8	5.60	10.30
9	5.85	10.55
10	6.00	10.70

Table 8-2
Utility under Various Reinsurance Arrangements

S_i	0.5	0.6	0.7	0.8	0.9	1.0
0	4.77	4.78	4.77	4.76	4.75	4.73
1	5.84	5.85	5.84	5.83	5.82	5.80
2	6.80	6.81	6.81	6.80	6.79	6.77
3	7.66	7.67	7.68	7.67	7.66	7.64
4	8.42	8.43	8.45	8.44	8.43	8.41
5	9.08	9.09	9.11	9.11	9.10	9.08
6	9.64	9.65	9.67	9.68	9.67	9.65
7	10.10	10.11	10.13	10.14	10.13	10.12
8	10.46	10.47	10.49	10.50	10.49	10.49
9	10.72	10.73	10.75	10.76	10.76	10.76
10	10.88	10.89	10.91	10.92	10.93	10.93

3.9. As another approach to our problem we can assume that a mutual company wants to keep its premiums as low as possible, but also wants to avoid the cost of collecting an extra contribution from the members if the premiums should prove insufficient.

To formalize this, let us assume:

(i)   To collect an extra contribution will cost a.
(ii) If the company at the end of the insurance period holds funds exceeding R, it must make a distribution to its members. The cost of a distribution is b.
(iii) The company wants to set its premium so that expected costs are minimized.

If the company collects an amount S as premiums from its members, the probability that an additional contribution will be necessary is

$$\int_S^\infty dF(x) = 1 - F(S)$$

The probability that funds at the end of the period shall exceed R is

$$\int_0^{S-R} dF(x) = F(S - R)$$

Hence expected costs are

$$a(1 - F(S)) + bF(S - R) = a - aF(S) + bF(S - R)$$

The company's objective will then be to maximize the utility function

$$U(S) = aF(S) - bF(S - R)$$

3.10.   The utility function in the preceding paragraph satisfies the Bernoulli hypothesis. It is easy to see that we have

$$U(S) = \int_0^\infty u(S - x)\, dF(x)$$

if $u(x) = 0$ for $x < 0$

   $u(x) = a$ for $0 \leqslant x < R$

   $u(x) = a - b$ for $R \leqslant x$

The first-order condition for a maximum is

$$\frac{dU}{dS} = aF'(S) - bF'(S - R) = 0$$

or $af(S) - bf(S - R) = 0$

where $f(x) = F'(x)$ is the frequency function.

From this condition we can determine S, and hence the optimal premium which the company should collect in advance from its members. It is interesting to note that this optimal premium will be independent of the traditional net premium

$$P = \int_0^\infty x\, dF(x).$$

This is not really surprising. There is no reason why our company should charge a net premium, loaded so that the probability of an extra collection becomes very small.

4. Conclusion

4.1.   The problem we have discussed in this paper seems to be of fundamental importance to a theory of insurance, and it is indeed surprising that it so far has received so little attention in the literature. The main reason for this neglect is probably that a rational analysis of the problem requires mathematical tools which only recently have become popular among economists. However, these tools have existed for a long time. As early as 1834 Barrois [1] applied the Bernoulli hypothesis in his book on the theory of fire insurance, a book in which one will find practically all the concepts used in this paper.

4.2.   Another reason why the problem has escaped attention may be that in insurance results will always depend on chance. A company which is very careless in analyzing the risks it is running, may with luck do extremely well. It is possible to be "right for the wrong reason" or vice versa. An insurance company may go bankrupt, even if the probability that this should happen was 0.0000001. However, such considerations can be made for most kinds of economic activity, and is no really satisfactory explanation.

4.3. It may be mere perfectionism to require that insurance companies more than other firms should pursue consistent objectives. An insurance manager may be more worried over the possibility of losing a million because a large risk is left without reinsurance, than over a similar loss due to some rather speculative investment of company funds. If a theorist points out that this is inconsistent, the manager can still insist that this is the way he feels about it. He may even justify this by explaining that he will be blamed by his Board for leaving the large risk without reinsurance, but not for a fall on the Stock Exchange. The theorist can then only meekly state that such attitudes should be considered irrational.

References

1. Barrois, Th. *Essai sur l'application du calcul des probabilités aux assurances contre l'incendie* (Lille: Imprimerie de L. Daniel, 1834).
2. Borch, K. Reciprocal reinsurance treaties seen as a two-person cooperative game. *Skandinavisk Aktuarietidskrift,* 1960, pp. 29–58.
3. ———. The utility concept applied to the theory of insurance. *ASTIN Bulletin* 1 (1961): pp. 245–255.
4. ———. Equilibrium in a reinsurance market. *Econometrica* 30 (1962): 424–444.
5. Neuman, J. von, and Morgenstern, O. *Theory of Games and Economic Behavior,* 2nd ed. (Princeton, 1947).

Part III
The Reinsurance Market

The bargaining situations discussed in Part II present very difficult problems if the two parties have to negotiate in isolation, without possibilities of calling in or appealing to any third party. If this should be the case, the two will have to find a solution on their own, on an ad hoc basis, or to agree on some general principle, which can be used to solve all, or certain classes, of bargaining situations.

Usually two insurance companies do not bargain as if they were on a desert island. There will be other companies around, and the two companies considered can try to reach an agreement based on what appears to be "accepted business practice," or either of them can contact a third company and try to conclude a more favorable agreement with the outsider. If there are many such outsiders in the market, the problem does not become simpler, but it becomes possible to analyze the situation with methods familiar from economic theory. It is usual to talk about the "reinsurance market," and it is clear that the situation of a number of companies, which can gain by an exchange of reinsurance, is similar to the classical model of a market of pure exchange.

The classical model is based on a number of behavioral assumptions, which may not always be realistic. It is, however, possible to make weaker assumptions and analyze the situation as an n-person game. These questions are discussed in Chapters 9 to 14.

If only proportional reinsurance is considered, the classical model of exchange can be applied without any complications. In this situation the following elements are taken as given:

(i) $F_i(x)$ = the claim distribution of the portfolio of company i ($i = 1, 2, \ldots, n$)
(ii) S_i = the reserves of company i
(iii) P_i = the market price (negative) of the portfolio of company i, i.e., the amount which the company must pay in order to be released from the obligation to meet claims made under the insurance contracts in the portfolio.
(iv) q_{ij} = the fraction which, after an exchange, company i holds of the portfolio initially held by company j
(v) $u_i(x)$ = the utility function representing the preference ordering of company i

In the initial situation the utility of company 1 is

$$U_1(1, 0, \ldots, 0) = \int_0^\infty u_1(S_1 - x)\, dF(x)$$

After exchange the utility will be

$$U_1(q_{11}, q_{12}, \ldots, q_{1n}) = \int u_1(S_1 - P_1 + q_{11}P_1 + q_{12}P_2 - q_{11}x_1 - q_{12}x_2$$

$$+ \ldots) \, dF$$

where F stands for the joint distribution of claim payments under the portfolios. If claims in the initial portfolios are stochastically independent, $F(x_1, x_2, \ldots, x_n)$ will be the product of the distributions $F_1(x), F_2(x), \ldots$.

The classical solution to the problem is then given by the equations

$$\frac{\partial U_i}{\partial q_{ij}} = \lambda_i P_j \tag{1}$$

$$\sum_{i=1}^{n} q_{ij} = 1 \tag{2}$$

$$\sum_{j=1}^{n} P_j q_{ij} = S_i + P_i \tag{3}$$

The solution will give the n^2 "quotas" q_{ij} and the n "prices" P_i. A solution exists under fairly general conditions, which are discussed in most textbooks of economic theory. The solution is "Pareto optimal," i.e., no other exchange can give all companies a higher utility.

In this model a portfolio is described by a probability distribution $F(x)$. The market price of the portfolio does, in general, not depend only on $F(x)$, but also on $S_1, \ldots, S_n$ and on the utility functions. This idea is, or was, apparently unfamiliar to many actuaries. In actuarial calculations it is usually assumed that the amount P, which has to be paid for reinsurance cover of a portfolio, should be determined exclusively by the stochastic properties of the portfolio. It is generally assumed that P should be the net premium, plus loadings proportional to the net premium, the standard deviation, and variance of the claim payments. Benktander [1] has, after a survey of earlier literature, suggested that one should consider

$$P = E + aE + b\sigma + c\sigma^2 \tag{4}$$

where

$$E = \int_0^\infty x \, dF(x)$$

$$\sigma^2 = \int_0^\infty (x - E)^2 \, dF(x)$$

If we require, in addition to (1) to (3), that (4) shall be satisfied for all the n portfolios, we will clearly run into difficulties if $n > 3$, as we add n new equations to the system, and only the three new unknowns, a, b, and c.

Condition (4) represents the conventional actuarial thinking, and observations indicate that many companies try to apply the condition in their transaction in the reinsurance market. This means that some of the equations in (1) to (3) may not be satisfied, and that the outcome of the transactions may not be Pareto optimal.

If nonproportional reinsurance arrangements are admitted, the problem becomes much more difficult. The companies can then exchange claim distributions of any form—not just fractions of their initial portfolios. This means that we can no longer analyze the situation as a classical market in which a finite number of commodities are traded. The classical model cannot, however, be dismissed entirely. If we take, instead of the given portfolios, as our basic commodities contingent claims, payable only if well-defined "states of the world" occur, the pure exchange model can be reformulated so that it leads to a Pareto optimal arrangement in equilibrium. This was demonstrated by Arrow in 1952, and the implications of his model are still being developed in the current work on economic equilibrium under uncertainty.

In the reinsurance market a "state of the world" can most naturally be described by the total amount of claims to be paid, i.e., $z = x_1 + x_2 + \ldots + x_n$. A general reinsurance arrangement between the companies can be defined by n functions $y_1(z), \ldots, y_n(z)$, where $y_i(z)$ is the amount to be paid by company i, if total claims are z. As all claims have to be paid, the functions must satisfy the condition $y_1(z) + y_2(z) + \ldots + y_n(z) = z$.

Chapter 9 gives a proof that a general reinsurance arrangement is Pareto optimal if and only if the y functions satisfy the conditions

$$u_i'(y_i(z)) = k_i u_1'(y_1(z)) \qquad i = 2, 3, \ldots, n \tag{5}$$

where k_i are nonnegative constants. If marginal utility is decreasing, i.e., if $u_i''(x) < 0$, (5) will define a unique n-tuple of y functions, for a given set of constants k_i. As these constants can be chosen arbitrarily, it follows that the set of Pareto optimal reinsurance arrangement is an $n - 1$ dimensional manifold. If the companies behave rationally, they should reach an arrangement in the Pareto optimal set. One must make additional behavioral assumptions if one wants to determine the particular Pareto optimal arrangement that the company will reach.

Arrow's approach to this problem is to introduce a price function $p(z) =$ the amount one has to pay in the market for a note (an "Arrow certificate"), promising to pay \$1 if the event "total claims $= z$" occurs. If the companies issue such certificates and trade in them as if they were commodities in the classical exchange model, an equilibrium will be reached, defined by a set of equations similar to (1) to (3). This equilibrium will be Pareto optimal, so that the corresponding arrangement must satisfy (5), and hence it will give $n - 1$ equations for the determination of the constants $k_2, k_3, \ldots, k_n$. This result is both important and interesting, but the underlying behavioral assumptions seem very artificial, at least in a reinsurance market.

A general reinsurance arrangement will be proportional only if the y functions are linear, i.e., if

$$y_i(z) = q_i z + a$$

The solution of (5) will be linear only if all utility functions belong to one of the following classes:

(i) $u_i(x) = k e^{\alpha_i x}$

(ii) $u_i(x) = (x + c_i)^\beta$

(iii) $u_i(x) = \log (x + c_i)$

or are positive linear transformations of such functions. A proof is given in [2]. This result implies that a proportional reinsurance arrangement can be Pareto optimal only if all companies virtually have identical utility functions. The functions in class (i) differ only by a scale factor, and those in classes (ii) and (iii) imply that all differences in preference can be explained by differences in "initial wealth."

Insurance companies conclude nonproportional reinsurance contracts, evidently because they prefer them to the more orthodox proportional arrangements. This must mean that there are substantial differences between the preferences of the companies, so that they cannot all be represented by utility functions belonging to one of the three classes. Since there is no evidence that insurance companies trade in "Arrow certificates," we must conclude that if they reach a Pareto optimal arrangement, they do so through a negotiation or bargaining process, which must be analyzed in the framework of game theory.

References

1.   Benktander, G. "Schadenhäufigkeit und Risikoprämiensatz als Funktion der Grösse," *Transactions of the 19th International Congress of Actuaries* 3 (1972): 170–192.
2.   Borch, K. "General Equilibrium in the Economics of Uncertainty," in Borch and Mossin (eds.), *Risk and Uncertainty* (London: MacMillan, 1968), pp. 247–264.

The Safety Loading of Reinsurance Premiums

1. Introduction

1.1. In the older forms of reinsurance, often referred to as "proportional" reinsurance, there is no real problem involved in determining the correct safety loading of premiums. It seems natural, in fact almost obvious, that reinsurance should take place on "original terms," and that any departure from this procedure would need special justification. The only problem which may be troublesome is to determine the three components of the gross premium, i.e., net premium, safety loading, and loading for expenses. The last of these components is calculated to cover costs connected with the direct underwriting, such as agent's commission, and does not in principle concern the reinsurer.

1.2. In nonproportional reinsurance it is obviously not possible to attach any meaning to "original terms." It is therefore necessary to find some other rule for determining the safety loading. The easiest solution is clearly to make the loading proportional to the net premium. However, this may be inconvenient, particularly for extremely skew forms of reinsurance, such as stop loss contracts and various kinds of catastrophe cover. For reinsurance contracts of this kind the net premiums may become practically negligible, so that the safety loading may amount to several thousand percent if the contract is to be acceptable to a reinsurer.

1.3. A more convenient rule may be to make the safety loading proportional to the *standard deviation* of the probability distribution of the claims which may be made under the contract. This has been proposed by a number of authors, right through the alphabet from Ammeter [2] to Wold [7]. The justifications given for this procedure vary a great deal, but they are all rather similar to the agruments which a manufacturer might put forward to justify what he considers a "fair" price for his product. However, the price which the manufacturer actually gets will be determined by what the market is willing to pay and not by considerations of fairness. It therefore seems necessary to investigate the mechanism of the reinsurance market in order to find a general solution to the problem of safety loading.

1.4. In a previous paper [4] we have studied the case of two insurance companies negotiating with the purpose of concluding a reciprocal reinsurance

121

treaty. We found that under certain assumptions there existed a unique treaty which was optimal in the sense that both companies would consider it the best bargain they could make in the given circumstances. We also found that if the companies had some preconceived ideas as to what constitutes a "fair" or "proper" price for reinsurance cover, they might be led to conclude a non-optimal treaty. In the present paper we shall generalize these results to an arbitrary number of companies.

2. A Model of the Reinsurance Market

2.1. Consider n insurance companies, each holding a portfolio of insurance contracts. The *risk situation* of company i ($i = 1, 2, \ldots, n$) is defined by the following two elements:

(i) The *risk distribution*, $F_i(x_i)$, which is the probability that the total amount of claims occurring under the contracts in the company's portfolio shall not exceed x_i
(ii) The *funds* S_i which the company has available to pay claims

We will assume that $x_1, \ldots, x_i, \ldots, x_n$ are stochastically independent. To this risk situation the company attaches a utility $U_i(S_i F_i(x_i))$. From the axioms of von Neumann and Morgenstern [6], often referred to as the Bernoullian hypothesis, it follows that

$$U_i(S_i, F_i(x)) = \int_0^\infty u_i(S_i - x_i) \, dF_i(x_i)$$

where $u_i(x)$ is the "utility of money" to company i. In the following it will be assumed that $u(x)$ is a continuous nondecreasing function of x, and that its two first derivatives exist. The assumptions necessary to prove the Bernoullian hypothesis as a theorem are discussed in some detail in a previous paper [4].

2.2. In this initial situation company i is committed to pay an amount x_i if the claims which occur under the contracts in portfolio i amount to x_i. In the reinsurance market the companies can conclude treaties which change their initial commitments. For instance, a reciprocal treaty between company i and company j can be defined by two functions $y_i(x_i, x_j)$ and $y_j(x_i, x_j)$, where $y_i(x_i, x_j)$ is the amount company i has to pay if claims in the two portfolios amount to x_i and x_j, respectively. Similarly $y_j(x_i, x_j)$ is the amount to be paid by company j. Since all claims must be paid, it follows that

$$y_i(x_i, x_j) + y_j(x_i, x_j) = x_i + x_j$$

2.3. The obvious generalization of these considerations, is to introduce a set of functions

$$y_i(x_1, x_2, \ldots, x_n) \qquad i = 1, 2, \ldots, n$$

such that $y_i(x_1, x_2, \ldots, x_n)$ is the amount company i has to pay if claims in the respective portfolios amount to $x_1, x_2, \ldots, x_n$. These functions must clearly satisfy the condition

$$\sum_{i=1}^{n} y_i(x_1, x_2, \ldots, x_n) = \sum_{i=1}^{n} x_i$$

This set of functions will define a unique set of treaties concluded by the n companies in the reinsurance market. These treaties will change the utility of company i from

$$\int_0^\infty u_i(S_i - x_i)\, dF_i(x)$$

to $\quad \int_0^\infty \ldots \int_0^\infty u_i(S_i - y_i(x_i, \ldots, x_n))\, dF_1(x_1) \ldots dF_n(x_n)$

For simplicity we will write x for the vector $\{x_1, \ldots, x_n\}$, so that the utility of the company after concluding the treaties can be written

$$U_i(y) = \int_R u_i(S_i - y_i(x))\, dF(x),$$

where $F(x)$ is the joint probability distribution of $x_1, \ldots, x_n$, and R stands for the positive orthant in the n-dimensional x-space. Further we will write y for the vector $\{y_1(x), \ldots, y_n(x)\}$.

2.4. If the companies act rationally, they will not conclude a set of treaties represented by a vector y, if there exists another set of treaties with a corresponding vector $\bar{y}$, such that

$$U_i(y) \leqslant U_i(\bar{y}) \qquad \text{for all } i$$

y will in this case clearly be inferior to $\bar{y}$. If there exists no vector $\bar{y}$ satisfying the above condition, the set of treaties represented by y will be referred to as Pareto optimal.

A Pareto optimal set of treaties will represent a stable equilibrium situation in the reinsurance market. Additional treaties concluded in this situation cannot increase the utility of any company without decreasing the utility of at least one other company.

2.5. We now assume that $y(x)$ is Pareto optimal, and consider the vector $\bar{y}(x)$ whose elements are given by

$$\bar{y}_i(x) = y_i(x) + \epsilon_i(x)$$

We find

$$U_i(\bar{y}) - U_i(y) = \int_R \left\{ u_i(S_i - y_i(x) - \epsilon_i(x)) - u_i(S_i - y_i(x)) \right\} dF(x)$$

If $\epsilon_i(x)$ is small in absolute value, this can be written

$$U_i(\bar{y}) - U_i(y) = - \int_R u_i'(S_i - y_i(x)) \, \epsilon_i(x) \, dF(x)$$

As we assumed that $y(x)$ is Pareto optimal, this difference cannot be nonnegative for all i.

2.6. It is easy to see that a *sufficient* condition that $y(x)$ is Pareto optimal, is that there exist $n - 1$ positive constants $k_2, \ldots, k_n$ such that

$$u_i'(S_i - y_i(x)) = k_i u_1' (S_1 - y_1(x))$$

If this condition is fulfilled, we have

$$U_i(\bar{y}) - U_i(y) = -k_i \int_R u_1' (S_1 - y_1(x)) \epsilon_i(x) \, dF(x)$$

Since we obviously must have

$$\sum_{i=1}^{n} \bar{y}_i(x) = \sum_{i=1}^{n} y_i(x) = \sum_{i=1}^{n} x_i$$

it follows that

$$\sum_{i=1}^{n} \epsilon_i(x) = 0 \qquad \text{for all } x$$

If we divide by k_i and sum over all i, we obtain

$$\sum_{i=1}^{n} \frac{1}{k_i} \left\{ U_i(\bar{y}) - U_i(y) \right\} = - \int_R u_1' (S_1 - y_1(x)) \sum_{i=1}^{n} \epsilon_i(x) \, dF(x) = 0$$

where $k_1 = 1$. Since $k_i > 0$ for all i, all terms in the sum on the left can be non-negative only if $U_i(\bar{y}) - U_i(y) = 0$ for all i. This will, however, imply $\epsilon_i(x) \equiv 0$ for all i. Hence we must have $\bar{y}(x) = y(x)$ which proves our statement.

2.7.   To prove that the condition is *necessary,* we shall show that if it is not fulfilled, it will be possible to find a set of functions $\epsilon_1(x), \ldots, \epsilon_n(x)$ not identically zero so that

$$U_i(\bar{y}) - U_i(y) \geqslant 0$$

for all i, the inequality being strict for at least one value of i.

Let

$$\epsilon_1(x) = a' \text{ over a set } A', \text{ where } u_1'(S_1 - y_1(x)) > u_2'(S_2 - y_2(x))$$

$$= a'' \text{ over a set } A'', \text{ where } u_1'(S_1 - y_1(x)) < u_2' - y_2(x))$$

$$= 0 \text{ for all points belonging neither to } A' \text{ nor } A''$$

$$\epsilon_2(x) = -\epsilon_1(x)$$

$$\epsilon_i(x) = 0 \quad \text{ for } i = 3, 4, \ldots, n$$

We find

$$U_1(\bar{y}) - U_1(y) = -a' \int_{A'} u_1'(S_1 - y_1(x))\, dF(x) - a'' \int_{A''} u_1'(S_1 - y_1(x))\, dF(x)$$

and

$$U_2(\bar{y}) - U_2(y) = a' \int_{A'} u_2'(S_2 - y_2(x))\, dF(x) + a'' \int_{A''} u_2'(S_2 - y_2(x))\, dF(x)$$

It is easily seen that, if a' and a'' are chosen so that

$$\frac{\int_{A''} u_1'(S_1 - y_1(x))\, dF(x)}{\int_{A'} u_1'(S_1 - y_1(x))\, dF(x)} < -\frac{a'}{a''} < \frac{\int_{A''} u_2'(S_2 - y_2(x))\, dF(x)}{\int_{A'} u_2'(S_2 - y_2(x))\, dF(x)}$$

both $U_1(\bar{y}) - U_1(y)$ and $U_2(\bar{y}) - U_2(y)$ will be positive. Since $U_i(\bar{y}) - U_i(y) = 0$ for $i = 3, 4, \ldots, n$, $y(x)$ is not Pareto optimal, provided that neither of the two sets A' and A'' are empty. Assume now that A' is empty, i.e., that

$$u_1'(S_1 - y_1(x)) < u_2'(S_2 - y_2(x)) \quad \text{ for all } x$$

Since the utility function is determined only up to a linear transformation, any relation between $u_1'(x)$ and $u_2'(x)$ must remain valid if $u_1'(x)$ is multiplied by an arbitrary constant c. However, unless $u_2'(S_2 - y_2(x)) = k_2 u_1'(S_1 - y_1(x))$, it will be possible to find a c, such that

$$cu_1'(S_1 - y_1(x)) < u_2(S_2 - y_2(x)) \qquad \text{for a set } A''$$

and $\quad cu_1'(S_1 - y_1(x)) > u_2(S_2 - y_2(x)) \qquad$ for a nonempty set A'

This completes the proof.

2.8. We have thus found that the functions $y_1(x), \ldots, y_n(x)$, which satisfy the conditions:

$$\left. \begin{aligned} u_i'(S_i - y_i(x)) &= k_i u_1'(S_1 - y_1(x)), \\[2mm] \sum_{i=1}^{n} y_i(x) &= \sum_{i=1}^{n} x_i, \end{aligned} \right\} \quad k_i > 0 \quad i = 2, 3, \ldots, n \qquad \begin{aligned} &(1)\\[6mm] &(2) \end{aligned}$$

define a Pareto optimal set of reinsurance treaties.

If we differentiate both equalities with respect to x_j, we obtain

$$\frac{\partial y_i(x)}{\partial x_j} u_i''(S_i - y_i(x)) = k_i \frac{\partial y_1(x)}{\partial x_j} u_1''(S_1 - y_1(x))$$

and $\displaystyle\sum_{i=1}^{n} \frac{\partial y_i(x)}{\partial x_j} = 1$

If we divide the first equation by $u_i''(S_i - y_i(x))$ and sum over all i, we obtain

$$1 = u_1''(S_1 - y_1(x)) \frac{\partial y_1}{\partial x_j} \sum_{i=1}^{n} \frac{k_i}{u_i''(S_i - y_i(x))}$$

It is easy to see that in general we have

$$\frac{\partial y_i(x)}{\partial x_j} = \frac{\dfrac{k_i}{u_i''(S_i - y_i(x))}}{\displaystyle\sum_{i=1}^{n} \dfrac{k_i}{u_i''(S_i - y_i(x))}}$$

where $k_1 = 1$. The right-hand side does not depend on j. Hence

$$\sum_{j=1}^{n} \frac{\partial y_i}{\partial x_j} dx_j = \frac{\partial y_i}{\partial x_k} \sum_{j=1}^{n} dx_j = \frac{\partial y_i}{\partial x_k} dz$$

for any value of k. It then follows that the vector function $y_i(x)$ must be a scalar function $y_i(z)$ of one single variable

$$z = \sum_{i=1}^{n} x_i$$

so that we have

$$\frac{dy_i(z)}{dz} = \frac{\dfrac{k_i}{u_i''(S_i - y_i(z))}}{\displaystyle\sum_{i=1}^{n} \frac{k_i}{u_i''(S_i - y_i(z))}}$$

2.9. The fact that $y_i(x)$ is a function of z alone means that the only Pareto optimal arrangement is that the companies should cede their entire portfolio to a pool, and then agree on some rule as to how payment of claims against the pool should be divided among the companies. There may be an infinity of such rules, since the positive constants $k_2, \ldots, k_n$ can be chosen arbitrarily.

If the companies conduct their reinsurance negotiations in a rational manner we will expect them, in some way, to end by concluding a Pareto optimal set of treaties. However, this assumption of rationality is not sufficient to determine which of the Pareto optimal sets the companies will arrive at. To make the problem determinate, i.e., to determine $k_2, \ldots, k_n$, it is necessary to make some *additional assumptions* about the manner in which the companies negotiate their way to a final set of treaties.

We shall not take up this general problem, which really is that of finding a unique solution to an n-person game [6]. The problem is extremely complex, particularly if there is no restriction on how companies can form coalitions to strengthen their bargaining position versus those outside the coalition.

3. Equilibrium Price in a Market

3.1. In para. 2.8 we used the notation $y_i(z)$ for the amount which company i had to pay if claims against the pool were z. $y_i(0)$, i.e., payment if there are no claims, can then obviously be interpreted as the company's net outlay of reinsurance premiums. If there is a market price for reinsurance, i.e., a price which has to be applied in all treaties, $y_i(0)$ will obviously be determined for all i, and this may enable us to determine the constants $k_2, \ldots, k_n$.

3.2. We shall first illustrate the part played by price in an ordinary commodity market. Assume that x units of a certain good can be sold for an amount of money $p(x)$. If the market is perfectly competitive, and if $p(x)$ is an equilibrium price, the x units must bring in the same amount of money regardless of whether they are sold in several lots, or in one single transaction. Hence if $x = x_1 + x_2$, we must have

$$p(x) = p(x_1 + x_2) = p(x_1) + p(x_2)$$

Apart from the trivial $p(x) = 0$, the only function which satisfies this equation is $p(x) = px$. Hence there exists a unit price which does not depend on the number of units included in any transaction.

3.3. In the reinsurance market the commodity traded is probability distributions. The price concept we need should make it possible to associate a number $P(F(x))$ to any probability distribution $F(x)$, so that $P(F(x))$ is the amount of money an insurance company can obtain by accepting to pay a claim which is a random variable with probability distribution $F(x)$.

As a natural extension of the concepts from commodity markets, we require that

$$P(F(x)) = P(F_1(x_1)) + P(F_2(x_2))$$

where $F(x)$ is the convolution of the two independent probability distributions $F_1(x_1)$ and $F_2(x_2)$.

There is clearly an infinity of functionals which satisfy this additivity condition. It is, for instance, satisfied by the cumulant generating function

$$\psi(t) = \log \varphi(t)$$

where $\varphi(t)$ is the characteristic function

$$\varphi(t) = \int_0^\infty e^{itx} \, dF(x)$$

It is inconvenient to work with a complex valued function, so in the following we will use the corresponding real functions

$$\varphi(t) = \int_0^\infty e^{-tx} \, dF(x)$$

and $\psi(t) = \log \varphi(t)$

which exist for any nonnegative value of t. The cumulants are given by the expansion

$$\psi(t) = \sum_{n=1}^{\infty} (-1)^n \frac{\kappa_n}{n!} t^n$$

3.4. It follows that for any nonnegative value of t, $\psi(t)$ can be interpreted as a price which satisfies the condition in the preceding paragraph. The same will hold for any linear combination of the form

$$c_1 \psi(t_1) + c_2 \psi(t_2) + \ldots$$

where $c_1, c_2, \ldots$ are constants. Similar expressions containing derivatives of $\psi(t)$ of any order will also satisfy the condition.

However, any such expression will be a linear combination of cumulants, so that we can write

$$P(F(x)) = \sum_{n=1}^{\infty} p_n \kappa_n = \sum_{n=1}^{\infty} b_n \psi^{(n)}(0)$$

where κ_n is the nth cumulant of the distribution $F(x)$. Here we must clearly place some restrictions on the coefficients p_n and b_n to ensure that the series converge. If these restrictions are met, the series will be the most general price concept which satisfies the additivity condition of para. 3.3. We shall not prove this, but we note that a safety loading proportional to the standard deviation is a price concept which does not satisfy the condition.

We shall require, as a continuity condition that $p_1 = 1$. If $F(x)$ is degenerate, so that all cumulants except the first vanish, we must have

$$F(x) = 0 \quad \text{for } x < \kappa_1$$

and $F(x) = 1 \quad \text{for } \kappa_1 \leqslant x$

Hence p_1 is the price of one monetary unit, to be claimed with certainty, and it is reasonable to require that this shall be unity.

3.5. In para. 3.3 we assumed that x_1 and x_2 were stochastically independent. If we drop this assumption and require that the condition

$$P(F(x_1 + x_2)) = P(F_1(x_1)) + P(F_2(x_2))$$

shall hold also when x_1 and x_2 are dependent, it is obvious that the only price concept which satisfies the condition is

$$P(F(x)) = \int_0^\infty x \, dF(x) = \kappa_1$$

This means that the risk situations are traded against cash payment equal to the expected amount of claims, or in insurance terminology that all reinsurance is done on a net premium basis.

3.6. The price concept we have introduced appears forbiddingly complicated, but it becomes fairly simple for some special distributions.
    For the normal distribution

$$N(x) = \frac{1}{\sigma\sqrt{2\pi}} e - \frac{(x - m)^2}{2\sigma^2}$$

we have

$$P(N(x)) = m + p_2\sigma^2$$

since all cumulants of higher order are zero.
    For the Poisson distribution

$$P(x) = \frac{m^x}{X!} e^{-m}$$

we have

$$P(P(x)) = m \sum_{i=1}^\infty p_i = \alpha m$$

since for this distribution, all cumulants are equal to m. This provides some justification for making the loading proportional to the net premium.
    We shall not pursue our discussion of the general case. In the following we shall analyze in some detail a very simple special case.

4. Discussion of a Special Case

4.1. From the formula at the end of para. 2.8 we see that the expressions for $y_i(z)$ will become particularly simple if all utility functions are polynomials of second degree. We shall therefore study the case where

$$u_i(x) = -a_i x^2 + x \quad \text{for all } i$$

This utility function gives acceptable results provided that a_i is positive and sufficiently small. This has been demonstrated in a previous paper [4].

If $a_i < 1/2S_i$, $u_i(x)$ will be increasing over the whole range from $-\infty$ to S_i. This is obviously a reasonable requirement, since it means that "no claims" is considered as the best possible result company i can get from its direct under-writing.

If $a_i \leqslant 1/2\Sigma S_j$ for all i, the regions where there is decreasing utility of money will be completely excluded from consideration. However, this condition may be too strong if the number of companies is great.

It is clear that a_i can be interpreted as a measure of the company's "risk aversion." If $a_i = 0$, the company will be indifferent to risk. Its sole objective will then be to maximize expected profits, ignoring all risk of deviations from the expected value.

4.2. From the formulas in para. 2.8 we find

$$y_i(z) = k_i \frac{z + \sum_{j=1}^{n} \dfrac{\frac{1}{2} - a_j S_j}{a_j}}{a_i \sum_{j=1}^{n} \dfrac{k_j}{a_j}} - \frac{\frac{1}{2} - a_i S_i}{a_i}$$

Hence the optimum arrangement is that company i shall pay a fixed quota

$$\frac{k_i/a_i}{\Sigma k_j/a_j} = q_i$$

of the amount of claims made against the pool. For $z = 0$ we find:

$$y_i(0) = q_i \sum_{j=1}^{n} \left(\frac{1}{2 a_j} - S_j \right) - \left(\frac{1}{2 a_i} - S_i \right)$$

4.3. The utility of company i in the initial situation is

$$U_i(x_i) = \int_0^{\infty} \left\{ -a_i(S_i - x_i)^2 + S_i - x_i \right\} dF_i(x_i)$$

or $U_i(x_i) = -a_i(S_i - P_i)^2 + S_i - P_i - a_i V_i$

where

$$P_i = \int_0^\infty x_i \, dF_i(x_i)$$

and $V_i = \int_0^\infty (x_i - P_i)^2 \, dF_i(x_i)$

4.4. We introduce the symbols

$$P = \int_0^\infty z \, dF(z) = \sum_{i=1}^n P_i$$

and $V = \int_0^\infty (z - P)^2 \, dF(z)$

Since $x_1, x_2, \ldots, x_n$ are stochastically independent, we have $V = \sum_{i=1}^n V_i$, and that $F(z)$ is then the convolution of $F_1(x_1), \ldots, F_n(x)$.

It is convenient to write $R_i = S_i - P_i$. R_i can be interpreted as the "free reserves" of company i.

The dealings in the reinsurance market will then change the utility of company i from

$$U_i(x_i) = -a_i R_i^2 + R_i - a_i V_i = \frac{1}{4a_i} - a_i \left\{ \left(\frac{1}{2a_i} - R_i \right)^2 + V_i \right\}$$

to $U_i(y) = \dfrac{1}{4a_i} - a_i q_i^2 \left\{ \left(\sum_{j=1}^n \left(\frac{1}{2a_j} - R_j \right) \right)^2 + \sum_{j=1}^n V_j \right\}$

4.5. If company i acts rationally, it will take part in these transactions only if they increase the company's utility, i.e., only if

$$U_i(x_i) < U_i(y)$$

From this condition we obtain the following inequality which must be satisfied for all i:

$$q_i^2 < \frac{\left(\dfrac{1}{2a_i} - R_i \right)^2 + V_i}{\left\{ \displaystyle\sum_{j=1}^n \left(\frac{1}{2a_j} - R_j \right) \right\}^2 + \displaystyle\sum_{j=1}^n V_j}$$

The condition $\Sigma_{j=1}^{n} q_j = 1$ will give a lower limit for q_i.

It is easy to see that these conditions in general will give an interval for the constants $k_2, \ldots, k_n$. We see that $U_i(y)$ will decrease when q_i increases. Hence the smaller q_i is, the more favorable will the corresponding set of reinsurance treaties be to company i.

4.6. The assumption that the utility of money is of the form $u(x) = -ax^2 + x$ implies that the companies will be indifferent to any change in the cumulants of the risk distribution, κ_n for $n > 2$. This means that no company is willing to pay anything to obtain a change which only affects the cumulants of higher order. It then follows that in the general expression for the price

$$P(F(x)) = \sum_{n=1}^{\infty} p_n \kappa_n$$

we must have $p_n = 0$ for $n > 2$. Hence the most general price in the special case we consider will be

$$P(F(x)) = P + pV$$

where P and V are respectively the mean and variance of $F(x)$.

4.7. The Pareto optimal arrangement described in para. 4.2 can obviously be brought about by a series of reciprocal treaties between two companies.

If we consider company i and company j, we see that Pareto optimality will be reached if company i cedes a quota q_j of its portfolio to company j, and in return accepts a quota q_i from company j. In the notation of para. 4.2, this means that company i should pay to company j the amount

$$q_j P_i + pq_j^2 V_i - q_i P_j - pq_i^2 V_j$$

where p is the market price applicable to all reinsurance transactions. Summing this for all $j \neq i$, we obtain

$$P_i \Sigma q_j - q_i \Sigma P_j + p\left\{ V_i \Sigma q_j^2 - q_i^2 \Sigma V_j \right\}$$

which is equal to

$$P_i - q_i \sum_{j=1}^{n} P_j + p\left\{ V_i \sum_{j=1}^{n} q_j^2 - q_i^2 \sum_{j=1}^{n} \right\} V_j$$

since $\Sigma_{j=1}^{n} q_j = 1$. However, this expression must be equal to the total net payment of company i, which, according to para. 4.2, is

$$y_i(0) = q_i \sum_{j=1}^{n} \left(\frac{1}{2a_j} - S_j \right) - \left(\frac{1}{2a_i} - S_i \right)$$

Hence we must have

$$p \left\{ V_i \sum_{j=1}^{n} q_j^2 - q_i^2 \sum_{j=1}^{n} V_j \right\} = q_i \sum_{j=1}^{n} A_j - A_i$$

where

$$A_j = \frac{1}{2a_j} - R_j \quad \text{and} \quad R_j = S_j - P_j$$

This expression for $i = 1, 2, \ldots, n$, together with $\Sigma_{j=1}^{n} q_j = 1$, gives a system of $n + 1$ equations for the determination of the $n + 1$ unknowns $q_1, \ldots, q_n$ and p_2. However, this system has no meaningful solution.

4.8. If we substitute

$$t_i = \frac{q_i}{\sum\limits_{j=1}^{n} q_j}$$

the equation corresponding to $i = 1$ becomes

$$p \left\{ V_1 \sum_{j=1}^{n} t_j^2 - t_1^2 \sum_{j=1}^{n} V_j \right\} = t_1 \sum_{j=1}^{n} t_j \sum_{j=1}^{n} A_j - A_1 \left(\sum_{j=1}^{n} t_j \right)^2$$

This is a quadratic form in $t_1, \ldots, t_n$ with a determinant

$$\begin{vmatrix} \alpha & \beta & \beta & \beta & \cdots \\ \beta & pV_1+A_1 & A_1 & A_1 & \cdots \\ \beta & A_1 & pV_1+A_1 & A_1 & \cdots \\ \beta & A_1 & A_1 & pV_1+A_1 & \cdots \\ \beta & A_1 & A_1 & A_1 & \cdots \\ \cdots & \cdots & \cdots & \cdots & \cdots \end{vmatrix}$$

where

$$\alpha = p\left(V_1 - \sum_{j=1}^{n} V_j\right) + A_1 - \sum_{j=1}^{n} A_j \quad \text{and} \quad \beta = A_1 = \tfrac{1}{2}\sum_{j=n}^{n} A_j$$

It is easy to see that this determinant is strictly negative for any $p > 0$. Hence the quadratic form is strictly negative for any $t_1, \ldots, t_n$, provided that $p > 0$. This obviously holds, also for $i = 2, \ldots, n$. For $p = 0$ we obtain the solution

$$q_i = \frac{A_i}{\sum_{j=1}^{n} A_j} = \frac{\frac{1}{2a_i} - R_i}{\sum_{j=1}^{n}\left(\frac{1}{2a_j} - R_j\right)}$$

4.9. We have thus found that the only solution consistent with our conditions is $p = 0$, i.e., that all reinsurance is made on a net premium basis.

However, even this solution is not acceptable if it gives one of the companies a lower utility than it has in the initial situation. We must also require that q_i satisfies the inequalities in para. 4.5. That $p = 0$ actually can lead to values of q_i which do not satisfy the inequalities has been demonstrated by an example in a previous paper [4].

4.10. The practical implication of these results can be stated as follows. If the companies believe that there is a certain market price for reinsurance, and apply this price to all their transactions, they will inevitably end in a situation which is not Pareto optimal. If some of the companies realize this, they may find a way, for instance, a reciprocal treaty between two companies which will increase the utility of both, without changing the utility of any other company.

However, a treaty of this kind will imply a price different from the one used in the first set of transactions. Hence there exists no market price which will lead to a Pareto optimal arrangement, if applied to all transactions.

4.11. The result which we have reached is in a way completely negative. It shatters any illusions which we may have held to the effect that reinsurance transactions are made in a perfectly competitive market, where competition brings about an equilibrium which also is an optimum.

It may be useful to examine ordinary commodity markets more closely, to see if we have any reason to be disappointed or surprised over our negative result. In the classical model an individual brings quantitites $x_0, y_0, z_0, \ldots$ of various goods to the market. Here he barters his goods with the other participants in the market. Classical economic theory has created order in this apparently confused situation by making two simple assumptions:

1. Each participant acts as if the market price of the various goods is given, i.e., as if nothing which he can do will change the price.
2. Each participant seeks to maximize a utility function.

From these assumptions it follows that:

1. Each participant will leave the market with quantities $x, y, z, \ldots$ which maximize his utility function $u(x, y, z)$ subject to the condition

$$p_1 x_0 + p_2 y_0 + p_3 z_0 + \ldots = p_1 x + p_2 y + p_3 z + \ldots$$

where $p_1, p_2, \ldots$ are the prices which make supply of each good equal to demand.
2. The distribution of goods resulting from these market transactions is Pareto optimal.

It is indeed surprising that it is possible to derive such a far-reaching result from some extremely simple assumptions. We have really no reason to expect that a few equally simple assumptions should create order in a reinsurance market, which is essentially different from the classical commodity market.

4.12. The difference is brought out clearly by the following point. In a commodity market, the "market value" of the goods an individual holds does not change. The so-called budget equation

$$p_1 x_0 + p_2 y_0 + \ldots = p_1 x + p_2 y + \ldots$$

must hold regardless of what transactions the individual does at the market price.

In para. 4.4 we found that the reinsurance treaties changed the variance of company i from V_i to $q_i^2 \Sigma_{j=1}^n V_j$. Since obviously

$$\sum_{j=1}^n V_j > \left(\sum_{j=1}^n q_i^2 \right)\left(\sum_{j=1}^n V_j \right)$$

there is nothing corresponding to the budget equation in a reinsurance market.

4.13. Reinsurance brokers should rejoice over our result. If there is no simple price mechanism which more or less automatically brings about an optimal situation, it seems that brokers must perform an essential function in reconciling different interests and desires, and possibly steering the market into an optimal situation.

5. Market Equilibrium under Uncertainty

5.1. The problem we have studied in this paper is really that of extending the classical Walras-Cassel model of market equilibrium to include risk. This is obviously a problem of fundamental importance to economic theory, and it is surprising that so few economists have taken it up for systematic study.

It appears that only Allais [1] and Arrow [3] have made any serious attempts to tackle the problem. Their results have recently been generalized by Debreu [5], but his treatment of the matter is too abstract to have any real bearing on our problem.

5.2. Allais [1] has proved that there exists an equilibrium price, which also is Pareto optimal, in a market for lottery tickets. However, his proof rests on the assumption that lottery tickets can be bought and sold only in integral numbers, i.e., one can buy one ticket, but not a 50% interest in two tickets. This is a rather serious limitation if one wants to interpret his model as a reinsurance market.

5.3. Arrow [3] has proved that a price mechanism will bring about a Pareto optimal equilibrium in a model which is considerably more general than required for our purpose. Firstly he deals with n different commodities, and secondly he allows himself the luxury of considering subjective probabilities. This may be necessary for a theory of stock exchanges, which apparently is what Arrow has in mind. However, in a reinsurance market such refinements are not essential.

Stripped of these refinements and presented in insurance terms, Arrow's model can be described as follows:

(i)   Company i has a utility of money $u_i(x) \cdot (i = 1, 2, \ldots, I)$.

(ii) As a result of its direct underwriting company i is committed to pay an amount x_{is} if "state of the world" s occurs ($s = 1, 2, \ldots, S$).

(iii) The company has funds amounting to S_i available for meeting these commitments.

(iv) The probability that state of the world s will occur is p_s.

The utility of company i in the initial situation is then

$$U_i(0) = \sum_{s=1}^{S} p_s u_i (S_i - x_{is})$$

5.4.   It is then assumed that the company pays an amount $g_s y_{is}$ in order to be assured of receiving the amount y_{is} if state of the world s occurs. This means that should this state of the world occur, the company will have to make a net payment of $x_{is} - y_{is}$.

The utility of the company after having made a series of such contracts will be

$$U_i(y) = \sum_{s=1}^{S} p_s u_i \left(\left\{ S_i - \sum_{s=1}^{S} g_s y_{is} \right\} - (x_{is} - y_{is}) \right)$$

If we maximize this function in a straightforward manner, we find:

$$\frac{\partial U_i(y)}{\partial y_{it}} = -g_t \sum_{s=1}^{S} p_s u_i' \left(\left\{ S_i - \sum_{s=1}^{S} g_s y_{is} \right\} - x_{js} + y_{is} \right)$$

$$+ p_t u_i' \left(\left\{ S_i - \sum_{s=1}^{S} g_s y_{is} \right\} - x_{it} + y_{it} \right)$$

The first-order conditions for maximum are

$$g_t \sum_{s=1}^{S} p_s u_i' (R_i - x_{is} + y_{is}) = p_t u_i' (R_i - x_{it} + y_{it}) \qquad t = 1, 2, \ldots, S$$

where we have put

$$S_i - \sum_{s=1}^{S} g_s y_{is} = R_i$$

If the utility function fulfills some reasonable conditions, these equations will lead to a solution of the form

$$y_{it} = f_i\left(\frac{p_t}{g_t}, x_{it}\right)$$

If $u_i'(x)$ is monotonicly decreasing, y_{it} will decrease with increasing g_t, and increase with increasing p_t and x_{it}. Since we obviously must have

$$\sum_{i=1}^{I} y_{is} = 0 \qquad \text{for all } s$$

we obtain S equations to determine the S prices $g_1, \ldots, g_s$. That these equations, under certain conditions have a nontrivial solution follows from Arrow's paper.

5.5. Arrow's price g_s depends on the probability p_s that state of the world s shall occur, *and* on the initial distribution among the companies of the amounts x_{is} which become payable if this state of the world should occur. The latter element is not included in our model, which assumes that the market price depends exclusively on the probability that a claim will occur. This is obviously the reason why we found that no equilibrium price exists.

We shall illustrate this by a practical example. Assume that the probability of total loss of an ocean liner worth $100 million is the same as the probability that a house worth $10,000 will be totally destroyed by fire. According to ordinary actuarial theory, an insurance company should demand the same premium for covering the house against total destruction by fire, as for paying out $10,000 if the ocean liner should be lost.

According to Arrow's theory, the company will demand different premiums for the two coverages. It is easy to show that under fairly reasonable assumptions, the company will—or can—ask a higher premium for covering a part of the ocean liner. The reason being that other companies in the market will feel uneasy about the large amounts they have to pay if the liner should be lost. Hence there will be a great demand for reinsurance cover of this particular risk, so that an uncommitted company can exact a high premium for such coverage.

5.6. Arrow's paper shows that it is possible to construct a model of a reinsurance market in which unrestricted competition will lead to an equilibrium which is Pareto optimal. In order to reach this result, he has to sacrifice the *principle of equivalence* which has been sacrosanct ever since the beginning of rational insurance.

This might perhaps have been expected. The principle of equivalence may have its proper place in ethics, rather than in a business world where everything depends on supply and demand. Whether insurance essentially is a business aiming at making money or a benevolent social service is a point which probably will never be finally settled. If we press the analogy with business to the utmost, as we have done in this paper, we should not be surprised that we either run into inconsistencies or have to sacrifice a principle deemed essential to insurance.

References

1. Allais, M. L'extension des théories de l'équilibre économique général et du rendement social au cas du risque, *Econometrica* 1953, pp. 269–290.
2. Ammeter, H. "The Calculation of Premium Rates for Excess of Loss and Stop Loss Reinsurance Treaties," in *Non-proportional Reinsurance,* edited by S. Vajda (Brussels, 1955) pp. 79–110.
3. Arrow, K. J. Le rôle de valeurs boursières pour la répartition la meilleure des risques, *Colloques Internationaux du Centre National de la Recherche Scientifique,* XL, pp. 41–48, Paris 1953.
4. Borch, K. "Reciprocal Reinsurance Treaties Seen as a Two-person Cooperative Game," *Skand. Aktuarietidskr.* 1960, pp. 29–58.
5. Debreu, G. *Theory of Value,* (New York: John Wiley & Sons, 1959).
6. Neumann, J. von and Morgenstern, O. *Theory of Games and Economic Behavior* (Princeton, 1944).
7. Wold, H. *Landsbygdens Brandförsäkringsbolags Maximaler och Återförsäkring* (Stockholm, 1936).

10 Equilibrium in a Reinsurance Market

This paper investigates the possibility of generalizing the classical theory of commodity markets to include uncertainty. It is shown that if uncertainty is considered as a commodity, it is possible to define a meaningful price concept, and to determine a price which makes supply equal to demand. However, if each participant seeks to maximize his utility, taking this price as given, the market will not in general reach a Pareto optimal state. If the market shall reach a Pareto optimal state, there must be negotiations between the participants, and it seems that the problem can best be analyzed as an *n*-person cooperative game.

The paper is written in the terminology of reinsurance markets. The theoretical model studied should be applicable also to stock exchanges and other markets where the participants seek to reach an optimal distribution of risk.

1. Introduction

1.1. The Walras-Cassel system of equations which determines a static equilibrium in a competitive economy is certainly one of the most beautiful constructions in mathematical economics. The mathematical rigor which was lacking when the system was first presented has since been provided by Wald [10] and Arrow and Debreu [4]. For more than a generation one of the favorite occupations of economists has been to generalize the system to dynamic economies. The mere volume of the literature dealing with this subject gives ample evidence of its popularity.

1.2. The present paper investigates the possibilities of generalizing the Walras-Cassel model in another direction. The model as presented by its authors assumes complete certainty, in the sense that all consumers and producers know exactly what will be the outcome of their actions. It will obviously be of interest to extend the model to markets where decisions are made under uncertainty as to what the outcome will be. This problem seems to have been studied systematically only by Allais [1] and Arrow [3] and to some extent by Debreu [7] who includes uncertainty in the last chapter of his recent book. It is surprising that a problem of such obvious and fundamental importance to economic theory has not received more attention. Allais ascribes this neglect of the subject to *son extrême difficulté.*

1.3.   The subject does not appear inherently difficult, however, at least not when presented in Allais' elegant manner. What seems to be forbiddingly difficult is to extend his relatively simple model to situations in the real world where uncertainty and attitude toward risk play a decisive part, for instance, in the determination of interest rates, share prices, and supply and demand for risk capital. Debreu's abstract treatment also seems very remote from such familiar problems. There are further difficulties of which Allais, particularly, seems acutely aware, such as the psychological problems connected with the elusive concepts of "subjective probabilities" and "rational behavior." In the present paper we shall put these latter difficulties aside. It then appears fairly simple to construct a model of a competitive market which seems reasonably close to the situations in real life where rational beings exchange risk and cash among themselves. The problem still remains difficult, but it seems that the difficulty is the familiar one of laying down assumptions which lead to a determinate solution of an n-person game.

1.4.   The reason why neither Allais nor Arrow has followed up his preliminary study of the problem is probably that their relatively simple models appear too remote from any really interesting practical economic situation. However, the model they consider gives a fairly accurate description of a *reinsurance market.* The participants in this market are insurance companies, and the commodity they trade is risk. The purpose of the deals which the companies make in this market is to redistribute the risks which each company has accepted by its direct underwriting for the public. The companies which gain from this redistribution of risks are ready to pay compensation in cash to the other companies. This is a real life example of just the situation which Allais and Arrow have studied in rather artificial models.

It seems indeed that the reinsurance market offers promising possibilities of studying how attitudes toward risk influence decision making and the interaction between the decisions made by the various participants. This problem has so far been studied mainly in the theory of investment and capital markets where one must expect that a large number of "disturbing factors" are at play. It is really surprising that economists have overlooked the fact that the problem can be studied, almost under laboratory conditions, in the reinsurance market.

2.   A Model of the Reinsurance Market

2.1.   Consider n insurance companies, each holding a portfolio of insurance contracts.

The *risk situation* of company i $(i = 1, 2, \ldots, n)$ is defined by the following two elements:

(i)   The *risk distribution*, $F_i(x_i)$, which is the probability that the total amount of claims to be paid under the contracts in the company's portfolio shall not exceed x_1.

(ii) The *funds*, S_i, which the company has available to pay claims.

We shall assume that $x_1, \ldots, x_n$ are stochastically independent. To this risk situation the company attaches a utility $U_i(S_i, F_i(x_i))$. From the so-called "Bernoulli hypothesis" it follows that

$$U_i(S_i, F_i(x_i)) = \int_0^\infty u_i(S_i - x_i)\, dF_i(x_i)$$

Here $u_i(S) = U_i(S, \epsilon(x))$, where $\epsilon(x)$ is the degenerate probability distribution defined by

$$\epsilon(x) = 0 \quad \text{for } x < 0$$

$$\epsilon(x) = 1 \quad \text{for } 0 \leqslant x$$

Hence $u_i(S)$ is the utility attached to a risk situation with funds S and probability of 1 that claims shall be zero. In the following we shall refer to the function $u_i(S)$ as the "utility of money to company i." We shall assume that $u_i(S)$ is continuous and that its first derivative is positive and decreases with increasing S.

2.2   Von Neumann and Morgenstern [9] proved the Bernoulli hypothesis as a theorem, derived from a few simple axioms. Since then there has been considerable controversy over the plausibility of the various formulations which can be given to these axioms. There is no need to take up this question here, since it is almost trivial that the Bernoulli hypothesis must hold for a company in the insurance business.

2.3.   In the initial situation company i is committed to pay x_i, the total amount of claims which occur in its own portfolio. The commitments of company i do not depend on the claims which occur in the portfolios of the other companies. In the reinsurance market the companies can conclude agreements, usually referred to as *treaties* which redistribute the commitments that the companies had in the initial situation.

In general these treaties can be represented by a set of functions:

$$y_i(x_1, x_2, \ldots, x_n) \quad i = 1, 2, \ldots, n$$

where $y_i(x_1, x_2, \ldots, x_n)$ is the amount company i has to pay if claims in the respective portfolios amount to $x_1, x_2, \ldots, x_n$. Since all claims have to be paid, we must obviously have

$$\sum_{i=1}^{n} y_i(x_1, \ldots, x_n) = \sum_{i=1}^{n} x_i$$

These treaties will change the utility of company i from

$$U_i(x) = \int_0^\infty u_i(S_i - x_i)\, dF_i(x_i)$$

to $\quad U_i(y) = \int_R u_i(S_i - y_i(x))\, dF(x)$

where $F(x)$ is the joint probability distribution of $x_1, \ldots, x_n$, and where R stands for the positive orthant in the n-dimensional x-space.

For simplicity we have written x and y, respectively for the vectors $\{x_1, \ldots, x_n\}$ and $\{y_1(x), \ldots, y_n(x)\}$.

2.4. If the companies act rationally, they will not conclude a set of treaties represented by a vector y if there exists another set of treaties with a corresponding vector $\bar{y}$, such that

$$U_i(y) \leqslant U_i(\bar{y}) \qquad \text{for all } i$$

with at least one strict inequality. y will in this case clearly be inferior to $\bar{y}$. If there exists no vector $\bar{y}$ satisfying the above condition, the set of treaties represented by y will be referred to as *Pareto optimal.* If the companies act rationally, the treaties they conclude must obviously constitute a Pareto optimal set.

2.5. It has been proved in a previous paper [6] that a necessary and sufficient condition that a vector y is Pareto optimal is that its elements, the functions $y_1(x), \ldots, y_n(x)$ satisfy the relations

$$u_i'(S_i - y_i(x)) = k_i u_1'(S_1 - y_1(x)) \tag{1}$$

$$\sum_{i=1}^{n} y_i(x) = \sum_{i=1}^{n} x_i \tag{2}$$

where $k_2, k_3, \ldots, k_n$ are positive constants which can be chosen arbitrarily.

The proof is elementary. It will not be repeated here since a rigorous statement is lengthy and rather tedious. Heuristically it is almost self-evident that if the condition is fulfilled, a change in y cannot increase the utility of all the companies, i.e., that the condition is sufficient. The proof that it is necessary is slightly less transparent.

2.6. Differentiation of the equations in the preceding paragraph with respect to x_j gives

$$u_i''(S_i - y_i(x)) \frac{\partial y_i}{\partial x_j} = k_i u_1''(S_1 - y_1(x)) \frac{\partial y_1}{\partial x_j}$$

and $$\sum_{i=1}^{n} \frac{\partial y_i}{\partial x_j} = 1$$

Dividing the first equation by $u_i''(S_i - y_i(x))$ and summing over all i, we obtain

$$u_1''(S_1 - y_1(x)) \frac{\partial y_1}{\partial x_j} \sum_{i=1}^{n} \frac{k_i}{u_i''(S_i - y_i(x))} = 1$$

where $k_1 = 1$.

It then follows that for any i and j we must have

$$\frac{\partial y_1}{\partial x_i} = \frac{\partial y_1}{\partial x_j}$$

This implies that the vector function $y_1(x)$ is a scalar function of one single variable

$$z = \sum_{i=1}^{n} x_i$$

It is easy to verify that in general we have

$$\frac{dy_i(z)}{dz} = \frac{\dfrac{k_i}{u_i''(S_i - y_i(z))}}{\displaystyle\sum_{j=1}^{n} \dfrac{k_j}{u_j''(S_j - y_j(z))}}$$

This means that the amount $y_i(z)$ which company i has to pay will depend only on $z = x_1 + \ldots + x_n$, i.e., on the total amount of claims made against the insurance industry. Hence any Pareto optimal set of treaties is equivalent to a pool arrangement, i.e., all companies hand their portfolios over to a pool, and agree on some rule as to how payment of claims against the pool shall be divided among the companies. In general there will be an infinity of such rules, since the $n-1$ positive constants $k_2, k_3, \ldots, k_n$ can be chosen arbitrarily. In general the utility of company i will decrease with increasing k_i ($i \neq 1$). Since the company will not be party to a set of treaties unless $U_i(y) \geqslant U_i(x)$ there must be an upper limit to k_i. We shall return to this question in Section 4.

2.7. The results reached in the preceding paragraphs correspond very well to what one could expect on more intuitive grounds. If all companies are averse to risk, it was to be expected that the best arrangement would be to spread the risks as widely as possible. It was also to be expected that the solution should be indeterminate, since no assumptions were made as to how the companies should divide the gain resulting from the greater spread of risks.

In the Walras-Cassel model there is a determinate equilibrium, i.e., unique Pareto optimal distribution of the goods in the market. The basic assumption required to reach this result is that each participant considers the market price as given, and then buys or sells quantities of the various goods so that his utility is maximized. In the following section we shall investigate the possibility of finding some equally simple assumptions which will bring a reinsurance market into an equilibrium.

3. The Price Concept in a Reinsurance Market

3.1. In insurance circles it is generally assumed that there exists a well defined market price, at least for some particular forms of reinsurance. It is also generally believed that Lloyd's of London is willing to quote a price for any kind of reinsurance cover.

If a market price exists, it must mean that it is possible to associate a number $P(F)$ to any probability distribution $F(x)$, so that an insurance company can receive the amount $P(F)$ from the market by undertaking to pay the claims which occur in a portfolio with risk distribution $F(x)$. It must also be possible for the company to be relieved of the responsibility for paying such claims by paying the amount $P(F)$ to the market.

3.2. Assume now that a company accepts responsibility for two portfolios with risk distributions $F_1(x_1)$ and $F_2(x_2)$. Assume further that x_1 and x_2 are stochastically independent and that $x = x_1 + x_2$ has the probability distribution

$F(x)$. It is natural to require that the company shall receive the same amount whether it accepts the two portfolios separately or in one single transaction. This means that we must have

$$P(F) = P(F_1) + P(F_2)$$

This additivity condition is clearly a parallel to the assumption in the classical model that the price per unit is independent of the number of units included in a transaction.

3.3. The additivity condition is obviously satisfied by a number of functionals. It is for instance satisfied by the cumulant generating function

$$\psi(t) = \log \varphi(t)$$

where $\varphi(t)$ is the characteristic function

$$\varphi(t) = \int_0^\infty e^{itx}\, dF(x)$$

As it is inconvenient to work with a complex valued function, we shall in the following use the corresponding real functions

$$\varphi(t) = \int_0^\infty e^{-tx}\, dF(x)$$

and $\psi(t) = \log \varphi(t)$

which exist for any nonnegative value of t. The cumulants are then given by the expansion

$$\psi(t) = \sum_{n=1}^\infty (-1)^{n-1} \frac{K_n}{n!} t^n$$

3.4. It follows that for any nonnegative value of t, $\psi(t)$ can be interpreted as a price which satisfies the additivity condition. The same will hold for any linear combination of the form

$$c_1\psi(t_1) + c_2\psi(t_2) + \ldots$$

where $c_1, c_2, \ldots$ are constants. Similar expressions containing derivatives of $\psi(t)$ of any order will also satisfy the condition.
It is obvious that any expression of this kind can be written as a sum of cumulants. Hence we can write

$$P(F) = \sum_{n=1}^{\infty} p_n \kappa_n$$

where $p_1, \ldots, p_n$ are constants.

It follows from a theorem by Lukacs [8] that this is the most general expression which satisfies the additivity condition.

3.5. Let now $\epsilon(x)$ be the degenerate probability distribution defined in para. 2.1.

$\epsilon(x - m)$ can then be interpreted as a risk distribution according to which the amount m will be claimed with probability 1. The price associated with this distribution will be

$$P(\epsilon(x - m)) = p_1 m$$

since $\kappa_n = 0$ for $1 < n$. We shall therefore require as a continuity condition that $p_1 = 1$.

3.6. We now assume that a market price of this form is given, and we consider a company in the risk situation $(S, F(x))$. The utility of the company in this situation is

$$U(S, F(x)) = \int_0^{\infty} u(S - x) \, dF(x)$$

If the company undertakes to pay a claim y with probability distribution $G(y)$, it will receive an amount $P(G)$. If x and y are stochastically independent this transaction will change the company's utility to

$$U(S + P(G), H(x)) = \int_0^{\infty} u(S + P(G) - x) d \left\{ \int_0^{\infty} F(x - y) \, dG(y) \right\}$$

$$= \int_0^{\infty} u(S + P(G) - x) \, dH(x)$$

where $H(x)$ is the convolution of $F(x)$ and $G(y)$.

If the company acts rationally, it will select among the portfolios available in the market one with a risk distribution $G_0(y)$ which maximizes $U(S + P(G), H(x))$. This function $G_0(y)$ can be considered as the amount of reinsurance cover which the company will *supply* at the given price.

3.7. The nature of the maximization problem appears more clearly if we introduce the cumulants explicitly in the formula of the preceding paragraph.

Let $f(t)$ and $g(t)$ be the characteristic functions of $F(x)$ and $G(y)$ respectively. The characteristic function of $H(x)$ is then $f(t)g(t)$, and if $H(x)$ has a derivative, we have

$$\frac{dH(x)}{dx} = \frac{1}{2\pi} \int_{-\infty}^{+\infty} e^{-itx} f(t)g(t) \, dt = \frac{1}{2\pi} \int_{-\infty}^{+\infty} e^{-itx} e^{\log f(t) + \log g(t)} \, dt$$

$$= \frac{1}{2\pi} \int_{-\infty}^{+\infty} \exp\left\{ -itx + \sum_{n=1}^{\infty} \frac{(it)^n}{n!} (k_n + \kappa_n) \right\} dt$$

where k_n and κ_n are the nth cumulants of $F(x)$ and $G(y)$, respectively. Hence the problem becomes that of determining the values of $\kappa_1 \kappa_2, \ldots, \kappa_n$ which maximize the expression

$$\int_0^{\infty} u \left(S - x + \sum_{n=1}^{\infty} p_n \kappa_n \right) \int_{-\infty}^{+\infty} \exp\left\{ -itx + \sum_{n=1}^{\infty} \frac{(it)^n}{n!} (k_n + \kappa_n) \right\} dt \, dx$$

It is interesting to note that the cumulants of different order appear as different commodities, each with its particular price. The "quantitites" $\kappa_1, \ldots, \kappa_n$, however, must satisfy certain restraints in order to be the cumulants of a probability distribution. These restraints will be of a complicated nature. A sufficient set of restraints can be derived from the Liapounoff inequalities

$$\frac{1}{n} \log m_n \leqslant \frac{1}{n+1} \log m_{n+1}$$

where m_n is the nth absolute moment about an arbitrary point. Since $G(y) = 0$ for $y < 0$, the inequalities must hold for the moments about zero of $G(y)$. It is easy to see that the sign of equality will hold only in the degenerate case when $G(y) = \epsilon(y - m)$.

The problem on the *supply* side of a reinsurance market thus appears to be similar to the problems of maximization under restraints which occur in some production models. It is clear that the problem will have a solution, at least under certain conditions.

3.8.   The problems on the *demand* side are more complicated. Assume that with a given price a company demands reinsurance cover corresponding to a probability distribution $G(y)$. This means that in order to be relieved of an obligation to pay a claim with a probability distribution $G(y)$, the company is willing to pay an amount

$$P(G(y)) = \sum_{n=1}^{\infty} p_n \kappa_n$$

where $\kappa_1, \ldots, \kappa_n$ are the cumulants of $G(y)$.

Assume now that the company can buy its reinsurance cover in two trans-actions, for instance by placing two portfolios with risk distribution $G(\frac{1}{2}y)$ with two different reinsurers. If the market price is applied to both transactions, the company will have to pay

$$2P(G(\tfrac{1}{2}y)) = \sum_{n=1}^{\infty} \frac{p_n}{2^{n-1}} \kappa_n$$

for the reinsurance cover. $2P(G(\frac{1}{2}y))$ will generally be different from $P(G(y))$. Hence the reinsurance arrangement which maximizes the company's utility will depend not only on the given price, but also on the number of reinsurers who are willing to deal at this price. This makes it doubtful if any meaning can be given to the term "market price" in a reinsurance market. We shall not at present discuss this problem in further detail. We shall, however, consider it again for a special case in Section 4.

4. Existence of an Equilibrium Price

4.1. In the preceding section we studied separately the demand and supply of reinsurance cover. It is fairly obvious, however, that if the companies shall reach the Pareto optimum which we found in Section 2.5, each company must act *both* as seller and buyer of reinsurance cover. In a previous paper [5] it was proved by a more direct approach that it will in general be to the advantage of a company to act in both capacities at the same time.

In this section we shall study whether a price mechanism can bring supply and demand into an equilibrium which also represents a Pareto optimal distribu-tion of the risks.

4.2. Since the problem is rather complex, we shall analyze only a special case. We assume that the utility of money to all companies can be represented by a function of the form

$$u_i(x) = -a_i x^2 + x \qquad \text{for } i = 1, 2, \ldots, n$$

We assume that a_i is positive and so small that $u_i(x)$ is an increasing function over the whole range which enters into consideration.

a_i can evidently be interpreted as a measure of the company's "risk aversion." If $a_i = 0$, the company will be indifferent to risk. Its sole objective will then be to maximize expected profits, ignoring all risk of deviations from the expected value. The greater a_i is, the more concerned will the company be about the possibility of suffering great losses.

From the formulas in para. 2.6 we find

$$\frac{dy_i(z)}{dz} = \frac{k_i/a_i}{\Sigma k_j/a_j} = q_i$$

Hence the optimum arrangement is that company i shall pay a fixed quota q_i of the amount of claims z made against the pool. It is easily verified that

$$y_i(z) = q_i z + q_i \sum_{j=1}^{n} \left(\frac{1}{2a_j} - S_j \right) - \left(\frac{1}{2a_i} - S_i \right) = q_i z + q_i \sum_{j=1}^{n} A_j - A_i$$

For $z = 0$ we find

$$y_i(0) = q_i \sum_{j=1}^{n} A_j - A_i$$

$y_i(0)$ is the amount (positive or negative) that company i has to pay if there are no claims. Hence $y_i(0)$ must be the differnce between the amount the company pays for the reinsurance cover it buys and the amount the company receives for the reinsurance cover it sells.

4.3. If $u(x) = -ax^2 + x$, the utility of the company in the initial situation is

$$U(0) = \int_0^\infty u(S - x)\, dF(x) = \int_0^\infty \left\{ -a(S - x)^2 + (S - x) \right\} dF(x)$$

$$= -a(S - \kappa_1)^2 + (S - \kappa_1) - a\kappa_2$$

where κ_1 and κ_2 are the first two cumulants, i.e., the mean and the variance of $F(x)$. We see that in this case the utility which the company attaches to a risk situation will depend only on the two first cumulants of the risk distribution. If the utility function $u(x)$ is of the form $-ax^2 + x$ for all companies, the cumulants of higher order can have no effect of the optimal arrangement. They will appear as "free goods" in the market, i.e., with price zero. Hence, in the expression for price we must have $p_n = 0$ for all $n > 2$. The amount paid for reinsurance cover of a risk distribution $F(x)$ will then be

$$P(F) = \kappa_1 + p_2 \kappa_2 = m + pV$$

if we drop the index of p_2, and write m and V for the mean and variance of $F(x)$, respectively.

4.4. We now consider two companies, i and j, with risk distributions $F_i(x_i)$ and $F_j(x_j)$ where x_i and x_j are stochastically independent. In a Pareto optimal set of reinsurance treaties the two companies will have to pay fixed quotas, q_i and q_j, of the claims made against the pool $z = \Sigma_{j=1}^{n} x_j$.

It is evident that a Pareto optimal arrangement will result if every pair of companies concludes a reciprocal treaty, according to which company i undertakes to pay $q_i x_j$ if claims against company j amount to x_j, and company j in return pays $q_j x_i$ if claims x_i are made against company i (i.e., q_i is the same for every j).

If m_i and V_i are the mean and variance of $F_i(x_i)$, company i will receive an amount $q_i m_j + pq_i^2 V_j$ for the reinsurance cover it gives company j. Similarly company i will have to pay out $q_j m_i + pq_j^2 V_i$ for the cover it receives from company j.

Hence the net payment from company i to company j will be

$$q_j m_i + pq_j^2 V_i - q_i m_j - pq_i^2 V_j$$

Summing this for all $j \neq i$, we obtain

$$m_i \Sigma q_j - q_i \Sigma m_j + p \left\{ V_i \Sigma q_j^2 \Sigma V_j \right\}$$

which is equal to

$$m_i - q_i \sum_{j=1}^{n} m_j + p \left\{ V_i \sum_{j=1}^{n} q_j^2 - q_i^2 \sum_{j=1}^{n} V_j \right\}$$

This expression, however, must be equal to the total net payment of company i, which according to para. 4.2 is

$$y_i(0) = q_i \sum_{j=1}^{n} A_j - A_i$$

Hence we must have

$$p \left\{ V_i \sum_{j=1}^{n} q_j^2 - q_i^2 \sum_{j=1}^{n} V_j \right\} - q_i \sum_{j=1}^{n} (A_j + m_j) + (A_i + m_i) = 0$$

This expression for $i = 1, 2, \ldots, n$, together with $\Sigma_{j=1}^{n} q_j = 1$ gives a system of $n + 1$ equations for the determination of the $n + 1$ unknowns $q_1, \ldots, q_n$ and p.

These equations are not independent, however, since the last one can be obtained by adding together the first n. Hence the system will give $q_1, \ldots, q_n$ as functions of p.

For $p = 0$ we find

$$q_i(0) = \frac{A_j + m_j}{\sum_{j=1}^{n} (A_j + m_j)}$$

Differentiating the equations with respect to p, we find

$$\left[\frac{dq_i(p)}{dp}\right]_{p=0} \sum_{j=1}^{n} (A_j + m_j) = V_i \sum_{j=1}^{n} q_j^2 - q_i^2 \sum_{j=1}^{n} V_j$$

Hence it follows from considerations of continuity that $q_i(p)$ will be real and positive when p lies in some interval containing zero.

4.5. We shall now assume that a price p is given, and study how company 1 can increase its utility by dealing in the market at this price.

(i) The company can *sell* reinsurance cover, i.e., it can accept responsibility for paying a claim with mean m_0 and variance W_1. For giving this cover the company will receive the amount $m_0 + pW_1$.

According to the formulas in para. 4.3, this transaction will change the utility of the company from

$$-a_1(S_1 - m_1)^2 + (S_1 - m_1) - a_1 V_1 = U_1(S_1 - m_1, V_1) = U_1(R_1, V_1)$$

to

$$-a_1(S_1 - m_1 + pW_1)^2 + (S_1 - m_1 + pW_1) - a_1(V_1 + W_1)$$

$$= U_1(R_1 + pW_1, V_1 + W_1)$$

Here $R_1 = S_1 - m_1$, which in insurance terminology is called the "free reserves" of the company, i.e., funds in excess of expected amount of claims. We see that the utility does not depend on m_0, but only on free reserves and variance.

(ii) The company can *buy* reinsurance cover from the $n - 1$ other companies, i.e., by paying the amounts $pv_2, \ldots, pv_n$ of its free reserves to the other companies, it can "get rid of" variances $v_2, \ldots, v_n$.

These transactions will leave the company with a variance

$$v_1 = V_1 \sum_{i=2}^{n} v_i - 2 \sum_{i \neq j} C_{ij}$$

where C_{ij} is the covariance between claims in the portfolios taken by companies i and j.

Since the utility of company 1 will increase with decreasing v_1, the company will seek to arrange its purchases so that C_{ij} is as great as possible, i.e., so that

$$C_{ij} = (v_i v_j)^{1/2}$$

This clearly means that there must be a perfect positive correlation between claims in the part of the original portfolio which the company retains and the parts which are reinsured. Hence we must have $v_i = q_i^2 V_1$ and $\Sigma_{j=1}^{n} q_j = 1$. This is the same as the result which we in para. 4.2 derived from the general condition for Pareto optimality of para. 2.5.

4.6. If the company buys and sells reinsurance cover in this way, its utility will become

$$U_1 \left(\left\{ R_1 + p \left(W_1 - \sum_{i=2}^{n} v_i \right) \right\}, \left\{ W_1 + \left(V_1^{1/2} - \sum_{i=2}^{n} v_i^{1/2} \right)^2 - V_1 \right\} \right)$$

The company will then seek to determine W_1, and $v_2, \ldots, v_n$ so that this expression is maximized.

The first-order conditions for a maximum are

$$\frac{\partial U_1}{\partial W_1} = -p \left\{ 2a_1 \left(R_1 + p \left(W_1 - \sum_{j=2}^{n} v_j \right) \right) - 1 \right\} - a_1 = 0$$

$$\frac{\partial U_1}{\partial v_i} = p \left\{ 2a_1 \left(R_1 + p \left(W_1 - \sum_{j=2}^{n} v_j \right) \right) - 1 \right\} + a_1 \frac{V_1^{1/2} - \sum_{j=2}^{n} v_j^{1/2}}{v_i^{1/2}} = 0$$

$i = 2, 3, \ldots, n$

Adding the first of these equations to the one obtained by differentiating with respect to v_i, we obtain

$$V_1^{1/2} - \sum_{j=2}^{n} v_j^{1/2} = v_i^{1/2}$$

Since this must hold for all i, we must have

$$v_i = \frac{1}{n^2} V_1 \qquad \text{for all } n$$

This means that regardless of what the price is, the company will seek to divide its portfolio into n identical parts, and reinsure $n - 1$ of these with the other companies.

Inserting the values of v_i in the first equation, we find

$$W_1 = \frac{n - 1}{n^2} V_1 + \frac{2p(1/2a_1 - R_1) - 1}{2p^2}$$

4.7.   In general we find that for a given price p, company i is willing to supply reinsurance cover for a variance

$$W_i = \frac{n - 1}{n^2} V_i + \frac{2p(1/2a_i - R_i) - 1}{2p^2}$$

The company will demand cover for a variance

$$W_i' = \frac{n - 1}{n^2} V_i$$

regardless of what the price is, provided that this variance can be divided equally between the $n - 1$ other companies.

It is obvious that in this case we cannot determine p by simply requiring that total supply shall be equal to total demand, i.e., from the "market equation"

$$\sum_{i=1}^{n} W_i = \sum_{i=1}^{n} W_i'$$

Instead we have the conditions that supply from company i must equal the sum of $1/(n-1)$ of the demand from the other $n-1$ companies, i.e.,

$$W_i = \frac{1}{n-1} \sum_{j \neq 1} W' = \frac{1}{n^2} \sum_{j \neq i} V_j$$

Hence p must satisfy the n equations

$$\frac{1}{n^2} \sum_{j=1}^{n} V_j - \frac{1}{n} V_i = \frac{2p(1/2a_i - R_i) - 1}{2p^2} \qquad i = 1, 2, \ldots, n$$

This is clearly impossible, except for special values of a_i, R_i, and V_i.

4.8. It is obvious from the preceding paragraph that unrestricted utility maximization with a given price has little meaning in our model. The procedure may, however, have some meaning if we introduce restrictions so that it necessarily leads to a Pareto optimal arrangement.

These restrictions can be formulated as follows. For all i and j, $j \neq i$, company i can satisfy its demand for reinsurance cover only by placing a part $q_j^2 V_i$ of its variance with company j.

Company i will then be willing to supply reinsurance cover for a variance

$$W_i = V_i \sum_{j \neq i}^{n} q_j^2 + \frac{2p(1/2a_i - R_i) - 1}{2p^2}$$

The n market equations from para. 4.7 will then take the form

$$q_i^2 \sum_{j=1}^{n} V_j - V_i \sum_{j=1}^{n} q_j^2 = \frac{2p(1/2a_i - R_i) - 1}{2p^2} \qquad i = 1, 2, \ldots, n$$

It is easy to see that these n equations, which are linear in q_i^2, have a determinant of rank $n-1$. Hence the equations have a solution only if the sum of the right hand sides is zero. This condition is satisfied:

(i) If the right-hand sides all vanish, i.e., if p tends to infinity. The corresponding values of q_i are then

$$q_i = \frac{V_i^{1/2}}{\displaystyle\sum_{j=1}^{n} V_j^{1/2}}$$

(ii) If

$$p = \frac{n}{2\displaystyle\sum_{j=1}^{n} (1/2a_j - R_j)}$$

This appears to be all that we can get, even from a diluted principle of utility maximization.

The result is not very satisfactory. The general assumptions which lead to these "equilibrium prices" are rather artificial, and it is easy to construct numerical examples where the result becomes meaningless.

From the formulas in para. 4.2 we see that the utility of company i will decrease with increasing q_i. The price we have found may lead to values of q_i which will give some companies a lower utility than they have in the initial situation. These companies will obviously refuse to trade at such a price.

The conditions which q_i must satisfy in order to give a meaningful solution are discussed in the paper [6] already referred to, and we shall not pursue the point further in the present paper.

5. The Models of Allais and Arrow

5.1. Both Allais [1] and Arrow [3] have proved that in models very similar to ours, there exists a price such that utility maximization, when this price is considered as given, will lead to a Pareto optimal situation. To explain the apparent contradiction with our result, we shall examine their models in some detail.

5.2. Allais [1] studied a model which essentially is a market for lottery tickets. The prize of the tickets is a normally distributed random variable with mean equal to one unit of money, and a given standard deviation. Allais proves that in this model there exists a market price for lottery tickets which will lead to a uniquely determined, optimal distribution of the risks.

The crucial assumption which Allais makes in order to reach this result is that lottery tickets can be bought and sold only in integral numbers, i.e., one can buy one ticket, but not a 50% interest in two tickets. It is obvious that when this assumption is given up, the Pareto optimum is no longer unique. The situation will be similar to the one we found in para. 2.7, which is an example of the familiar problem that an n-person game has an indeterminate solution. To make it determined, one will have to make some assumptions about how the participants form coalitions to buy packages of lottery tickets.

5.3.   In the model of Allais there is only one kind of lottery ticket. If tickets are indivisible as Allais assumes, it is almost trivial that there must exist a price which leads to a Pareto optimal situation. The problem will change completely, however, if the model is generalized by the introduction of several kinds of tickets, i.e., tickets where the prize is drawn from different probability distributions. The problem can be handled as we did in the preceding sections if one accepts the Bernoulli hypothesis. Allais [2] has emphatically rejected this hypothesis, however, and thus barred the most obvious, and probably the only way to generalize his model.

5.4.   The model studied by Arrow [3] is far more general. He considers n different commodities, and he assumes that each participant in the market may have his own subjective probabilities. In this paper we shall disregard both these refinements. The generalization to n commodities appears inessential when our main objective is to study the interplay of different attitudes toward risk and uncertainty. The subjective probabilities play a key part in Arrow's model, but it seems unnecessary to introduce them in a study of a reinsurance market. When a reinsurance treaty is concluded, both parties will survey all information relevant to the risks concerned. To hide information from the other party is plain fraud. Whether two rational persons on the basis of the same information can arrive at different evaluations of the probability of a specific event, is a question of semantics. That they may act differently on the same information is well known, but this can usually be explained assuming that the two persons attach different utilities to the event. In some situations, for instance in stock markets, it may be useful to resort *both* to subjective probabilities and different utility functions to explain observed behavior. This seems, however, to be an unnecessary complication in a first study of reinsurance markets.

5.5.   When simplified as indicated in the preceding paragraph, Arrow's model can be described as follows:

(i)   Company i has a utility of money $u_i(x)$, $i = 1, 2, \ldots, I$.

(ii) As a result of its direct underwriting the company is committed to pay an amount x_{is} if "state of the world" s occurs, $s = 1, 2, \ldots, S$.

(iii) The company has funds amounting to S_i available for meeting the commitments.

(iv) The probability that state of the world s shall occur is p_s ($\Sigma_{s=1}^{S} p_s = 1$). The utility of company i in the initial situation is then

$$U_i(0) = \sum_{s=1}^{S} p_s u_i(S_i - x_{is})$$

where x_{is} may be zero for some s.

5.6. It is then assumed that there exists a price vector $g_1, \ldots, g_s, \ldots, gS$, so that the company can pay an amount $g_s y_{is}$, and then be assured of receiving the amount y_{is} if state of the world s occurs. This means that should this state occur, the company will have to make a net payment of $x_{is} - y_{is}$. If the company makes a series of such contracts, its utility will change to

$$U_1(y) = \sum_{s=1}^{S} p_s u_i \left(\left\{ S_i - \sum_{s=1}^{S} g_s y_{is} \right\} - (x_{is} - y_{is}) \right)$$

where y_{is} may be positive or negative.

Differentiating with respect to y_{it}, we find

$$\frac{\partial U_i(y)}{\partial y_{it}} = -g_t \sum_{s=1}^{S} p_s u_i' \left(\left\{ S_i - \sum_{s=1}^{S} g_s y_{is} \right\} - x_{is} + y_{is} \right)$$

$$+ p_t u_i' \left(\left\{ S_i - \sum_{s=1}^{S} g_s y_{is} \right\} - x_{it} + y_{it} \right)$$

Since we have placed no restrictions on y_{it}, the first-order conditions for a maximum will be

$$g_t \sum_{s=1}^{S} p_s u_i' \left(S_i - \sum_{s=1}^{S} g_s y_{is} - x_{is} + y_{is} \right) = p_t u_i' \left(S_i - \sum_{s=1}^{S} g_s y_{is} - x_{it} + y_{it} \right)$$

$$t = 1, 2, \ldots, S$$

5.7. We now assume that the utility function is of the same simple form as in Section 4, i.e., that

$$u_i(x) = -a_i x^2 + x \qquad i = 1, 2, \ldots, I$$

The first-order conditions for a maximum will then become

$$2a_i g_t \sum_{s=1}^{S} p_s \left(S_i - \sum_{s=1}^{S} g_s y_{is} - x_{is} + y_{is} \right) - g_t =$$

$$2a_i p_t \left(S_i - \sum_{s=1}^{S} g_s y_{is} - x_{it} + y_{it} \right) - p_t$$

By some rearrangement this system of equations can be written

$$(g_t - p_t)\left(\frac{1}{2a_i} - S_i \right) + g_t \sum_{s=1}^{S} p_s x_{is} - p_t x_{it} =$$

$$g_t \sum_{s=1}^{S} p_s y_{is} - p_t y_{it} - (g_t - p_t) \sum_{s=1}^{S} g_s y_{is}$$

$$t = 1, 2, \ldots, S \qquad \text{and} \qquad i = 1, 2, \ldots, I$$

y_{is} is the amount (positive or negative) which company i will receive if state of the world s occurs. Since this amount necessarily must be paid out by the other companies, we must have

$$\sum_{i=1}^{I} y_{is} = 0 \qquad \text{for all } s$$

Hence if we sum the equations over all i, the right-hand side will disappear, so that we get the system

$$(g_t - p_t) \sum_{i=1}^{I} \left(\frac{1}{2a_i} - S_i \right) + g_t \sum_{s=1}^{S} p_s \sum_{i=1}^{I} x_{is} - p_t \sum_{i=1}^{I} x_{it} = 0 \qquad t = 1, 2, \ldots, S$$

From this we obtain

$$g_t = p_t \frac{X_t + A}{X + A}$$

where

$$A = \sum_{i=1}^{I} A_i = \sum_{i=1}^{I} \left(\frac{1}{2a_i} - s_i \right)$$

$$X_s = \sum_{i=1}^{I} x_{is} \quad \text{and} \quad X = \sum_{s=1}^{S} p_s X_s$$

The complete solution of the system is given by

$$x_{it} - y_{it} = q_i X_t$$

and

$$q_i = \frac{A_i + \displaystyle\sum_{s=1}^{S} g_s x_{is}}{A + \displaystyle\sum_{s=1}^{S} g_s X_s}$$

where

$$\sum_{i=1}^{I} q_i = 1$$

5.8.   This solution implies that company i ($i = 1, 2, \ldots, I$) shall pay a fixed quota q_i of the total claim payment, regardless of which state of the world may occur. Hence the solution belongs to the set of Pareto optimal arrangements that we found in para. 4.2.
Since

$$\sum_{s=1}^{S} g_s x_{is} = \sum_{s=1}^{S} p_s \frac{X_s + A}{X + A} x_{is} = \frac{1}{X + A} \sum_{s=1}^{S} p_s (A x_{is} + X_s x_{is})$$

$$= \frac{1}{X+A} \left\{ Am_i + Xm_i + \sum_{s=1}^{S} p_s(X_s - X)(x_{is} - m_i) \right\}$$

$$= m_i + \frac{\displaystyle\sum_{s=1}^{S} p_s(X_s - X)(x_{is} - m_i)}{X+A} = m_i + \frac{C_i}{X+A}$$

where $m_i = \Sigma_{s=1}^{S} p_s x_{is}$, and since $X = \Sigma_{i=1}^{I} m_i$, we have

$$q_i = \frac{A_i + m_i + \dfrac{C_i}{X+A}}{\displaystyle\sum_{j=1}^{I}(A_j + m_j) + \dfrac{\text{var } X_s}{X+A}}$$

It is interesting to compare this with the expression which we found in para. 4.4 for the case $p = 0$.

5.9.   The difference between Arrow's model and ours obviously lies in the price concept. In Arrow's model there is a price associated with every state of the world. The price will be the same for all states which lead to the same amount of total claim payment.

Our model is essentially a drastic simplification. Instead of the really infinite number of prices considered by Arrow, we have introduced one single price, a specific *price of risk*. We found that this price would have to be a vector with an infinite number of elements. If the utility function has the simple form studied in Section 4, the number of elements is reduced to two. However, in this case a competitive equilibrium cannot in general be a Pareto optimal distribution of risks.

5.10.   The price in Arrow's model increases with the probability of a particular state of the world, and with the total amount to be paid if this state occurs. In insurance this means that a reinsurer who is asked to cover a modest amount if a certain person dies, will quote a price increasing with the total amount which is payable on the death of this person.

Such considerations are not unknown in insurance practice. It is well known that it can be difficult, i.e., expensive to arrange satisfactory reinsurance of particularly large risks. Practice seems here to be ahead of insurance theory, however, which still is firmly based on the *principle of equivalence,* i.e., that "net premiums" should be equal to the expected value of claim payments.

To apply Arrow's theory to stock market speculation we just have to reverse the signs of the formulas in this section.

We then find that the price of a certain share will depend not only on its "intrinsic value," but also on the number of such shares in the market. This may seem reasonable, although it implies that one pays more for a chance of getting rich alone, than for an identical chance of getting equally rich together with a lot of other speculators. The implication is that even in a model using essentially classical assumptions, there is a positive price attached to "getting ahead of the Joneses," and this may be a little unexpected.

6. The Problem seen as an *n*-Person Game

6.1. We noted in para. 2.6 that a Pareto optimal set of reinsurance treaties was equivalent to a pool arrangement. Once the pool was established, the companies had to agree on some rule as to how each company should contribute to the payment of claims against the pool. In the special case which we considered in Section 4, this rule was that each company should pay a fixed proportion of these claims, regardless of its size. The quotas which each company should pay remained to be fixed, however.

When the problem is presented in this way, it seems natural to consider it as a problem of bargaining and negotiation which logically should be analyzed in the terms of the theory of games. A priori it appears unlikely that there should exist some price mechanism which automatically will lead the companies to such a rather special arrangement as a Pareto optimal set of treaties.

6.2. In general an *n*-person game has an indeterminate solution. To get a determinate solution, we must make *additional assumptions* about how the companies negotiate their way to an agreement.

The point is brought out clearly by the special case studied in Section 4. The usual assumptions of game theory leave the quotas $q_1, \ldots, q_n$ undetermined, except for the restriction $\Sigma q_i = 1$. The solution has, so to speak, $n - 1$ "degrees of freedom." During the negotiations each company will try to get the smallest possible quota for itself.

We then lay down the additional rule that the same price must be applied to all the reciprocal treaties which constitute a Pareto optimal set. This amounts really to a ban on "price discrimination" or a partial ban on coalitions. The rule leaves only the price *p* to be determined by negotiation, so that the number of degrees of freedom is reduced to one.

6.3. From the expressions in para. 4.4 we can conjecture that a given price *p* will divide the companies in two groups or coalitions. One group will benefit from a higher price, the other from a lower one. The higher the price, the more companies will be in the latter group. The "equilibrium price" must then be determined so that it divides the companies in two groups, which in some unspecified manner are equal in strength. There are obviously a number of possible ways in which the concept "strength" can be defined, and hence a number of possible determinate solutions. We shall, however, not explore these possibilities in the present paper.

6.4.   In real life reinsurance treaties are concluded after lengthy negotiations, often with brokers acting as intermediaries. The concept of prevailing market prices plays a part in the background of these negotiations, but the whole situation is more similar to an n-person game than to a classical market with utility maximization when the price is considered as given.

Little is known about the laws and customs ruling such negotiations in the reinsurance market. It seems, however, that further studies of this subject should be a promising, if not the most promising, way of gaining deeper knowledge of attitudes toward risk and the decisions which rational people make under uncertainty.

References

1. Allais, Maurice. "L'Extension des Théories de l'Équilibre Économique Général et du Rendement Social au Cas du Risque," *Econometrica*, 1953, pp. 269–290.
2. ——. "Le Comportement de l'Homme Rationnel devant le Risque: Critique des Postulates et Axiomes de l'École Américaine," *Econometrica*, 1953, pp. 503–546.
3. Arrow, Kenneth J. "Le Rôle de Valeurs boursières pour la Répartition la meilleure des Risques," *Colloques Internationaux du Centre National de la Recherche Scientifique*, XL, Paris, 1953, pp. 41–48.
4. Arrow, Kenneth J. and Gerard Debreu. "Existence of an Equilibrium for a Competitive Economy," *Econometrica*, 1954, pp. 265–290.
5. Borch, Karl. "An Attempt to Determine the Optimum Amount of Stop Loss Reinsurance," *Transactions of the XVI International Congress of Actuaries*, vol. II, pp. 597–610.
6. ——. "The Safety Loading of Reinsurance Premiums," *Skandinavisk Aktuarietidskrift*, 1960, pp. 163–184.
7. Debreu, Gerard. *Theory of Value* (New York: John Wiley & Sons, 1959).
8. Lukacs, E. "An Essential Property of the Fourier Transforms of Distribution Functions," *Proceedings of the American Mathematical Society*, 1952, pp. 508–510.
9. Neumann, J. von, and O. Morgenstern. *Theory of Games and Economic Behavior* (Princeton: Princeton Univ. Press, 1944).
10. Wald, Abraham. "Über einige Gleichungssysteme der mathematischen Ökonomie," *Zeitschrift für Nationalökonomie*, 1936, pp. 637–670. English translation, *Econometrica*, 1951, pp. 368–403.

11

A Contribution to the Theory of Reinsurance Markets

In this paper we shall generalize some results recently published in this journal [1]. We shall also seek to illustrate the problem by a fairly detailed discussion of a simple numerical example.

1. Summary of Previous Results

1.1. We shall consider n insurance companies and we assume that company i $(i = 1, 2, \ldots, n)$ is the risk situation $(S_i, F_i(x_i))$.

Here $F_i(x_i)$ is the probability that the amount of claims under the insurance contracts which the company holds, shall not exceed x_i, and S_i is the funds which the company can draw upon to pay claims. We shall assume that the duration of the contracts is so short that we can ignore interest earned on the funds, and we shall further assume that all premiums have been paid in advance, i.e., that they are included in S_i.

The purpose of the company's reinsurance arrangement is to improve the risk situation which the company has reached as a result of its direct underwriting. The word "improve" implies that the company must have some criterion which enables it to decide whether one risk situation is better than another. One can obtain a criterion of this kind by attaching a "utility" index $U(S, F(x))$ to the risk situation $(S, F(x))$, so that this index increases when the risk situation improves.

1.2. If one is not to run into inconsistencies, the index must satisfy the condition

$$U(S, F(x)) = \int_0^\infty u(S - x)\, dF(x)$$

Here

$$u(S - a) = U(S, \epsilon(x - a))$$

where $\epsilon(x)$ is the degenerate probability distribution. In other words $u(S - a)$ is the utility of a risk situation with funds S, and probability 1 that claims shall amount to a. It is convenient to refer to the function $u(S - a)$ as the "utility of

165

money," since it represents the utility attached to the situation where the amount of money $S - a$ is held in hand. This function determines the company's attitude to risk, and it may of course differ from one company to another.

The condition above, often referred to as the *Bernoulli hypothesis,* appears essential to any theory where preferences depend only on preferences for events which are certain, and on the probability that such events may occur. This has been demonstrated by von Neumann and Morgenstern [7], and its implications for insurance have been discussed in some detail in a previous paper [2]. The only alternative to the Bernoulli hypothesis seems to be that preference orderings over risk situations have nothing to do with probabilities, a line developed with considerable vigor by Shackle [8].

1.3.   The most general collective reinsurance arrangement our n companies can make is to agree that company i shall pay an amount $y_i(x_1, x_2, \ldots, x_n)$ if claims in the portfolios of the n companies amount to $x_1, \ldots, x_n$ respectively.

We call an arrangement "collective" if it depends only on the total amount of claims $x_1, \ldots, x_n$, and not on how these claims are made up of claims under particular insurance contracts.

In the initial situation the utility of company i is

$$U_i(x_i) = \int_0^\infty u_i(S_i - x_i)\, dF_i(x_i)$$

where $u_i(x)$ is the utility of money to company i.

The reinsurance arrangement will give the company the utility

$$U_i(y) = \int_R u_i(S_i - y_i(x))\, dF(x)$$

where $F(x)$ is the joint probability distribution of $x_1, \ldots x_n$, and the integral is taken over positive orthant R.

1.4.   If our companies act rationally, they will reach a reinsurance arrangement which is *Pareto optimal,* i.e., an arrangement so that there exists no other arrangement which will give all companies a higher utility. In the paper [1] already referred to it has been proved that an arrangement is Pareto optimal if, and only if, the corresponding functions $y_1, \ldots, y_n$ satisfy the conditions

$$k_i\, u_i'(S_i - y_i) = k_j\, u_j'(S_j - y_j)$$

where $k_1, \ldots k_n$ are arbitrary positive constants. The result can also be derived from a general theorem by Kuhn and Tucker [5].

If $u_i'(x_i), i = 1, \ldots, n$, are monotonic, decreasing functions it follows that y_i is a nondecreasing function $y_i(x)$ of one single variable $x = x_1 + \ldots + x_n$.

1.5. A reinsurance agreement implies that an insurance company receives an amount $P(F(x))$ when it accepts to pay a claim x which has a probability distribution $F(x)$. The transformation $P(F(x))$ will define the price of this reinsurance cover.

Let now x_1 and x_2 be stochastically independent variates with probability distributions $F_1(x_1)$ and $F_2(x_2)$, and let $F(x)$ be the distribution of $x = x_1 + x_2$. If the transformation $P(F(x))$ is to define a price concept in any acceptable sense, it must satisfy the conditions

$$P(F(x)) = P(F_1(x_1)) + P(F_2(x_2))$$

It follows from a theorem by Lukacs [6] that any transformation of a probability distribution which satisfies these conditions can be written in the form

$$P(F(x)) = \sum_{n=1}^{\infty} p_n \kappa_n$$

where $p_1, \ldots, p_n \ldots$ are constants, and $\kappa_1, \ldots, \kappa_n \ldots$ are the cumulants of $F(x)$. As a continuity condition we require that $p_1 = 1$, i.e., that

$$P(\epsilon(x - a)) = a$$

In the following we shall investigate the conditions under which a price of this kind can exist in a reinsurance market.

2. The Reinsurance Market

2.1. If our n companies make a reinsurance arrangement which is not Pareto optimal, there will exist potential intercompany transactions which will increase the utility of all participating companies. It seems natural to assume that a clever manager or a shrewd broker will discover such possibilities and negotiate the relevant transactions through. Hence we must assume that the companies ultimately will end up with an arrangement which is Pareto optimal, i.e., with an arrangement represented by a set of functions $y_1(x), \ldots, y_n(x)$ which satisfy the condition of para. 1.4.

2.2. There is, however, an infinity of reinsurance arrangements which satisfy this condition, since the n parameters $k_1, \ldots, k_n$ were left undetermined. The only restriction we can place upon the parameters is that an acceptable Pareto optimal arrangement must not give any company a lower utility than it has in the initial situation. It is easy to see that this will place some restrictions on the values of $k_1, \ldots, k_n$ which lead to acceptable arrangements.

2.3. We shall now investigate if a price mechanism can bring about an acceptable Pareto optimal arrangement. As a first step we assume that the same price has to be used to settle *all* intercompany transactions. This essentially amounts to a ban on *price discrimination*.

Let $\kappa_j^{(i)}$ be the jth cumulant of the distribution $F_i(x_i)$. Let further $h_j^{(i)}$ be the jth cumulant of the risk distribution which company i has in a Pareto optimal situation, i.e., the coefficient of $(it)^{(j)}$ in the expansion

$$\log \int_0^\infty e^{ity(x)}\, dF(x) = \sum_{j=1}^\infty \frac{(it)^j}{j!} h_j^{(i)}$$

If all transactions are settled at the price $\{p_1, \ldots, p_j, \ldots\}$, we must have

$$\sum_{j=1}^\infty p_j \kappa_j^{(i)} - \sum_{j=1}^\infty p_j h_j^{(i)} = y_i(0)$$

for all $i = 1, 2, \ldots, n$

Here the term on the right-hand side, $y_i(0)$ is the amount company i has to pay if there are no claims, i.e., the company's net outlay of reinsurance premiums. The first term on the left-hand side can be interpreted as the amount the company has to pay in order to be relieved of all responsibility for claims against its original portfolio. The second term respresents the amount which the company receives by accepting the new portfolio.

2.4. Since $p_1 = 1$, the equations in the preceding paragraph can be written

$$\sum_{j=2}^\infty p_j \left\{ \kappa_j^{(i)} - h_j^{(i)} \right\} = y_i(0) - \kappa_1^{(i)} + h_1^{(i)} \qquad i = 1, 2, \ldots, n$$

These n equations are linear in p_j. Hence in the price vector $p = \{ p_2, \ldots, p_j, \ldots \}$ we can choose all elements except n arbitrarily, and determine these from the equations. We can for instance choose $p_j = 0$ for $j > n + 1$, and determine $p_2, \ldots, p_{n+1}$ from the equations. This means that to any Pareto optimal arrangement there will in general correspond an infinity of acceptable price vectors.

It appears, however, that an acceptable price vector in general must have at least n nonzero elements. In the paper already referred to [2] it was shown that if the utility of money $u(x)$ could be represented by a polynomial of degree m, the utility attached to any risk situation would be completely determined by the m first cumulants of the risk distribution. This obviously implies that $p_j = 0$ for $j > m$, since otherwise the companies would pay nonzero amounts for changes in the risk situation which do not change the utility.

This means that if $m < n + 1$, it will not be possible to reach an arbitrary Pareto optimal arrangement if the same price must be applied to all inter-company transactions. Hence the ban on price discrimination introduced in para. 2.3 will reduce the set of acceptable Pareto optimal arrangements. For $m > n + 1$, there will in general exist one or more prices consistent with any Pareto optimal arrangement.

2.5.   The findings in the preceding paragraph are obviously related to familiar results in the classical theory of commodity markets. In such markets there will in general be a set of Pareto optimal situations, of which only a subset is consistent with the conditions that the same price must be applied to all transactions. Under very general conditions one can prove that there will exist only one Pareto optimal situation, and hence only one price, for which supply is equal to demand.

This means that if this *equilibrium price* is announced in the market, the total amount of the commodity offered for sale will equal the amount demanded. The behavioral assumption behind this classical model is about as follows. Each participant in the market takes the equilibrium price as given an unchangeable. He then buys or sells at this price until his utility is maximized.

This model has been the corner stone of classical economic theory, at least since the days of Walras. The only difficulty about the model is to explain how traders arrive at considering the equilibrium price as given. However, in many situations one can find good reasons for assuming that traders behave in this manner.

2.6.   In order to adapt the reasoning of classical commodity trade to the reinsurance market, we shall formulate our problem as follows.

We assume that the utility of company i can be expressed as a function of the funds S_i and the cumulants of the risk distribution $\kappa_1^{(i)}, \ldots, \kappa_j^{(i)}, \ldots$, i.e.,

$$U_i = U_i(S_i - \kappa_1^{(i)}, \kappa_2^{(i)}, \ldots, \kappa_j^{(i)}, \ldots)$$

Assume then that the company takes the market price vector $\{p\}$ as given, and that the company's transactions at the market price give it a risk distribution with cumulants $h_1^{(i)}, \ldots, h_j^{(i)}, \ldots$. The company's utility will then be

$$U_i\left(S_i + \sum_{j=1}^{\infty} p_j \left\{h_j^{(i)} - \kappa_j^{(i)}\right\}, h_2^{(i)}, h_3^{(i)}, \ldots\right)$$

If the company acts rationally, it will determine $h_1^{(i)}, \ldots, h_j^{(i)}, \ldots$ so that U_i is maximized. This is the problem we must solve. However, if the solution shall also be Pareto optimal, the following two conditions must be satisfied:

(i) $h_1^{(i)}, \ldots, h_j^{(i)}, \ldots$ are the coefficients of the expansion

$$\log \int_0^\infty e^{ity \, i(x)} \, dF(x) = \sum_{j=1}^\infty \frac{(it)^j}{j!} h_j^{(i)}$$

where $F(x)$ is the probability distribution of $x = x_1 + \ldots + x_n$.

(ii) $y_1(x), \ldots, y_n(x)$ satisfy the conditions

$$k_i u_i'(S_i - y_i(x)) = k_j u_j'(S_j - y_j(x))$$

for some positive values of $k_1, \ldots, k_n$.

2.7. The mathematical problem outlined in the preceding paragraph appears to be a formidable one, and we shall not try to solve it in full generality.

In the following we shall confine our study to some special cases in which the Pareto optimal arrangements are of a particular simple form. We shall assume that

$$y_i(x) = q_i x + y_i(0)$$

where q_i is a constant. This means that company i will pay a fixed quota q_i of the total amount of claims x, regardless of the size of this amount.

In the paper [1] already referred to, it has been proved that

$$\frac{dy_i(x)}{dx} = \frac{\dfrac{k_i}{u_i''(S_i - y_i(x))}}{\displaystyle\sum_{j=1}^n \dfrac{k_j}{u_j''(S_j - y_j(x))}}$$

Under our assumption the right-hand side must be independent of x for all i.

It is easy to see that this will be the case if $u_i'(x)$ and $u_j'(x)$ differ only by a linear transformation, i.e., if for any i and j there are constants A, B, and C such that

$$u_i(x) = A u_j(x) + Bx + C$$

This condition is obviously satisfied if all $u_i(x)$ are polynomials of second degree, a case which has previously been studied in some detail [1 and 3].

2.8.   The assumption in the preceding paragraph implies that we have

$$h_j^{(i)} = q_i^j \sum_{i=1}^{n} \kappa_j^{(i)} = q_i^j \kappa_j$$

where q_i is the quota of company i. We must obviously have

$$\sum_{i=1}^{n} q_i = 1$$

The condition in para. 2.3 then becomes

Form 1:

$$\sum_{j=1}^{\infty} p_j \left\{ \kappa_j^{(i)} - q_i^j \kappa_j \right\} = y_i(0)$$

Here we can, as already mentioned, interpret the left-hand side as the difference between the amount company i has to pay if it cedes the total of its portfolio, and the amount the company receives by accepting a quota q_i of the market.

However, when the Pareto optimal arrangement is a set of quota share treaties, we can also apply another argument.

We can assume that company i retains a quota q_i of its portfolio and cedes quotas q_t $(t \neq i)$ to the $n - 1$ other companies. For this the company has to pay $\sum_{j=1}^{\infty} \{ p_j \kappa_j^{(i)} \sum_{t \neq i} q_t^j \}$. Similarly we assume that the company accepts a quota q_i of the portfolios of the other companies, and receives the amount $\sum_{j=1}^{\infty} \{ p_j \sum_{t \neq i} \kappa_j^{(t)} q_j^t \}$. This leads to the equation

$$\sum_{j=1}^{\infty} p_j \left\{ \kappa_j^{(i)} \sum_{t \neq i} q_t^j - \sum_{t \neq i} \kappa_j^{(t)} p_i^j \right\} = y_i(0)$$

or

Form 2:

$$\sum_{j=1}^{\infty} p_j \left\{ \kappa_j^{(i)} \sum_{t=1}^{n} q_t^j - q_i^j \kappa_j \right\} = y_i(0)$$

which obviously is different from Form 1 above.

2.9. The two forms are identical if

$$\sum_{j=2}^{\infty} p_j \kappa_j^{(i)} \left(1 - \sum_{t=1}^{n} q_t^j \right) = 0 \quad \text{for} \quad i = 1, \ldots, n$$

If this condition is fulfilled, the "market value" of the company's portfolio will not change if all transactions in the market are settled at the same price. In commodity markets this condition holds almost trivially. We shall see in the following that we run into serious difficulties if we require that the condition shall be satisfied in a reinsurance market.

However, if we do not require that the condition shall be fulfilled, we arrive at the embarrassing situation of having two equally acceptable solutions.

3. A Numerical Example

3.1. To illustrate the results in Section 2, we shall analyze a particularly simple case in some detail. We assume that the utility of money is given by

$$u_i(x) = (x - a_i)^3 + b_i \quad \text{for all} \quad i$$

This choice of utility function implies that the marginal utility of money is increasing for large positive amounts. In most economic applications this is unreasonable. However, the point does not appear to be particularly important in our case, since it is the behavior of the utility function for large negative values which is relevant to insurance. We shall, however, assume that a_i is so great that marginal utility is decreasing for all positive amounts in the range we consider. If company i is in the risk situation $(S_i, F_i(x))$ its utility will be

$$U_i(0) = \int_0^{\infty} (S_i - a_i - x)^3 \, dF(x) + b_i$$

$$= (S_i - a_i - \kappa_1^{(i)})^3 + 3(S_i - a_i - \kappa_1^{(i)}) \kappa_2^{(i)} - \kappa_3^{(i)} + b_i$$

expressed by the cumulants of $F_i(x)$. Here we assume that $a_i > S_i$, so that marginal utility of money is decreasing in the range considered.

3.2. The Pareto optimal arrangements are in this case given by the conditions

$$k_i(S_i - a_i - y_i(x))^2 = k_j(S_j - a_j - y_j(x))^2$$

or $$k_j^{-1/2}(S_i - a_i - y_i(x)) = k_i^{-1/2}(S_j - a_j - y_j(x))$$

Summing these equations over all j, we obtain

$$y_i(x) = \frac{k_i^{-1/2} x}{\displaystyle\sum_{j=1}^{n} k_j^{-1/2}} + S_i - a_i - \frac{k_i^{-1/2}}{\displaystyle\sum_{j=1}^{n} k_j^{-1/2}} \sum_{j=1}^{n} (S_j - a_j)$$

or $$y_i(x) = q_i x + S_i - a_i - q_i \sum_{j=1}^{n} (S_j - a_j)$$

To simplify these expressions, we introduce the symbols

$$R_i = S_i - \kappa_1^{(i)} = \text{the free reserves of company } i$$

$$A_i = a_i - R_i$$

and $$\sum_{j=1}^{n} A_j = A$$

Hence we have

$$U_i(0) = b_i - A_i^3 - 3A_i\kappa_2^{(i)} - \kappa_3^{(i)}$$
and $y_i(x) = q_i x + q_i A - A_i$

It is easy to see that this Pareto optimal arrangement will give company i the utility

$$U_i(q_i) = b_i - q_i^3 \left\{ A^3 + 3A\kappa_2 + \kappa_3 \right\}$$

The arrangement is acceptable only if q_i is so small that

$$U_i(q_i) \geqslant U_i(0)$$

3.3. We shall now assume that $n = 3$, and choose convenient numerical values for the parameters. These values are given in Table 11-1.

We have chosen b_i so that the utility in the initial situation, i.e., $U_i(0)$, is zero for all companies. This has obviously no significance. It only means that we have chosen the origin in a convenient way on the scale which measures utility.

3.4. Table 11-2 gives $U_i(q_i)$ for some selected values of q_i. Each cell in the table gives the utility of companies 1, 2, and 3 in descending order.

Since an arrangement which gives any company a negative utility is unacceptable, only the cells printed in italic type need to be considered.

The table illustrates how the interests of the three companies are opposed in this bargaining situation. Company 1 will try to obtain agreement on a cell as far to the left as possible, company 2 will try to get as high up in the table as possible, whilst company 3 will hold out for a cell in the lower right-hand corner of the table.

3.5. So far each cell given in italics in Table 11-2 is acceptable. In order to obtain a more determinate solution, we lay down the restriction that all intercompany transactions must be settled at the same price, i.e., that there must be no price discrimination. We found, however, in para. 2.8 that this restriction is ambiguous.

Form 1 of para. 2.8 in this example becomes

$$(1 - 3q_1{}^2) p_2 + (1 - 4q_1{}^3) p_3 = 8q_1 - 2$$

$$(1 - 3q_2{}^2) p_2 + (1 - 4q_2{}^3) p_3 = 8q_2 - 3$$

$$(1 - 3q_3{}^2) p_2 + (2 - 4q_3{}^3) p_3 = 8q_3 - 3$$

Table 11-1
Values of the Parameters

i	1	2	3
a_i	3	5	4
b_i	15	37	38
R_i	1	2	1
$x_2{}^{(i)}$	1	1	1
$x_3{}^{(i)}$	1	1	2
$U_i(0)$	0	0	0
$U_i(q_i)$	$15 - 588\, q_1{}^3$	$37 - 588\, q_2{}^3$	$38 - 588\, q_3{}^3$

These 3 equations have solutions in p_2 and p_3 only if

$$
\begin{vmatrix}
2 - 8q_1 & 1 - 3q_1^2 & 1 - 4q_1^3 \\
3 - 8q_2 & 1 - 3q_2^2 & 1 - 4q_2^3 \\
3 - 8q_3 & 1 - 3q_3^2 & 2 - 4q_3^3
\end{vmatrix} = 0
$$

This condition together with $q_1 + q_2 + q_3 = 1$ gives us two equations for the determination of q_1, q_2, and q_3. This means that in general one quota, say q_1, can be chosen arbitrarily. The other two, q_2 and q_3, and hence also p_2 and p_3 will then be determined. Hence the ban on price discrimination means that all cells denoted by italics in Table 11-2 are no longer acceptable solutions to our problem. It is easy to see that the solutions which satisfy the new condition are given by a curve in the $q_1 q_2$ plane, or if one prefers by a curve through the cells in Table 11-2.

We also see that if p_2 and p_3 are given, it will not in general be possible to find quotas q_1, q_2, and q_3 which satisfy the two conditions. This means that if a price is imposed on the market, so that the companies have to settle all reinsurance transactions at this price, it will be impossible to reach a Pareto optimal arrangement.

Table 11-2
Utility of Three Companies in Pareto Optimal Situations

	q_1					
q_2	0.20	0.22	0.24	0.26	0.28	0.30
0.30	10.30	8.74	6.87	4.67	2.09	−0.12
	21.12	21.12	21.12	21.12	21.12	21.12
	−35.50	−27.03	−19.23	−12.08	−5.56	0.37
0.32	10.30	8.74	6.87	4.67	2.09	−0.12
	17.73	17.73	17.73	17.73	17.73	17.73
	−27.03	−19.23	−12.08	−5.56	0.37	5.74
0.34	10.30	8.74	6.87	4.67	2.09	−0.12
	13.89	13.89	13.89	13.89	13.89	13.89
	−19.23	−12.08	−5.56	0.37	5.74	10.57
0.36	10.30	8.74	6.87	4.67	2.09	−0.12
	9.57	9.57	9.57	9.57	9.57	9.57
	−12.08	−5.56	0.37	5.74	10.57	14.89
0.36	10.30	8.74	6.87	4.67	2.09	−0.12
	4.74	4.74	4.74	4.74	4.74	4.74
	−5.56	0.37	5.74	10.57	14.89	18.73
0.40	10.30	8.74	6.87	4.67	2.09	−0.12
	−0.63	−0.63	−0.63	−0.63	−0.63	−0.63
	0.37	5.74	10.57	14.89	18.73	22.12

3.6. We shall now consider Form 2 of para. 2.7. In our example the equations become

$$(-2q_1^2 + q_2^2 + q_3^2) p_2 + (-3q_1^3 + q_2^3 - q_3^3) p_3 = 8q_1 - 2$$

$$(q_1^2 - 2q_2^2 + q_3^2) p_2 + (q_1^3 - 3q_2^3 + q_3^3) p_3 = 8q_2 - 3$$

$$(q_1^2 + q_2^2 - 2q_3^2) p_2 + (2q_1^3 + 2q_2^3 - 2q_3^3) p_3 = 8q_3 - 3$$

It is easy to see that in this case the determinant will be zero for all values of q_1, q_2, and q_3, so that the equations will always have solutions in p_2 and p_3. This means that there corresponds one price vector (p_2, p_3) to each Pareto optimal arrangement, i.e., to each cell in Table 11-2.

3.7. From the formula in para. 2.9 we find that the two forms are identical if

$$q_1 = {}^2\!/_8 = 0.25 \qquad q_2 = q_3 = {}^3\!/_8 = 0.375$$

This corresponds to the price $p_2 = p_3 = 0$.
The utilities in this point are

$$U_1 = 5.81 \qquad U_2 = 6.13 \qquad U_3 = 7.13$$

We see from Table 11-2 that this is a reasonable solution, which all three companies may well settle for. However, $p_2 = p_3 = 0$ means that this arrangement is reached by settling all reinsurance transactions on a net premium basis. This is not entirely unreasonable. A company may well find it advantageous to accept reinsurance without any safety loading in the premium, if it at the same time obtains the right to cede a part of its own portfolio on the same conditions.

However, the *net premium principle* leads to a reasonable result in our example, because of the particular numerical values chosen for the parameters. In another paper [4] it has been shown that the principle can lead to solutions which are unacceptable because they violate the last condition of para. 3.2, i.e., give some company a lower utility than it has in the initial situation.

3.8. As a last illustration we shall consider the Pareto optimal arrangement corresponding to

$$q_1 = 0.26 \quad \text{and} \quad q_2 = q_3 = 0.37$$

The utilities in this case are

$$U_1 = 4.67 \qquad U_2 = 7.22 \qquad U_3 = 8.22$$

This also appears to be a reasonable arrangement, although rather unfair to company 1.

If we apply Form 1, we find that this arrangement is inconsistent with our ban on price discrimination. It appears in fact that there is discrimination against company 1.

If we apply Form 2, we find the price vector $p_2 = 0.58$ and $p_3 = 0$. Hence it appears that this arrangement implies that the companies have agreed to ignore the third moments of the claim distribution when calculating the safety loadings. This may be a practical rule, but it is rather unfavorable to company 1.

4. Conclusion

It is generally believed that there exists a market for reinsurance, and that the price of various kinds of reinsurance cover is determined by supply and demand in this market. From the example which we have discussed, it appears that this market is not ruled by the simple laws known from the classical theory of commodity markets, discussed in para. 2.5.

Reinsurance is obviously an economic activity, and it is rather disappointing that ordinary economic theory is unable to analyze this activity. It is, however, fairly clear that the solution to our problem must be sought in the general theory of n-person games. The theory of games [7] is a generalization of classical economic theory, and appears to hold considerable promise of being able to tackle the problems which we have discussed along more orthodox lines in the present paper.

References

1.   Borch, K. "The Safety Loading of Reinsurance Premiums," *Skandinavisk Aktuarietidskrift,* 1960, pp. 163–184.
2.   ——. "The Utility Concept Applied to the Theory of Insurance," *ASTIN Bulletin* 1 (1961): 245–255.
3.   ——. "Equilibrium in a Reinsurance Market," *Econometrica* 30 (1962): 424–444.
4.   ——. "Uncertainty and Market Equilibrium," *Metroeconomica* 13 (1961): 139–155.
5.   Kuhn, H. W. and Tucker, A. W. "Nonlinear programming," *Proceedings of the Second Berkeley Sumposium,* Berkeley, 1951, pp. 481–492.
6.   Lukacs, E. An essential property of the Fourier transforms of distribution functions. *Proceedings of the American Mathematical Society,* 1952, pp. 508–510.
7.   Neumann, J. von, and Morgenstern, O. *Theory of Games and Economic Behavior,* 2nd ed. (Princeton, 1947).
8.   Shackle, G. L. S., *Decision, Order and Time,* (Cambridge, 1961).

12

Recent Developments in Economic Theory and their Application to Insurance

1. Introduction

1.1. The very title of this paper may cause some surprise, since economic theory so far has found virtually no application in insurance. Insurance is obviously an economic activity, and it is indeed strange that general economic theory should seem inapplicable to insurance.

This apparent paradox may to some extent be explained by the historic development. Actuarial mathematics and the essential scientific basis of insurance were developed into a self-contained and fairly complete theory long before economists could claim the name of science for their subject. Actuaries and other insurance people may from time to time have turned to economic theory for help on their problems. In most cases they must have turned away in disappointment, being convinced that actuarial mathematics was well ahead of general economic theory.

1.2. The last point is brought out clearly in a paper on the safety loading of insurance premiums which Tauber [19] presented at the Sixth International Congress of Actuaries in Vienna in 1909. In the introduction to this paper Tauber seems to consider risk bearing as a service and appears to assume that it like all other goods and services must have a *price,* determined by supply and demand in the market. Tauber did not develop this idea, apparently because the economic theory of his time was utterly unable to analyze the problem. That his approach was sound, and the problem can be formulated and solved by modern economic theory, has been indicated in a previous paper [6].

1.3. During the last 30 years there has been an extremely rapid development in economic theory. The "General Theory" of Keynes [12] which appeared in 1936, is usually considered to have caused a revolution in economic theory. However, this "revolution" has not lead to any developments which seem to have an immediate application in insurance. Post- and pre-Keynesian economics are equally powerless when confronted with the problem which Tauber tried to formulate. It is therefore premature to conclude from the title of this paper that economic theory has caught up with actuarial science, and that the theory of insurance has now become a part of a general theory comprising all economic activities.

1.4.   The developments which we shall discuss in this paper all have their
origin in one single book: *Theory of Games and Economic Behavior,* published
in 1944 by von Neumann and Morgenstern [16]. When this book appeared, it
was predicted that it would lead to a revolution in economic thought, even more
fundamental than the one caused by Keynes' "General Theory." This revolution
has not materialized, and it seems that the basic ideas of game theory have been
rather slow in gaining acceptance among economists. The reason may be simply
that the theory is *too* revolutionary, and that the game theoretical approach
plays havoc with the traditional methods of economic analysis.

Even if game theory to some extent has been ignored, the subject has been
developed rapidly since 1944. A bibliography published in 1959 [20] lists more
than 1000 books and papers, most of which have appeared during the less than
15 years which had elapsed since the theory was first presented. However, most
of the papers listed are written by mathematicians, and the bibliography as a
whole confirms the impression that economists in general have not yet grasped
the real significance of game theory. It may be appropriate that actuaries should
take the lead in putting this extremely versatile theory to practical use, since the
theory probably is beyond the mathematical capacity of the rank and file
economists.

1.5.   Game theory has been a fashionable topic in mathematical circles for
more than a decade, and it is natural that we find a number of attempts to apply
the theory to insurance problems. However, most of these applications, e.g., [2],
[4], [17], and [18], are based on the equivalence between the simplest nontrivial
game and the linear programming model, and they deal with insurance problems
which are fairly trivial. In this paper we shall try to show that there are other
parts of game theory which can be applied to the really important problems of
insurance.

2.   The Theory of Games

2.1.   In this section we shall, as briefly as possible, introduce the essential
concepts of game theory.

An n-person game in the so-called *normal* form consists of the following
three elements.

(i)   A set of n players, $1, 2, \ldots, n$.
(ii) n sets of *strategies* $X_1, \ldots, X_n$.
(iii) n real-valued *payoff* functions $M_1, \ldots, M_n$ defined over the members of
       the sets $X_1, \ldots, X_n$.

The game is played as follows: Each player chooses a strategy from the set available to him, i.e., player i chooses a strategy x_i, which is a member of X_i. If the strategies chosen by the n players are $x_1, x_2, \ldots, x_n$, player i will receive the "payoff" $M_i(x_1, \ldots, x_n)$. Hence the payoff function $M_i(x_1, \ldots, x_n)$ is interpreted as the *gain* to player i when the strategies $x_1, \ldots, x_n$ are used. This gain can be the monetary value of the profit or loss which the player makes by participating in the game. More generally one can interpret M_i as the *utility* which player i attaches to this gain.

2.2. If player i is *rational*, he will try to choose his strategy x_i, so that his payoff M_i becomes as great as possible. However, M_i depends not only on x_i which player i can choose freely. The payoff M_i will depend also on the strategies x_j, $j \neq i$, chosen by the $n - 1$ other players. In general player i will have no influence on the choices made by the other players. Hence his problem is not just to maximize a given function over the set X_i. To determine the best strategy, he must either anticipate the choices of the other players, or he must seek an agreement with them as to what strategies should be chosen.

2.3. It is evident that the model we have described can be used to analyze a great number of situations in economic life. It also seems that by formulating the problems in the terms of game theory, we come to grips with the real essentials in such situations.

These essentials were usually "assumed away" in classical economic theory. It is generally assumed that each economic agent, producers, consumers, savers, investors, etc., in a sense takes the world as given, and chooses the strategy which will maximize his particular "payoff." The assumption implies that the choices made by all other agents are known, at least in a stochastical sense, and that they are independent of the choice made by the particular agent we consider. In most economic situations such assumptions are obviously unrealistic, but they are still made, also in modern theory. The whole "programming" approach to economic problems is based on assumptions of this kind.

The *homo economicus* of classical economics has in the modern theory of "decision making under uncertainty" been replaced by *homo stochasticus*. However, the agent which we really should study is *homo politicus*, the man who makes decisions and acts, fighting or cooperating, with other men pursuing objectives similar to his own.

Haavelmo [11] has recently, in a presidential address to The Econometric Society, admitted that modern mathematical economics often has given poor results when applied to problems in real life. One explanation may be that economists usually have studied a nonexistent variety of *homo sapiens*.

2.4. The simplest nontrivial game is usually referred to as the *two-person zero-sum game*. Here $n = 2$ and

$$M_2(x_1, x_2) = -M_1(x_1, x_2)$$

For this case one can prove that there exist two probability distributions $F_1(x_1)$ and $F_2(x_2)$ defined over the sets X_1 and X_2, so that

$$\min_{x_2 \epsilon X_2} \int_{X_1} M_1(x_1, x_2)\, dF_1(x_1) = \max_{x_1 \epsilon X_1} \int_{X_2} M_1(x_1, x_2)\, dF_2(x_2)$$

This is the famous *minimax theorem* which was first proved by von Neumann [15]. A discussion between Frechet [9, 10] and von Neumann [14] gives some interesting information on the history of this theorem.

The essential idea behind the theorem is that a player must choose his strategy by some random device. If he does not do this, the opponent can guess his strategy and adjust his own strategy accordingly. By selecting the proper random device, i.e., the proper probability distribution, a player can secure for himself a certain expected gain, regardless of what strategy the opponent chooses. The theorem states that these expected gains which both players can secure for themselves, have the same absolute value. Hence none of the players can obtain a greater expected gain if the opponent behaves rationally, i.e., if he chooses the proper random device.

2.5.   The minimax theorem is a really deep mathematical theorem, and it has had a profound influence on statistical thinking during the last decade. The economic problems which can be formulated as two-person zero-sum games appear to be rather trivial. However, the solution of a two-person zero-sum game, i.e., the problem of determining the probability distribution $F_1(x_1)$ and $F_2(x_2)$ is as von Neumann himself has pointed out, equivalent to solving a linear programming problem and its dual. Linear programming has proved to be a very useful technique for solving a number of problems in economic analysis, and it is through this backdoor that game theory has found most of its applications in economics. The papers referred to in para. 1.5 are, as we pointed out, all based on this equivalence between linear programming and the simplest of all games.

2.6.   Game theory as a whole will have rather restricted applications in economics if M_i is interpreted only as the monetary value of the gain which player i makes in the game. However, by interpreting M_i as the *utility* which player i attaches to this gain, von Neumann and Morgenstern open vast new fields of application for game theory.

This idea is due to Bernoulli [3] who in 1738 proposed that rational people act so that they maximize, not expected gain, but expected utility of the gain. This principle has played a certain although modest part in statistical theory, but was ignored by most economists until von Neumann and Morgenstern [16] revived it. To Bernoulli the principle was merely a plausible hypothesis. Von Neumann and Morgenstern proved that the principle could be derived as a *theorem* from a few simple and apparently very acceptable axioms.

2.7. From this short discussion it appears that the two aspects of game theory which should be most promising for immediate application to problems in insurance, are the following:

(i)   The utility concept derived from the Bernoulli principle.
(ii) The analysis of n-person conflict situations, i.e., situations where parties whose interests are opposed can gain by cooperating.

Both aspects have been discussed in considerable detail in a number of recent publications. In the present paper it should therefore be sufficient to give only a brief summary of the essential ideas, illustrated by some simple applications.

3. The Approach of Classical Economic Theory

3.1. Before discussing in more detail the application of game theory, it may be useful to survey briefly the traditional economic approach to some of the problems in insurance.

The reason why classical economic theory is unable to deal with insurance, is clearly that uncertainty has no place in this theory. The theory assumes that an entrepreneur has full and certain knowledge of future prices and cost when he decides how much to invest in a new factory, where it shall be located and how much it shall produce. This assumption is obviously unrealistic, and most economists replace it by an assumption that the entrepreneur's *expectation* of prices and cost determine his decisions. Practically the whole economic theory is based on this assumption. The theory is internally consistent, and it cannot be refuted when confronted by reality—as long as one does not venture into making statements as to how entrepreneurs form their expectations from the information available to them.

3.2. At a fairly early stage in the development of mathematical economics, authors began more or less tacitly to assume that the expectations of a "rational" entrepreneur would be equal to the *mathematical expectation* in the precise sense given to this term in the theory of probability.

It is obviously not self-evident that the vague concept "entrepreneurial expectations" is identical to, or even connected with the well defined statistical concept "expected value." Suppose for instance that an entrepreneur is considering the marketing of a new product, which may prove either to be worthless, or to sell for $20 per unit, with equal probability. The assumption implies that this entrepreneur, if he is rational, should act as if he was certain the product would sell for $10 a unit.

Marshall [13, page 332] discusses this question briefly, and in very cautious terms. He concludes that "the evils of uncertainty must count for something," and seems to assume that the entrepreneur will act as if he was certain to get a lower amount, say $9 per unit of his product.

3.3.   Many economists do not seem to share the prudence of Marshall, and they confidently assume that entrepreneurs try to maximize *expected profits*, and hence that they keep stocks so that expected storage costs are minimized, locate factories so that expected transportation costs are minimized, etc. This assumption may be justified as a first approximation in some cases, but it cannot be generally valid. If it were, i.e., if businessmen invariably made the decisions which maximize expected profits, they would never take any insurance. As an insurance premium necessarily is greater than the expected loss, a businessman will inevitably reduce his expected profits if he takes insurance to cover some of the risks which he is running.

Hence it appears that a large part of economic theory is based on assumptions which make insurance outright irrational, which of course means that the theory is unable to recognize and analyze insurance as an economic activity.

3.4.   The cause of these difficulties is evidently the assumption that a rational man should seek to maximize expected profits, an assumption which can be traced back at least to Pascal. However, the well-known "St. Petersburg Paradox" shows that the hypothesis can lead to absurd results when pushed to extremes. The solution which Bernoulli [3] proposed to the paradox has been strangely ignored by actuaries and economists alike.

In the following we shall see that Bernoulli's assumption that a rational man seeks to maximize expected *utility* will make it possible to bring insurance into a general theory of economic activities.

4. The Utility Concept

4.1.   In a paper [5] presented to the ASTIN Colloquium in 1961, it was demonstrated that a utility concept appears to be an essential element in a complete theory of insurance. In that paper we considered an insurance company holding a portfolio of fully paid insurance contracts. If the duration of all contracts is so short that we can ignore interest, the *risk situation* of the company will be completely determined by the following two elements:

(i) $F(x)$ = the probability that claims payable under the contracts shall not exceed x
(ii) S = the funds which the company holds and can draw upon to pay claims

If a manager of an insurance company shall be able to make intelligent decisions, he must have some *preference ordering* over the set of all risk situations, i.e., he must have some criterion which enables him to decide whether one risk situation is better than another.

4.2. The preference ordering over the set of risk situations $(S, F(x))$ can be represented by a *utility index*, or a functional $U(S, F(x))$. Von Neumann and Morgenstern [16] have shown that if the preference ordering is consistent in a particular sense, the Bernoulli principle can be proved as a theorem. Hence we must have

$$U(S, F(x)) = \int_0^\infty u(S - x)\, dF(x)$$

where

$$u(S) = U(S, \epsilon(x))$$

Thus $u(S)$ is the utility attached to the degenerate risk situation $(S, \epsilon(x))$ where the company holds funds amounting to S, and where the probability is one that claims shall be zero. The function $u(x)$ can be interpreted as the *utility of money* to the insurance company.

The Bernoulli principle states that the utility attached to any risk situation can be expressed as a linear combination of the utility attached to degenerate risk situations. The theorem is obviously related to the familiar theorem that any n linearly independent vectors can be taken as a basis which spans the whole n-dimensional Euclidian space. In many cases the most convenient basis consists of "degenerate" vectors of the type $(1, 0, 0, \ldots, 0), (0, 1, 0, \ldots, 0) \ldots$. The Bernoulli principle is nothing but a generalization of this theorem to a space of infinitely many dimensions.

4.3. In the paper [5] referred to we showed that a utility concept was necessary in order to determine the optimal reinsurance arrangement. In the present paper we shall study a different aspect of insurance, which also will illustrate how a utility concept appears essential for a rational formulation of the problem.

We shall consider an insurance company which underwrites only one kind of insurance contracts, and we shall assume that this particular kind of contract has the claim distribution $F(x)$. The net premium of this insurance will then be

$$P = \int_0^\infty x\, dF(x) = m$$

We assume further that the company accepts such insurance contracts against a gross premium $(1 + \lambda)P$.

If the company underwrites n contracts, its total funds will amount to $S + n(1 + \lambda)P$ and the claim distribution of its portfolio will be

$F^{(n)}(x)$ = the nth convolution of $F(x)$ with itself.

4.4. In the simplest nontrivial case the utility of money can be represented by a function of the form

$$u(x) = -ax^2 + x$$

When the utility function has this form, it is easy to show that the utility attached to the risk situation $(S, F(x))$ is given by

$$U(S, F(x)) = S - m - a(S - m)^2 - aV$$

where m and V are the mean and the variance of $F(x)$. With a portfolio of n contracts, the utility of the company will be

$$U(S + n(1 + \lambda)P, F^{(n)}(x)) = S + n\lambda P - a(S + n\lambda P)^2 - anV$$

With this expression we can formulate and solve a number of problems. We can, for instance, assume that λ is given by market conditions, and determine the value of n, i.e., the number of contracts which will maximize the utility of the company.

4.5. We shall not solve the problems outlined in the preceding paragraph when the utility function has the form $u(x) = -ax^2 + x$. This utility function has been studied in considerable detail in previous papers [6, 7], so that a complete solution will be a mere repetition of calculations already published.
    Instead we shall assume

$$u(x) = -e^{-ax}$$

It is of course of no significance that utility in this case is negative. We can always add a positive constant to the utility function without altering the under-lying preference order.
    For this utility function we find

$$U(S, F(x)) = -\int_0^\infty e^{-a(S-x)}\, dF(x) = -e^{-aS}\, \varphi(a)$$

If the integral

$$\varphi(a) = \int_0^\infty e^{ax}\, dF(x)$$

exists, $\varphi(a)$ will be the characteristic function of $F(x)$ (for the argument $-ai$).
    Hence a portfolio of n stochastically independent insurance contracts each with a claim distribution $F(x)$, will give the company a utility

$$U(S + n(1 + \lambda)P, F^{(n)}(x)) = -e^{-a(S+n(1+\lambda)P)} \{\varphi(a)\}^n$$

4.6.   In the last formula of the preceding paragraph it is convenient to write

$$V(n, \lambda) = \log(-U) = n \log \varphi(a) - aS - an(1 + \lambda)P$$

As $V(n, \lambda)$ will decrease with increasing U, the company will seek to maximize $V(n, \lambda)$.

We see that $V(n, \lambda)$ is linear in n. Hence the problem mentioned in para. 4.4 is trivial when the utility of money has this particular shape. For a given λ, the company will seek to underwrite as many contracts as possible if

$$a(1 + \lambda)P > \log \varphi(a)$$

If the inequality is reversed, the company will not underwrite any contract of this kind.

4.7.   We arrive at more interesting problems if we assume that n depends on λ, i.e., that we have

$$n = n(\lambda)$$

where $n(\lambda)$ is a function which increases with decreasing λ. Here we can interpret $n(\lambda)$ as the market demand for this particular insurance contract. The lower the "price" λ, the greater the demand n. In practice it appears that insurance has a very low price elasticity. A more realistic interpretation may be to assume that n can be increased by using a part of the loading for sales promotion, such as advertising.

If the function $n(\lambda)$ is given, we can determine the value of λ which maximizes the company's utility. The first-order condition for a maximum is

$$\frac{\partial V}{\partial n} \frac{dn}{d\lambda} + \frac{\partial V}{\partial \lambda} = 0$$

If we assume that $n(\lambda)$ is linear, i.e., that

$$n(\lambda) = n_0 - \alpha\lambda$$

the condition is reduced to

$$\alpha \log \varphi(a) = an_0 - \alpha aP(1 + 2\lambda)$$

from which we can determine the desired value of λ.

4.8. The problem which we have discussed in the preceding paragraphs is of obvious practical importance, and it has frequently been discussed in insurance literature. However, it appears difficult, if not impossible to come to grips with the problem unless the objectives of the insurance company are formulated in an operational manner. Such formulation of the problem requires a utility concept— or something equivalent.

4.9. It is interesting to note that the Bernoulli principle was used as early as 1834 by Barrois [1] in his study of fire insurance. Barrois considered the following problem:

> A man who has total assets amounting to S, owns a house worth R and there is a probability p that the house may be destroyed by fire. He can insure his house against fire by paying a premium Q. Shall he, or shall he not take this insurance?

Barrois introduced a utility function $u(x)$ which measures the utility attached to an amount x of money, and shows that a rational person will take insurance if, and only if

$$u(S - Q) > pu(S - R) + (1 - p) u(S)$$

This inequality says that the person prefers to have his assets reduced from S to $S - Q$ with certainty, rather than risk a reduction to $S - R$ with probability p.

By this simple device Barrois has solved Marshall's problem of determining the amount a rational person should pay to avoid the "evils of uncertainty." He has also provided the analytical tools which Tauber 75 years later sought in vain in economic theory.

Following Bernoulli, Barrois assumes that $u(x) = \log x$. However, like Bernoulli himself, he seems aware that other nondecreasing functions may serve equally well. Barrois should certainly be recognized as one of the pioneers in the theory of insurance. It seems incidentally that the place in the history of insurance which is rightfully his, is about to be occupied by Alice Morrison, who according to a recent paper by Williams [23] was the first to apply Bernoulli's principle to insurance problems. Miss Morrison's work has apparently not been published, but it was rewarded with a Ph.D. by Iowa State University in 1949.

4.10. Barrois was a contemporary of Cournot, whose work also was forgotten by the following generation of economists. Referring to Cournot, Walras [22, page 20] wrote in 1900:

> "Si la France du XIXme siècle, qui a vu naître la science nouvelle, s'en est complètement désintéressée, cela tient à cette conception d'une étroitesse bourgeoise de la culture intellectuelle qui l'a partagée en deux

zones distinctes: l'une produisant des calculateurs dépourvus de connaissances philosophiques, morales, historiques, économiques, et l'autre où fleurissent des lettrés sans aucunes notions mathématiques"

It may be unfair to make this comment on the France of today, but the remark may have some address to modern actuaries. Barrois has been quoted fairly regularly in the insurance literature—also in *The ASTIN Bulletin.* However, none of the conscientious bibliographers who have referred to Barrois' paper seem to have realized that the paper contains the key to the whole theory of the economics of uncertainty.

Actuaries are certainly not "calculateurs" without any culture, but they do occasionally take a too narrow view of their function. Insurance is an economic activity, and the actuary should not ignore the economic environment in which his company works.

5. Conflict Situations

5.1. Another paper [8] presented to this colloquium discusses the rating of different risk groups in an insurance collective. This is a typical conflict situation. Each group wants to pay the lowest possible premium, and the total amount of premium to be paid will be lowest if all groups can agree to join and form one single company. Hence the groups as a whole will gain if they cooperate. However, the interests of the various groups are opposed, since each group will want to secure for itself the greatest possible share of the collective gain which results from the cooperation. If a group is dissatisfied with its share of this gain, it can threaten to leave the company, and it can try to bribe other groups to join it in setting up a rival company. The remaining groups will then have to consider whether they shall offer the dissident group a higher share, or accept the break up of the big company.

5.2. Economic theory has nothing to offer when it comes to analyzing a problem like the one we have outlined. Most economists will probably dismiss the problem all together as not belonging to economics but to some under-developed branch of psychology.

The paper [8] referred to offers a solution, which may, or may not, be considered as the final answer. However, whether this solution is accepted or not, it is clear that game theory has something to offer, and that it is through this theory we may hope to gain complete mastery of the problem.

5.3. We get a better basis for comparing game theory and classical economic theory if we study the reinsurance market.

As a starting point we consider n insurance companies, which as a result of their direct underwriting find themselves in the risk situations determined by the elements $F_i(x_i)$ and S_i $(i = 1, 2, \ldots, n)$.

Using the notation of para. 4.2, we find that company i attaches the following utility to its initial risk situation

$$U_i = \int_0^\infty u_i(S_i - x_i) \, dF_i(x_i)$$

If $x_1, \ldots, x_n$ are stochastically independent, and if for all i we have $u_i(x_i) > 0$ and $u_i''(x_i) < 0$ over the whole range which enters into consideration, it is fairly easy to show that there are reinsurance arrangements which will increase the utility of all the companies. Hence the situation is similar to the one described in para. 5.1. All companies stand to gain if they cooperate, i.e., if they conclude reinsurance treaties with each other. However, there is a conflict of interest as to how this gain should be distributed among the companies. It is clear that the problem can be analyzed in terms of game theory, and that we can arrive at a solution similar to the one given for the problem discussed in the paper [8] already referred to.

5.4. Assume now that the companies make some reinsurance arrangements so that the utility of company i changes from $U_i{}^0$ to $U_i{}^1$.

If no company will participate in an arrangement which reduces its own utility, we must have

$$U_i{}^0 \leqslant U_i{}^1 \qquad \text{for all } i$$

If there exists no arrangement which will give company i the utility $U_i{}^2$ such that

$$U_i{}^1 \leqslant U_1{}^2 \qquad \text{for all } i$$

the arrangement corresponding to $U_i{}^1$ is said to be *Pareto optimal.*

If the n companies act rationally, we must assume that they somehow reach a Pareto optimal reinsurance arrangement. It is obviously irrational to settle for some other arrangement, since it will then be possible to increase the utility of all companies by switching to a Pareto optimal arrangement.

5.5. In the paper [6] already referred to it has been shown that the Pareto optimal arrangements in a reinsurance market are determined by n functions $y_1(x), \ldots, y_n(x)$ which satisfy the conditions

$$k_i u_i'(S_i - y_i(x)) = k_j u_j'(S_j - y_j(x))$$

where $k_1, \ldots, k_n$ are positive constants, and $x = x_1 \ldots + x_n$ and where $y_i(x)$ is the amount which company i has to pay if the total amount of claims is x.

The constants $k_1, \ldots, k_n$ can be chosen arbitrarily, subject to some rather trivial restrictions which we shall not discuss here. Hence the solution we have arrived at is indeterminate. Our assumption that the companies behave rationally, implies that they will reach some Pareto optimal arrangement, but the assumption is not sufficient to determine which articular arrangement they will settle for. In order to obtain a determinate solution, i.e., to determine the values of $k_1, \ldots, k_n$, we must make *additional assumptions* about how the companies behave in the reinsurance market.

5.6.   The indeterminate character of the solution is brought out quite clearly by a simple example studied in the paper [7] already referred to. In this paper we assumed that the utility of money to company i was given by

$$u(x) = x - a_i x^2 \quad i = 1, 2, \ldots, n$$

The constant a_i can be interpreted as a measure of the company's risk aversion, and may differ from one company to another.

It can then be proved that a Pareto optimal reinsurance arrangement between the n companies will give company i the utility

$$U_i = \frac{1}{4a_i} - q_i^2 \, a_i \, A \quad i = 1, 2, \ldots, n$$

Here A is a positive "universal constant" for this particular market. The parameters $q_1, \ldots, q_n$ can be chosen arbitrarily, subject to the restrictions:

(i) $q_1 + q_2 + \ldots q_n = 1$
(ii) $q_i \geqslant 0$ for all i

Company i will obviously want q_i to be as small as possible. However, this leads to a conflict with the desires of the other companies, which also want their particular q to be as small as possible. Hence the n companies have to bargain their way to a compromise.

The companies have to reach agreement on a set of numbers $q_1, \ldots, q_n$ which satisfy the conditions above. This is the problem, reduced to its bare essentials. It is quite clear that in order to obtain a determinate solution, we must make some assumptions as to how the companies negotiate their way to an agreement.

5.7.   In some previous papers [6, 7] we have approached the problem in the manner of classical economic theory. We have assumed with Tauber [19] that reinsurance cover is a service, and that as any other service it must have its price. We have further assumed that there exists an equilibrium price which will make supply and demand for this service equal.

In the classical theory of commodity markets, it is assumed that all traders in the market take the equilibrium prices for each commodity as given and unalterable, and buy and sell at these prices until their utility is maximized. One can then show that the market will reach a Pareto optimal situation. In this Pareto optimal situation, the commodities are distributed among the traders in such a way that any further exchanges will reduce the utility of some of the participants.

In the following we shall seek to transfer this behavioral assumption to the reinsurance market, and see if the price mechanism which leads the classical commodity market to a Pareto optimum can be generalized so that it can fulfill the same function in a reinsurance market.

5.8.   In a reinsurance market a company accepts liability for a portfolio of insurance contracts with claim distribution $F(x)$ against payment of an amount P. Since there is no natural "unit of insurance cover," there is no obvious way in which P and $F(x)$ can be connected. Hence our first problem is to define a price concept which can be meaningfully applied to the transactions in a reinsurance market.

In the paper [6] already referred to, it has been shown that a transformation of the form

$$P(F(x)) = \sum_{j=1}^{\infty} p_j \kappa_j$$

is the only one which satisfies the essential requirements of a price concept. Here $p_1, \ldots, p_j, \ldots$, are constants, and κ_j is the jth cumulant of the probability distribution $F(x)$.

The transformation $P(F(x))$ must be interpreted as the amount one has to pay for reinsurance cover for a portfolio with claim distribution $F(x)$.

5.9.   Under certain conditions a price of this form can be an equilibrium price, i.e., can lead to a balance between supply and demand for reinsurance cover in the market. It has, however, been shown in another paper [7] that if the companies take an equilibrium price of this kind as given, and set out to do the transactions which will maximize their utility, they will in general end up with a situation which is not Pareto optimal. In this situation there will be transactions—at other prices—which will increase the utility of all the participating companies. If the companies act rationally, they will carry out these transactions and reach a Pareto optimal situation. However, these latter transactions can obviously not be governed by the price mechanism of classical economic theory.

5.10.   The reinsurance problem appears at first sight to be a problem which can be analyzed in terms of classical economic theory, once the objectives of the companies have been formulated in an operational manner by the help of Bernoulli's utility concept. However, closer investigations show that economic theory can only take us part of the way. The problem is in its very essence a problem of cooperation between parties who have conflicting interests, and who are free to form and break any coalitions which may serve their particular interests. Classical economic theory is powerless when it comes to analyze such problems. The only theory which at present seems to hold some promise of being able to sort out and explain this apparently chaotic situation, is the theory of games.

6.   A General Theory of Insurance

6.1.   In the preceding sections we have assumed that all players act rationally. We shall now assume that one player, say player n, does not act rationally. We shall refer to this player as *Nature,* and assume that he burns down houses, sinks ships, and in general plays havoc with the carefully laid plans of the other players. However, Nature is not completely erratic in its behavior. We shall assume that there exists a probability distribution $F(x_n)$ defined over the set X_n, and that this distribution can be determined, at least to a useful approximation by observing the behavior of Nature.

The $n-1$ other players who act rationally must take the erratic behavior of Nature into account when choosing their strategies. A single player, acting on his own, can do little to protect himself against Nature. However, groups of players can cooperate, and for instance form insurance companies—or in game theory—coalitions to spread the harmful effects of Nature's behavior. These coalitions can again make reinsurance arrangements so spread the effects even further.

6.2.   It is evident that the whole insurance activity can be seen as a game played by a large number of reasonably rational players against an erratic, and generally hostile Nature. The function of the actuary in this game is to study the probability distribution $F(x_n)$ and provide the information which forms the basis of the decisions made by the players individually, and by those responsible for managing their coalitions, i.e., the directors of insurance companies.

The concept "game against nature" was introduced by Wald [21] in 1950. The concept has proved extremely useful by providing a link between modern statistical theory and game theory and stucies of economic behavior. It also appears that by adopting this concept, it should be possible to construct a unified theory for all aspects of insurance. This will of course be a formidable task, which it may take decades to complete. In the present paper we have only touched upon a few points which illustrate the power of game theory when it comes to solving problems which it is difficult even to formulate in a meaningful manner in the terms of earlier theories.

7. Conclusion

7.1. In this paper we have tried to show that game theory can be applied to a number of problems in insurance, problems to which earlier theories have been unable to offer satisfactory solutions. The literature we have quoted seems to indicate that an increasing number of actuaries are becoming aware of the possibilities of game theory, and that they will find far more ingenious applications for the theory than we have been able to suggest.

7.2. We have, however, tried to show something more than this. We have sought to demonstrate that game theory is not just another new mathematical device which may be handy in an insurance company. The real purpose of this paper has been to show that game theory is indeed a necessary—maybe even a sufficient—basis on which a unified general theory of insurance can be constructed.

References

1. Barrois, T. "*Essai sur l'application du calcul des probabilités aux assurances contre l'incendie,*" Mémoires de la Société Royale des Sciences de l'Agriculture et des Arts de Lille, 1834, pp. 85–282.
2. Baumgartner, U. "Abschätzung von Reserven mit spieltheoretischen Methoden," *Bulletin de l'Association des Actuaires suisses* 1961, pp. 223–274.
3. Bernoulli, D.: "Exposition of a New Theory on the Measurement of Risk," *Econometrica,* 1954, pp. 23–46. Translation of a paper in Latin published in St. Petersburg 1738.
4. Bierlein, D. "Spieltheoretische Modelle für Entscheidungssituationen des Versicherers," *Blätter der Deutschen Gesellschaft für Versicherungsmathematik* 1958, pp. 461–469.
5. Borch, K. "The Utility Concept Applied to the Theory of Insurance," *The ASTIN Bulletin,* vol. 1, pp. 245–255.
6. ——. "The Safety Loading of Reinsurance Premiums," *Skandinavisk Aktuarietidskrift,* 1960, pp. 163–184.
7. ——. "Equilibrium in a Reinsurance Market."*Econometrica,* 1962, pp. 424–444.
8. ——. "Application of Game Theory to some Problems in Automobile Insurance," *The ASTIN Bulletin,* vol. II, pp. 208–221.
9. Frechet, M.: "Emile Borel, initiator of the theory of psychological games and its application," *Econometrica,* 1953, pp. 95–96.

10. ——. "Commentary on the Three Notes of Emile Borel," *Econometrica*, 1953, pp. 118–124.

11. Haavelmo, T. "The Role of the Econometrician in the Advancement of Economic Theory," *Econometrica*, 1958, pp. 351–357.

12. Keynes, J. M. *The General Theory of Employment, Interest and Money*, (London, 1936).

13. Marshall, A. *Principles of Economics*, 8th Ed. (London, 1920).

14. Neumann, J. von. "Communication on the Borel Notes," *Econometrica*, 1953, pp. 124–127.

15. ——. "Zur Theorie der Gesellschaftsspiele," *Mathematische Annalen*, 1928, pp. 295–320. English translation *Annals of Mathematical Studies*, no. 40, pp. 13–42.

16. —— and O. Morgenstern. *Theory of Games and Economic Behavior* (Princeton, 1944).

17. Nolfi, P. "Zur mathematischen Darstellung des Nutzens in der Versicherung," *Bulletin de l'Association des Actuaires suisses* 1957, pp. 395–407.

18. ——. "Die Berücksichtigung der Sterblichkeitsverbesserung in der Rentenversicherung nach der Optimalmethode der Spieltheorie," *Bulletin de l'Association des Actuaires suisses* 1959, pp. 29–48.

19. Tauber, A. "Über Risiko und Sichereitszuschlag." *Report of the Sixth International Congress of Actuaries*, Vienna, 1909, pp. 781–842.

20. Thompson, D. M. and G. L. Thompson. "A Bibliography of Game Theory," *Annals of Mathematical Studies*, no. 40, pp. 407–453.

21. Wald, A. *"Statistical Decision Functions"* (New York, 1950).

22. Walras, L. *Elements d'Economie Politique Pure*, Edition definitive. (Paris: Tirage Pichon & Durand-Auzias, 1952).

23. Williams, C. A. "Game Theory and Insurance Consumption," *The Journal of Insurance*, December 1960, pp. 47–56.

13

Ends and Means in Actuarial Science

1. Introduction

1.1. When a branch of science is in rapid development, it may be useful to look back from time to time and reconsider the means available and the ends which we want to achieve. There has hardly been any startling innovation in actuarial science during the last decades, but there has been an explosive development in theoretical statistics and the branches of mathematics, which in the past have provided the actuary with most of his tools. This opens a vast field of new possibilities which the actuary already has begun to explore. If however, he shall be able to make the most of these possibilities, the explorations must be carried out with a clear purpose.

1.2. If we read between the lines of actuarial journals, we get the impression that the actuary is a very modest sort of person. The task of the actuary appears— in his own opinion—to consist of providing the facts and figures which are used by his superiors who draw up company policy and make the final decisions. How these decisions actually are made, seems to be of little concern to the actuary.

There is something paradoxical about this situation. The actuary is undisputed master of the means, but shows little interest in the ends which these means are supposed to serve. In the following we shall try to illustrate this by discussing a few simple examples.

1.3. The traditional task of the actuary is to calculate the *expected value* of the payments which will be made under an insurance contract. The central concepts of actuarial science, *net premium* and *technical reserves,* are by definition equal to such expected values. However, few actuaries seem to have questioned whether these concepts are relevant to the actual decisions which must be made in an insurance company.

To drive the point home, let us consider an insurance contract under which the only possible payment is $1 million, and assume that this payment has to be made only if an event with probability 0.0 001% should occur. The net premium for this contract is clearly $1, but has this any significance whatsoever? Would not any reinsurer in his senses consider this a ridiculously low premium for a catastrophe cover—even if all administrative costs were paid by the cedent?

1.4. Actuaries have of course realized long ago that the net premium is not

197

everything. An ingenious actuary may point out that the standard deviation of payments under the contract considered is $1000, and he may suggest that $3000 is a suitable premium.

This is however hardly more relevant than the net premium. The contract is completely described when we have specified the amount and the probability that it shall become payable. We obtain no new information by calculating the standard deviation and other statistics. The problem, and the whole problem, is to determine the premium which the reinsurer considers adequate compensation for accepting the risk. This is necessarily a subjective judgment which the re-insurer must take alone. The actuary may be right in considering this decision as outside his realm, but he is wrong if he fails to recognize that such subjective judgments must enter as data in any application of actuarial science.

In the following we shall indicate how these judgments can be formulated in an operational manner and brought into practical actuarial work. We shall find it convenient to present the problem in terms of reinsurance rather than direct insurance.

2. Formulation of the Problem

2.1. As a slight generalization of the example in the Introduction, we shall consider an insurance contract which stipulates that an amount S shall be paid if an event with probability p should occur. We shall assume that a reinsurer is deliberating if he should accept this contract against a premium P. His gain will of course depend on his decision, and on whether the event occurs or not, i.e., on the *state of the world.* This is illustrated by Table 13–1, a *payoff matrix.*

2.2. It is reasonable to assume that the contract will be accepted for a sufficiently large P. For instance, if $P = S$, the reinsurer cannot possibly lose by accepting. Similarly for $P = 0$, he cannot possibly gain if he accepts.

Formally we state the assumption as follows:

There exists a number P_1 such that:

The reinsurer will accept the contract if $P \geqslant P_1$

Table 13–1
Gain of the Reinsurer

Decision	State of the World	
	Event occurs	Event does not occur
Contract accepted	$-(S - P)$	P
Contract not accepted	0	0

The reinsurer will not accept the contract if $P < P_1$.

P_1 is the lowest premium against which the reinsurer is willing to provide cover for the risk under consideration.

The actuary may suggest that this minimum premium should be determined by some formula like

$$P_1 = pS$$

or $P_1 = pS + 3S\sqrt{p(1-p)}$

If pressed to defend this suggestion, the actuary would probably refer to the "law of large numbers" or something equivalent. However, if it is obvious that this law does not apply, the actuary's argument will evidently be irrelevant.

2.3.   The decision involved is essentially a decision as to how the reinsurer should run his business. He can do this in a prudent manner, or he can run great risks. No matter which course the reinsurer chooses, the decision remains his. He will be a pure escapist if he tries to force the actuary to make the decision for him through some calculations which they both should know must be irrelevant. He could just as well consult an astrologer as to whether the critical event will occur or not, since this really is the problem which worries him.

2.4.   If the reinsurer shall be able to make the decisions which are required, he must have some *decision rule.* In the simple situation we have considered, the rule can be given as a function of two variables

$$P_1 = P(p, S)$$

which determines the lowest premium at which the reinsurer will cover a risk defined by the pair (p, S). This decision rule can be interpreted as the *business policy* of the reinsurer. Once this is given, the actuary will have the clear-cut task of estimating probabilities and compute premiums.

If the reinsurer conducts his business in a rational manner, his decision rule must satisfy some consistency conditions. We shall return to these conditions later, since they can best be discussed in a more general context.

2.5.   We have discussed this simple model to demonstrate that it is necessary to separate the responsibilities of the policy maker and the technician in order to give a satisfactory analysis of the situation.

The model is obviously too simple to give an adequate representation of any problem from insurance in real life. There is however no particular difficulty involved in constructing a more general model. In the following we shall study the case where payments are represented by an arbitrary stochastic variable, and it is also possible to analyze the case where the relevant probabilities are only partially known.

In these more general models it will also be necessary to separate the responsibilities. This is of course only what we should have expected. It would really have been astonishing if the introduction of ignorance and computational complications could simplify the task, so that the technicians could solve it alone. When the problem is formulated so bluntly, it becomes notably absurd to seek algorithms which will give "correct" premiums and "optimal" reinsurance arrangements without any reference to the policy of the insurance company in question.

3. A More General Model

3.1. We shall now consider an insurance contract which is such that the total amount paid to cover claims is a stochastic variable x, with a distribution $F(x)$. We shall refer to $F(x)$ as the *claim distribution* of the contract.

If an insurance company has a well-defined business policy, it must have a rule which determines the lowest premium P at which the company will underwrite a contract with claim distribution $F(x)$.

This means that a business policy can be represented by an operator T which maps or projects the set of all probability distributions on the real line, i.e.,

$$T\{F(x)\} \to P$$

3.2. In para. 2.4 we mentioned that a policy would have to satisfy certain consistency conditions, at least if the policy should be considered as rational in any acceptable sense of the word.

In order to illustrate this, let us consider two claim distributions $F(x)$ and $G(x)$, and assume

$$T\{F(x)\} \to P(1)$$

$$T\{G(x)\} \to P(0)$$

and $P(0) < P(1)$

A *probability mixture* of the two distributions is defined by

$$\alpha F(x) + (1 - \alpha) G(x) \quad \text{where } 0 \leqslant \alpha \leqslant 1$$

This can again be interpreted as a claim distribution generated by a random device which selects $F(x)$ with probability α, and $G(x)$ with probability $1 - \alpha$.

The minimum premium required to cover this distribution must then be given by the same transformation. Let us write this

$$T\{\alpha F(x) + (1 - \alpha)G(x)\} \rightarrow P(\alpha)$$

The consistency condition is then that $P(\alpha)$ shall be continuous and increase steadily from $P(0)$ to $P(1)$ as α increases from 0 to 1.

3.3. The condition in the preceding paragraph appears very innocent, and most people will feel intuitively that it should be satisfied by any rational business policy. The condition is however sufficient to prove the following:

There exist a transformation U and a real valued function u(x) such that:

$$U\{F(x + P)\} = \int_0^\infty u(P - x)\, dF(x) = u(0)$$

where P is the minimum premium which according to the policy is required to cover a contract with claim distribution $F(x)$.

This result can be interpreted as follows:

The function $F(x + S)$ is defined for $x \geqslant -S$.

Hence it can be taken as the distribution of an insurance contract which can lead to negative claims, i.e., to a profit for the company. This means that $F(x + S)$ represents a contract under which the company receives the amount S as compensation for accepting liability for a claim with distribution $F(x)$.

Let us now consider a degenerate distribution $F(x) = \epsilon(x - a)$ (i.e., claims will be equal to a with probability one), and assume that the company underwrites this "risk" against a premium Q. Applying the transformation U, we obtain

$$U\{\epsilon(x + Q - a)\} = u(Q - a)$$

However, this contract is obviously equivalent to a transaction where the company receives the amount $Q - a$ as an outright gift. Hence $u(Q - a)$ can be interpreted as the *utility* attached to the amount $Q - a$, and the function $u(x)$ as the *utility of money*.

The transformation U assigns a utility to any insurance contract. If for instance we have

$$U\{F(x + S)\} = u(R)$$

this means that the contract represented by $F(x + S)$ is equivalent to (has the same utility as) a direct gift, or a certain profit of R.

The basic result at the beginning of this paragraph simply states that to accept a contract at the minimum premium is equivalent to a gift equal to zero. The importance of the result lies in the fact that it gives us a function $u(x)$ which represents the business policy, i.e., the rule which makes it possible to quote a minimum premium for each claim distribution.

If we assume that the company seeks to build up a portfolio of insurance contracts which, according to its business policy, is equivalent to the highest possible profits, receivable with certainty, we have an operational formulation of the company's objectives. The ends of actuarial science will then consist of determining the obtainable portfolio which has maximum utility.

3.4.   The result which we have outlined above was first proposed by Daniel Bernoulli [2] as a hypothesis as to how rational people would make decisions under uncertainty. The relevance of the hypothesis to insurance was noted by Bernoulli himself and by others, among them Laplace. In 1834 Barrois [1] used the Bernoulli hypothesis to develop a fairly complete theory of fire insurance.

Von Neumann and Morgenstern [6] proved that the Bernoulli hypothesis could be derived as a theorem from a few very weak assumptions, and made it one of the corner stones in their theory of games. In this paper we have made far stronger assumptions, and it is then possible to derive the Bernoulli hypothesis from one of the classical results in analysis, the Riesz representation theorem [7].

3.5.   To illustrate the application of the Bernoulli principle, we shall consider an insurance company and assume:

(i)   The company's business policy can be represented by a function $u(x)$.
(ii)   The company holds a portfolio of insurance contracts with the claim distribution $F(x)$.
(iii) The company's funds amount to S.

To this initial situation the company will attach the utility

$$U(S, F) = \int_0^\infty u(S - x)\, dF(x)$$

We shall then assume that this company is invited to give reinsurance cover to a portfolio with claim distribution $G(y)$ against a premium P. For simplicity we shall assume that x and y are stochastically independent and we shall write

$$H(x) = \int_0^\infty F(x - y)\, dG(y)$$

for the convolution of $F(x)$ and $G(y)$.

If the company accepts the proposed reinsurance contract, it will reach a risk situation with the utility

$$U(S + P, H) = \int_0^\infty u(S + P - x)\, dH(x)$$

Hence the company will accept the proposed contract if and only if

$$U(S + P, H) > U(S, F)$$

The equation

$$U(S + P, H) = U(S, F)$$

will then determine the lowest premium at which this company will agree to cover a portfolio with claim distribution $G(x)$.

3.6. Let us now assume that an actuary has to quote a premium for reinsurance cover of a certain portfolio. In order to do this he must of course obtain all possible knowledge about the claim distribution of the portfolio, i.e., $G(x)$. However, the example we have discussed shows that this is not enough. In order to quote a premium the actuary must also consider:

(i)   The present situation of his own company, i.e., S and $F(x)$ in the example
(ii) The business policy of the company, i.e., the function $u(x)$

These two elements are often overlooked in actuarial studies of reinsurance problems. There is however a third element which is almost invariably ignored in actuarial literature, although in practice it may be more important than any of the others.

3.7. There is no obvious reason why the actuary should quote the lowest possible premium, i.e., the premium determined by the equation at the end of para. 3.5. If his company has a rational business policy, the actuary will also take into account *what the cedent is prepared to pay.*
In their daily work actuaries are certainly aware of this, but the same simple fact of life seems to escape them when they write theoretical papers about reinsurance. There are necessarily two parties to a reinsurance contract, and it seems rather futile to study the problem without considering both parties. However, it is hard to find a single paper on, say, maximum retention, which even considers the possibility the reinsurers may be unwilling to play on the author's conditions.

3.8. To illustrate the point, we shall return to the example in para. 2.1 and look at the situation from the point of view of the ceding company. The pay-off matrix will be

Table 13-2
Loss of the Cedent

	State of the World	
Decision	*Event occurs*	*Event does not occur*
Reinsure	P	P
Do not reinsure	S	0

We assume that there exists a number P_2, so that the potential cedent will insure if and only if $P \leqslant P_2$. If $P > P_2$ he will prefer to carry the whole risk himself.

Comparing with para. 2.2, we see that no reinsurance contract will be concluded if $P_2 < P_1$.

If $P_2 > P_1$, it will be to the advantage of both parties to conclude a contract at a premium P which satisfies the condition $P_1 < P < P_2$.

This is however an indeterminate result. There is no natural rule which enables us to single out one particular premium in the interval as the "correct" one; or to formulate the problem in a less normative way, there is no theory which can "predict" the premium that the two parties will agree upon.

3.9. The last two paragraphs have brought us close to some of the central ideas of economic theory. With a slight change of emphasis we could start afresh, and consider insurance cover or simply "security," as a commodity which is bought and sold. There is an evident demand for this commodity, if the price is not exorbitant, and there are companies which are willing to supply the commodity if they consider the price satisfactory. It is then tempting to put aside all actuarial ideas as to how premiums should be calculated, and instead follow economic theory, assuming that the price is determined so that supply is equal to demand.

This approach to insurance has been discussed in some detail in other papers, e.g., [3] and [5], so we shall not develop it any further here.

This approach should ultimately lead to an integration of actuarial science and economic theory. One should however note that insurance markets are considerably more complicated than the markets studied in classical economic theory. It has for instance been demonstrated that a unique equilibrium price will usually not exist in a reinsurance market [4]. It may therefore take some time before we reach this attractive goal.

4. Conclusion

4.1. In this paper we have tried to show that actuaries have developed means of considerable sophistication, without always being quite clear as to which ends these means should serve.

It is not for the actuary to specify the ends i.e., the overall policy of his company. In his work the actuary should take the ends as given. If they are not given, it is his right—and his duty—to insist that those who are responsible should spell out the policy in an operational manner. Only if this is done, will it be possible for the actuary to develop the appropriate means.

4.2.   This may all sound fairly obvious, and be quite simple in theory. However, in practice it is not so easy to establish such a clear cut division of responsibilities. One reason is that ends and means are interwoven in a very intricate pattern—as we have tried to demonstrate in this paper.

It is obvious that one cannot devise the proper means without knowing the ends. It is less obvious, but equally true that one cannot define the ends without some understanding of the available means. This should imply that the actuary must take a prominent part in the formulation of company policy, and he must consider how far the objectives of this policy can be achieved in a world where other companies pursue similar objectives.

However, this is just what actuaries do in real life—in spite of the much narrower functions which they are given in actuarial literature, so there is apparently a discrepancy between theory and practice. If this should be the case, this paper will indicate how theory can be modified and brought in harmony with practice.

References

1.   Barrois, T. "Essai sur l'application du calcul des probabilités aux assurances contre l'incendie," *Memoires de la Société Royale des Sciences,* Lille 1834, pp. 85–282.
2.   Bernoulli, D. "Exposition of a New Theory on the Measurement of Risk," *Econometrica,* 1954, pp. 23–46. Translation of the paper published in St. Petersburg in 1738.
3.   Borch, K. "The Safety Loading of Reinsurance Premiums," *Skandinavisk Aktuarietidsskrift,* 1960, pp. 163–184.
4.   ——. "Equilibrium in a Reinsurance Market," *Econometrica,* 1962, pp. 424–444.
5.   ——. "Recent Developments in Economic Theory and their Application to Insurance," *The ASTIN Bulletin,* 1963, pp. 322–341.
6.   Neumann, J. von and O. Morgenstern. *Theory of Games and Economic Behavior* (Princeton, 1944).
7.   Riesz, F. "Sur les opérations fonctionelles linéaires," *Comptes Rendus,* 1909, pp. 974–976.

14   The Economic Theory of Insurance

1. Introduction

1.1. Under Subject 4 at this Congress we have discussed the practical application of modern statistical techniques in different branches of insurance. During the last decades, there has been an almost explosive development in theoretical statistics and related branches of mathematics. I think it has been very useful to survey the techniques which have been developed, and find out if they can be used in insurance.

1.2. There may, however, be some danger in this approach. When new *means* become available, we should of course have an open mind, and examine these means in order to see if they can serve our *ends.* We should, however, not get so excited over the power of new techniques, that we distort our ends just for the sake of being able to apply the means.

Linear programming, to take an example, is a powerful tool, which has proved extremely useful in many, apparently very different fields. There is, however, little point in using this technique in insurance, unless we have problems which consist of determining the maximum of a linear expression, subject to linear restraints. If there are problems in insurance which can be cast in this form, with sufficient approximation, then linear programming is obviously useful. If, however, we lose something essential by reformulating our problems in this way, linear programming may become a dangerous temptation, which we should resist.

1.3. In this paper I shall take a different approach. I shall try to take a good and hard look at the ends, with the hope that this will enable us to specify the means which we require. If these means already exist, all is well. If we cannot find any suitable techniques in the mathematician's armory, we will have to do our own basic research, and develop the tools we need.

A generation ago, the subject "applied mathematics" consisted mainly of techniques which had proved extremely useful in classical physics. These techniques were used with considerable enthusiasm and little success in economics and other social sciences. The new statistical techniques which excite us today have to a large extent been developed to solve problems in quantum mechanics and telecommunications. We may therefore ask ourselves if we have any reason to expect these techniques to be useful in actuarial work.

207

This point has been made with considerable force by von Neumann and Morgenstern ([5], page 6) who make the blunt statement: "It is unlikely that a mere repetition of the tricks which served us so well in physics, will do for the social phenomena too." They sum up their view: "It is therefore to be expected— or feared—that mathematical discoveries of a stature comparable to that of calculus will be needed in order to produce decisive success in this field [i.e., economics] ."

It is in this spirit we shall try to analyze the ends and means of actuarial science.

2. The Principle of Equivalence

2.1. To illustrate the point which I want to make, we shall begin by discussing an extremely simple example.

Consider an insurance contract under which the only possible payment is an amount of one monetary unit. We shall assume that this amount becomes payable if, and only if an event with probability p should occur.

This contract will define the following *claim distribution:*

0 with probability $1 - p$

1 with probability p

The *net premium* of the contract is by definition p.

2.2. We shall next assume that an insurance company offers the contract we have described to the public, at a premium $x > p$. We shall assume that there is a *demand* for the insurance cover given by this contract, and that demand depends on the premium. We shall formalize this by assuming that the company will be able to sell $n = n(x)$ contracts if the premium is set at x. It is natural to assume that $n(x)$ will increase with decreasing x.

The problem is now to determine the premium x at which the company should offer this insurance contract in the market. This seems to be a very simple problem, and we ought to solve it in a satisfactory manner, before we tackle more complicated problems, or embark on the more ambitious task of constructing a general theory of insurance.

2.3. In classical theory our simple problem is solved by applying the *principle of equivalence.* According to this principle, the premium should be equal to expected claim payments + administrative costs. This means that x should be determined by

$$x = p + \frac{1}{n} C(n)$$

where $C(n)$ is the cost involved in selling and managing a portfolio of n contracts. If we assume that costs can be split up into "fixed" and "variable" costs, we can write

$$C(n) = C_1 + nC_2$$

The premium will then be given by the equation

$$x = p + C_2 + \frac{C_1}{n(x)}$$

We have assumed that $n(x)$ decreases with increasing x. This means that both sides of the equation will increase with x, so that the equation may have any number of solutions, depending on the shape of the function $n(x)$.

2.4. The principle of equivalence gives a neat solution to our simple problem—if we are prepared to disregard the somewhat academic question about existence and uniqueness of the roots of the main equation. To solve the problem in practice, we have to know:

(i)   The basic probability p
(ii) The cost elements C_1 and C_2
(iii) The function $n(x)$

To obtain this knowledge, we will usually have to resort to statistical methods, or to be more precise, the techniques of statistical *estimation.*

The traditional task of the actuary is to provide the best possible estimate of p. He is also frequently called upon to supply estimates of C_1 and C_2, since this often requires statistical analysis.

The determination of the last element, the function $n(x)$ is usually considered as being outside the duties of the actuary.

In most cases it will probably be the sales manager of the company or a market research department, who is responsible for guessing or estimating the shape of $n(x)$.

2.5. The function $n(x)$ represents the demand or the market for the insurance contract under consideration. These are economic concepts, and this indicates that our problem cannot be satisfactorily solved, unless we bring in some elements of economic theory.

In some cases it may be possible to determine the "correct" premium without knowing the number of contracts which will be sold. This will be the case if $n(x)$ is approximately constant, or in terms of economics, if insurance has a "low price elasticity." It may seem fairly safe to assume that this actually is the case, if there is no evidence that lower premiums will lead to a significant increase in sales. One should, however, bear in mind that a reduction in the premium or an increase in the agent's commission, come to the same thing for the company, but that they may have very different effects on sales. If we ignore, or "assume away" $n(x)$ in our calculations, we may therefore lose something which is essential to the problem we set out to study.

3. Operational Research and the Theory of Risk

3.1.   If an insurance contract is offered to the public at a premium determined by the principle of equivalence, the *expected* profits on this transaction will be zero. The absence of profits is unpleasant in business, but this is not the point which we want to discuss here.

If an insurance company consistently makes losses on its operations, the company will sooner or later be unable to fulfill its part of the insurance contracts. This means of course that the "insurance" contracts do no longer serve the very purpose for which they were designed, i.e., to provide almost absolute security to the insured persons.

These considerations indicate that the premium must be set higher than dictated by the principle of equivalence. It is, however, an open question *how much higher* the premium should be, so that the simple problem discussed in para. 2.2 is still unsolved.

3.2.   The simple problem is rarely explicitly formulated in actuarial literature, and no general solutions have been suggested. It is, however, undeniable that the problem exists, and it has not been completely ignored. I think we can distinguish at least three different ways in which authors have tried to attack the problem:

(i) The problem can be dismissed as too simple. It is obvious that the problems we meet in practice are vastly more complicated, and "practical" men may well claim that they have to spend their time solving these more "serious" problems. It is most likely that they have to make their decisions without full knowledge of the true probability p and of the exact shape of the demand function $n(x)$, and that they claim that these decisions are rational or correct. However, if the simple problem is put aside for such reasons, the implications are that the problem becomes easier to solve if we bring in complications, and that ignorance can help us to make the right decisions.

(ii) One can add a *safety loading* to the premium determined by the principle of equivalence, so that expected profit becomes positive. This idea has probably originated in economic theory, where it is felt that expected profits should be greater the greater the "risks" are. However, economic theory has not so far, been very successful in defining the concept of "risk" and establish its relations to expected profits.

(iii) One can take the *probability of ruin* as a starting point. In our simple example this means that we consider the probability that the company will suffer a loss if the insurance contract is offered at a premium x. This approach is usually taken in actuarial literature; it is often referred to as the theory of risk. This theory is in many ways very attractive, but it has found few applications in practice. The reason—I believe—that the theory does not come to grips with the real problems as practicing actuaries see—or feel—them.

3.3.   We shall now try a different approach to the problem, and in doing so we shall ignore the cost elements. This involves no loss of generality, since these elements can be brought in explicitly at any stage in the argument.

If an insurance company has underwritten n contracts against a premium x, the outcome can be any result between the two extremes:

(i)   A loss of $n(1 - x)$, if all contracts lead to a claim.
(ii)   A profit of nx, if no claims are made.

In general the profit z (positive or negative) will have a probability distribution determined by

$$\Pr(z \leqslant nx - y) = \sum_{j \geqslant y} \binom{n}{j} p^{j}(1 - p)^{n-j}$$

where n depends on x.

3.4.   From these considerations we see that the decision to offer an insurance contract to the public at a premium x will give the company a profit which is a stochastic variable. The probability distribution of this variable will depend on x, the claim distribution, and the demand function. This means that the choice of a market premium x implies the choice of a *profit distribution.*

If we now assume that an insurance company has some rules which enable it to decide on the premium at which the contract should be offered, it must also have a rule which makes it possible to pick out the best or the *most preferred* among the obtainable profit distributions. This rule will represent the company's willingness to assume risk, or its *risk policy*, or to use still another term, the *objectives*, which the company wants to pursue.

3.5.   The choice of policy or objectives is by its very nature a subjective decision. It is not possible to state categorically that it is right or wrong if the company underwrites a given risk. It may, however, be possible to state whether a particular underwriting decision is consistent or not with the overall objectives of the company.

In order to formalize these ideas, we shall assume:

(i)   An insurance company has a *complete preference ordering* over the set of all profit distributions. This ordering will represent the company's policy, and in every situation the company will seek to make the decision which leads to the most preferred among the attainable profit distributions.

(ii) The company's preference ordering is *consistent*. This term obviously requires a precise definition, a point which we shall not take up here. The different possible definitions have been studied in detail by a number of authors, e.g., Savage [6], and the application to insurance has been discussed in another paper [2].

3.6. From these assumptions it follows trivially that it is possible to assign a real number or an index $U\{F\}$ to any profit distribution $F(z)$ so that

$$U\{F\} > U\{G\}$$

if and only if $F(z)$ is preferred to $G(z)$.

It follows further that there exists a real valued function $u(z)$ such that

$$U\{F\} = \int_{-\infty}^{+\infty} u(z)\, dF(z)$$

This result is far from trivial. It was first proved by von Neumann and Morgenstern [5] in 1947. Since then a number of other proofs have been published, for instance in the book by Savage [6] already referred to.

The implication of this result to our problem is that any consistent rule for determining the premium for an insurance contract can be represented by a function $u(z)$. This function is usually referred to as a *utility* function, because it can be interpreted as the utility assigned to an amount of money equal to z. The concept "utility of money" plays a central part in classical economic theory, and it is interesting to note that this concept also appears necessary for further development of the theory of insurance.

3.7. In order to illustrate the application of the ideas developed in the preceding paragraph, we shall study an example, slightly less trivial than the one introduced in para. 2.1. We shall find it convenient to make some changes of notation.

We shall consider an insurance company and assume:

(i)   The company's policy can be represented by a utility function $u(x)$.
(ii) The company's initial capital (or free reserves) is S.
(iii) The company considers offering the public an insurance contract with a claim distribution $F(x)$.

(iv) The premium for this contract is fixed as P, for instance by tariff agreement or government regulation.

(v) If the company spends an amount s on advertising and sales promotion, it will be able to sell $n = n(s)$ contracts.

The problem is then to determine the optimal amount s which should be spent on sales promotion.

By a straightforward application of the results in para. 3.6 we find that s should be determined, so that the following expression is maximized:

$$\int_0^\infty u(S + nP - s - x)\, dF^{(n)}(x)$$

where $F^{(n)}(x)$ is the nth convolution of $F(x)$ with itself.

This value of s will lead to the profit distribution which according to the company's policy is considered the best attainable.

3.8. In the example above we have *reformulated* our original problem so that our task finally was reduced to maximizing a mathematical expression. This approach to a problem is typical of *operational research*. This term is often used loosely about a group of more or less interrelated mathematical techniques. However, the essential idea, and the real art of operational research lies, not in solving a particular class of mathematical problems, but in formulating the problem so that these mathematical techniques can be applied.

3.9. If the formulation given in para. 3.7 comes to grips with the problem as practicing actuaries see it, they should be able to decide in general terms on the kind of mathematical techniques which are required to solve the problem. The choice of specific techniques can probably best be made in each particular case, depending on the nature of the three functions $u(x)$, $n(s)$, and $F(x)$.

Of these three functions, $F(x)$ is well known to any actuary, and $n(s)$ represents a concept which should be familiar to company actuaries who keep in contact their colleagues in the market research department. The utility function $u(x)$ may, however, seem strange and unfamiliar to many actuaries. The function represents the company's policy, and so far, little is known about the general shape of these utility functions. The main reason for this lack of knowledge is that few companies are very specific when they make public statements about their policy. This may mean that companies simply do not have a well-defined policy. It may, however, also mean that companies consider their policy a business secret. The companies may have good reasons for doing this. For instance, in negotiations over a reinsurance treaty, it must be important for a company to hide that its real policy is to obtain cover almost at any cost.

We shall not pursue this subject any further. The possible shape of the utility function is discussed in some detail in another paper [1], and the problem has recently been studied by Welten [7].

3.10. Our formulation does of course oversimplify the real problem, and this may mean that we have lost something which is essential—or to put it another way—that we have solved the wrong problem—a problem which cannot occur in practice.

The two most serious aspects of our simplifying assumptions appear to be:

(i)   We have studied an isolated decision to be taken once and for all. This means that we have ignored any implications the decision may have on the future of the company.

To meet objections on this point, we can formulate the problem in terms of a dynamic model. An attempt in this direction has been made in another paper [4].

(ii) We have assumed that the company was alone in the market, or that our company reached its decision without considering the decisions or actions which competing companies might take.

We shall discuss this point in the following chapter, and we shall see that this leads us toward an economic theory of insurance.

4.   Risk and Economic Theory

4.1.   In para. 3.7 we assumed that there existed a function $n(s)$ which determined the number of insurance contracts n which our company could sell if an amount s was spent on sales promotion. This function represented the market situation which confronted the company.

If more than one company operates in the market, the situation cannot be represented by a single function of one variable. If there are k companies, we may get an adequate description of the situation by specifying k functions

$$n_i(s_1, \ldots, s_k) \qquad i = 1, 2, \ldots, k$$

Here n_i is the number of contracts which company i will sell if the k companies spend the amounts $s_1, \ldots, s_i, \ldots, s_k$ to promote their sales.

4.2.   In this model the task of company i will still be to maximize a mathematical expression of the same form as the one we considered at the end of para. 3.7. However, this expression will now depend on the k variables $s_1, \ldots, s_k$, and company i controls only one of these. The remaining $k - 1$ variables are controlled by the other companies, and they will seek to use this control to pursue objectives which may be different, and even directly opposed to those of the company under consideration. This means that company i cannot select an optimal s_i without knowing or guessing the values which the other companies will select for $s_1, \ldots, s_{i-1}, s_{i+1}, \ldots, s_k$. These other companies, will, however, be in exactly the same kind of dilemma, so the whole situation becomes a *game* as to who can outguess whom.

4.3. It is obvious that the situation we have described is essentially different and more complicated than the situations which we analyzed in Section 3. It is also obvious that the companies in this situation cannot reduce their problems to the simple maximizing problem considered in para. 3.8. Such a reduction of the problem is the very essence of the approach which leads to operational research. If this reduction is impossible, we must look for a different approach.

4.4. The situation we have described is not very different from the classical model of a market where several sellers or producers compete for the favor of a large number of buyers or consumers. Classical economic theory has been able to analyze such markets in a rather satisfactory manner, and it is natural to try if this theory can provide an approach which leads to a solution to our problem.

This leads us to consider insurance cover as a commodity for which there is a *demand,* depending on the price. We must then assume that some persons or institutions are willing and able to *supply* this commodity, and that the amount they will supply depends on the price.

If the supply and demand functions meet certain conditions, there exists a unique price which will make total supply in the market equal to total demand.

This price is referred to as the *equilibrium price.*

4.5. The basic assumption of the classical market theory is that the traders behave in a passive manner, in the sense that they take the price as given and unchangeable, and decide how much they want to buy or sell at this price. If the traders make their decisions on the basis of a price different from the equilibrium price, supply and demand will be unequal, and this will generate forces which push the price toward the equilibrium price.

The crowning achievement of the classical theory was to prove that if all traders made their decisions on the basis of the equilibrium price, the market would reach a *Pareto optimal* state. This means roughly that the market is in a state where no trader can improve his situation, except at the expense of others. This means that the price mechanism establishes a rational arrangement in a market which initially seemed to be a chaos of conflicting interests. This again led classical economists to claim that free competition would lead to "the best of all possible worlds."

4.6. If we try to apply the ideas of classical economic theory to an insurance market, we will run into difficulties almost immediately. One of the first difficulties is that there is no natural unit of insurance cover, so that it seems impossible to define *price* in a meaningful way. There are other difficulties of an even more fundamental nature, but I shall not deal with them here, since they have been discussed in detail in another paper [3].

Even if many of the basic concepts of classical economic theory are meaningless or inapplicable in an insurance market, the most fundamental of them all, Pareto optimality, can be defined fairly easily. It is therefore natural to take this concept as our starting point. This leads us to the *theory of games* [5], which in this context must be seen as a far-reaching generalization of the more orthodox economic theories.

4.7. The basic assumption in the theory of *n*-person games is that rational players will somehow come to a Pareto optimal arrangement. This leads to another difficulty, since there usually will be an infinity of such arrangements.

To illustrate this, we can again consider the example of paras. 4.1 to 4.2. In this example there may well be a unique advertising expenditure which will be optimal for the *k* companies, seen as a group. There will, however, be infinitely many ways in which this expenditure and its fruits can be divided among the *k* companies.

To obtain a determinate solution to such problems, we must make *additional assumptions* about how the parties behave during negotiations or bargaining. In game theory such behavioral assumptions concern the ways in which the players form *coalitions* in order to cooperate during the negotiations towards a Pareto optimal arrangement.

Classical economic theory reached a determinate solution, i.e., a unique equilibrium price by making the "additional assumption" that traders passively adjusted to prices, as if they were given by some *deus ex machina*. This assumption may be realistic or not; the point in the present context is that it has no meaning when applied to an insurance market. We must find other assumptions of about the same strength if we want to treat insurance as an economic activity, and analyze it within the framework of a general economic theory.

5. Concluding Remarks

5.1. The point I have tried to make in this paper is that the ends should guide our choice of means. We should not adjust the ends in order to create new applications for means which happen to be fashionable.

A good actuary should of course explore new mathematical techniques and find out if they can be of help in his work. I do, however, not believe that this is the most pressing need, neither in the actuarial profession nor in the insurance industry.

5.2. In Section 3 I have tried to show that the methods of operational research can be successfully applied only in insurance companies which have a well-defined policy—or to put it tautologically—companies which can spell out their objectives in an operational manner.

In Section 4 I have indicated that there are situations in which the methods of operational research fall short. Mathematical methods which may prove useful in these situations, have been developed in game theory. The methods appear powerful, but we cannot hope to use them successfully unless we are quite clear about the objectives—the objectives of persons and companies, when they act individually, and when they act in groups where the members have partially conflicting interests.

5.3. The stress on objectives really means that we need more factual knowledge before we start experimenting with new mathematical techniques. We need to know more about man's need for security and willingness to take risks before we devise the insurance which will solve his problems.

It may be fitting to terminate this paper by quoting the conclusions Von Neumann and Morgenstern reached in their analysis of the application of mathematical methods in economic theory: "The underlying vagueness and ignorance has not been dispelled by the inadequate and inappropriate use of a powerful instrument that is very difficult to handle [5, pages 4-5]."

References

1. Borch, K. "Reciprocal Reinsurance Treaties," *The ASTIN Bulletin*, vol. 1, pp. 170-191.
2. ——. "The Utility Concept applied to the Theory of Insurance," *The ASTIN Bulletin*, vol. 1, pp. 245-255.
3. ——. "Equilibrium in a Reinsurance Market," *Econometrica*, vol. 30, pp. 424-444.
4. ——. "Payment of Dividend by Insurance Companies," *Transactions of the 17th International Congress of Actuaries*, vol. III, pp. 527-540.
5. Neumann, J. von and O. Morgenstern. *Theory of Games and Economic Behavior*, 2nd edition (Princeton, 1947).
6. Savage, L. J. *The Foundations of Statistics* (New York, 1954).
7. Welten, C. P. "Reinsurance Optimization by Means of Utility Functions," *Actuariële Studiën*, February 1964, pp. 166-175.

Part IV
The Dynamic Theory of Insurance

The models discussed in Parts I to III are all of static nature. It was usually assumed that the situation of an insurance company could be completely described by one single probability distribution $F(x - S)$, where x represents claim payments, and S reserves available for paying claims. The problem for the management of the company was to obtain a more advantageous distribution by different actions—usually by reinsurance arrangements.

In real life the distribution $F(x - S)$ will change, virtually every day, as claims are paid, old insurance contracts expire, and new contracts are under-written. The changes may not be substantial, but they undoubtedly occur, and this means that the company really should revise its reinsurance arrangements almost on a day to day basis. In practice this is neither possible nor desirable. It is, therefore, a clear need for a more general, dynamic theory, which can be applied in a changing world.

The pioneer in developing a dynamic theory of insurance was Filip Lundberg. The elements of his theory were first presented in his dissertation at the University of Uppsala in 1903. A more complete development of the theory was presented at the International Congress of Actuaries in Vienna in 1909. The main ideas of this theory can be summarized in the following three points:

(i) Each insurance contract defines a claim distribution. The claim distribution $F(x)$ of a portfolio of insurance contracts will be the convolution of the distributions defined by the contracts in the portfolio—provided that claims under different contracts are stochastically independent. In theory $F(x)$ can then be computed for any portfolio, but in practice a prohibitive amount of computation may be involved, even in a small insurance company. Lundberg suggested another decomposition of $F(x)$. He considered the two elements:

$Q(n, t)$ = the probability that n claims shall occur in a period of length t

$R(x)$ = the probability distribution of the size of an arbitrary single claim

The claim distribution of the portfolio, for a period of length t, will then be:

$$F(x, t) \sum_{n=0}^{\infty} Q(n, t)R^{(n)}(x)$$

Here $R^{(n)}(x)$ is the nth convolution of $R(x)$ with itself, and $R^{(0)}(x) = 1$. Under reasonable and fairly general assumptions the number of claims will follow the Poisson distribution, so that

219

$$Q(n, t) = e^{-mt} \frac{(mt)^n}{n!} \qquad n = 0, 1, 2, \ldots$$

By a suitable choice of units we can take $m = 1$, so that the claim distribution becomes

$$F(x, t) = e^{-t} \sum_{n=0}^{\infty} \frac{t^n}{n!} R^{(n)}(x)$$

This result of Lundberg's is of considerable importance. It brings time into the model, and it makes it practically possible to estimate the claim distribution from data which are easily available from the company's statistical records. In this estimation process it is not necessary to consider the claim distribution of individual insurance contracts. Lundberg's theory is, therefore, usually referred to as the *collective theory of risk.*

(ii) The reserves S in the static model has to be redefined in the dynamic model. It is natural to write $S(t)$, the reserves at time t in the following form:

$$S(t) = S(0) + P(t)$$

where $P(t)$, which may be a stochastic process, is the total amount of premium received by the company during the time interval $(0, t)$. Lundberg makes a transformation from chronological time to "operational time," or to "entropy time," so that $P(t) = (1 + \lambda)$, and

$$\int_0^{\infty} x \, dF(x, t) = t$$

The constant λ can then be interpreted as the "safety loading" of the insurance premiums. We can then write

$$S(t) = S(0) + (1 + \lambda)t = S + (1 + \lambda)t$$

and consider the distribution $F(x - S - (1 + \lambda)t)$. The introduction of operational time makes it possible to present the theory in a more elegant manner, but it also makes it more difficult to apply the theory in practice. In a dynamic economic theory one cannot ignore interest, and interest is computed according to real or "chronological" time, and not according to "operational" time.

(iii) Let accumulated claims during the period $(0, t)$ be x_t. The distribution of this stochastic variable is $F(x, t)$. If $x_t > S + (1 + \lambda)t$, the company will not be solvent at time t. Lundberg considered the probability

$$\psi(S, \lambda, T) = \text{Pr} \left\{ \min (S + (1 + \lambda)t - x_t \geqslant 0 \right\} t \, \epsilon \, T$$

where T is some set, such as an interval on the real line, or a discrete set of points on the line. If T is the whole positive half of the real line, the probability is usually written $\psi(S, \lambda)$, giving the probability that the company will remain solvent at any time in the future. The probability $\psi(S, \lambda)$, or $\psi(S, \lambda, T)$ gives a measure of the quality of the insurance company— or of the credibility of the contracts it has underwritten—provided that it continues its operations in the same manner in an infinite future. Usually the management of the company can take action to control the process, and this will make the probability $\psi(S, \lambda)$ irrelevant.

Lundberg's ideas had little impact during the first two decades after the presentation of his theory. His ideas did, however, gradually become known among Scandinavian actuaries, who during the years 1930 to 1950 took them up and developed them intensively. Today it is easy to see that this work in a sense led the theory into a "blind alley," because it converged on deriving approximate expressions for the irrelevant probability $\psi(S, \lambda)$. De Finetti brought the theory out of the blind alley with the paper he presented to the International Congress of Actuaries in 1957. He observed that the probability that the company would remain solvent forever, $\psi(S, \lambda)$, would be zero, unless the company allowed the reserve capital to grow without limit. It does not appear likely that insurance companies should operate in a manner which will allow unlimited accumulation of capital. In most countries the law or usual business practice will oblige an insurance company to pay dividends, to policyholders or shareholders as the case may be, when reserves exceed certain levels. Any policy of this kind does, however, imply that ruin is certain sometime in the future.

De Finetti suggested that one could consider, as an alternative to the probability of ruin, the "expected life" of the company, or the expected discounted value of the dividends which the company pays before the inevitable ruin. These suggestions have turned out to be extremely germane. They have given a new life to the stagnating actuarial risk theory, by opening the door for the application of modern control theory and adaptive programming to problems in insurance.

Chapter 15 is a shortened version of a paper presented at the International Congress of Actuaries in 1964. A faulty discussion of a special case, with a numerical example, has been omitted.

The paper develops the ideas of De Finetti, but by an oversight his paper from the Congress in 1957 is not mentioned. Instead, references are given to work by Shubik, Thompson, and Miyasawa, who have studied the same models, applied to more general economic problems, without specific reference to insurance.

Chapters 16 and 17 develop different aspects of the model and illustrate its features by detailed discussion of two numerical examples. In one of the examples the claim distribution is discrete, and in the other absolutely continuous. Chapter 18 gives a relatively broad survey of the development of the actuarial theory of risk. The paper was presented to the Royal Statistical Society in London in 1967. It was followed by a discussion which indicates that the prob-

lems in actuarial risk theory are very similar in their structure to problems en-
countered in different branches of social and natural sciences, and that most of
these problems can be analyzed and solved with the same mathematical tools.

A complete policy in a dynamic model will dictate the decision to be made
in every conceivable situation, which may occur in the future. If a decision
problem of this kind—in a particular situation—is considered in isolation, i.e., as
a static decision problem, it must be based on a utility function of the von
Neumann–Morgenstern type. In the static problems, discussed in the three first
chapters, it was in a sense assumed that the company's management would have
to seek their soul and determine the utility function which best represented their
attitude to risk. It appears that if management has a well-defined long-term
objective, such as to maximize the expected discounted value of the company's
payments, a static utility function can be derived from these objectives. This
question is discussed in Chapter 19.

In the theories of Lundberg and De Finetti it is assumed that the stream of
profitable business, which flows into the company, is independent of the company's reserves. This assumption may not be very realistic, but it has rarely been
questioned. The assumption implies that with positive reserves, no matter how
small, the company has the power to attract profitable business and is allowed to
operate. The company may then have a considerable value. If on the other hand
the reserves fall below zero by an infinitesimal amount, the company is not
allowed to operate, and its value will be zero. It does not seem reasonable that
such discontinuities should occur in economic life.

In Chapter 20 the problem is discussed, and the value of the "goodwill" of
an insurance company is determined. This may lead to a more realistic theory. It
does not happen very often that an insurance company goes bankrupt. If a
company with a faithful group of customers is in difficulties because its reserves
are too low, it will usually be taken over by, or merge with, another company.

The models discussed in this part can be given many different interpretations.
The most popular among these leads to the problem of determining the optimal
lifetime consumption-saving plan. The problem was formulated by Ramsey [5],
and has been generalized and studied in detail, i.a., by Hakansson [2], Phelps
[4], and Yaari [6].

In some respects the models become easier to handle if they are formulated
in terms of continuous time. With this formulation, a number of results from the
theory of diffusion can be applied. In my opinion, the problems of insurance can
most naturally be formulated in discrete time. Other authors, i.a., Gerber [1]
and [2] have, however, preferred to work with continuous time, and have presented results which it seems difficult to reach with discrete methods.

References

1. Gerber, H. "Entscheidungskriterien für den zusammensetzten Poisson-Prozess," *Mitteilungen der Vereinigung Schweizerischen Versicherungsmathematiker,* 1969, pp. 185–228.
2. Gerber, H. "Abschätzung der Ruinwahrscheinlichkeit mit den Methoden der Fluktuationstheorie für Zufallswege," *Skandinavisk Aktuarietidskrift,* 1969, pp. 171–173.
3. Hakansson, N. H. "Optimal Investment and Consumption Strategies under Risk, an Uncertain Lifetime, and Insurance," *International Economic Review,* 1969, pp. 443–466.
4. Phelps, E. "The Accumulation of Risky Capital," *Econometrica,* 1962, pp. 729–743.
5. Ramsey, F. P. "A Mathematical Theory of Saving," *The Economic Journal,* 1928, pp. 543–559.
6. Yaari, M. "Uncertain Lifetimes, Life Insurance, and the Theory of the Consumer," *Review of Economic Studies,* 1965, pp. 137–150.

15

Payment of Dividend by Insurance Companies

1. Introduction

1.1. An insurance contract gives the insured a right to claim certain amounts of money from the insurance company if some specified events should occur. If insurance is to serve its real purpose, the insured must be virtually certain that the company is able to meet its contractual obligations. This means that an insurance company must keep "special reserves" or "surplus funds" in addition to its technical reserve, which by definition is equal to the mathematical expectation of claim payments under the contracts in the company's portfolio.

An insurance company will usually acquire its surplus funds by adding a "safety loading" to the premiums, so that these funds can be expected to grow as time goes by. In practice, most insurance companies will pay out a dividend— to shareholders or policyholders as the case may be—when surplus funds in some sense become "larger than necessary." However, theory has so far not been able to lay down any really satisfactory rules as to how large these funds should be before the company can consider paying dividends. In this paper, we shall try to bridge the gap between present theory and current insurance practice.

1.2. We shall begin by considering the following situation:

At the end of an underwriting period an insurance company finds itself with a surplus S, and considers the possibility of paying out an amount s as dividend. The amount not distributed as dividend, $S - s$, will be kept by the company as a "special reserve" during the following underwriting period. The purpose of this reserve is to enable the company to meet contingencies in later periods, and to *safeguard future dividend payments.*

The problem is to determine s when S is given. This clearly means that the company must balance the desirability of paying a high dividend today against the desirability of being able to pay dividends in the future.

1.3. The problem we have outlined is obviously of central importance in insurance, but it has seldom been explicitly formulated and discussed in actuarial literature.

The usual approach in modern actuarial theory is to consider S as given at some point of time, for instance when the company enters into business, and

225

then calculate Lundberg's *probability of ruin*. If this probability turns out to be too high, either S must be increased, or the company has to make reinsurance arrangements so that the ruin probability is brought down to an acceptable level.

However, Lundberg's probability of ruin is calculated under the assumption that the surplus earned by the company is retained in the special reserve during *all* future periods. Only under this assumption will the probability of ruin be smaller than one. This means, of course, that the special reserve must be allowed to increase to infinity. Any dividend policy which keeps the special reserve finite makes it virtually certain that the company will be ruined some time in the future.

A theory of risk which cannot accommodate the fact that insurance companies sometimes pay dividends is obviously unrealistic. In the following we shall try to outline a more realistic theory. In doing so, we shall draw on mathematical techniques which have been developed fairly recently, and which so far do not seem to have been applied to problems in insurance.

2. A Simple Solution

2.1. In para. 1.2 we mentioned that the purpose of maintaining a "special reserve" is not just to avoid ruin, but also to safeguard future dividend payments. The latter purpose is clearly the more general, since dividend payments necessarily will stop if the company is ruined.

These considerations naturally lead us to make the tentative assumption that an insurance company seeks to maximize the expected value of dividend payments, discounted in a suitable manner. We shall formulate the problem as follows:

Let S be the surplus held by the company at the beginning of period 1, and let s_t be the dividend paid at the end of period t. The problem of the company is then to determine the sequence $s_0, s_1, \ldots, s_t, \ldots$ which maximizes

$$E\left[\sum_{t=0}^{\infty} v^t s t\right]$$

where v is a discount factor, which for the time being will be considered as constant over time.

2.2. The expected value of future dividend payments will clearly depend on the initial surplus S which the company holds at the beginning of period 1. We shall therefore write $V(S)$ for the expected discounted value of an *optimal* dividend sequence and define this function by

$$V(S) = \max E \left[\sum_{t=0}^{\infty} v^t st \right] \tag{1}$$

We shall assume that this function exists, and that it has the following properties:

(i) $V(S) = 0$ for $S < 0$, i.e., if there is no initial surplus, the company is not allowed to operate, and no dividends can ever be paid.
(ii) $V(S)$ is continuous everywhere, except possibly for $S = 0$.

2.3.   We now consider an insurance company which in each period holds a portfolio of insurance contracts with claim distribution $F(x)$, i.e., $F(x)$ is the probability that the total amount of claims in a period shall not exceed x.
    We shall assume that $F(x) = 0$ for $x < 0$, and that the derivative $f(x) = F'(x)$ exists, and is continuous for all nonnegative x.
    The net premium of this portfolio is by definition

$$P_1 = \int_0^{\infty} xf(x)\, dx$$

We shall assume that the gross premium collected by the company is

$$P = P_1 + P_2$$

where P_2 is a positive safety loading.

2.4.   We now assume that our company at the end of an arbitrary period has a surplus S. If the company pays out a dividend s, and then again underwrites the portfolio just described, its funds at the end of the following period will be

$$S - s + P - x$$

For an arbitrary value of s, we must have

$$V(S) \geqslant s + v \int_0^{\infty} V(S - s + P - x)f(x)\, dx$$

$V(S)$ is by definition the discounted expected value of an *optimal* sequence of dividend payments. The inequality merely states that an arbitrary payment s cannot increase $V(S)$. If, however, s is an optimal payment, the sign of equality must hold. Hence the function $V(S)$, if it exists, must satisfy the equation

$$V(S) = \max_{0 \leqslant s \leqslant S} \left[s + v \int_0^{\infty} V(S - s + P - x)f(x)\, dx \right] \tag{2}$$

2.5. We now consider the function

$$w(s) = s + v \int_0^\infty V(S - s + P - x)f(x)\, dx \qquad (3)$$

which we shall write in the following form

$$w(s) = s + U(S - s + P)$$

Differentiating this function, we obtain

$$w'(s) = 1 - U'(S - s + P)$$

If $w(s)$ has a maximum for a value s' in the interval $0 < s' < S$, s' must be a root of the equation

$$U'(S - s + P) = 1 \qquad (4)$$

Hence, if s' is an optimal dividend payment when the surplus is S, $s' + \sigma$ will be an optimal payment when surplus is equal to $S + \sigma$.

It then follows that if $w(s)$ has a maximum in the interval $(0, S)$ the optimal dividend payment is determined by an equation of the form

$$s = S - Z \qquad \text{if } S > Z \qquad (5)$$

$$s = 0 \qquad \text{if } S \leqslant Z$$

This means that the company will let surplus accumulate up to a limit Z, and distribute as dividend any surplus in excess of Z.

3. Discussion of the Simple Solution

3.1. The problem which we have discussed has been studied in several different contexts during the last few years. This is really what we should expect, since the mathematical model we arrived at can be given a number of different interpretations. The model can for instance be applied to inventory situations in which the firm will have to go out of business if demand in any period should exceed stocks.

The model can be interpreted more generally as a "survival game" played against "nature" or against a player using a random strategy.

The methods which were used in solving the problem are not entirely new. It is, however, only recently that these methods have been systematically studied, and brought together in a fairly self-contained theory. The main contributions are due to Bellman [1], who has introduced the term *dynamic programming* for this class of methods.

3.2.   Shubik and Thompson [8] have studied a special case of our problem. In their model the random variable x can take only the values -1 and +1, with probabilities p and $1 - p$, respectively. For this case they find a simple and elegant solution.

The results of Shubik and Thompson have been generalized by Miyasawa [6], who studied the case where $F(x)$ is an arbitrary discrete probability distribution. Miyasawa's general solution is extremely complex. This seems to be unavoidable, since the simple solution [5] which we found for the continuous case is next to meaningless for discrete probability distributions. However, it may be premature to conclude that the continuous case is essentially simpler, since we have not carried out a full discussion of our solution. It is clear that [4] for some probability distributions may have multiple solutions, and that this will lead to a number of difficulties.

3.3.   The discount factor v which was introduced in para. 2.1 has nothing to do with interest rate which the company may earn on its funds. Interest is in fact completely irrelevant in our model. When an amount s has been declared as a dividend, it becomes the absolute property of the shareholders (or policyholders) and cannot be used to pay future claims against the company. It is this removal of the uncertainty which matters, not whether s is actually paid out or continues to be administered by the company.

v represents a *preference system* for the timing of dividend declarations. The assumption that $v < 1$ means that an early declaration is preferred to a later one, or more loosely that it is considered desirable to remove as much uncertainty as early as possible. The preference may of course be reversed if the later payments are considerably greater than the earlier ones.

The preference for earlier payments implies that an *impatience element* (Minderschätzung) must exist in the economy. This suggestion was first made by Böhm-Bawerk [2], and it seems to have been accepted by most writers on economic theory. There has, however, been a considerable controversy over both the implications of the impatience assumption, and the mathematical formulation of this assumption. A penetrating and essentially nonmethematical study of the problem made by Morgenstern [7] in 1934 sums up the classical position, and exposes it to a severe criticism.

3.4.   The most systematic mathematical discussion of the problem appears to be a recent study by Koopmans [5].

Koopmans defines a utility function $u(s_1, s_2, \ldots, s_t, \ldots)$ over an infinite sequence of payments. From some innocent-looking assumptions about this function he proves that we must have

$$u(s_1, \ldots, s_t + \sigma, \ldots, s_{t+i}, \ldots) > u(s_1, \ldots, s_t, \ldots, s_{t+i} + \sigma, \ldots)$$

for any positive i and σ. This means that the existence of an impatience element can be derived as a mathematical consequence of some more basic assumptions about timing preferences.

3.5. The most critical of Koopmans' assumptions appears to be his Postulate 3, which in our terms can be stated as follows:

For any positive σ and for any payment sequence $s_1, \ldots, s_2, \ldots, s_t, \ldots,$ the following inequality must hold

$$u(s_1 + \sigma, s_2, \ldots, s_t, \ldots) > u(s_1, s_2, \ldots, s_t, \ldots)$$

It is reasonable to assume that an insurance company will prefer the dividend sequence $(2, 2, 2, 2, \ldots)$ to $(1, 2, 2, 2, \ldots)$. If, however, the company considers a reduction in dividend as a minor catastrophe, the sequence $(2, 1, 2, 2, \ldots)$ may not be preferred to $(1, 1, 2, 2, \ldots)$. It is, of course, possible to find reasons for dismissing such preferences as "irrational," but there will still be some doubt about the general validity of the postulate. If the postulate is strengthened, so that we require the inequality

$$u(s_1 + \sigma_1, s_2 + \sigma_2, s_3, \ldots, s_t, \ldots) > u(s_1, s_2, \ldots, s_3, \ldots, s_t, \ldots)$$

to hold for any payment sequence, and for any positive σ_1 and σ_2, it follows from a result by Debreu [4] that the utility function must be of the form

$$u(s_1, \ldots, s_t, \ldots) = \sum_{t=1}^{\infty} v^{t-1} u(s_t)$$

This is a very strong result, which we shall study in more detail in para. 4.2.

3.6. In most economic situations it is natural, or even necessary, to assume that an element of impatience exists. This does not seem to be the case in the situation which we have studied. We will not run into any difficulties by assuming that insurance companies are "patient," i.e., that $v > 1$. This will mean that immediate dividend payments are given little importance in relation to the probability of staying in business and being able to pay dividends in the future. For large v we would expect the company to approach the behavior assumed in Lundberg's theory, i.e., to retain all underwriting profits in order to increase the probability of survival. This does not, however, appear directly as a limiting case in our model. Our results are valid only if the function $w(s)$ introduced in para. 2.5 has a maximum in the interval $0 < s < S$.

4. Generalization of the Model

4.1. Our simple solution implied that no dividend should be distributed if the surplus of the company was less than an amount Z determined by (4). If the surplus becomes greater than Z, the whole excess should immediately be paid out as dividend.

It is obvious that this dividend policy may lead to considerable fluctuations in payments from one period to another. Such fluctuations are considered as undesirable by most insurance companies. In practice, these fluctuations can be reduced by transferring the excess $S - Z$ to a special *dividend reserve,* and make payments from this reserve at the steady or steadily increasing rate which most companies seem to prefer.

However, a sophisticated company may consider fluctuations even in the transfers to the dividend reserve as undesirable. It is therefore worth while seeking to generalize the model so that it explicitly takes into account this preference for stable payments.

4.2. From the result of Debreu [4] referred to in paragraph 3.5 it follows that it will be difficult, if not impossible, to generalize the model by assuming that the discount rate v varies over time. It is, however, possible to introduce a utility function $u(x)$, and define $V(S)$ by

$$V(S) = \max \left[u(s) + v \int_0^\infty V(S - s + P - x) f(x)\, dx \right] \tag{6}$$

which is a generalization of (2).

If $u(s)$ increases more slowly than s, the company will attach a lower utility to an immediate dividend increase than to a maintained rate in the future. Generally speaking this means that the current dividend rate will not be increased before it is reasonably certain that the higher rate can be maintained in the future.

As in para. 2.5 we can write

$$w(s) = u(s) + U(S - s + P)$$

Differentiating, we obtain the condition

$$u'(s) - U'(S - s + P) = 0$$

which determines the optimal dividend $s = s(S)$ when the special reserve amounts to S. Differentiating again, with respect to S, we obtain

$$u''(s) \frac{ds}{dS} - \left(1 - \frac{ds}{dS}\right) U''(S - s + P) = 0$$

or $\dfrac{ds}{dS} = 1 - \dfrac{u''}{u'' + U''}$

$u''(s)$ will usually be negative (decreasing marginal utility of money), and the same will hold for U'' provided that the probability distribution is of the kind one usually finds in insurance problems. Hence we will under very general conditions have

$$\frac{ds}{dS} < 1$$

This means that if S increases in a successful underwriting period, only a part of the increase will be paid out as dividend immediately, the remainder being kept in the special reserve to safeguard future dividend payments. It therefore seems that the model (6) gives a more realistic representation of company objectives than the simple model studied in Section 2.

4.3. In our model we assumed that claims in any given period were independent of the amount of claims paid in preceding periods. This assumption has been made in practically all previous studies in the theory of risk.

In our model it is fairly easy to relax the independence assumption. If $f(x_2|x_1)$ is the frequency function of claims in period 2, if claims in period 1 amounted to x_1, we can define

$$V(S) = \max_{s_1, s_2} \; [s_1 + v \int_0^\infty (s_2 + v \int_0^\infty V(S - s_1 - s_2 - x_1 - x_2) f(x_2|x_1) \, dx_2) f(x_1) \, dx_1]$$

and determine the dividend payments s_1 and s_2 which satisfy the equation.

We shall not at present discuss this general problem. It is not clear what kind of interperiod dependence one should look for in insurance, and it is doubtful if the problem can be discussed in a rational manner, unless we make specific assumptions about how the premium P is adjusted to changes in the probability distribution.

4.4. In our model we have not considered reinsurance. It would obviously be desirable to take this point into consideration, and assume that at the end of each period the company has to make two decisions:

(i)   How much of the surplus from the last period should be paid out as dividend

(ii) How should the portfolio underwritten in the next period be reinsured

If we assume that all kinds of reinsurance cover have their prices in the market, it is possible to give a formal solution to this problem. However, the market price must be determined by demand and supply of reinsurance cover, and it has been proved in a previous paper [3] that stable prices cannot exist in a reinsurance market. Hence the direct approach to the problem will not lead to a realistic solution.

The problem can be analyzed in terms of the general theory of n-person games, but we shall not discuss this possibility in the present paper.

5. Conclusions

5.1. It is generally recognized that subjective elements must play an important part in any theory of risk. There can be no universal or objectively "correct" answer to questions as to what reserve funds an insurance company should keep, or what reinsurance arrangements it should seek. It is, however, possible to find solutions which are optimal when the subjective elements are given, and spelled out in an unambiguous manner. This latter problem is not always easy. The subjective elements are usually referred to in a vague manner as "attitude to risk," "degree of prudence," etc., and cannot easily be expressed in an operational form.

5.2. In the preceding paragraphs we have shown that the attitude to risk can be completely determined by the two elements

(i)   The discount factor v which is to be applied to future dividend payments
(ii) The utility function $u(s)$

It is, however, possible to use other elements, which may look different, but which must be mathematically equivalent to the two considered in this paper.

An insurance company can for instance apply the rule of thumb that it will keep a special reserve so that the probability of ruin in the next period is just equal to a certain number π. This company will have a well defined attitude to risk, or a "risk policy," defined by a single number π. However, it is clear that this risk policy can also be defined by a linear utility function $u(s) = s$, and a discount rate v.

5.3. More generally we can assume that an insurance company divides profits earned between dividends and special reserves so that a generalized utility function $U(s, \pi)$ is maximized. This function will define the company's risk policy, but this policy can also be determined by a pair $(v, u(s))$.

In general a consistent risk policy can be defined in many different ways, so that the policy makers of an insurance company have a considerable choice of expressions when they want to spell out the objectives of the company. It appears, however, that definition by means of a discount factor v and a utility function $u(s)$ is the most convenient form when it comes to determining the actions which are optimal under the given objectives.

References

1.   Bellman, R. *Dynamic Programming* (Princeton 1957).
2.   Böhm-Bawerk, E. von. *Positive Theorie des Kapitals* (Vienna, 1889).
3.   Borch, K. "Equilibrium in a Reinsurance Market," *Econometrica, 1962,* pp. 424–444.
4.   Debreu, G. "Topological Methods in Cardinal Utility Theory," *Mathematical Methods in the Social Sciences* (Stanford, 1960), pp. 16–26.
5.   Koopmans, T. C. "Stationary Ordinal Utility and Impatience," *Econometrica,* 1960, pp. 287–309.
6.   Miyasawa, K. "An Economic Survival Game," *Journal of the Operations Research Society of Japan,* April 1962.
7.   Morgenstern, O. "Das Zeitmoment in der Wertlehre," *Zeitschrift für Nationalökonomie,* 1934, pp. 433–458.
8.   Shubik, M. and Thompson, G. L. "Games of Economic Survival," *Naval Research Logistics Quarterly,* 1959, pp. 111–124.

16

Control of a Portfolio of Insurance Contracts

1. Introduction

1.1. In this paper we shall consider a *given* portfolio of insurance contracts, and we shall study the following two problems:

(i)   How should this portfolio be reinsured?
(ii) What reserves should the company maintain to pay claims which will be made under the contracts in the portfolio?

This means that we shall ignore all questions as to how the company acquired the portfolio, i.e., some of the most important questions concerning management control of insurance companies, such as rating policy, underwriting control, etc.

1.2. Even the two simple problems, which are singled out for study in this paper, cannot be solved unless we specify the objectives and the external circumstances of the company.

It is obvious that the reinsurance problem cannot be solved unless we know something about the company's "attitude to risk," and about the cost of obtaining cover for various kinds of risk in the reinsurance market.

It is also obvious that we cannot solve the reserve problem unless we specify the safety requirements, which the company has to satisfy. We shall see in the following that we may also have to specify the portfolios, which the company expects to underwrite in the future.

2. The Basic Model

2.1. We shall now consider an insurance company, which has underwritten a portfolio of short-term insurance contracts. We shall assume:

(i) $F(x)$ = probability that claim payments under these contracts shall not exceed x
(ii) P = amount of premiums, which the company collected by underwriting the portfolio
(iii) S = initial capital of the company

235

When all contracts in the portfolio have expired, the company will hold a capital

$$y = S + P - x$$

It is clear that y is a stochastic variable with the distribution

$$G_0(y) = F(S + P - y) \qquad y \leqslant S + P$$

It is convenient to refer to $G_0(y)$ as the *profit distribution* associated with the portfolio.

2.2. By reinsurance arrangements it may be possible for the company to change the profit distribution.

Let us assume that the company by suitable reinsurance arrangements can obtain any of the profit distributions $G_1(y), \ldots, G_n(y), \ldots$. The problem is then to determine the "best" among these attainable distributions. In order to solve this problem, we must know the company's *preference ordering* over the set of attainable profit distributions. Such preference orderings have been discussed in other papers [2] and [3] . It has been shown that if the ordering is consistent, there exists a function $u(x)$ which represents the ordering in the sense that

$$\int_{-\infty}^{+\infty} u(y)\, dG_i(y) > \int_{-\infty}^{+\infty} u(y)\, dG_j(y)$$

if and only if the profit distribution $G_i(y)$ is preferred to $G_j(y)$.

This result, due to von Neumann and Morgenstern [5], gives us an attractive operational formulation of the reinsurance problem. However, this formulation is useful only if we know something about the shape of the *utility* function $u(x)$, which represents the preference ordering. We shall see in the following that we can obtain some information about this function by placing our, essentially static, problem in its natural dynamic setting.

2.3. In our model there is a probability

$$1 - F(S + P)$$

that the company shall be unable to pay the claims, which are made under the contracts in the portfolio.

Let us now assume that somebody—the company's management or the government inspector—decides that the company cannot operate unless this probability is smaller than α.

This means that if the requirement is not satisfied, i.e., if

$$1 - F(S + P) > \alpha$$

the company must either obtain additional capital, or seek a reinsurance arrangement, so that the condition is met.

If, on the other hand,

$$1 - F(S + P) \leqslant \alpha$$

there is no obvious reason why the company should risk all its capital in the insurance business. It is natural to assume that the company in this case will pay a dividend s, determined by the equation

$$1 - F(S + P - s) = \alpha$$

This gives us a solution to the reserve problem, provided that α is given, for instance by regulations imposed by the government. If there are no such regulations, the company can pay out all its assets as dividend, and calmly face certain ruin. However, experience tells us that insurance companies do not behave in this way. All available evidence indicates that they want to *survive* and stay in business. This observation naturally leads us to consider dynamic models.

2.4.   Let us now assume that our company in each successive period receives a premium P by underwriting a portfolio with a claim distribution $F(x)$. Further let S be the initial capital of the company.

We shall then tentatively assume that the company considers Z as a sufficient reserve for the portfolio in question, i.e., whenever its capital exceeds Z, the excess will be paid out as dividend. This means of course that the acceptable ruin probability is $\alpha = 1 - F(Z + P)$.

Let now s_t be the dividend paid after the tth underwriting period, and consider the expected discounted value of the sequence of dividend payments:

$$V(S, Z) = E\left\{ \sum_{i=0}^{\infty} v^t s_t \right\}$$

It is easy to see that $V(S, Z)$ must satisfy the integral equation

$$V(S, Z) = v \int_0^{s+P} V(S + P - x, Z)\, dF(x)$$

for $0 \leqslant S \leqslant Z$.

By definition we have

$$V(S, Z) = S - Z + V(Z, Z) \qquad \text{for } S > Z$$

If we assume that the company has to go out of business if it loses all its capital, we have

$$V(S, Z) = 0 \quad \text{for } S < 0$$

2.5. It is possible to solve the integral equation in the preceding paragraph by classical means. The solution will, however, be exceedingly complex, and we shall not attempt to discuss the problem in its full generality.

It is not surprising that our model leads to rather formidable mathematical problems, since it is direct generalization of the collective risk theory. In fact, our model reduces to that of Lundberg if we let Z go to infinity, i.e., if we assume that the company never considers any dividend payment.

2.6. To get some idea about the nature of the solution, we shall consider the special case

$$F(x) = 1 - e^{-x}$$

The integral equation can then be written

$$V(S, Z) = ve^{-S-P} \int_0^{S+P} V(x, Z)e^x \, dx \quad S < Z$$

or by omitting Z for simplicity

$$V(S) = ve^{-S-P} \int_0^{S+P} V(x)e^x \, dx$$

Differentiation with respect to S gives

$$V'(S) = vV(S + P) - ve^{-S-P} \int_0^{S+P} V(x)e^x \, dx$$

Adding this to the original equation, we obtain the differential-difference equation

$$V'(S) + V(S) - vV(S + P) = 0$$

It is easy to see that this equation has a solution of the form

$$V(S) = e^{\alpha S}$$

where α satisfies the characteristic equation

$$\alpha + 1 - ve^{\alpha P} = 0$$

This equation has infinitely many roots, which all are simple. This means that the general solution of our differential-difference equation is of the form

$$V(S) = \sum_r c_r e^{\alpha_r S}$$

where the sum is taken over all roots of the characteristic equation. c_r are constants, which must be determined so that the "boundary conditions"

$$V(S, Z) = S - Z + V(Z, Z) \qquad S > 0$$

$$V(S, Z) = 0 \qquad\qquad\qquad S < 0$$

are satisfied.

We shall not pursue this subject any further, since it has been discussed in considerable detail in the literature, e.g., in a recent book by Bellman and Cooke [1]. Instead we shall study an even simpler example.

3. The Simplest Possible Case

3.1. We shall now consider an insurance company which in each operating period receives a premium of 1 by underwriting a portfolio of insurance contracts, which can lead to the claim payments.

Either 0 with probability p
or   2 with probability $q = 1 - p$

This means that the company in each period engages in a gamble, which can lead to either a loss or a gain of one unit. We shall assume that $p > q$, i.e., that the gambles are favorable to the company.

We shall further assume that the company has an initial capital S, and that the game will terminate if the capital becomes negative, i.e., that the company will have to go out of business if it becomes insolvent.

If the sole objective of the company is to stay in business as long as possible, it is obvious that the company will never pay any dividend.

In order to obtain a nontrivial model, we shall assume that the company wants to pay dividends, and that its overall objective is to maximize the expected discounted value of the dividends, which will be paid during the company's lifetime.

3.2. The model which we have outlined was first studied by Shubik and Thompson [6], and it has been discussed in some detail in another paper [4].

Shubik and Thompson proved that the optimal dividend policy is to let the capital increase up to an amount Z, and then pay out any excess as dividend immediately.

Let now $w_n(S, Z)$ be the probability that the first dividend shall be paid after n periods, provided that:

S = the initial capital of the company

Z = the capital which the company decides to accumulate before any
      dividend is paid

At this stage of our analysis there is no loss of generality if we assume that S and Z are integers.

It is easy to see that this probability must satisfy the recurrence relation

$$w_{n+1}(S, Z) = pw_n(S + 1, Z) + qw_n(S - 1, Z)$$

subject to the boundary conditions

$$w_0(S, Z) = 0 \quad \text{for } S \leqslant Z$$
$$w_0(S, Z) = 1 \quad \text{for } S > Z$$
$$w_n(S, Z) = 0 \quad \text{for } S > Z \text{ and } n > 0$$
$$w_n(S, Z) = 0 \quad \text{for } S < 0$$

3.3. Let us now introduce the generating function

$$W(S, Z) = \sum_{n=0}^{\infty} v^n w_n(S, Z)$$

It is easy to see that this function must satisfy the difference equation

$$W(S, Z) = pvW(S + 1, Z) + qvW(S - 1, Z)$$

The boundary conditions are easily established. Taking these into account, we find that the difference equation has the solution

$$W(S, Z) = \frac{r_1^{s+1} - r_2^{s+1}}{r_1^{Z+2} - r_2^{Z+2}}$$

where r_1 and r_2 are the roots of the characteristic equation

$$r = pvr^2 + qv$$

If the variable v is interpreted as a discount factor, $W(S, Z)$ will be the expected discounted value of the first unit paid as dividend.

3.4. Let now, as in para. 2.4, $V(S, Z)$ stand for the expected discounted value of the dividends which our company will pay during its lifetime.

Since we have assumed that S and Z are integers, the first dividend will be 1, and it will be paid when the company's capital reaches $Z + 1$. When this dividend has been paid, the company will enter the next operating period with a capital Z.

From these considerations it follows that for $0 \leqslant S \leqslant Z$,

$$V(S, Z) = \left\{ 1 + V(Z, Z) \right\} W(S, Z)$$

By putting $S = Z$, we obtain

$$V(Z, Z) = \frac{W(Z, Z)}{1 - W(Z, Z)}$$

and $$V(S, Z) = \frac{W(S, Z)}{1 - W(Z, Z)}$$

or $$V(S, Z) = \frac{r_1^{S+1} - r_2^{S+1}}{(r_1^{Z+2} - r_2^{Z+2}) - (r_1^{Z+1} - r_2^{Z+1})}$$

It is easy to see that there is a unique value of Z, independent of S, which will maximize $V(S, Z)$. However, some caution is required, since we so far have assumed that S and Z both are integers.

For $S > Z$ we have by our definition of the dividend policy

$$V(S, Z) = S - Z + V(Z, Z)$$

and for $S < 0$ we have obviously

$$V(S, Z) = 0$$

3.5. It may be useful to illustrate these results by a simple numerical example. For this purpose we shall take $r_1 = 1.1$ and $r_2 = 0.7$. These values correspond approximately to

$$p = 0.565, \quad q = 0.435 \quad v = 0.983$$

Table 16-1 gives the value of $V(S, Z)$ for some selected values of S and Z.

We see that in this example the optimal dividend policy is given by $Z = 5$, at least as long as we only admit integral values of Z. To complete our analysis we

Table 16-1
$V(S, Z)$ = Expected discounted value of dividend payments
Z = Capital required before dividends can be paid

S = Initial Capital	0	1	2	3	4	5	6
0	1.25	1.49	1.70	1.83	1.89	1.89	1.82
1	2.25	2.69	3.05	3.30	3.40	3.40	3.27
2	3.25	3.69	4.19	4.52	4.67	4.67	4.49
3	4.25	4.69	5.19	5.56	5.79	5.79	5.56
4	5.25	5.69	6.19	6.56	6.81	6.82	6.55
5	6.25	6.69	7.19	7.56	7.81	7.83	7.50

should of course investigate the meaning of nonintegral values of Z. We shall, however, ignore this problem since it is not very relevant to the main purpose of the present paper.

3.6. We have so far indicated how the reserve problem can be solved for a given portfolio. In order to do this, we had to make assumptions about the portfolios, which the company expects to underwrite in the future—i.e., to examine the static problem in a dynamic setting.

In order to attack the reinsurance problem, let us first assume that our insurance company has adopted an optimal dividend policy, corresponding to a certain integral number Z.

If the company at the beginning of a period holds a capital $S < Z$, the expected discounted value of its future dividend payments is given by

$$V(S, Z) = K \left\{ r_1^{S+1} - r_2^{S+1} \right\}$$

where K is independent of S.

Let us further assume that at this point the company is offered an insurance contract of the type

Gain R_1 with probability α
Loss R_2 with probability $1 - \alpha$

We can think of this as an invitation to provide short-term reinsurance cover for another company.

If our company accepts the offer, the expected value of its future dividend payments will become

$$\alpha V(S + R_1, Z) + (1 - \alpha) V(S - R_2, Z)$$

If the company maintains the overall objective of maximizing the expected discounted value of the dividends which will be paid during its whole lifetime, it will accept the offer if and only if

$$\alpha\, V(S + R_1, Z) + (1 - \alpha)\, V(S - R_2, Z) > V(S, Z)$$

This means, however, that the company will make its decision as if it wanted to maximize expected utility, with $V(S, Z)$ serving as the utility function.

In some earlier papers [2, 3] it has been pointed out that a rational theory of reinsurance must be based on a utility concept. This is, however, not a very useful result, unless we know something about the shape of the utility function, which the company seeks to maximize. The considerations above show that this function can be taken as determined by the long-term objectives of the company —at least when the company acts as reinsurer.

3.3.   Before we analyze the company's own reinsurance arrangements, we should note that the expression which we found for $V(S, Z)$ in para. 3.4 is valid only for integral values of S and Z. If we want to interpret $V(S, Z)$ as a utility function, it is necessary to define it also for nonintegral values of S.

If S and Z are integers, we have:

(i)   The first dividend cannot be paid earlier than after $Z - S + 1$ periods, and this dividend will necessarily be equal to 1.

(ii) The company can be forced out of business at the earliest after $S + 1$ periods.

Let now $[S]$ be the largest integer not exceeding S. If S is not an integer, we have, assuming that Z is an integer

(i)   The first dividend will be equal to $S - [S]$, and it can be paid at the earliest after $Z - [S]$ periods.

(ii) Ruin can at the earliest occur after $[S] + 1$ periods.

With these observations we can just repeat the argument used in paras. 3.3 and 3.4.

When S is not an integer, we have to substitute $[S]$ and $Z - 1$ for S and Z; hence the generating function will be

$$W(S, Z) = W([S], Z - 1)$$

and we have, since the first dividend will be $S - [S]$:

$$V(S, Z) = \left\{ S - [S] + V(Z, Z) \right\} W([S], Z - 1)$$

THE DYNAMIC THEORY OF INSURANCE

This expression can be written

$$V(S, Z) = \{S - [S]\} \frac{r_1^{[S+1]} - r_2^{[S+1]}}{r_1^{Z+1} - r_2^{Z+1}} + V([S], Z)$$

From this we see that the function $V(S, Z)$ has jumps for integral values of S. Between the jumps $V(S, Z)$ will increase linearly with S.

Table 16–2 below gives the value of $V(S, 5)$ for some selected values of S for the numerical example introduced in para. 3.5.

3.8. It is obvious that our insurance company—acting as reinsurer—can make some decisions, which will seem very peculiar to an outside observer. Let us as an illustration assume that the company's capital is $S = 1.75$. If the company has adopted the optimal dividend policy, defined by $Z = 5$, the expected discounted value of future dividend payments will be

$$V(1.75, 5) = 3.73$$

Let us now assume that the company is offered a premium of 0.5 if it will cover a risk with the claim distribution

0 with probability 0.33
1 with probability 0.67

Any actuary worthy of the name will advise against accepting this offer. If, however, the company accepts the offer in spite of actuarial orthodoxy, the expected discounted value of the future dividend payments will increase to

$$0.33 V(2.25, 5) + 0.67 V(1.25, 5) = 3.94$$

Hence it is to the advantage of the company to accept this offer, even if it is grossly unfair.

Table 16–2
$V(S, 5)$ = Expected discounted value of dividend payments for an optimal dividend policy

S	$V(S, 5)$	S	$V(S, 5)$
0	1.89	1.75	3.73
0.25	1.95	2.00	4.67
0.50	2.01	2.25	4.82
0.75	2.07	2.50	4.97
1.00	3.40	2.75	5.12
1.25	3.51	3.00	5.79
1.50	3.62	3.25	5.97

If we want to justify this paradox, we would have to argue that the company is uncomfortably close to ruin. Hence it appears worth while to take a chance—against unfavorable odds—to get out of the danger zone. It may, however, not be easy to sell this argument to the general manager of the company.

3.9.   To illustrate the effect of reinsurance, let us assume that the company reinsures a quota share $1 - k$ of its portfolio on "original terms," i.e., the company retains a quota k. We shall assume that this arrangement is made for one underwriting period only, i.e., we exclude any long-term reinsurance treaties. Let $V(S, Z, k)$ be the expected discounted value of future dividend payments under this short-term reinsurance arrangement. Our problem is then to determine

$$\max_{0<k<1} (V(S, Z, k))$$

It is easy to see that we have

$$V(S, Z, k) = vp V(S + k, Z) + vq V(S - k, Z)$$

and for the two extremes:

$$V(S, Z, 1) = V(S, Z)$$

$$V(S, Z, 0) = v V(S, Z)$$

Since $V(S, Z)$ is piecewise linear, the maximum must occur, either for $k = 1$, or at one of the jumps.

From this it follows that the optimal retention is:

$$k = 1 \qquad \text{for } S - [S] \leqslant \tfrac{1}{2}$$
$$k = S - [S] \qquad \text{for } S - [S] > \tfrac{1}{2}$$

Intuitively this means that the company should reinsure to avoid the possibility of a downward jump in $V(S, Z)$, if this can be done without losing a possibility of an upward jump. This kind of solution is sometimes referred to as "bang-bang control."

4.   Concluding Remarks

4.1.   In the preceding paragraphs we have tried to formulate the control problems of insurance companies in an operational manner, and we have indicated how these problems can be solved. It appears that this formulation of the problems leads to a generalization of the collective risk theory, created by F. Lundberg. It also appears that fairly advanced mathematical tools will be required to analyze these problems in full generality. The author expects to discuss this subject in more detail in a later paper.

4.2. Some of the results indicated in this preliminary paper, may appear paradoxical. It is worth noting that this is not due to the extreme simplicity of the model which we have studied. The paradoxes are caused by the discontinuities of the function $V(S, Z)$, and such discontinuities will occur also in more general models. The basic integral equation in para. 2.4 may in general only have a piecewise continuous solution for $S < Z - P$. From this it follows that an insurance company occasionally should accept an actuarially unfair contract—if the company seeks to maximize the expected, discounted value of its dividend payments.

References

1. Bellman, R. and Cooke, K. L. *Differential-Difference Equations*, (Academic Press, 1963).
2. Borch, K.: "The Utility Concept Applied to the Theory of Insurance," *The ASTIN Bulletin*, Vol. 1, pp. 245–255.
3. Borch, K.: "The Objectives of an Insurance Company," *Skandinavisk Aktuarietidskrift*, 1962, pp. 162–175.
4. Borch, K. "The Optimal Management Policy of an Insurance Company," *Proceedings of the Casualty Actuarial Society*, vol. 51. pp. 182–197.
5. Neumann, J. von and Morgenstern, O. *Theory of Games and Economic Behavior*, 2nd edition (Princeton, 1947).
6. Shubik, M. and Thompson, G. "Games of Economic Survival," *Naval Research Logistics Quarterly*, 1959, pp. 111–123.

17

Dynamic Decision Problems in an Insurance Company

1. Introduction

1.1. In this paper we shall consider some of the decisions which have to be made in the normal course of business in an insurance company. We shall see that the "right" decisions can be found only when the problems are analyzed in their proper dynamic context.

As examples of the decision problems which we shall study, we can mention the following:

(i) What premium rates should be quoted on the insurance contracts, which the company offers to the public?
(ii) How much should the company spend to promote the sale of its policies?
(iii) When should the company refuse to underwrite a proposed insurance contract?
(iv) How shall the company reinsure its portfolio of insurance contracts?
(v) What reserve funds should an insurance company keep?
(vi) How shall the company's funds be invested?

Any actuary will be familiar with such problems, and he will probably feel that these problems cannot be satisfactorily solved with the methods offered by the classical actuarial theory.

1.2. In some earlier papers [1, 2] it has been argued that such problems can best be solved in the framework of *utility* theory. As an illustration we shall take problem (iii) in the preceding paragraph, and consider an insurance company in the following situation:

(i) The company has a capital S.
(ii) The company holds a portfolio of insurance contracts which will lead to a total payment of x to settle claims. $F_1(x)$ is the distribution of the variate x.

When all contracts in the portfolio have expired, the company will have a capital

$$z_1 = S - x$$

z_1 is a variate with the distribution

$$G_1(z_1) = 1 - F_1(S - z_1) \qquad z_1 \leqslant S$$

Let us now assume that this company is offered an amount P, if it will accept an insurance contract (a reinsurance treaty) with claim distribution $F_2(y)$. If the company accepts, its capital when all contracts have expired will be

$$z_2 = S + P - x - y$$

The distribution of this variate will be

$$G_2(z_2) = 1 - H(S + P - z_2) \qquad z_2 \leqslant S + P$$

If the variates x and y are stochastically independent, the distribution H will be the convolution of F_1 and F_2.

1.3.   If the company considered in the preceding paragraph, accepts the offer, it must in some sense find the distribution G_2 better than G_1. In order to compare two arbitrary distributions and select the best, the company must have a *preference ordering* over the set of all probability distributions.

A preference ordering of this kind must obviously depend on "subjective" elements, such as the cmpany's willingness to assume risks. The ordering can usually be described in several different ways. If the ordering is consistent in the precise sense, defined by von Neumann and Morgenstern [8] , it can be described in a particularly simple way. In this case there exists a function $u(x)$, so that $G_2(x)$ is preferred to $G_1(x)$ if and only if

$$\int_{-\infty}^{+\infty} u(x)\, dG_2(x) > \int_{-\infty}^{+\infty} u(x)\, dG_1(x)$$

The function $u(x)$ is usually referred to as the *utility function,* because it can be interpreted as the utility associated with an amount of money equal to x. From our point of view it is, however, sufficient to consider $u(x)$ as a convenient way of describing a preference ordering.

1.4.   The utility theory of von Neumann and Morgenstern is mathematically elegant, and in many ways very attractive. It can, however, not be of much practical use, unless we know something about the shape of the utility function, which represents the preference ordering of our insurance company.

As an approach to this problem we can ask what is the utility of the capital, left with the company, when all contracts in the portfolio have expired. It seems that we can answer this question only if we know something about the future plans of the company, i.e., the kind of insurance business which the company expects to underwrite in later periods. This naturally leads us to consider the essentially static decision problem in a dynamic setting.

2. A Simple Dynamic Model

2.1. As a first approach to a dynamic formulation of the problem, we shall consider an insurance company which operates under the following conditions:

(i)   The company has an initial capital S.
(ii) In each successive underwriting period the company makes a profit x, which is a variate with distribution $F(x)$ The profit in any period is stochastically independent of profits in other periods.
(iii) If the company's capital becomes negative at the end of an underwriting period, the company is ruined, and will go out of business.
(iv) If at the end of a period the company's capital exceeds Z, the excess will be paid out as dividend immediately.

This model is a *random walk* with an absorbing barrier at $S = 0$, and a reflecting barrier at $S = Z$.

If we let Z go to infinity, i.e., if we assume that the company never will pay any dividends, we obtain the model which forms the basis of Lundberg's "collective theory of risk" [7]. This assumption is not very realistic, and the resulting theory has not found many practical applications, although it may have stimulated further research. This has been pointed out, e.g., by de Finetti [6], who first studied the far richer theory we obtain by adding a reflecting barrier to the model.

2.2. To illustrate the possibilities of de Finetti's generalization, let us first consider the function

$D(S, Z)$ = expected number of operating periods before ruin occurs

From the conditions in para. 2.1 it follows that

$D(S, Z) = 0$ for $S < 0$

$D(S, Z) = D(Z, Z)$ for $S > Z$

For $0 \leqslant S \leqslant Z$ it is easy to see that $D(S, Z)$ must satisfy the integral equation

$$D(S, Z) = 1 + \int_{-S}^{\infty} D(S + x, Z)\, dF(x)$$

De Finetti studied the special case where

$F(x) = 0$ for $x < -1$

$F(x) = 1 - p$ for $-1 \leqslant x < 1$

$F(x) = 1$ for $1 \leqslant x$

In this case the integral equation reduces to the difference equation

$$D(S, Z) = 1 + pD(S + 1, Z) + (1 - p)D(S - 1, Z)$$

This equation can be solved by elementary methods, and the nature of the solution has been discussed in some detail in another paper [4].

As a more general case, let us assume that $F(x)$ is continuous, and that a density function $f(x) = F'(x)$ exists.

The integral equation can then be written

$$D(S, Z) = 1 + \left\{ 1 - F(Z - S) \right\} D(Z, Z) + \int_0^z D(x, Z)f(x - S)\, dx$$

This is an equation of Fredholm's type, with the simple kernel $f(x - S)$, and it can be solved by different methods. We can, for instance, form the iterated kernels

$$f^{(1)}(x - S) = f(x - S)$$

$$f^{(n)}(x - S) = \int_0^z f^{(n-1)}(x - t)f(t - S)\, dt$$

and obtain the Liouville-Neumann expansion

$$D(S, Z) = 1 + \left\{ 1 - F(Z - S) \right\} D(Z, Z) + \sum_{n=1}^{\infty} f^{(n)}(x - S)\, dx$$

$$+ D(Z, Z) \sum_{n=1}^{\infty} \int_0^z \left\{ 1 - F(Z - x) \right\} f^{(n)}(x - s)\, dx$$

We determine $D(Z, Z)$ by requiring the solution to be continuous at $S = Z$. This gives the equation

$$D(Z, Z) = 1 + \left\{ 1 - F(0) \right\} D(Z, Z) + \sum_{n=1}^{\infty} \int_0^z f^{(n)}(x - Z)\, dx$$

$$+ D(Z, Z) \sum_{n=1}^{\infty} \int_0^z \left\{1 - F(z - x)\right\} f^{(n)}(x - z)\, dx$$

2.3. If at the end of underwriting period t the company's capital S_t exceeds Z, the excess $s_t = S_t - Z$ will be paid out as dividend—to share holders or policy holders, as the case may be. Hence the company will make a sequence $s_0, s_1, \ldots, s_t, \ldots$ of dividend payments. This sequence is a discrete stochastic process.

Let us now consider the expected discounted value of these payments, i.e.,

$$E\left\{\sum_{t=0}^{\infty} v^t s_t\right\}$$

where $0 < v < 1$ is a discount factor.

Since this obviously depends on the initial capital S, and on the reserve requirements represented by Z, we shall write

$$V(S, Z) = E\left\{\sum_{t=0}^{\infty} v^t s_t\right\}$$

From the conditions in para. 2.1 it follows that

$$V(S, Z) = 0 \qquad\qquad \text{for } S < 0$$

$$V(S, Z) = S - Z + V(Z, Z) \qquad \text{for } S > Z$$

For $0 \leqslant S \leqslant Z$ the function $V(S, Z)$ must satisfy the integral equation

$$V(S, Z) = v \int_{-S}^{z-s} V(S + x, Z)\, df(x) + v \int_{z-s}^{\infty} \left\{V(Z, Z) + x + S - Z\right\} df(x)$$

For the simple discrete case considered in the preceding paragraph, the integral equation reduces to the difference equation

$$V(S, Z) = vp V(S + 1, Z) + v(1 - p)V(S - 1, Z)$$

This case has been discussed by de Finetti [6], and in more detail in some other papers [3, 4].

If $F(x)$ is continuous and a density function exists, the integral equation can be written

$$V(S, Z) = v \int_0^z V(x, Z) f(x - S)\, dx + v \int_z^{\infty} \left\{V(Z, Z) + x - Z\right\} f(x - S)\, dx$$

This is again an equation of Fredholm's type. It can be solved by forming the iterated kernels and taking the Liouville-Neumann expansion:

$$V(S, Z) = v \left\{ 1 - F(Z - S) \right\} V(Z, Z)$$

$$+ v \int_z^\infty xf(x + Z - S)\, dx + \sum_{n=1}^\infty v^n \int_0^z f^{(n)}(x - S)\, dx$$

$$+ V(Z, Z) \sum_{n=1}^\infty \int_0^z \left\{ 1 - F(z - x) \right\} f^{(n)}(x - s)\, dx$$

To determine $V(Z, Z)$, we require the solution to be continuous at $S = Z$ and obtain

$$V(Z, Z) = v \left\{ 1 - F(0) \right\} V(Z, Z) + v \int_0^\infty xf(x)\, dx$$

$$+ \sum_{n=1}^\infty v^n \int_0^z f^{(n)}(x - Z)\, dx$$

$$+ V(Z, Z) \sum_{n=1}^\infty \int_0^z \left\{ 1 - F(z - x) \right\} f^{(n)}(x - z)\, dx$$

2.4.   It is clear that the two functions $D(S, Z)$ and $V(S, Z)$ are relevant to a number of decisions which have to be made in an insurance company.
   For instance:

(i)   If the objective of the company is to maximize the expected discounted value of its dividend payment, we are led to seek the value of Z, which maximizes $V(S, Z)$, for given S.

(ii)   If the required reserve Z is given, and the objective of the company is to survive as long as possible, we have some information about how the company will make its reinsurance decisions.

To illustrate this, let us assume that the company receives an offer of the type we considered in para. 1.2. If the offer is accepted, the expected duration of life of the company will be

$$\int_0^\infty D(S + P - y, Z)\, dF_2(y)$$

If the company pursues its overall objective in a consistent manner, it will accept the offer only if this increases the expected life, i.e., if

$$\int_0^\infty D(S + P - y, Z)\, dF_2(y) > D(S, Z)$$

This means, however, that the company makes its decision as if its preference ordering over probability distributions is represented by the utility function $D(S, Z)$. Hence it appears that the static decision problem considered in Section 1 is solved almost automatically when the problem is placed in its natural dynamic context.

It is possible to discuss such decision problems in full generality. To bring out the main features of the problems, it is, however, sufficient to discuss a special case. In the following we shall do this, and we shall indicate when the results derived from the special case have general validity.

3. A Special Case

3.1. In general Fredholm's integral equation has no simple explicit solution. We are therefore led to seek a case where the basic distribution $F(x)$ has a form giving a solution which can be discussed in detail by fairly elementary methods.

As a reasonably realistic example, we could consider the case:

$$f(x) = e^{x-p} \quad x \leqslant P$$

$$f(x) = 0 \quad x > P$$

We can interpret this to mean that our company in each operating period receives an amount of premiums P, and accepts a portfolio with the claim distribution $F(x) = 1 - e^{-x}$. It is natural to assume that $P > 1$, so that the game is favorable to the company.

It has been shown in another paper [5] that the integral equation in this case reduces to a differential-difference equation, which has a solution given by a finite expression. This expression is, however, far from simple and is not very suitable for detailed discussion.

3.2. As another example, let us consider

$$f(x) = k\alpha e^{-\alpha x} \quad \text{for } x > 0$$

$$f(x) = (1 - k)\alpha e^{\alpha x} \quad \text{for } x < 0$$

The value of $f(x)$ for $x = 0$ does not matter. We shall assume that $\frac{1}{2} < k < 1$, i.e., that the underwriting is favorable to the company.

The obvious objection to this probability distribution is that it does not put any upper limit to the gain, which the company can make in a single underwriting period. We can justify our choice of $f(x)$ simply by its mathematical convenience.

We can also assume that the company invests its funds in very speculative shares, which may give a very high yield.

The integral equation from para. 2.3 can now be written as follows:

$$V(S) = v(1-k)\alpha e^{-\alpha}S \int_0^S V(x)e^{\alpha x}\,dx + vk\alpha e^{\alpha S}\int_0^S V(x)e^{-\alpha x}\,dx$$

$$+ vk\,V(Z)e^{\alpha(S-Z)} + \frac{vk}{\alpha}e^{\alpha(S-Z)}$$

For simplicity we have written $V(S)$ for $V(S,Z)$, since there should be no risk of misunderstanding.

3.3. Differentiating the integral equation twice with respect to S, we obtain

$$V'(S) = v(1-k)\alpha V(S) - vk\alpha V(S)$$

$$- v(1-k)\alpha^2 e^{-\alpha S}\int_0^S V(x)e^{\alpha x}\,dx + vk\alpha^2 e^{\alpha S}\int_S^z V(x)e^{\alpha x}\,dx$$

$$+ vk\alpha V(Z)e^{\alpha(S-Z)} + vke^{\alpha(S-Z)}$$

and $V''(S) = v(1-2k)\alpha V'(S) - v\alpha^2 V(S)$

$$+ v(1-k)\alpha^3 e^{-\alpha S}\int_0^S V(x)e^{\alpha x}\,dx + vk\alpha^3 e^{\alpha S}\int_S^z V(x)e^{-\alpha x}\,dx$$

$$+ vk\alpha^2 V(Z)e^{\alpha(S-Z)} + vk\alpha e^{\alpha(S-Z)}$$

From these expressions it is easy to see that $V(S)$ must satisfy the differential equation

$$V''(S) - \alpha^2 V(S) = v(1-2k)\alpha V'(S) - v\alpha^2 V(S)$$

or $(1-v)\alpha^2 V(S) + v(1-2k)\alpha V'(S) - V''(S) = 0$

Hence our integral equation is reduced to a homogeneous differential equation of the second order with constant coefficients. The general solution of this equation is:

$$V(S) = C_1 e^{r_1 S} + C_2 e^{r_2 S}$$

Here C_1 and C_2 are arbitrary constants, and r_1 and r_2 are the roots of the characteristic equation

$$r^2 - v(1 - 2k)\,\alpha\,r - (1 - v)\alpha^2 = 0$$

We find

$$r_1 = \frac{\alpha}{2}\left\{v(1 - 2k) + (v^2(1 - 2k)^2 + 4 - 4v)^{\frac{1}{2}}\right\}$$

$$r_2 = \frac{\alpha}{2}\left\{v(1 - 2k) - (v^2(1 - 2k)^2 + 4 - 4v)^{\frac{1}{2}}\right\}$$

It is easy to verify that both roots are real, and that $r_1 > 0, r_2 < 0$.

3.4. The constants C_1 and C_2 must be determined so that the general solution of the differential equation also is a solution of the integral equation. Substituting the general solution in the integral equation, we find

$$C_1 e^{r_1 S} + C_2 e^{r_1 S} = \frac{v(1 - k)\alpha}{r_1 + \alpha}\, C_1 \left\{e^{r_1 S} - e^{-\alpha S}\right\}$$

$$+ \frac{v(1 - k)\alpha}{r_2 + \alpha}\, C_2 \left\{e^{r_2 S} - e^{-\alpha S}\right\} + \frac{vk\alpha}{r_1 - \alpha}\, C_1 \left\{e^{(r_1 - \alpha)Z + \alpha S} - e^{r_1 S}\right\}$$

$$+ \frac{vk\,\alpha}{r_2 - \alpha}\, C_2 \left\{e^{(r_2 - \alpha)Z + \alpha S} - e^{r_2 S}\right\} + vkC_1\, e^{(r_1 - \alpha)Z + \alpha S}$$

$$+ vkC_2 e^{(r_2 - \alpha)Z + \alpha S} + vk\alpha e^{\alpha(S - Z)}$$

We shall write this expression as follows:

$$\left\{1 - \frac{v(1 - k)\alpha}{r_1 + \alpha} + \frac{vk\,\alpha}{r_1 - \alpha}\right\} C_1 e^{r_1 S} +$$

$$\left\{1 - \frac{v(1 - k)\alpha}{r_2 + \alpha} + \frac{vk\,\alpha}{r_2 - \alpha}\right\} C_2 e^{r_2 S} -$$

$$\left\{\frac{vk\,r_1}{r_1 - \alpha}\, e^{(r_1 - \alpha)Z}\, C_1 + \frac{vk\,r_2}{r_2 - \alpha}\, e^{(r_1 - \alpha)Z} C_2 + \frac{vk}{\alpha}\, e^{-\alpha Z}\right\} e^{\alpha S} +$$

$$\left\{ \frac{v(1-k)\alpha}{r_1+\alpha} C_1 + \frac{v(1-k)\alpha}{r_2+\alpha} C_2 \right\} e^{-\alpha S} = 0$$

This equation must hold for all values of S. Hence the four expressions in braces must be zero.

It is easy to verify that the two first of these expressions, i.e., the coefficients of $e^{r_1 S}$ and $e^{r_2 S}$ are zero when r_1 and r_2 are the roots of the characteristic equation.

We then obtain the following two equations for the determination of C_1 and C_2:

$$\frac{r_1 e^{r_1 Z}}{r_1 - \alpha} C_1 + \frac{r_2 e^{r_2 Z}}{r_2 - \alpha} C_2 = -\frac{1}{\alpha}$$

$$\frac{1}{r_1 + \alpha} C_1 + \frac{1}{r_2 + \alpha} C_2 = 0$$

The determinant of these equations is

$$D = \frac{r_1 e^{r_1 Z}}{(r_1 - \alpha)(r_2 + \alpha)} - \frac{r_2 e^{r_2 Z}}{(r_1 + \alpha)(r_2 - \alpha)}$$

and we find

$$C_1 = \frac{-1}{\alpha(r_2 + \alpha)D} \qquad C_2 = \frac{1}{\alpha(r_1 + \alpha)D}$$

This gives us the following explicit expression for the expected discounted value of the dividend payments:

$$V(S, Z) = \frac{1}{\alpha D} \left\{ \frac{e^{r_2 S}}{r_1 + \alpha} - \frac{e^{r_1 S}}{r_2 + \alpha} \right\}$$

This expression is maximized for the value of Z which minimizes the absolute value of D, i.e., the value determined by the equation

$$\frac{dD}{dZ} = \frac{r_1^2 e^{r_1 Z}}{(r_1 - \alpha)(r_2 + \alpha)} - \frac{r_2^2 e^{r_2 Z}}{(r_1 + \alpha)(r_2 - \alpha)} = 0$$

or $\quad e^{(r_1 - r_2)Z} = \dfrac{r_2^2 (r_1 - \alpha)(r_2 + \alpha)}{r_1^2 (r_1 + \alpha)(r_2 - \alpha)}$

This value of Z is clearly unique, and independent of S, i.e., there exists a unique optimal level for the company's reserves. The result does, however, not seem to hold in the general case.

3.5. By similar considerations we find that $D(S) = D(S, Z)$ must satisfy the integral equation

$$D(S) = 1 + (1 - k)\alpha e^{-\alpha S} \int_0^S D(x)e^{\alpha x}\, dx$$

$$+ k\alpha e^{\alpha S} \int_z^S D(x)\, e^{-\alpha X}\, dx + k e^{\alpha(S-Z)} D(Z)$$

Differentiating twice, we find that the integral equation can be reduced to the differential equation

$$(2k - 1)\alpha D'(S) + D''(S) + \alpha^2 = 0$$

The general solution of this equation is

$$D(S) = C_1 e^{-(2k-1)\alpha S} - \frac{\alpha}{2k - 1} S + C_2$$

where C_1 and C_2 are constants which must be determined so that the solution also satisfies the integral equation.

By a procedure similar to the one used in para. 3.3, we find

$$C_1 = -\frac{2k}{(2k - 1)^2} e^{(2k-1)\alpha Z}$$

$$C_2 = \frac{k}{(2k - 1)^2(1 - k)} e^{(2k-1)\alpha Z} - \frac{1}{2k - 1}$$

and $D(S, Z) = \dfrac{k}{(2k - 1)(1 - k)} e^{(2k-1)\alpha Z} - \dfrac{2k}{(2k - 1)^2} e^{(2k-1)\alpha(Z-S)}$

$$- \frac{1}{2k - 1}(1 + \alpha S)$$

3.6. To illustrate these results with a numerical example, let us take $\alpha = 1$, $r_1 = 0.1$, and $r_2 = -0.3$.

This corresponds to $\nu = 0.97$ and $k = 0.603$. We then find:

$$V(S, Z) = \frac{143\, e^{0.1S} - 91\, e^{-0.3S}}{16\, e^{0.1Z} + 21\, e^{-0.3Z}}$$

and $D(S, Z) = 37.5\, e^{0.2Z} - 5\,(1 + S) - 30\, e^{0.2Z(Z-S)}$

Table 17–1 gives the value of the function $V(S, Z)$ for some selected values of S and Z. It is easy to verify that this function takes its maximal value for $Z = 3.45$.

Table 17–2 gives the value of the function $D(S, Z)$ for the same values of S and Z.

4. The Decision Problems

4.1. The example we have discussed in Section 3 brings out an obvious, but often overlooked truth: We cannot find the right decision unless we really know what we want. This may sound trivial, but our discussion indicates that it may not always be so easy to spell out what we want in an unambiguous way.

To illustrate the point, let us assume that we are the majority shareholders of an insurance company. We may then want to make the expected life of our

Table 17–1

$V(S, Z)$ = Expected discounted value of dividend payments

S \ Z	0	1	2	3	4	5
0	1.41	1.57	1.68	1.74	1.73	1.68
1	2.41	2.74	2.93	3.02	3.02	2.94
2	3.41	3.74	4.03	4.16	4.16	4.04
3	4.41	4.74	5.03	5.21	5.20	5.14
4	5.41	5.74	6.03	6.21	6.19	6.02
5	6.41	6.74	7.03	7.21	7.19	6.98

Table 17–2

$D(S, Z)$ = Expected duration of life of the company

S \ Z	0	1	2	3	4	5
0	2.5	4.2	6.2	8.7	11.7	15.4
1	2.5	5.8	9.6	13.3	19.0	25.2
2	2.5	5.8	11.2	16.7	23.6	32.4
3	2.5	5.8	11.2	18.3	27.0	37.0
4	2.5	5.8	11.2	18.3	28.6	40.4
5	2.5	5.8	11.2	18.3	28.6	42.0

company as long as possible. This implies, however, that the company should never pay any dividend, and this may not be quite what we want. Our second thought may then be to maximize the expected discounted value of the dividend payments which will be made over the lifetime of the company. However, is this really what we want?

4.2. To throw some light on these questions, let us assume that at the end of an underwriting period our company has a capital $S = 4$. Let us further assume that the actuary of the company asks us to make one of the following four decisions:

(i)   Set the reserve requirement at $Z = 3$, and pay a dividend $s = 1$. This will give:
      Expected dividend payment $V(4,3) = 6.21$
      Expected life $D(4,3) = 18.3$
(ii) Set the reserve requirement at $Z = 3.45$ and pay a dividend $s = 0.55$. This will give:
      Expected dividend payment $V(4, 3.45) = 6.23$
      Expected life $D(4, 3.45) = 22.7$
(iii) Set the reserve requirement at $Z = 4$, and pay no dividend. This will give:
      Expected dividend payment $V(4,4) = 6.19$
      Expected life $D(4,4) = 28.6$
(iv) Set the reserve requirement at $Z = 5$, and pay no dividend. This will give:
      Expected dividend payment $V(4,5) = 6.02$
      Expected life $D(4,5) = 40.4$

Is it obvious that we in this situation select decision (ii)? Some people may well be willing to sacrifice some dividends in order to prolong the life of the company, and they may go in for decision (iv).

4.3. Our discussion indicates that we should be very careful in spelling out the *objectives* of our insurance company, before we get too excited over the advanced methods of operations research. These methods are powerful, and they will always give us the right solution, but this may be the solution to the wrong problem.
     If the general manager of our insurance company wants to run the company strictly as a business enterprise, he will probably always seek out the decisions which maximize $V(S, Z)$. If, however, he is concerned with the social respon-sibility of the company, and the security which it offers to policy holders, he may also consider $D(S, Z)$ when making his decisions. He will probably try to balance the two elements, but it is not easy to specify how this should be done.
     The general manager and his board must, however, solve this problem, and it seems that they must do it themselves, without much help from actuaries and other experts on operations research.

References

1. Borch, K.: "The Utility Concept applied to the Theory of Insurance," *The ASTIN Bulletin* 1 (1962): 245–255.
2. ———. "The Objectives of an Insurance Company," *Skandinavisk Aktuarie-tidskrift,* 1962, pp. 162–175.
3. ———. "Dividend Policies, *Statsøkonomisk Tidsskrift,* 1965, pp. 183–201.
4. ———. "Control of a Portfolio of Insurance Contracts," *The ASTIN Bulletin* 4 (1966): 59–71.
5. ———. "Una generalizacion de la teoria del riesgo colectivo," *Anales del Instituto de Actuarios Españoles,* 1965, pp. 13–30.
6. Finetti, B. de. "Su una Impostazione Alternativa della Teoria Collettiva del Rischio," *Transactions of the XV International Congress of Actuaries,* 1957, Vol. 2, pp. 433–443.
7. Lundberg, F. "Ueber die Theorie der Rückversicherung," *Transaction of the VI International Congress of Actuaries,* 1909, Vol. 1, pp. 877–955.
8. Neumann, J. von and O. Morgenstern. *Theory of Games and Economic Behavior,* 2nd edition (Princeton, 1947).

18

The Theory of Risk

The classical theory of risk is reviewed. It is shown to be a static theory, and this is adduced to be its main disadvantage. A dynamic theory was introduced by Lundberg in 1909. This is discussed and Lundberg's achievement is re-affirmed. However, it is pointed out that this theory, in spite of extensive mathematical development, has found virtually no application in practice. The major difficulty lies in the formulation of insurance problems in a convincing way. In the last section a new approach is called for. A model incorporating dynamic features of Lunberg's collective risk theory with more realistic constraints is investigated. Possible directions for future research are suggested.

1. Historical Note

The word "risk" is used colloquially in many different senses, but has also been defined as a precise technical term in a number of different contexts.

Economists will generally recall Frank Knight's [19] sharp distinction between the concepts of "risk" and "uncertainty." In Knight's terminology *risk* is present in a situation where an action can lead to several different, mutually exclusive outcomes each of known probability. If these probabilities are unknown, the situation will in Knight's language contain *uncertainty*. The development of the Bayesian approach to statistics and decision theory seems to have made Knight's distinction between the concepts obsolete, or at least to indicate that the distinction is not essential to a systematic study of the subject.

Statisticians will probably associate risk with Wald's [28] theory of statistical decision functions. Wald defines risk as the sum of expected cost of experimentation and expected loss due to wrong terminal decisions, when a particular decision function is used. This is a concept which appears to be essential in a theory of rational decisions, but the technical term chosen by Wald may have been unfortunate. In recent years authors have preferred words such as "pay-off," which do not have so many colloquial connotations as risk.

In insurance the word "risk" has a long tradition, and has been used in many different senses. It is generally assumed that it was first used as a precisely defined mathematical concept by Tetens [27] in a work on life annuities. In this work Tetens proposed to attach the name risk to what we today would describe as "one-half of the mean deviation." This terminology, now obsolete, persisted in actuarial circles at least up to the Second World War, and led to the development of *risk theory,* a term which still has a well-defined meaning to most actuaries. It is this theory which we shall discuss in the following sections.

It will become apparent that actuarial risk theory has, to a large extent, developed outside the mainstream of probability theory and mathematical statistics. It is difficult now to explain why this should have happened. One reason may be that for a long time insurance—together with gambling—was the only practical application of probability theory. Actuaries had the field to themselves, and tended to formulate their results as solutions to insurance problems, without taking the trouble of explaining their general nature. As probability theory found other applications, it was apparently easier to rediscover the results than to trace them in existing literature, where they were hidden behind clouds of insurance jargon.

2. The Classical Theory of Risk

To present the actuarial theory of risk in its proper setting, it is necessary to restate some of the elements in the theory of insurance. The basic concept in insurance is the *insurance contract.* In its simplest form an insurance contract will give a person—the insured—the right to claim an amount of money, S, from the company, if certain events should occur. To be entitled to this right, the insured pays the company a premium P.

If the probability of events leading to a claim is p, the premium is determined so that

$$P = pS \tag{1}$$

This equation illustrates the *principle of equivalence,* which constitutes the very foundation of insurance theory. In its general form, this principle states that the expected value of claim payments under a contract should be equal to the expected value of premiums received.

Strictly speaking the equation determines the so-called *net premium.* In practice one must add to this premium a "loading" to cover the expected administrative costs of the company. We shall, however, ignore these costs, since they do not raise any new questions of principle; such costs can be brought into our formulae at any stage, if it should be desirable.

A more general insurance contract is defined by a probability distribution $F(x)$, where $F(x)$ is the probability that claim payments under the contract shall not exceed x. The net premium for this contract is, by the principle of equivalence,

$$P = \int_0^\infty x \, dF(x) \tag{2}$$

As a more complicated example, let us consider a contract according to which a person undertakes to pay a premium P at the beginning of each year as long as he lives. In return the insurance company undertakes to pay an amount S at the end of the year in which he dies.

Let q_t be the probability that the person considered shall die in year t. As obviously

$$q_1 + q_2 + \ldots q_t + \ldots = 1$$

the expected claim payment will be S. Expected premium receipts bill be

$$P(q_1 + 2q_2 + \ldots + tq_t + \ldots)$$

We could use these two observations to determine the premium by the principle of equivalence. For a contract of long duration, we should, however, take into account the interest earned by accumulated funds. This leads us to determine the premium from the equation

$$P\{q_1 + (1+v)q_2 + (1+v+v^2)q_3 + \ldots\} = S\{vq_1 + v^2 q_2 + v^3 q_3 + \ldots\}$$

where $v = (1+i)^{-1}$, and i is the rate of interest. This illustrates the general principle of equivalence: The *expected discounted values* (or the "present values") of premium receipts and claim payments must be equal.

Classical actuarial mathematics consists of estimating probabilities and computing expected discounted values. These problems are not always easy, since it is possible to draw up very complicated insurance contracts. The problems are, however, by no means unique to insurance. The development of operational research has shown that mathematical problems of this kind may occur in any industry, and that the real difficulty is to discover the problems and to give them a suitable formulation.

Let us now consider two insurance contracts. Under the first the only possible claim is $S_1 = 100$, and the probability that it shall be paid is $p_1 = 0.1$. The second contract is of the same form, but with $S_2 = 1,000$ and $p_2 = 0.01$.

The principle of equivalence will lead to the same premium, $P = 10$, for both these contracts. Most people will, however, feel that the second contract is more dangerous, or "riskier" than the first, and that this ought to be reflected in the premium. In some cases it may be possible to dismiss this argument with an appeal to the law of large numbers, which is, after all, the real basis of insurance.

In order to obtain a measure of the risk of a contract, Tetens [27] defined risk as expected loss to the company, if the contract leads to a loss. Applied to the first example of the preceding paragraph, this gives the risk as

$$R = \int_P^\infty (x - P)\, dF(x) = \frac{1}{2} \int_0^\infty |x - P|\, dF(x) \tag{3}$$

For the two examples above, we find the risks

$$R_1 = \tfrac{1}{2}\{0.9 \times 10 + 0.1 \times 90\} = 9$$

$$R_2 = \tfrac{1}{2}\{0.99 \times 10 + 0.01 \times 990\} = 9.9$$

It is usually more convenient to work with the standard deviation than with the mean deviation, so the idean of Tetens naturally led to suggestions that risk should be defined as M, where M is determined by the equation

$$M^2 = \int_0^\infty (x - P)^2 \, dF(x) \tag{4}$$

This concept was discussed in considerable detail by Hausdorff [18], and is usually associated with his name, although it has been studied earlier by other authors. For the examples above we find $M_1 = 30$ and $M_2 = 99$.

The pioneers of the theory of risk are not very clear when it comes to explaining the practical use which should be made of the different measures of risk. There seems to have been a vague feeling that some amount, proportional to the risk, should be added to the net premium as a "safety loading," but this was first explicitly suggested by Wold [29].

It is interesting to note that few actuaries seem to have recognized the significance of the work by Daniel Bernoulli [5] on the problem we now refer to as the "St Petersburg paradox." Bernoulli suggested that mathematical expectation should be replaced by "moral expectation," a concept which we today know as *expected utility*.

In modern terms Bernoulli's idea can be expressed as follows: The company has a *preference ordering* over the set of all insurance contracts. This ordering can be represented by a utility function $u(x)$, in the sense that the expected utility

$$\int_0^\infty u(P - x) \, dF(x) \tag{5}$$

is greater, the higher the contract is placed in the preference ordering.

The company will then accept an insurance contract only if it is preferred to a degenerate contract, which is certain to give neither loss nor gain. This means that the premium Q must be determined so that

$$u(0) \leqslant \int_0^\infty u(Q - x) \, dF(x)$$

The function $u(x)$ can be interpreted as the *utility of money*, and it is usually assumed that $u'(x) > 0$ and $u''(x) < 0$, i.e., the marginal utility of money is decreasing. From these assumptions it follows that $Q \geqslant P$, so that we obtain the "safety loading" which was mentioned above.

The ideas of Bernoulli were taken up by Barrois [27] , who used them to develop a fairly complete and surprisingly modern theory of fire insurance. To illustrate this, let us assume that the wealth of a person is S, and that he may suffer a loss from fire x, where x is a variate with the distribution $F(x)$. If the utility function for money of this person is $w(x)$, he is willing to pay a premium Q to be insured against the loss, provided that

$$\int_0^\infty w(S - x)\, dF(x) \leqslant w(S - Q)$$

A premium which satisfies this inequality, as well as the inequality in the preceding paragraph, should be acceptable to both the person to be insured and the insurance company. The insurance contract will then increase the expected utility of both parties.

The work of Barrois seems to have been ignored by following generations of actuaries. The ideas of Bernoulli reappeared in insurance literature only when the game theory of von Neumann and Morgenstern [22] had made utility fashionable, and demonstrated that this concept must occupy a central position in any theory of decisions under risk and uncertaintly. The first who applied modern utility theory to insurance was Nolfi [23] , and his results have been developed by a number of other authors, including Borch [7] .

The ideas of Bernoulli and Barrois indicate that the logical approach to the subject should be to consider insurance cover as a commodity, which is bought and sold. The premium must then be considered as a price, which is determined by supply and demand in the market. This should, as demonstrated in another paper [8] , lead to an economic theory of insurance, and to ideas which in general may be rather unfamiliar to actuaries and statisticians.

It is in some ways surprising that the development of mathematical economics during the last 80 to 100 years has had next to no influence on the theory of risk developed by actuaries. One explanation may be the reputation for integrity and high moral standards which the insurance industry seeks to maintain. These standards led actuaries to seek general rules for determining "correct loadings" and "fair premiums." They may have been well aware that some people might be prepared to pay more than a "fair premium" for insurance cover, but the idea of exploitation in order to make profits seems not to have commended itself to the traditional thinking in the insurance world. This is directly opposed to the thinking in economics, where it is assumed—usually without question—that a "rational" person will charge the price which the market is willing to pay.

After this digression, we return to the theory of risk. There are no real difficulties involved in computing the risk, R or M, for insurance contracts far more complicated than those considered earlier. The expressions may, however, be exceedingly complex, and in life insurance they will have to be recalculated for each year in which the contract runs, since the probability of dying will vary with a person's age. The relevant formulae can be found in older actuarial literature. We shall, however, neither reproduce nor discuss these formulae, since they seem to have found little application in practice.

Let us consider instead a portfolio of n independent insurance contracts, with premiums $P_1, P_2, \ldots, P_n$ and risks $M_1, M_2, \ldots, M_n$. We can then define the risk of the portfolio, M, by the equation

$$M^2 = M_1^2 + M_2^2 + \ldots + M_n^2 \tag{6}$$

Let the company's gain on this portfolio be a variate z. If the premiums are determined by the principle of equivalence, the expected value of this variate will evidently be zero, i.e., $E\{z\} = 0$. If n is large, z will under certain conditions be approximately normally distributed, with standard deviation M.

If the company holds a reserve fund S, in addition to the premiums collected for contracts in force, the expression

$$\alpha = \Pr\{z < -S\} = \frac{1}{M\sqrt{2\pi}} \int_{-\infty}^{-S} \exp\left\{-\frac{1}{2}\left(\frac{x}{M}\right)^2\right\} dx = \Phi\left(-\frac{S}{M}\right) \tag{7}$$

will give the probability that the company shall not be able to fulfil its commitments under the contracts in the portfolio. This probability, which is referred to as the *probability of ruin*, has become the central concept in the theory of risk.

The ideas outlined in the preceding paragraph make it possible to give the theory of risk some operational content.

The starting point is usually an assumption that the probability of ruin must be kept below a certain level, which represents the acceptable maximum. If S is so great that the ruin probability is smaller than this maximum, the company can pay a part of its reserve fund out as dividends—to share holders or policy holders, as the case may be. If S is so small that the ruin probability exceeds the acceptable level, the company may obtain additional guarantee capital, or it may seek a reinsurance arrangement, which will reduce the risk, and hence the probability of ruin. Usually the latter alternative is chosen, and as a result of the theory of risk became almost identical with the theory of reinsurance in actuarial literature.

The argument above implies that the company must obtain additional reserve funds as its volume of business grows. Theoretically the company could obtain these funds by calling upon share holders to put up more equity capital. In practice, these funds will usually be obtained from the company's customers by a loading of the premium. One usually assumes that the loading is proportional to the net premium, so that the premium actually paid under contract i is $(1 + \lambda)P_i$. The expected gain on the company's portfolio will then be

$$E\{z\} = \lambda P \tag{8}$$

where $P = P_1 + P_2 + \ldots + P_n$.

The probability of ruin will then be

$$\Pr\{z < -S\} = \Phi\left(-\frac{S + \lambda P}{M}\right) \tag{9}$$

In actuarial literature it is usually assumed that the maximum acceptable probability of ruin is decided outside the insurance industry, for instance, that it is imposed by the government as a solvency condition which the companies must satisfy.

An insurance company will then take α as given. It is natural to assume that the reserve fund S also is given and unchangeable, at least in the short run. The problem of the company will then be to determine the optimal loading factor λ. In order to make this a well-defined problem, we will have to specify the objectives of the company, and the conditions at which reinsurance can be obtained. If we do this, we will have a problem typical of operational research.

The actuaries who created the classical theory of risk, could not be expected to formulate their problem with the precision required by modern operational analysis. They probably came nearest to it when they sought to determine the value of λ which would leave the reinsured proportion of the portfolio constant when the volume of business increases. However, even this problem is without meaning, unless the nature of the insurance contracts and the conditions or reinsurance are specified.

The loading factor λ may, however, also have to be taken as given—it may be determined by competition in the market, or by government control of insurance premiums. The only decision left to the company will then be to choose the most favorable reinsurance arrangement. This means, as we have observed earlier, that the theory of risk is reduced to a theory of reinsurance, and as pointed out in Borch [8], already referred to, that the whole problem should be analyzed in terms of economic theory.

The foundation of insurance is the law of large numbers. It turns out, however, that the number of insurance contracts in the portfolio of a company is not usually "large enough," i.e., one cannot apply the law and ignore deviations from expected values. The theory of risk was developed to analyze these deviations, and the classical theory fell back on the central limit theorem, and assumed that the deviations were normally distributed. It seems, however, that the number of contracts is also usually too small to justify this assumption, as has been pointed out by a number of actuaries, *inter alios* by Cramér [13], who suggests that this is the main reason why the theory has found so little application in practice.

Cramér's criticism certainly contains a good deal of truth, but one may think of other explanations. It seems likely that the amount of computation required to apply the theory has played a part in its neglect. With electronic computers it may, however, be feasible to apply the theory in practice. Insurance companies are required to compute their reserves, i.e., the expected value of claims to be paid under the contracts in hand at the end of an accounting period. It should not be impossible to do some additional calculations and provide an estimate of the probability that total claim payments will be below the assets of the company. The practical usefulness of an estimate of this kind seems, however, to be very doubtful. The estimate is bound to be a fairly rough approximation, and it may obviously be very misleading. It should further be evident that one single number—the probability of ruin—cannot give a complete description of the real situation of the company.

The probability of ruin gives us the probability that the company shall be unable to meet the commitments under the contracts it holds at a certain moment. But this is a static measure; before these contracts have expired, it is likely that the company will have underwritten a large number of new contracts, and this may substantially change the company's ability to pay claims made under contracts in the original portfolio.

These considerations indicate that we need a dynamic theory of risk, in order to come to grips realistically with the problems of insurance companies. The fact that the classical theory of risk is essentially static is probably the main reason why it has found little application in the real, dynamic world. Arguments of this kind form the starting-point of the theory of Lundberg, which we shall discuss in the following section.

3. The Collective Risk Theory

The collective theory of risk was created by Lundberg [20], and has been developed by a relatively small group of actuaries, mainly Scandinavians. The theory seems to have found even less practical application than the classical theory discussed earlier, which Lundberg's followers usually refer to as the "individual theory of risk." The reason is, as we shall see, that Lundberg's theory does not, according to practicing actuaries, come to grips with the problems of insurance companies.

Lundberg's papers contain exceptionally penetrating analysis, and a very high degree of mathematical originality, and they have certainly not received the attention which they deserve. It is natural to compare Lundberg with Bachelier. Both studied problems connected with stochastic processes in continuous time about 30 years before this concept had been rigorously defined [1], and the work of both was ignored and practically forgotten.

It is not easy to explain why the significance of Bachelier's work should have been overlooked. In the case of Lundberg it is, however, easy to see that part of the explanation lies in his style.

Lundberg's mathematicl arguments were—and probably still are—too advanced for most actuaries and practical insurance people. His results are, however, almost invariably presented in actuarial terms, so that it is very hard for a mathematician without knowledge of insurance to see that some of the results are mathematical theorems of quite general validity.

Lundberg's theory has been developed in a number of papers, but most of these are written in a style which appeals neither to the mathematician nor to the practical insurance man. It may be quite natural for some members of a small group, working on a very special set of problems, to write mainly for the other initiated members of the group. It is, however, surprising that so few of the group have tried to write survey articles to inform the outsider. Cramér has written two good survey articles [13, 14], but they appear in publications which are not easily accessible. There is also a comprehensive survey by Segerdahl [25], which is of a rather limited value, since it does not contain any references to original papers.

Lundberg considered an insurance company as a container, or as a dam, to use the more popular current statistical term. Into this dam flows a continuous stream of premiums, and out of the dam goes a sequence of claim payments.

He then considered a model consisting of the following three elements:

(i)   The stream of premiums, $P(t)$ = the total value of premiums received in the period $(0, t)$.
(ii) $q(n, t)$ = the probability that n claims occur in the period $(0, t)$.
(iii) The probability distribution of individual claims, $G(x)$ = the probability that if a claim should occur, the amount payable will not exceed x.

This is a very general model. The most important restriction is the assumption that $G(x)$ does not depend on t and n. The restriction may be lifted, but few authors seem to have studied such generalizations. The reason is probably that it is not quite clear what kind of dependence one should assume in insurance problems.

From the three elements it follows that the probability that claim payments in the period $(0, t)$ shall not exceed x is given by the formula

$$F(x, t) = \sum_{n=0}^{\infty} q(n, t)G^{(n)}(x) \tag{10}$$

where $G^{(n)}(x)$ for $n > 0$ is the nth convolution of $G(x)$ with itself, and $G^{(0)}(x)$ = $H(x)$, where $H(x)$ is the Heaviside function defined by

$$H(x) = \begin{cases} 1 & \text{for} \quad x \geq 0 \\ 0 & \text{for} \quad x < 0 \end{cases}$$

$F(x, t)$ can obviously be considered as the claim distribution for a portfolio of insurance contracts, which all expire in the period $(0, t)$. If claim payments under different contracts are stochastically independent, $F(x, t)$ can be obtained as the convolution of all the claim distributions, defined by the contracts in the portfolio. Hence the second moment about the mean of $F(x, t)$ will be the square of the risk M^2, by analogy with (4).

These observations illustrate the elegance and power of Lundberg's method. With his approach it is no longer necessary to consider each contract in the portfolio in order to determine the probability distribution of the total amount of claim payments. Instead this distribution is built up from the two elements $q(n, t)$ and $G(x)$, from two distributions which it should be possible to estimate from the records of the company. From this point of view it seems natural to refer to Lundberg's theory as the collective theory of risk. It is, however, clear that the real innovation of the theory lies in its *dynamic* aspects, and it would have been preferable to use this word to distinguish Lundberg's theory from the essentially static, classical risk theory.

The discrete distribution $q(n, t)$ can be interpreted as the mechanism which generates claims. One can make assumptions about this mechanism, and deduce some of the properties of the distribution. This question has been studied by many actuaries, and, as one would expect, the assumptions which appear most natural differ from one branch of insurance to another. Lundberg himself worked with the stationarity and time-independence assumptions which lead to the Poisson process

$$q(n, t) = e^{-\alpha t} \frac{(\alpha t)^n}{n!}$$

The claim distribution then becomes the compound Poisson process

$$F(x, t) = e^{-\alpha t} \sum_{n=0}^{\infty} \frac{(\alpha t)^n}{n!} G^{(n)}(x) \tag{11}$$

The expected value of the claim payments x_t during the period $(0, t)$ is then

$$E\{x_t\} = \int_0^{\infty} x \, dF(x, t) = \alpha t \bar{x} \tag{12}$$

where

$$\bar{x} = \int_0^{\infty} x \, dG(x)$$

It is convenient to choose the unit of time such that

$$E\{x_t\} = t$$

There is, however, more than just convenience involved. It will clearly always be possible to make a transformation of the time scale, so that expected claim payments in any period are equal to the length of the period. This means that the stationarity assumptions, which lead to the Poisson process, are unnecessary if we work with this transformed "operational time."

Operational time is one of Lundberg's most ingenious concepts. It is closely related to the "entropy time" used in theoretical physics, and it makes it possible both to simplify the theory and to extend its validity. It seems, however, that this concept has also been the main obstacle to practical application of the theory.

The principle of equivalence implies that the net premium received by the company during a period of length t in operational time must be equal to t, the expected claim payments during the period. If there is a loading λ, the amount of premium received by the company during the period will be

$$P(t) = (1 + \lambda)t$$

Let us now assume that the company has an initial capital S_0. At time t, the capital will then be

$$S_t = S_0 + (1 + \lambda)t - x_t \tag{13}$$

This means that the development of the company's capital is described by a stochastic process with independent increments. It was a remarkable achievement of Lundberg to penetrate to the very core of the risk problem, and arrive at this formulation, which at his time could not be given with full mathematical rigour.

If the capital S_t is negative at time t, the company is insolvent or ruined. As a natural generalization of the classical probability of ruin, we are then led to study

$$\Pr \left\{ \min S_t \geqslant 0 \right\}$$

for t belonging to a suitable subset of the positive real line. If we select a subset consisting of one single point, we are back in the classical theory.

A practical insurance man may suggest a subset consisting of a sequence $t_1, t_2, \ldots, t_n$, corresponding to the dates of the n next valuations, or to the ends of the n next accounting years. He will then be interested in the probability that the company shall be solvent at all these dates, and presumably take some action if this probability falls below the acceptable minimum. It is, however, not easy to answer such practical questions, because the theory works with operational time. In order to obtain a simple and elegant theory, one has paid a heavy cost in the form of difficulties in practical applications.

If we take a subset consisting of an interval $(0, T)$, we are led to study the probability

$$\Pr\left\{ \min_{0 \leqslant t \leqslant T} S_t \geqslant 0 \right\} = R(S_0, T) \tag{14}$$

that the company shall be solvent during the whole period $(0, T)$. It is probably fair to say that most of the work in the collective risk theory has been concerned with deriving approximate expressions for $R(S, T)$ for large T. These expressions may be extremely complicated, but there are no serious mathematical problems involved. As we would expect, the expressions become simpler if we go to the limit, so let us write

$$\lim_{T \to \infty} R(S, T) = R(S) \tag{15}$$

where we have omitted the subscript on S. $R(S)$ is the probability that a company with initial capital S shall never become insolvent. We shall sketch a derivation of the integral equation satisfied by $R(S)$.

The probability that the first claim shall occur at time t is $e^{-t}dt$. The probability that this claim shall amount to x is $g(x)dx$, where $g(x) = G'(x)$. Provided that $x < S + (1 + \lambda)t$, the company will not be ruined by the first claim, and the probability that it shall remain solvent in the future will be $R(S + (1 + \lambda)t - x)$. By integrating over the relevant domains of t and x we obtain the integral equation

$$R(S) = \int_0^\infty e^{-t} \left\{ \int_0^{S+(1+\lambda)t} R(S + (1 + \lambda)t - x)g(x)\,dx \right\} dt \tag{16}$$

To simplify the expression we substitute $y = S + (1 + \lambda)t$, and write the equation

$$R(S) = \frac{1}{1 + \lambda} \int_S^\infty \exp\left(-\frac{y - S}{1 + \lambda} \right) \left\{ \int_0^y R(y - x)g(x)\,dx \right\} dy$$

The easiest way of solving this equation seems to differentiate and take Laplace transforms. Differentiation with respect to S gives

$$(1 + \lambda)R'(S) = R(S) - \int_0^S R(S - x)g(x)\,dx \tag{17}$$

Multiplying this equation by e^{-sS} (Re $s > 0$) and integrating over S from 0 to ∞, we obtain

$$(1 + \lambda)(s\psi(s) - R(0)) = \psi(s) - \psi(s)\,\phi(s)$$

or $$\psi(s) = \frac{(1 + \lambda)R(0)}{(1 + \lambda)s - 1 + \phi(s)} \tag{18}$$

Here $\psi(s)$ is the Laplace transform of $R(S)$, i.e.,

$$\psi(s) = \int_0^\infty e^{-sS} R(S) \, dS$$

and $\phi(s)$ is the Laplace transform of $g(x)$.

From the expression found for $\psi(s)$, we can find $R(S)$ itself by taking the inverse Laplace transform. It is easy to see that $\psi(s)$ under certain conditions can be represented by a convergent series of powers of $\phi(s)$, so that $R(S)$ can be expressed as an infinite series of convolutions of $g(x)$ with itself. The constant $R(0)$ can be determined, for instance by Tauberian methods, and one finds

$$R(0) = \frac{\lambda}{1 + \lambda}$$

In the preceding paragraphs we have solved our problem in a purely formal manner. We have done this in order to gain some insight into the nature of the problem. The results can be derived in a rigorous manner, by methods which by now are fairly standard, and which can easily be found in the literature, for instance in the textbook by Feller [16]. It is, however, remarkable that these results were achieved—admittedly in a heuristic manner—by Lundberg in the first decade of this century.

The methods we have outlined can be applied also for finite values of T, to determine $R(S, T)$. This will not lead to any essentially new difficulties, but it is clear that the explicit expressions will be even more complicated than in the limiting case.

The collective risk theory was created when few actuaries had even an electric desk calculator. It is therefore natural that the early development of the theory should have concentrated on deriving simple approximate expressions for $R(S)$ and $R(S, T)$. This has led to results which in many ways are impressive, but which are of little theoretical or practical interest today. The arrival of electronic computers has shifted the focus of interest to algorithms for computing the convolutions of high order, which enter in the series in the preceding paragraph. Some recent papers in this field [6] seem to have a considerable general interest. The fact remains, however, that—in spite of these developments—collective risk theory has found virtually no application in practice.

To illustrate the point, let us assume that an insurance company has to make a decision with regard to, say, loading and reinsurance. The company will then need a criterion for comparing the merits of the different possible decisions. The collective risk theory suggests that one should compute the probability that the company will never be ruined, provided that the decision, once it is made, can never be changed. One should then make the decision which gives the highest value to this "probability of survival." It does not seem very likely that insurance companies should wish to make their decisions in this manner, and there is certainly no reason why experts should advise companies to do so.

These considerations indicate that there is a need for a radical reformulation of the basic model behind Lundberg's theory. In the following section we shall discuss this question, which so far has received little attention.

4. The Modern Risk Theory

It is doubtful if one should talk about modern risk theory as a continuation of the theories discussed in the two preceding sections. All results in these older theories can today be considered as special cases of more general results in pure or applied mathematics created without any reference to insurance. It is clear that these general results can be applied to the problems of insurance, and it is likely that the future development of "risk theory" in our sense will consist of finding such applications. Actuaries no longer have the whole field of probability theory to themselves, nor do they have to create their own tools as they proceed from one problem to the next. The task of a modern actuary is above all to analyze and find the right formulation of his problem. The mathematical tools he needs to solve it are almost certain to be available.

As an illustration, we shall first discuss a model due to de Finetti [17], which has been generalized and studied in more detail by Borch [10-12].

The capital of our company at time t was given in equation (13), and the expected value of the capital is

$$E\left\{S_t\right\} = S_0 + (1 + \lambda)\, t - E\, x_t\ = S_0 + \lambda t \tag{19}$$

This means that the capital can be expected to grow to infinity with t. De Finetti observed that this is a most unrealistic model, and assumed that there must be an upper limit, say Z, to the amount of capital which an insurance company would want—or be allowed—to accumulate. This assumption implies, however, that the company is certain to be ruined some time in the future, i.e., $R(S_0) = 0$, so that all the results of the collective risk theory become irrelevant.

The model suggested by de Finetti can be described as follows:

(i)   The company has an initial capital S.
(ii) In each operating period the company underwrites a portfolio of insurance contracts with a claim distribution $F(x)$. We shall assume $F(x) = 0$ for $x \leqslant 0$.
(iii) In each operating period the company collects an amount of premium P.
(iv) If at the end of an operating period the company's capital exceeds Z, the excess is paid out—as dividend or taxes, as the case may be.
(v)   If at the end of an operating period the capital is negative, the company is ruined, and has to go out of business.

In this model the company's capital performs a *random walk,* and there is an absorbing barrier at $S = 0$, and a reflecting barrier at $S = Z$. If we let Z go to infinity, we obtain the model of Lundberg. The introduction of a finite reflecting barrier makes the model far more intresting, and makes it possible to ask a number of new questions.

As a first example we shall find the expected number of periods during which the company will operate, i.e., the "expected life" of the company. Since this number obviously will depend on the initial capital S, and on the upper limit Z, we shall denote it by $D(S, Z)$.

From the definition of the process it follows that

$$D(S, Z) = 0 \qquad \text{for } S < 0$$

$$D(S, Z) = D(Z, Z) \qquad \text{for } S > Z$$

For $0 \leqslant S \leqslant Z$, $D(S, Z)$ must satisfy the integral equation

$$D(S, Z) = 1 + \int_0^{S+P} D(S + P - x, Z)\, dF(x) \tag{20}$$

This is easily verified by using an argument similar to that used in setting up equation (16). The equation can be solved by standard methods, which we shall discuss below. De Finetti considered only the special case where $P = 1$, and where x can take only the values 0 and 2. The integral equation then reduces to the difference equation

$$D(S, Z) = 1 + pD(S + 1, Z) + qD(S - 1, Z)$$

where

$$\Pr\{x = 0\} = p$$

$$\Pr\{x = 2\} = q = 1 - p$$

If $p > q$, the solution of the difference equation is

$$D(S, Z) = \frac{p}{(p - q)^2} \left\{ \left(\frac{p}{q}\right)^{Z+1} - \left(\frac{p}{q}\right)^{Z-S} \right\} - \frac{S + 1}{p - q} \tag{21}$$

It is obvious that $D(S, Z)$ will go to infinity with Z, and that the probability of ruin may then become smaller tha one. It is a well-known classical result that the probability of ruin in the limit is

$$1 - R(S) = \left(\frac{q}{p}\right)^S$$

By some elementary manipulations we find that

$$D(S + 1, Z) - D(S, Z) = \frac{1}{p - q} \left\{ \left(\frac{p}{q}\right)^{Z-S} - 1 \right\}$$

from which it follows that $D(S, Z)$ increases with S.

As a second example, let us assume that excess capital is paid out as dividends, and let $V(S, Z)$ be the expected discounted value of the dividend payments, which the company will make during its lifetime. As in the preceding paragraph we have

$$V(S, Z) = 0 \qquad\qquad \text{for } S < 0$$

$$V(S, Z) = S - Z + V(Z, Z) \qquad \text{for } S > Z$$

For $0 \leqslant S \leqslant Z$ we see that $V(S, Z)$ must satisfy the integral equation

$$V(S, Z) = v \int_0^{S+P} V(S + P - x, Z) \, dF(x) \tag{22}$$

where v is a discount factor.

In the special case considered by de Finetti, the integral equation reduces to the difference equation

$$V(S, Z) = vp V(S + 1, Z) + vq V(S - 1, Z)$$

whose solution is

$$V(S, Z) = \frac{r_1^{S+1} - r_2^{S+1}}{r_1^{Z+2} - r_2^{Z+2} - r_1^{Z+1} + r_2^{Z+2}} \tag{23}$$

where r_1 and r_2 are the roots of the characteristic equation

$$r = vpr^2 + vq$$

It is easy to verify that both roots are positive, and that $r_1 > 1, r_2 < 1$. It then follows that $V(S, Z)$ will increase with S, as we would expect. It follows also that $V(S, Z)$ will go to zero as Z goes to infinity—i.e., if dividend payments are postponed indefinitely. There may, however, be a value of $Z > 0$, which maximizes $V(S, Z)$ and may in a sense be considered as the "optimal" reserve capital for the company. This observation has been made by Shubik and

THE THEORY OF RISK 277

Thompson [26] in a study of economic problems not having any formal connection with insurance.

The special case, studied by de Finetti, clearly gives some information about the general shape of the functions $D(S, Z)$ and $V(S, Z)$. To investigate this question in more detail, we shall study the continuous case, assuming that a density function $f(x) = F'(x)$ exists. Omitting the argument Z, we can write the integral equation (20) as follows:

$$D(S) = 1 + \int_0^{S+P} D(S + P - x)f(x)\, dx$$

$$\text{or} \quad D(S) = 1 + D(Z)F(S + P - Z) + \int_0^Z f(S + P - x)D(x)\, dx \qquad (24)$$

This is an equation of Fredholm's type. To solve it, we form the iterated kernels

$$f^{(0)}(S + P - x) = \delta(S - x)$$

where δ is the Dirac δ-function,

$$f^{(n)}(S + P - x) = \int_0^Z f(S + P - t)f^{(n-1)}(t + P - x)\, dt \qquad n = 2, 3, \ldots$$

The solution is then given by the Neumann expansion

$$D(S) = 1 + D(Z) \sum_{n=0}^{\infty} \int_0^Z f^{(n)}(S + P - x)F(x + P - Z)\, dx$$

$$+ \sum_{n=1}^{\infty} \int_0^Z f^{(n)}(S + P - x)\, dx \qquad (25)$$

The terms in the expansion are integrals over a finite range of products of density functions—or "truncated convolutions." It is therefore obvious that the series converges, and gives a solution of the integral equation. The unknown $D(Z)$ is determined by requiring the solution to be continuous to the right at $S = Z$. This gives

$$D(Z) = 1 + D(Z) \sum_{n=0}^{\infty} \int_0^Z f^{(n)}(Z + P - x)F(x + P - Z)\, dx$$

$$+ \sum_{n=1}^{\infty} \int_0^Z f^{(n)}(Z + P - x)\, dx$$

$$\text{or} \quad D(Z) = \frac{1 + \sum_{n=1}^{\infty} \int_0^Z f^{(n)} (Z + P - x)\, dx}{1 - \sum_{n=0}^{\infty} \int_0^Z f^{(n)} (Z + P - x)F(x + P - Z)\, dx}$$

The continuous solution is obviously unique.

The series will usually converge fairly rapidly for small values of Z, so it is possible to compute $D(Z)$ and $D(S)$ with only a reasonable amount of labor. In general it is, however, impossible to find an explicit and simple expression for the function $D(S)$, and study its properties by elementary means. It may therefore be useful to discuss a special case, which gives a fairly simple expression. The basic idea is to reduce Fredholm's integral equation to an equation of a simpler kind.

Let us assume

$$f(x) = e^{-x} \quad x \geqslant 0$$

The integral equation will then become

$$D(S) = 1 + e^{-S-P} \int_0^{S+P} D(x)e^x \, dx \tag{26}$$

Differentiating with respect to S, we find

$$D'(S) = -e^{-S-P} \int_0^{S+P} D(x)e^x \, dx + D(S + P)$$

adding this to the original equation, we obtain

$$D(S) + D'(S) = 1 + D(S + P) \tag{27}$$

This is a differential-difference equation, valid for $0 \leqslant S \leqslant Z$.

We shall now solve this equation, following a procedure developed by Bellman and Cooke [4]. It is, however, convenient first to make a change in the notation, which will give the results in a more familiar form. We shall write

$$t = Z - S$$

and $u(t) = D(S)$

The equation then becomes

$$u(t) - u'(t) - u(t - P) = 1 \tag{28}$$

which is valid for $0 \leqslant t \leqslant Z$. In the following we shall assume that the equation also holds for $Z < t$, although the solution in this domain is irrelevant to our concrete problem. For $t \leqslant 0$ we have the boundary condition $u(t) = D(Z) = c$.

Taking the Laplace transform, we obtain (when $\mathrm{Re}\, s > 0$)

$$\int_0^\infty u(t)e^{-st}\, dt - \int_0^\infty u'(t)e^{-st}\, dt - \int_0^\infty u(t-P)e^{-st}\, dt = \frac{1}{s}$$

which reduces to

$$\left\{1 - s - e^{-sP}\right\} \int_0^\infty u(t)e^{-st}\, dt = \frac{1}{s}\left\{1 + c - cs - ce^{-sP}\right\}$$

provided that s is sufficiently large. For the Laplace transform of $u(t)$ we therefore find

$$u^*(s) = \int_0^\infty u(t)e^{-st}\, dt = \frac{c}{s} + \frac{1}{s(1 - s - e^{-sP})} \tag{29}$$

The inversion of the expression $(1 + s - e^{-sP})^{-1}$ is discussed in another context by Feller [15]. Since a factor s^{-1} in the transform corresponds to an indefinite integration with respect to t in the original, easy manipulations of Feller's result yield

$$u(t) = c + \sum_{n=0}^\infty \left\{1 - e^{t-nP}\sum_{j=0}^n \frac{(-1)^j}{j!}(t-nP)^j\right\}H(t-nP) \tag{30}$$

In the interval, $NP \leqslant t \leqslant (N+1)P$, this may be written

$$u(t) = c + N + 1 - \sum_{n=0}^N e^{t-nP}\left\{1 - (t-nP) + \ldots + (-1)^n \frac{(t-nP)^n}{n!}\right\}$$

or $u(t) = c + 1 + \left[\frac{t}{P}\right] - A(t)$

where $[t/P]$ is the greatest integer not exceeding t/P, and $A(t)$ stands for the sum on the right-hand side. It is easy to verify that this function is continuous for $0 < t$.

To determine the constant c, we return to the integral equation (26) and note that

$$D(-P, Z) = u(Z + P) = 1$$

It then follows that

$$c = A(Z + P) - 1 - \left[\frac{Z}{P}\right]$$

and $u(t) = A(Z + P) - \left[\frac{Z}{P}\right] - A(t) + \left[\frac{t}{P}\right]$ (31)

Returning to our original notation, we find the following expression for the solution:

$$D(S, Z) = \sum_{n=0}^{\left[\frac{Z}{P}\right] + 1} e^{Z - (n-1)P} \left\{ 1 + \ldots \frac{(-1)^n}{n!} (Z - (n-1)P)^n \right\}$$ (32)

$$- \sum_{n=0}^{\left[\frac{Z - S}{P}\right]} e^{Z - S - nP} \left\{ 1 + \ldots \frac{(-1)^n}{n!} (Z - S - nP)^n \right\} - \left[\frac{Z}{P}\right] + \left[\frac{Z - S}{P}\right]$$

The function $V(S, Z)$ can be found by similar methods, as shown in another paper [9]. The expression will, however, be even more complicated than the one we have found for $D(S, Z)$—essentially because the boundary conditions are more complicated for the differential-difference equation satisfied by $V(S, Z)$.

To obtain really simple expressions for the two functions, we can assume that the *gain* of the company has the density function

$$f(x) = k\alpha e^{-\alpha x} \qquad \text{for } x > 0$$

$$f(x) = (1 - k)\alpha e^{\alpha x} \qquad \text{for } x < 0$$

In this case there is no upper limit to the company's gain, so the example may not be quite appropriate to an insurance company. It may, however, be accepted as a reasonable approximation, and the example may provide an adequate model for companies in other lines of business, as has been shown in another paper [12].

With this assumption, the integral equation (20) becomes

$$D(S) = 1 + (1 - k)\alpha e^{-\alpha s} \int_0^S D(x)e^{\alpha x} \, dx + k\alpha e^{\alpha S} \int_S^Z D(x)e^{-\alpha x} \, dx$$

$$+ ke^{\alpha(S-Z)} D(Z)$$ (33)

Differentiating twice, we find that the integral equation can be reduced to the differential equation

$$(2k - 1)\alpha D'(S) + D''(S) + \alpha^2 = 0$$

and the general solution of this equation is

$$D(S) = C_1 e^{-(2k-1)\alpha S} - \frac{\alpha}{2k - 1} S + C_2 \tag{34}$$

where C_1 and C_2 are constants, which must be determined so that the solution also satisfies the integral equation.

Similarly we find that the integral equation (22) can be written as

$$V(S) = v(1 - k)\alpha e^{-\alpha S} \int_0^S V(x)e^{\alpha x}\, dx + vk\alpha e^{\alpha S} \int_S^Z V(x)e^{-\alpha x}\, dx$$

$$+ vk V(Z)e^{\alpha(S-Z)} + \frac{vk}{\alpha} e^{\alpha(S-Z)} \tag{35}$$

Differentiating this twice, we find that the integral equation can be reduced to the differential equation

$$(1 - v)\alpha^2 V(S) + v(1 - 2k)\alpha V'(S) - V''(S) = 0$$

which has the general solution

$$V(S) = C_1 \exp(r_1 S) + C_2 \exp(r_2 S) \tag{36}$$

Here r_1 and r_2 are the roots of the characteristic equation

$$r^2 - v(1 - 2k)\alpha r - (1 - v)\alpha^2 = 0$$

and the constants C_1 and C_2 must be determined so that the general solution of the differential equation also is a solution of the integral equation.

To get some idea of the shape of the two functons, we shall take a numerical example in which $\alpha = 1$, $v = 0.97$ and $k = 0.603$. We then find:

$$V(S, Z) = \frac{143e^{0.1S} - 91e^{-0.3S}}{16e^{0.1Z} + 21e^{-0.3Z}}$$

and $D(S, Z) = 37.5e^{0.2Z} - 5(1 + S) - 30e^{0.2(Z-S)}$

Tables 18–1 and 18–2 give the value of $D(S, Z)$ and $V(S, Z)$ for some selected values of S and Z.

The two functions $D(S, Z)$ and $V(S, Z)$ obviously have some relevance to practical problems. If the objective of an insurance company is to maximize the expected discounted value of the dividends it will be able to pay before ruin, it will clearly set its "reserve requirements" at the level Z which maximizes $V(S, Z)$. This level, which the company will consider its optimal reserve, may not give the insured an adequate security. The company may therefore—on its own initiative, or following instructions from the government—set the reserves at a higher level, for instance a level such that $D(S, Z)$ is above a certain acceptable minimum. The objective of the company can then be expressed as

max $V(S, Z)$

subject to the condition

$D(S, Z) > D_0$

where D_0 is the acceptable minimum expected life.

It does not make sense to assume that the company's objective is to maximize $D(S, Z)$, since this implies that the company will never pay any dividend. It is, however, possible to assume that its objective can be expressed as

max $\{\alpha \log V(S, Z) + (1 - \alpha) \log D(S, Z)\}$

Here α and $1 - \alpha$ can be interpreted as the relative weights given to the company's objectives as a profit-making business concern, and the objectives which spring from its obligation to provide adequate security to the public. A high weight on the second group of objectives may be imposed by the government, or it may be due to a desire of the directors and the employees of the company to secure their own position by giving the company a long expected life.

The two objectives suggested in the preceding paragraph show that the modern theory makes it possible to give an operational formulation of the basic

Table 18–1
$D(S, Z)$ = Expected life of the company

S \ Z	0	1	2	3	4	5	6
0	2.5	4.2	6.2	8.7	11.7	15.4	19.1
1	2.5	5.8	9.6	13.3	19.0	25.1	33.0
2	2.5	5.8	11.2	16.7	23.6	32.4	42.7
3	2.5	5.8	11.2	18.3	27.0	37.0	49.8
4	2.5	5.8	11.2	18.3	28.6	40.4	54.6
5	2.5	5.8	11.2	18.3	28.6	42.0	57.9
6	2.5	5.8	11.2	18.3	28.6	42.0	59.5

problems in insurance. If, for instance, the objective of the company is to maximize a function of of the type suggested, one can determine the optimal value of Z, i.e., the optimal dividend policy. One can, however, also select the best of the available reinsurance arrangements, and the best underwriting policy—provided of course that these concepts can be defined precisely.

This seems to open a vast field for further generalizations, a field which so far has not been explored at all. To illustrate the possibilities, let us return to the stochastic process S_t of (13).

Let us assume that the company reinsures a quota k of its portfolio, against a premium $(1 + \pi)k$ per unit of time. This means that the reinsurer will pay a proportion k of all claims, and that the company itself will pay the remainder $(1 - k)$. The reinsurance arrangement will change the stochastic process to

$$S_t(k) = S_0 + (1 - k + \lambda - \pi k)t - (1 - k)x_t \tag{37}$$

It is natural to assume $\pi > \lambda$, i.e., that the loading on reinsurance is higher than on the direct underwriting, since we cannot neglect the cost of the reinsurance arrangement.

The real problem of the company now is to find the value of k which gives the "best" of the stochastic processes in the set we have defined. The problem can obviously be generalized by assuming that other types of reinsurance are available.

However, there is no sense in talking about the "best stochastic process," unless one has some rule or criterion for deciding when one process should be preferred to another, i.e., a *preference ordering* over a set of stochastic processes. This points to the need for a generalization of the Bernoulli principle, which was shown in Section 2 to give a very convenient representation of preference orderings over a set of probability distributions. So far there does not seem to have been any attempt to extend this principle to sets of stochastic processes. It is, however, evident that such a generalization will present some very intricate mathematical problems.

Table 18-2
$V(S, Z)$ = Expected discounted value of dividend payments

S \ Z	0	1	2	3	4	5	6
0	1.41	1.57	1.68	1.74	1.73	1.68	1.60
1	2.41	2.74	2.93	3.02	3.02	2.94	2.70
2	3.41	3.74	4.03	4.16	4.16	4.04	3.84
3	4.41	4.74	5.03	5.21	5.20	5.14	4.88
4	5.41	5.74	6.03	6.21	6.19	6.02	5.70
5	6.41	6.74	7.03	7.21	7.19	6.98	6.60
6	7.41	7.74	8.03	8.21	8.19	7.98	7.53

A preference ordering over the elements of a set is essentially a mapping from the set to the real line. The two functions $D(S, Z)$ and $V(S, Z)$ give such mappings from a set of stochastic processes, and will therefore represent preference orderings; so also will any combination of them. These orderings will, however, be of a special kind, and it is clearly desirable to study preference orderings of a more general nature. An insurance company may, for instance, be interested, not only in the expected discounted value of its dividend payments, but also in avoiding large variations in these payments from one year to another. Such a desire for stability seems to be important in practice, but it is not taken into account in the preference ordering represented by $V(S, Z)$, and seems very difficult to formulate mathematically.

These considerations indicate that the real difficulty is to formulate the insurance problem, i.e., to describe with sufficient precision what the company really wants to achieve. Once this is done, it may not be so difficult to discover how the objective should be reached: to determine the decision which selects the best of the attainable stochastic processes.

The most unrealistic assumptions in the models we have discussed seem to be:

(i)   The stationarity assumptions, which imply that the nature of the company's business will never change. These assumptions become less drastic than they may seem at first sight, if we introduce operational time.
(ii) The assumption that the probability laws governing the process are completely known.
(iii) The implicit assumption that a decision once it has been made cannot be changed.

The real life situations, which these models should represent are rather different. The reserve capital of an insurance company can obviously be considered as a stochastic process, but the laws governing the process will usually be known only partially. As time passes, the company may acquire more knowledge about these laws, for instance by statistical analysis of the current claim payments. The company will then have to decide if, in view of the new knowledge, existing reinsurance arrangements or plans for future dividend payments should be changed.

In general the problem of the company will be to devise:

(i)   An *information system*: a system for observing the stochastic process as it develops
(ii) A *decision function*: a set of rules for translating the observations into action

The optimal solution to this problem should enable the company to control the process so that it develops in the way which is considered best, according to some preference ordering over sets of stochastic processes.

The possible generalizations of the risk theory, which we have outlined in the preceding paragraph, should lead to models which contain all the essential elements of the real problems in insurance companies. The models are, however, so general that they can be given a number of other interpretations, and applied to a wide range of practical problems in different fields.

We have now reached the point where the actuarial theory of risk again joins the mainstream of theoretical statistics and applied mathematics. Our general formulation of the actuary's problem leads directly to the general theory of *optimal control processes* or *adaptive control processes*, a theory which it is natural to associate with the names of Bellman [3] and Pontryagin [24]. This theory has grown out of problems in engineering, and it is appropriate, as suggested by Bellman, to place its origin in the paper which Maxwell read to the Royal Society of London [21].

The theory of control processes seems to be "tailor-made" for the problems which actuaries have struggled to formulate for more than a century. It may be interesting and useful to meditate a little over how the theory would have developed, if actuaries and engineers had realized that they were studying the same problems and joined forces 50 years ago. A little reflection should teach us that a "highly specialized" problem may, when given the proper mathematical formulation, be identical to a series of other, seemingly unrelated problems.

References

1. Bachelier, L. *Théorie de la speculation* (Paris. Thesis, 1900).
2. Barrois, T. "Essai sur l'application du calcul des probabilités aux assurances contre l'incendie," *Mém. Soc. Sci. Lille,* 1834, pp. 85–282.
3. Bellman, R. *Adaptive Control Processes—A Guided Tour* (Princeton University Press, 1961).
4. Bellman, R., and Cooke, K. *Differential-Difference Equations* (New York: Academic Press, 1963).
5. Bernoulli, D. "Specimen theoriae novae de mensura sortis," *Commentarii academiae scientarum imperialis Petropolitanae,* 1738. (English translation: *Econometrica,* 22, 23–36.)
6. Bohman, H. and Esscher, F. "Studies in Risk Theory with Numerical Illustrations," I. *Skand. Aktuar.,* 1963, pp. 173–225.
7. Borch, K. The Utility Concept Applied to the Theory of Insurance. *The ASTIN Bulletin,* 1, (1961): 245–255.
8. ——. "Equilibrium in a Reinsurance Market," *Econometrica,* 30, (1962): 424–444.
9. ——. "Una generalización de la teoria del riesgo colectivo," *An. Inst. Actuar. Españoles,* 5 (2), (1965): 13–30.

286 THE DYNAMIC THEORY OF INSURANCE

286 THE DYNAMIC THEORY OF INSURANCE

10. ——. "Control of a Portfolio of Insurance Contracts." *The ASTIN Bulletin*, 4, (1966): 59–71.
11. ——. "Dynamic Decision Problems in an Insurance Company," *The ASTIN Bulletin*, (1967).
12. ——. "Die optimale Dividendenpolitik der Unternehmen," *Unternehmensforschung* 11 (1967): 131–143.
13. Cramér, H. "On the Mathematical Theory of Risk," *Skandia Jubilee Volume*, Stockholm, 1930.
14. ——. "Collective Risk Theory," *Skandia Jubilee Volume*. Stockholm, 1955.
15. Feller, W. "A Problem in the Theory of Counters," papers presented to Richard Courant, New York, 1945.
16. ——. *An Introduction to Probability Theory and its Applications*, vol. 2. (New York and London: Wiley, 1966).
17. Finetti, B. de."Su una impostazione alternativa della theoria collettiva del rischio," *Trans. XV Int. Congr. Actuaries* 2 (1957): 433–443.
18. Hausdorff, F. "Das Risico bei Zufallsspielen," *Leipziger Berichte* 49 (1897): 497–548.
19. Knight, F. *Risk, Uncertainty and Profits* (Houghton, Mifflin, 1921).
20. Lundberg, F. "Über die Theorie der Rückversicherung," *Trans. VI Int. Congr. Actuaries* 1 (1909): 877–955.
21. Maxwell, J. C. "On Governors," *Proc. Roy. Soc. Lond.* 16 (1868): 270–283.
22. Neumann, J. von and Morgenstern, O. *Theory of Games and Economic Behavior*. (Princeton University Press, 1944).
23. Nolfi, P. "Zur mathematischen Darstellung des Nutzens in der Versicherung," *Bull. Actuaires Suisses* 57 (1957): 395–407.
24. Pontryagin, L. S., Boltyanskii, V. G., Gamkrelidze, R. V., and Mischenko, E. F. *Mathematical Theory of Optimal Processes* (New York: Wiley, 1962).
25. Segerdahl, C. O. "A Survey of Results in the Collective Theory of Risk," *Studies in Probability and Statistics–The Harald Cramér Volume* (New York: Wiley, 1959), pp. 276–299.
26. Shubik, M. and Thompson, G. "Games of Economic Survival," *Naval Res. Logist. Quart.*, 6 (1959): 111–124.
27. Tetens, J. N. *Einleitung zur Berechung der Leibrenten und Anwartschafen* (Leipzig, 1786).
28. Wald, A. *Statistical Decision Functions* (New York: Wiley, 1950).
29. Wold, H. *Landsbygdens Brandförsäkringsbolags Maximaler och Återförsäkring* (Stockholm, 1936).

Discussion on Professor Borch's Paper

Professor J. Gani: It gives me great pleasure to propose the vote of thanks to Professor Borch for his informative and stimulating survey of insurance risk problems. I must confess directly my embarrassment that this duty should have fallen, almost accidentally, to me. Unlike several members of the Royal Statistical Society present here this evening, I have little knowledge of actuarial mathematics, and no experience of risk problems other than that of a proposer in search of the most favorable terms for a motor or life insurance contract. In view of so serious a handicap, I feel I can comment on Professor Borch's paper only in the broadest layman's terms.

The paper opens with a review of classical risk theory. This is concerned with such problems as the determination of insurance premiums to be charged against claims, the calculation of risks for portfolios of insurance contracts, and the computation of probabilities of ruin. The methods used are those of classical probability theory, and include the application of the law of large numbers. The time variable appears to play no role, the discussion being limited to the position of a company at a particular instant. As a result, Professor Borch suggests that the theory has proved inadequate for the study of real-life situations.

With the development of collective risk theory by Lundberg and the Scandinavian school, we enter the realm of time-dependent stochastic processes. Starting with capital S_0, and receiving premiums at the rate $(1 + \lambda)$ per unit time, a company subject with probability $q(n, t)$ to n claims in the interval $(0, t)$ whose amounts $y_1, y_2, \ldots, y_n$ are independently and identically distributed, each with the d.f. $G(x)$, will have the capital

$$S_t = S_0 + (1 + \lambda)t - x_t$$

at time $t \geqslant 0$. The random variable x_t is the sum of all claims y_i in $(0, t)$.

If, in Figure 18-1, y_n were such that $S_t < 0$ at that instant, ruin would follow. It is, of course, necessary for a healthy company to remain solvent; Professor Borch has outlined the derivation of the limiting probability $R(S_0)$ of solvency in the particular case where the arrival process for claims is Poisson, and the claims themselves have a continuous distribution with p.d.f. $g(x) = G'(x)$. For other detailed results in connection with this and associated problems, the papers of Arfwedson [1, 2] and Prabhu [15] may be of interest. The latter in particular relates methods in collective risk theory to those in queueing and storage, possibly more familiar to some among us, myself included.

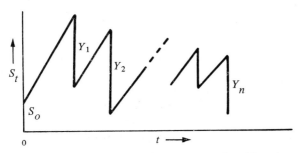

Figure 18-1. The capital of a company plotted against time.

If, in our model

$$E(x_t) \geqslant (1 + \lambda)t$$

the probability of solvency $R(S_0, T)$ of the company will tend to zero as $T \to \infty$. I have wondered if, in this case, the behavior of the distribution of the capital S_T, conditional on solvency, might not be worth investigating. In a notation similar to that used in the paper, this would be

$$\frac{\Pr\left\{S_T \leqslant s; \min_{0 \leqslant t \leqslant T} S_t \geqslant 0\right\}}{\Pr\left\{\min_{0 \leqslant t \leqslant T} S_t \geqslant 0\right\}} = \frac{H(s, T; S_0, 0)}{R(S_0, T)}$$

It would be interesting to establish the general conditions under which this expression would lead to a limiting distribution as $T \to \infty$. This might provide the analogue in insurance risk of the quasi-stationary distributions which have arisen in genetic problems, and been studied by Darroch and Seneta [7], Seneta and Seneta [16] and Vere-Jones [17].

In the section on modern risk theory, we are presented with a model of de Finetti's, studied in more detail by the author. This is a discrete-time equivalent of Lundberg's model with an upper reflecting barrier at $S = Z$, which corresponds to the payment as dividends or taxes of any capital in excess of Z. Quantities such as the expected life of the company $D(S_0, Z)$, and the expected discounted value of dividends $V(S_0, Z)$ are considered, and solutions provided for these under various assumptions.

Finally, the possible objectives of a company are set out in operational terms: these could be to maximize the dividends $V(S_0, Z)$ subject to the condition of keeping the expected life of the company above a certain minimum $D(S_0, Z) > D_0$. Alternatively, if α, $1 - \alpha$ are the relative weights to be given to dividends and expected life, respectively, then the company's objective might be to maximize, say,

$$\alpha \log V(S_0, Z) + (1 - \alpha) \log D(S_0, Z)$$

This type of formulation seems to indicate more realistically the basic problems of an insurance company. It is with an elaboration of the latter problems, and a reminder of the lack of realism of some of the assumptions previously made that the paper terminates.

Professor Borch's conclusion that actuarial problems lead directly to the theory of optimal control processes has made me, for one, resolve that I must learn more of them. I should like, once again, to thank him for his most instructive survey which has suggested to me stochastic problems with realistic applications, which would repay further research.

Professor P. G. Moore: A paper on the theory of risk is a statistically rare event, particularly at this Society, but in addition, as the author states, it is also true that the so-called theory of risk has not been applied greatly by actuaries or statisticians over recent years, particularly in the United Kingdom. It is noteworthy that the present paper does not contain a single reference to a paper in either the *Journal of the Institute of Actuaries* or the *Journal* of this Society. This is a puzzling phenomenon to which I think we should seek an answer. The possible answers seem to lie in two directions: is the theory relevant, and is it practicable?

First the relevance. Most actuaries are concerned with life assurance where the business is primarily of a long-term character and of a dynamic and continuing nature. Given also that the bulk of business is on a with-profit basis, and thus having a substantial loading to the basic premium, a cushion is provided to the fund that is in turn continually being built up, thus allowing the emerging results in the fund to be used to guide future policy decisions concerning both new business and the monetary value to be attached to existing business, i.e., an information system allied to a decision procedure. There are, however, a number of situations where the theory is more directly relevant, particularly if an office is looking carefully at each class of business separately. For example, Benjamin [3, page 165] considers a maturity guarantee on an equity-linked contract of the following form. A basic premium of 1 p.a. is invested in equity units for N years. All dividends are invested. A guarantee is given under the policy conditions that the maturity value will not be less than N. What loading should be made on the basic premium to charge for the guarantee? This is the kind of situation that is now becoming more common with a number of insurance linked trusts. Benjamin puts forward a possible solution to the problem based on certain assumptions regarding the possible movements of equity prices. His solution makes use of a simulation model to estimate the loading required. This leads on to the second point: is the theory practicable? For a mixed bag of policies, the amount of calculation could appear frightening, and I suspect that it would, in most cases, be impossible without electronic computation. Even actuaries blanch at computation when it reaches a critical level. Hence even if it were relevant, I doubt if the necessary calculation could be carried out, purely because of the great deal of effort and calculating power required on a fairly continuous basis.

In non-life insurance, however, the theory would seem, at a quick glance, to have considerably greater relevance and might be easier to apply. In non-life insurance there are usually a large number of short-term contracts renewable, at the insurer's option, at regular intervals. The happening of a claim is of a probabilistic nature, as is the size of the claim itself when it arises. As the claims which arise take quite a long time—in relationship to the length of the contract—to be agreed and settled, correspondingly large reserves are required at the end of any accounting period. This seems to be the theory of risk situation and it is perhaps ironic that actuaries do not in general deal in non-life insurance, although notable personal exceptions, such as R. E. Beard, spring to mind, and a paper of his [2] shows up the problems that exist, particularly on the question of adequate reserves in non-life business—a point that has particular relevance in the light of events over the last few months. Basically, it can be argued that the insurance company reserves should be of two kinds, a "specific" reserve based on the running results achieved by the business, and a "fluctuations" reserve, for which methods of risk theory could provide quantitative assessment. Arbitrary levels of "fluctuation" reserves, such as seem to be implied by the Board of Trade free asset requirement of £50,000, may penalize some companies or benefit other companies and are thus as unsatisfactory as are many of the rules used for judging companies by comparing reserves with turnover, rather than on a proper study of the nature of the possible variations. For the specific reserves, or solvency margins, methods are required to ensure that the system is a dynamic one and that these reserves are being kept right up to date. The latest Companies Act attempts to improve the situation, but does not appear to have completely solved it. Thus I feel that it is perhaps a good moment of time when we should strive to interest the non-life insurance world in the theory of risk and some of its ramifications.

I would accordingly like to add my congratulations to those of the opener and to thank the author for his stimulating paper. I have much pleasure in seconding the vote of thanks.

The vote of thanks was put to the meeting and carried unanimously.

Professor S. Vajda: I am very happy to have this opportunity of welcoming one of the very few who have contributed to the practical use of the theory of games in operational research. He did this in his work on reinsurance, to which he refers very briefly, but Professor Borch was too modest to quote his own papers. The first paper of his which he quotes dates from 1961, whereas he has written on reinsurance for the Brussels International Congress of Actuaries in 1960.

Professor Borch has mentioned Alfred Tauber. Tauber was of course a mathematician. He is the man after whom the Tauberian theorems in mathematics are called; but he was not the only mathematician interested in actuarial problems. For instance, Mittag-Leffler, well known for his work in the theory of functions, was an actuary, and Karl Friedrich Gauss, one of the greatest mathematicians, has written a very early paper on an actuarial problem. In more recent times, Edward Helly who was a well-known topologist, worked as an actuary. Professor Borch mentions the curious fact that mathematicians have been interested in actuarial problems and actuaries have had to deal with mathematics, and yet there seems to be so little contact between them. In those countries of Central Europe which I know something about it is very simple to explain why mathematicians worked in actuarial offices. They just could not get any other

job as mathematicians except in insurance companies, so they carried on with
their mathematics as a hobby, and they got their salaries for their actuarial work.

Professor Borch gives a reason why this contact was not as happy as it
might have been. He suggests in a rather roundabout way that this has something
to do with the integrity which is so highly esteemed in the insurance world. Now
I am certainly the last one to suggest that integrity is lacking in the insurance
world, but I do not really believe that this is a very good or very conclusive
reason. I rather think that Professor Moore, the seconder of the vote of thanks,
has mentioned one of the reasons, at least as far as life insurance is concerned.
The advent of with-profit policies makes the probability of ruin arbitrarily small;
an appropriate loading of premiums provides a cushion, as Professor Moore has
mentioned. I believe this is the main reason why practical insurance men were
not particularly interested in the theory of risk. There is a point here connected
with this cushioning of the probability of ruin by with-profit policies. If you
load the premiums in order to make this probability very small, then as the life
insurance policy progresses towards maturity, the standard deviations get smaller
and therefore it is not necessary any more to retain the same high loadings as
were advisable to begin with, therefore part of the loadings can be repaid to the
policy holder in the form of a bonus. I wrote a paper about this as a contribution
to the International Congress of Actuaries held in Stockholm in 1930.

Professor Borch describes Philip Lundberg's scheme which was not concerned with life insurance at all, but mainly with fire insurance. Now I believe
that the Lundberg scheme has a vital flaw, namely the introduction of "operational time." Professor Borch explains in a most interesting way that it is the
introduction of operational time which makes it possible to apply some theory
of stochastic processes. This is so, but on the other hand I believe that the
introduction of operational time did not give this theory any chance of ever
being applied. Operational time means that you measure time in such a way that
during unit time, a unit amount of premiums is being received by the insurance
company. But if an insurance company expands (and insurance companies did
expand and I hope they still do), then operational time contracts all the time and
this makes it very difficult to apply it in any way to the time of valuations, or to
any other time at which you want to sample what has happened. I believe that it
would have been wiser, and it would have been perhaps more profitable, if the
concept of birth and death process had been applied to insurance companies.
Deaths mean of course paying claims, and births mean new policies being underwritten. From this point of view we must emphasize what Professor Borch says,
that the most important restriction is the assumption that $G(x)$ does not depend
on t and n. There is another point which one ought to consider as well, and this
is $q(n, t)$ This depends on n and t, where t stands for the period 0 to t; however,
one ought to consider q as a function of the period from t_1 to $t_1 + t$. In other
words q changes not only with the length of time (i.e., t), but also with the
epoch.

Another aspect of stochastic processes which failed to be sufficiently developed in actuarial work is a consideration of the pure death process. I am not talking of the stochastic progress of the portfolio of a company, but of a stochastic process as applied to a group of assured of the same age, a "cohort" as it is sometimes called. The original, very naive actuarial theory was developed by assuming that out of a number of l_x assured of age x, l_{x+1} will survive another year, then l_{x+2}, and so on, and that these numbers were precisely known. This was the way in which Tauber taught me my actuarial mathematics. But this of course is quite unrealistic. There is a certain probability that out of l_x, $l_{x+1} + \epsilon$ will be left, where ϵ is a random variable. This is a stochastic process about which one can ask such questions as the probability distribution of the discounted value of all claims paid by the company during the next n years. The technique required is very similar to that which Professor Borch applies to his functions V. A number of papers have dealt with this approach, in particular some submitted to the International Congress of Actuaries in Lucerne, 1940, the Congress that never took place. (But the papers were published.)

Finally, I would like to say that I hope that Professor Borch's contribution to our proceedings marks an epoch in the history of mathematical applications to actuarial science, and I should express the hope that the theory of risk will, from now on, cease to be almost a monopoly of the Scandinavian and Swiss actuaries, but that others will be stimulated by Professor Borch's contribution.

Dr. J. A. Bather: Both the examples discussed in Section 4 seem to depend for their explicit solution on special knowledge of the overshoot. In the case studied by de Finetti, there is essentially no overshoot beyond the barriers and in the case of the double-exponential step distribution, any overshoot is also exponential. Another way of avoiding difficulties near $S = 0$ and $S = Z$ is to assume a diffusion model in continuous time. This gives explicit and apparently sensible solutions for the expected time to ruin and the expected dividend before ruin. In addition, it is relatively easy to solve simple control problems for this type of model.

Let the process $\{S_t\}$ have independent normal increments with $E(\delta S) = \lambda \delta t$ and $E(\delta S^2) = \sigma^2 \delta t + o(\delta t)$. Then $D(S)$ satisfies the differential equation

$$\tfrac{1}{2}\sigma^2 \, D''(S) + \lambda D'(S) + 1 = 0$$

and boundary conditions $D(0) = 0$ and $D'(Z) = 0$. The solution is

$$D(S) = \theta^{-1} \left\{ e^{\theta Z}(1 - e^{-\theta S}) - \theta S \right\}$$

where $\theta = 2\lambda/\sigma^2$, which is comparable with (34).

It is not difficult to treat k, the reinsurance quota, as a control parameter and maximize the expected dividend before ruin, at least if there is no discounting of future profits. We have, following the notation of (37),

$$E(\delta S) = \left\{ (\lambda - \pi) + (1 - k)(1 + \pi) \right\} \delta t, \quad E(\delta S^2) = (1 - k)^2 \sigma^2 \delta t + o(\delta t)$$

The dynamic programming equation for the maximum expected dividend $V(S)$ is

$$\max_{0 \leqslant k \leqslant 1} [\tfrac{1}{2}\sigma^2(1 - k)^2 V''(S) + \left\{ (\lambda - \pi) + (1 - k)(1 + \pi) \right\} V'(S)] = 0$$

with boundary conditions $V(0) = 0$, $V'(Z) = 1$. The maximum, at $k = k(S)$, is given by differentiation:

$$(1 - k)\sigma^2 V''(S) + (1 + \pi) V'(S) = 0$$

Then k can be eliminated and we are left with

$$V''(S) + \phi V'(S) = 0$$

where

$$\phi = \frac{(1 + \pi)^2}{2\sigma^2(\pi - \lambda)}$$

The solution is

$$V(S) = \phi^{-1} e^{\phi Z}(1 - e^{-\phi S})$$

so that the optimal reinsurance quota is $k = (1 + 2\lambda - \pi)/(1 + \pi)$, which does not depend on S, Z or σ^2. Hence, the expected rate of increase in reserves is $\pi - \lambda$, which is exactly opposite to the effect of full reinsurance with $k = 1$. On replacing θ by ϕ in the previous equation for $D(S)$, we find that

$$V(S) = S + (\pi - \lambda)D(S)$$

This result may well represent an oversimplification. For example, the use of a discount rate leads to a non-linear differential equation and, presumably, to a nontrivial control procedure. However, there are many other possible modifications which could be examined in the search for a more realistic, but still manageable formulation of the optimization problem. In particular, would it be reasonable to assume that the company, when bankrupt, can be rescued at a cost Z and allowed to continue operation? I would be grateful to have Professor Borch's comments on this.

Mr. L. P. Foldes: I should like to comment briefly on three points arising from Professor Borch's interesting paper. First, may I add to his list of surveys of actuarial theory the French text by Dubourdieu [8]. This work is accessible to the outsider who is familiar with ordinary elementary probability, and follows an approach very similar to that of Professor Borch's paper.

Secondly, I wanted to comment briefly on the economic justifiability of the principle of equivalence, but since it is so late I shall just say one sentence. In the form in which Professor Borch has stated it, namely that "the expected value of claim payments under a contract should be equal to the expected value of premiums received," this principle has all the usual weaknesses of any economic theory which assumes that prices must necessarily be adjusted to average costs of production.

Finally, I should like to comment on the following passage (page 283): "The real problem of the company now is to find the value of k which gives the 'best' of the stochastic processes in the set we have defined. . . . However, there is no sense in talking about the 'best stochastic process' unless one has some rule or criterion for deciding when one process should be preferred to another, i.e., a *preference ordering* over a set of stochastic processes. This points to the need for a generalization of the Bernoulli principle, which was shown in Section 2 to give a very convenient representation of preference orderings over a set of probability distributions. So far there does not seem to have been any attempt to extend this principle to sets of stochastic processes." Please note that in this passage Professor Borch refers to three distinct concepts: that of the decision rule or criterion, that of preference ordering, and that of Bernoullian utility. The assumption that a person decides according to a preference ordering is more restrictive that the assumption—which is presumably indispensable—that he follows a decision rule or criterion; and the assumption that his ordering can be represented by a Bernoullian utility function is more restrictive still. There is, of course, still a good deal of disagreement as to the postulates which are reasonable even in the case of theories which apply to *individuals*. The point which I want to emphasize is that additional difficulties arise when we consider insurance *companies* (or other companies which bear risk). A company is an organization, that is to say, a social sytem, one of whose functions is the resolution of conflict among its participants. It is not generally reasonable to impose on the decision procedures of an organization the same requirements of consistency as are appropriate in the case of an individual. It may therefore be inadvisable to place too much emphasis on the notions of ordering and utility in devising decision criteria. An alternative approach might be to start from the observation that the interests of particular groups of participants in an organization are often closely tied to the values taken by particular numerical variables. For example, in Professor Borch's case of an insurance company the policy holders and creditors are interested in the risk of default $(1 - R)$, or in the expected life of the company before ruin (D), while shareholders are interested in the capitalized value of dividends (V). It would be interesting to consider systematically the possibility of a theory of decision criteria for insurance companies or other organizations based on such "indicative" variables. As a tentative suggestion, the variables related to the interests of the most important groups of participants might reasonably be incorporated in the criterion function, while other variables could be introduced into suitable inequality constraints. An approach of this kind might help to justify the use of such criterion functions as

$$\max \left\{ \alpha \log V + (1 - \alpha) \log D \right\},$$

which Professor Borch uses in the last section of his paper.

Mr. S. Benjamin: I was glad that Professor Borch called this the "theory of risk" and not the "theory of insurance," because I would not recognize the theory of risk as being the important thing in insurance. I look at insurance primarily as an economic activity and as in any economic activity first of all the variables do not obey the law of large numbers, and secondly problems of smoothing become very important; This is true of insurance. Professor Vajda mentioned just now the fact that, for historical reasons, certainly in this country, we have reached a stage where a lot of insurance, especially life insurance, is run mostly on the basis of with-profit policies, and where problems of equity, e.g., in obtaining equity between one generation and another, require more attention than any questions of risk. In fact, in practice, questions of risk very rarely arise at any stage. If you take the case of a company just starting, for instance, the sort of question they will ask their adviser is: "At what level should we reassure?" Now, mathematically you can approach this question by the methods of the theory of risk—and nowadays you can get a numerical answer probably more easily by simulation than by analytical methods anyway. But essentially you are in the position of having to ask the new management what function q and what function G should be used before they have actually written any business. So it becomes a little difficult to apply a theory of this type in that situation.

In fact, as in all economic affairs, there are other variables which seem to swamp the situation and do in practice enable you to take a decision on other lines, because other things are more important. In particular, in this case, with a new company where you would on the face of it be very concerned with their probability of ruin, you will in fact get much more real discussion on the value of λ—that is to say, what the loading should be and what you consider the premium expenses should be. What you do about this will probably swamp the effect of fluctuations, even in the simplified but very real practical case, for example, of a small new motor insurance company. (I hasten to say that actuaries have not had anything to do with the recent, much criticized motor insurance companies.) In such a case you have a portfolio of policies where some claims have occurred and you could probably investigate the claim distribution, but it won't help very much. There aren't enough claims and you don't know what the big ones are going to be. You can look at the claims you have had so far, and you can look at the unexpired risk (that is to say, how many policy-years there are

left on which you need to set aside money) and the orders of mganitude which you
might find will indicate that they ought to have a reserve for claims not yet paid,
including those of unexpired risk, of the order of, say £800,000, but however
crudely you measure the fluctuation on this you will assess an outside fluctuation of the order of £50,000. This will be due partly to the fact that they will be
reassured at a very low level, say, £2,500.

Now £50,000 is a large sum of money, especially if it is a company which
has a capital of only £50,000, and I think it follows that £50,000 is insufficient
capital for an insurance company in British conditions. However, the fact remains that you have still got to decide quite separately what should be set aside
for future expenses, and you find that you can argue this on all sorts of bases. If
it is a small company which wishes to set aside as little as possible, that is to say
wants to set up a low reserve, then it will be tempted to argue from an accounting point of view that it could run off its existing business with, say, £5,000 for
expenses, and only need set aside £5,000. But you find on any crude formula
that, on the basis of their own recent running expenses, they could not possibly
run on such a tight reserve for future expenses and that they really need an
amount of the order of £150,000, which swamps the estimated £50,000 for an
outside fluctuation reserve. So in fact you spend much more of your time argu-
ing the implications of setting up a reserve for outstanding expenses on a strong
or weak basis, compared with the time spent on any mathematical calculations
that you might make on the fluctuation reserve and the sophistication of the
theory of risk.

The question was posed earlier in the discussion as to whether you could
usefully consider a company that went bankrupt and then had some money in-
jected into it. You can. The problem appears as a continuing decision process
because, for example, if things aren't going too well one thing you can do is to
lower your premium rates, and if by doing that you get more business, you
would probably lower your unit costs, which would have an equivalent effect.
For example, a typical non-life premium may require approximately 20-25% for
expenses and commission. The rest, roughly speaking, has got to cover the risk,
and may leave a profit margin of anywhere between +5 and –5%. What you do
about your expenses is very important indeed, so that you are continually
taking a decision via your premium rates as to what you will do by way of
injecting more capital into the company. This indeed is one of the major managerial decisions that anyone involved in running an insurance company has to
make. There are also serious problems of overlapping generations which the
paper omits. You need to provide equity between the different generations. The
whole approach of the paper here tends to make one think in terms of the policyholders as if they were a sort of homogeneous whole and that you can treat
them all the same. You can't treat them all the same, and for serious reasons of
both equity and competition you have got to give, and you have got to demonstrate that you are giving, equity to different generations of policyholders.

The only times that I personally have been involved in direct applications of the theory of risk are, in fact, in small cases such as relatively small insurers and especially reinsurers.

Running insurance appears to us very much as an economic activity, involving smoothing considerations, and in practice the only way in which you can really look at this sort of continuing problem is by some method of standard costing. Although we do not like to say so, the development of valuation methods in standard actuarial life-work has been through a standard costing method. This compares interestingly with Professor Borch's remark on p. 284, concerning a general problem of the company. A standard actuarial valuation is designed to provide information and a decision procedure. When an actuary does a valuation using a rate of interest of 2½% and a mortality table which is out of date he is not pretending that this is what is going to happen. He is doing a valuation on that basis because, amongst other problems, he has got to do some smoothing and he has got to take a decision at the end of the valuation, and the standard method is an adequate way of doing this. In fact, I do not think that these two parts are independent. Any method by which you look at a varying process in order to make a decision has got to contain some smoothing, and the way in which you actually carry out that smoothing will influence the decision you make. Indeed, if you use a seriously wrong actuarial valuation basis in valuing a company you can get yourself into a position of feedback with fluctuations which are difficult to control, and the main decision that you have to take is that of how you are going to control the emergence of surplus via the smoothing.

I wonder if we have arrived at a situation where aiming at "the best," with too much "optimizing," means that we can be in danger of nut running anything well. I agree with the last speaker that a company contains a conflict of interests, and a lot of managerial methods and decisions have to be designed to bring those interests together. For instance, in Professor Borch's paper he talks about paying out a dividend. One would almost think that this is against the interests of the policyholders, because it pays out money away from the company. But most life insurance companies pay a dividend which is based on their surplus and they pay a bonus to their policyholders calculated on the same basis so that the two are brought into line.

It is this conflict of interest, this economic process and the smoothing that is involved which are the main problems which completely outweigh any applications of the theory of risk. But it is a very interesting subject.

Dr. I. J. Good: I should like to make two disconnected comments, one formal and one philosophical. The formal comment relates to equation (10), and to the restrictiveness of the model on which it is based. The assumption that all the contracts of the insurance company are of the same size can be removed without difficulty. If, for a typical contract, $G_r(x)$ is the probability that if a claim should occur it will not exceed x, then the unconditional probability of this event at time t is

$$1 - p_r(t) + p_r(t)G_r(x)$$

where $p_r(t)$ is the probability that, by time t, a claim will have occurred. Therefore, if the various contracts are statistically independent, which is a big assumption, the probability that the total claim payments in the period $(0, t)$ will not exceed x is

$$\int_{-\infty}^{\infty} \prod_r \left\{ 1 - p_r(t) + p_r(t) \int_0^{\infty} e^{2\pi iuy}\, dG_r(y)\, dy \right\} e^{-2\pi iux}\, du$$

Regarding the calculation of the Fourier transforms one can approximate them by discrete Fourier transforms and then calculate them by the streamlined method of Good [11, 12] and Cooley and Tukey [5].

The philosophical comment concerns the distinction mentioned on page 261 between risk and uncertainty. Risk is supposed to correspond to cases where probabilities are known and uncertainty corresponds to cases where they are unknown. But in my opinion probabilities are never known and they are never unknown. By this paradoxical-sounding statement I mean that probabilities never have a sharp numerical value and on the other hand the lower and upper probabilities ae never 0 and 1. Probabilities lie in intervals of lengths strictly between 0 and 1. I am of course referring here to the following theory of probability:

"The ordinary mathematical theory of precise probabilities can be regarded as a black box whose input consists of judgments of probability inequalities and whose output consists of discernments of probability inequalities. In Mark II, utilities are incorporated both in the black box and in the peripheral equipment. Further peripheral equipment can be appended to cope with other types of judgments." (See [9, 10, 13]. In my contribution to the discussion of a paper by Smith [18] I may have given the impression that the black-box theory had been given an *a priori* justification by B. O. Koopman, but I have since found that Koopman proved something different. Although I published the theory in 1950, having used it for many years previously, the first convincing *a priori* justification was given by C. A. B. Smith in 1965.

Mr. G. D. Gwilt: Professor Borch's paper deals with a subject which appears to be quite fundamental to insurance. Why then do we largely if not completely ignore the theory of risk in determining life assurance premiums and reassurance levels in this country? I think the answer lies in the fact that in one important respect the underlying probability laws are almost completely unknown. I refer to the laws governing the rate of interest used in the calculation of premiums. The most usual policy up to the present has been the endowment assurance under which a sum assured is paid at the end of a certain period or on the previous death of the life assured.

In the case of the shorter term contracts at the lower ages mortality hardly affects the premiums which thus depend mainly on interest. My guess is that in practice a decision as to what rate of interest to use is of far greater importance than a decision as to what contingency loading to use. Indeed in practice such a conservative estimate of the future interest rate is used that its effect swamps that of the λ.

Professor Borch also discusses the problem of what dividends or bonuses to pay. It seems to me that this problem certainly requires investigation. Unfortunately, especially in the case of a mutual life assurance, it is almost impossible to formulate the aims of the company. Since the company is run for the benefit of the with-profit policyholders the existing policyholders would wish their future bonuses to be maximized. This implies maximizing $V(S, Z)$ subject to the payment of claims of existing policyholders. This implies closing the fund to new business. But this penalizes possible future members of the company. Is this inconsistent with the professed aims of a mutual company? The aim in practice is probably to maximize $V(S, Z)$ subject to bonuses being uniform throughout actual time and subject to a gradual increase in size of company. A final requirement, of course, is that the company should never fail.

Another problem facing a mutual life assurance company is how to decide the proportion of policies which should not participate in the profits. Theoretically, participating policyholders pay a larger premium than non-participating policyholders in order to provide reserve capital to support the latter whose profits are then repaid to the former.

Professor Borch replied briefly at the meeting and subsequently in writing as follows:

I am grateful to the discussants, both for their general remarks and for the specific suggestions they have made. Most of them have mentioned literature which I should have referred to. In the paper I have tried to refer to the publication where a particular idea was first formulated, and this made it necessary to give 29 references. It would have been useful to refer also to some recent papers illustrating how these ideas have been developed and rediscovered in different contexts. I am sorry that I did not do this in order to give added emphasis to my main point—that a mathematical model can be given many different concrete interpretations. I have referred to the work by Bachelier on prices at the Paris stock exchange. I should have mentioned that a few years later Einstein arrived at the same mathematical model in his studies of Brownian motion.

Out of common courtesy I should have given some references to papers in the *Journal* of this Society. This would have been easy. In recent years the *Journal* has published a number of papers on the theory of "passage times," which contain results from collective risk theory as special cases.

While on the subject of references, I must express my thanks to Professor Vajda, who before the meeting pointed out that I had overlooked a paper which A. Tauber presented at the International Congress of Actuaries in 1909. In this paper Tauber suggests that the loading should be proportional to the variance, and that it should be determined by supply and demand in the insurance market. I can only apologize for this omission, which is the more vexing, since I have referred to this paper myself in a note published in 1961.

Professor Gani has given a short and very elegant summary of the paper—more elegant than the paper itself or any summary which I could have given. He then suggests a mathematical problem which seems to be deep and to have a considerable interest in itself. If we decide to attack this problem, we should however realize we will be doing research in pure mathematics, and not expect the results to find immediate practical application in, say, insurance. I can see a number of problems—of equal mathematical interest—which are directly relevant to the real world problem which we set out to study. I shall therefore try not to be sidetracked in my future work, although it may be difficult to resist the temptation offered by Professor Gani in this very interesting problem.

Professor Vajda does not seem to be quite happy about my remarks on integrity, and I can agree that they are not well put. I think Mr. Foldes hit the nail on the head with his reference to production costs. The idea behind most actuarial work seems indeed to be that the company *should* charge a premium equal to the expected value of claim payments and expenses, plus a loading *necessary* to provide adequate security for the insured. This is of course ethics and not economics—hence the word integrity. It is evident that insurance must be seen as an economic activity, a point also made by Mr. Benjamin. Insurance companies—at least some of them—want to make profits by selling services which the public is willing to pay for, and then they need both actuarial mathematics and economic analysis. It is surprising that we find hardly a trace of economic thinking in actuarial literature. Tauber's voice is a lone one, and he does not seem to have followed up the idea he presented in 1909.

It may be useful to consider the conventional actuarial mathematics as a special kind of cost accounting. The cost accountant cannot tell top management the price which should be charged for the products of the company, but—backed by statistics—he can state that certain prices will lead to losses.

It is usually convenient and elegant to work with continuous time, so the model outlined by Dr. Bather seems promising. It is, however, desirable to relax the assumption about normality, and the model may then lose most of its attractive simplicity.

Without discounting the dividend payments it is difficult to give meaning to the concept of optimal reserve capital. For $v = 1$, it is easy to show that $V(S, Z)$ will increase to infinity with Z. Even if one disregards this mathematical argument, it seems reasonable to assume that an early dividend payment is preferred to a later one. Discounting at a constant rate is a convenient, but by no means

the only way of formalizing this "impatience," or preference for earlier payments.

Dr. Bather mentioned the possibility that a bankrupt insurance company
may be rescued. This raises a number of questions which are interesting both
from the theoretical and practical point of view. In the theory of risk it is
usually assumed that the company plays an infinite sequence of favorable
gambles. There is then no obvious reason why the company should have to
liquidate if its capital should become negative. It is practically certain that the
company will recover in the long run, if it is allowed to continue operating. If
the company's capital has fallen to $-S$, a rescue operation should be a profitable
investment provided that $S + Z < V(Z, Z)$.

The crucial assumption is of course that a company of doubtful solvency is
still able to attract favorable business. The whole queston raised by Dr. Bather
certainly deserves further study. It may well belong to an area where insurance
practice is ahead of theory. If a "sound" insurance company runs into temporary
difficulties, it will probably be rescued, no matter what the theory of risk may
have assumed. Liquidation may be the only possibility if the company is not
sound, i.e., if it can attract only unfavorable business.

Mr. Foldes points out that the decision rule of a group or of a company may
not satisfy the postulates which are generally accepted as reasonable for a
rational individual. This is well known, and the point has been driven home with
force by Arrow, but I am not certain if it is very important in practice.

A decision rule is essentially a rule for picking out one element in a given
set. If the rule is not to lead to contradictions when applied to different subsets,
it must be derived from a preference ordering over the original set. If it is not,
the rule may lead to decisions such as A preferred to B, B preferred to C, and C
preferred to A. People may make such "mistakes," but I do not think they make
them consistently. If I met a person who did, I could certainly make a fortune
by using him as a reliable "money pump." If he had A, I could induce him to pay
one pound to have A exchanged against C, and then to pay another pound to get
B instead of C, and further one pound to get A instead of B, and so on. If a
preference ordering over a set of stochastic variables is free from contradictions
of this kind, it can be represented by a Bernoulli utility function. In practice the
three concepts may therefore not be so very different.

I agree with most of what Mr. Benjamin has said, but I would like to add
some emphasis to his remarks about "equity between generations," a point also
discussed by Mr. Gwilt. This is a very important problem, which we seem curi-
ously reluctant to face. The problem appears most clear-cut in with-profit life
insurance. Higher profit payments to the present generation of policyholders
obviously mean lower payments to following generations, and may also mean
that the probability of ruin becomes non-negligible. Several discussants have
argued that the development of with-profit life insurance has reduced the practical importance of the problems studied in the theory of risk. If this is correct,

one may assume that the with-profit policy will usually favor future generations at the expense of present policyholders.

The problem is, however, much more general. It will exist in any plan for economic development where there is a choice between high immediate consumption or investment which will bring higher consumption later. The problem also exists in an educational system. Should the best people educate the next generation, or should they make a more immediately useful contribution to society? Problems of this kind are seldom discussed and they are usually "solved" in a haphazard manner. Since the problem appears in a very clear-cut manner in insurance, it may be useful to discuss it in this context in order to gain deeper insight into its general nature.

Formula (10) is derived without assuming that the company's portfolio consists of identical insurance contracts. In a heterogeneous portfolio $G(x)$, which is the probability that an arbitrary claim shall not exceed x, will be a weighted average of distributions, and this is really what Dr. Good suggests. The important distribution is obviously $F(x, t)$, and practical considerations should determine whether we build it up from estimates of Lundberg's $q(n, t)$ and $G(x)$ or of Good's $p_r(t)$ and $G_r(x)$.

I am grateful to the discussants who have suggested possible generalizations of the theory. I should, however, like to conclude by offering my own suggestions.

In the models we have discussed, the state of the company at a given time is described by a single number S_t. It would be desirable instead to consider a vector $(S_1(t), S_2(t), \ldots, S_n(t))$, where the elements can be interpreted as the different entries in the company's balance sheet at time t. The task of management will then be to steer this stochastic vector process so that it develops in the best possible way. If initially the probabilistic laws governing the process are known only partially, the development of the process will provide information which can be "fed back" and used to improve the steering. This is of course just what insurance companies do in practice and it would be desirable to have a suitable theoretical framework for analyzing this activity.

In such a theory, management of an insurance company would be considered as a "game against nature." It is, however, clear that in general the development of one company will depend on the activity of other companies. This means that the companies are engaged in a game against each other, and that a general theory of insurance should be constructed in the framework of the theory of games.

References in the Discussion

1. Arfwedson, G. "Research in Collective Risk Theory: I," *Skand. Aktuar.* 37 (1954): 191–223.

———. "Research in Collective Risk Theory: II," *Skand. Aktuar.* 38 (1955): 53-100.

2. Beard, R. E. "Some Actuarial Aspects of Non-life Insurance Company Management," *Het Verzekerings Archief* 42 (1965): 296-324.

3. Benjamin, S. "Putting Computers on to Actuarial Work," *J. Inst. Actuar.* 92 (1966): 134-192.

4. Borch, K. Una generalización de la teoria del riesgo colectivo, *An. Inst. Actuar. Españoles* 5 (2) (1965): 13-30.

5. Cooley, J. W. and Tukey, J. W. An algorithm for the machine calculation of complex Fourier series. *Maths of Computation* 19 (1965): 297-301.

6. Cramér, H. "Collective Risk Theory," *Skandia Jubilee Volume* (Stockholm, 1955).

7. Darroch, J. N., and Seneta, E. "On Quasi-stationary Distributions in Absorbing Discrete-time Markov Chains," *J. Appl. Prob.* 2 (1965): 88-100.

8. Dubourdieu, J. *Théorie mathématique du Risque dans les Assurances de Répartition* (Paris: Gauthier-Villars, 1952).

9. Good, I. J. *Probability and the Weighing of Evidence* (London: Griffin, 1950).

10. ———. "Rational decisions," *J. R. Statist. Soc.* B, 14 (1952): 107-114.

11. ———. "The Interaction Algorithm and Practical Fourier Analysis," *J. R. Statist. Soc.* B, 20 (1958): 361-372.

12. ———. "The Interaction Algorithm and Practical Fourier Analysis: An Addendum," *J. R. Statist. Soc.* B, 22 (1960): 372-375.

13. ———. "Subjective Probability as a Measure of a Non-measurable Set," in *Logic, Methodology and Philosophy of Science: Proc. 1960 Int. Congr. Stanford* (ed. Y. Bar-Hillel) (Amsterdam: North-Holland, 1962), pp. 319-329.

14. ———. "Contribution to the Discussion on Paper by C. A. B. Smith," *J. R. Statist. Soc.* A, 128 (1965): 494-495.

15. Prabhu, N. U. "On the Ruin Problem of Collective Risk Theory," *Ann. Math. Statist.,* 32 (1961): 757-764.

16. Seneta, E. "Quasi-stationary Distributions and Time-reversion in Genetics," *J. R. Statist. Soc.* B, 28 (1966): 253-277.

17. Seneta, E., and Vere-Jones, D. "On Quasi-stationary Distributions in Discrete-time Markov Chains with a Denumerable Infinity of States," *J. Appl. Prob.* 3 (1966): 403-434.

18. Smith, C. A. B. "Personal Probability and Statistical Analysis," *J. R. Statist. Soc.* A, 128 (1965): 469-499.

19

Risk Management and Company Objectives

1. Introduction

1.1. Most people dislike risk, and are willing to pay something to get rid of it. The function of an insurance company is to accept and carry risk against compensation, usually in the hope of making profits. Whether a risk should be accepted and retained will then depend on the profit which it may bring the company. The basis of the company's risk management must then be some rule for trade-off between risk and profit potential. It is not easy to formulate a general rule of this kind, and this is the problem which will be discussed in the following.

1.2. We shall first discuss a simple static model, that by now is almost classic, but which leaves a number of open questions. We shall then show that some of these questions find simple answers when the static problem is considered in its natural dynamic context.

2. A Static Model

2.1. We shall consider an insurance company in one single operating period. The situation we shall study is specified by the following three elements:

(i) S = the company's capital or free reserves at the beginning of the period.
(ii) P = premiums earned during the period.
(iii) y = claims paid during the period—a stochastic variable with distribution $G(y)$. $(y \geqslant 0)$.

At the end of the period the company's capital will be $T = S + P - y$.
The profit in the period will be $x = P - y$. T and x are stochastic variables with distributions

$$F(T) = 1 - G(S + P - T) \qquad T \leqslant S + P$$

$$F(x) = 1 - G(P - x) \qquad x \leqslant P$$

2.2. If the company has a choice of different reinsurance arrangements or

305

rate structures, it will also have a choice of different profit distributions. To make intelligent decisions in this situation, the company will need a rule which states when one profit distribution shall be preferred to another. If a rule of this kind is consistent, it can be represented by a *utility function* $u(x)$, and expressed as follows:

$F(x)$ is preferred to $H(x)$ if, and only if

$$\int_0^\infty u(x)\, dF(x) > \int_0^\infty u(x)\, dH(x)$$

The utility function describes the company's "risk policy," or its preference ordering over the set of obtainable profit distributions. This preference ordering may depend on the company's capital, and it is then more convenient to compare the distributions of T, the capital at the end of the period. We shall illustrate this with a few examples.

2.3.   Let us assume that the company considers reinsuring a quota $1 - k$ of its portfolio on original terms. The capital at the end of the period will then be $T = S + k(P - y) = S + kx$. The "expected utility" of this reinsurance arrangement will be

$$U(k) = \int_0^\infty u(S + k(P - y))\, dG(y)$$

The problem is then to determine the value of k, which maximizes this expression. The solution will give the optimal retention quota.

As another illustration, let us consider a company holding a portfolio with claim distribution $G_1(y_1)$, and write

$$V(S) = \int_0^\infty u(S + P - y_1)\, dG_1(y_1)$$

Let us now assume that this company is offered an amount Q if it will cover a portfolio with claim distribution $G_2(y_2)$. The variables y_1 and y_2 are assumed stochastically independent. If the company accepts the offer, expected utility will be

$$\int_0^\infty u(S + P + Q - z)\, dH(z) = \int_0^\infty V(S + Q - y_2)\, dG_2(y_2)$$

Here $H(z)$ is the distribution of $z = y_1 + y_2$, i.e., the convolution of G_1 and G_2. The company will accept the offer only if it leads to an increase in expected utility, i.e., if

$$V(S) < \int_0^\infty V(S + Q - y)\, dG_2(y)$$

This shows that $V(S)$ also can be interpreted as a utility function to be used for decisions.

2.4. As further illustrations we shall present a few simple utility functions which have been used in actuarial literature.

$$u(y) = y$$

$$U(k) = S + k \left\{ P - \int_0^\infty y \, dG(y) \right\}$$ (i)

If the premium P is greater than expected claim payments, $U(k)$ is maximized for $k = 1$, i.e., when the company retains the whole portfolio on its own account.

$$u(y) = 1 - e^{-y}$$

$$U(k) = 1 - e^{-S-kP} \int_0^\infty e^{ky} \, dG(y)$$ (ii)

Here $U(k)$ is maximized by the value of k which satisfies the equation

$$P \int_0^\infty e^{ky} \, dG(y) = \int_0^\infty y \, e^{ky} \, dG(y)$$

This value is independent of S, i.e., the optimal retention does not depend on the free reserves.

$$u(y) = y + a \quad \text{for } y \geqslant 0$$

$$u(y) = 0 \quad \text{for } y < 0$$

$$U(k) = (S + kP + a)G\left(\frac{S}{k} + P\right) - k \int_0^{(S/k) + P} y \, dG(y)$$ (iii)

Here a can be interpreted as a measure of how anxious the company is to avoid ruin. Some elementary calculations will show that the optimal quota k increases with S, and decreases with increasing a.

$$u(y) = y - e^{-y}$$

$$U(k) = S + k \left\{ P - \int_0^\infty y \, dG(y) \right\} - e^{-S-kP} \int_0^\infty e^{ky} \, dG(y)$$ (iv)

If as an illustration we take $G(y) = 1 - e^{-y}$, we find that the optimal quota is determined by the equation:

$$(P - 1)(1 - k)^2 = (1 + kP - P)e^{-S-kP}$$

Table 19–1

Free Reserves	Optimal Retention
2.2	50%
2.8	60%
3.6	70%
4.5	80%
6.9	90%

For $P = 1.2$ we obtain the numerical values shown in Table 19–1.

2.5. These simple examples may be taken to mean that a well defined utility function is virtually indispensable for intelligent risk management in an insurance company. If the company pursues consistent objectives, formulated in an operational manner, these objectives can be represented by a utility function. Actuaries and company directors do, however, not seem to spend much time discussing the shape of the utility function behind their decisions. The explanation for this apparent lack of concern over basic objectives, may be that the simple one-period model, which we have outlined, does not represent any relevant situation in real life. We shall, therefore, indicate how the model can be generalized.

3. A Dynamic Model

3.1. The capital S which the company holds at the end of an operating period, can be retained as free reserves in following periods. The company may, however, consider paying out an amount s as dividend, and enter the next operating period with $S - s$ as free reserves. De Finetti [2] has suggested that the company's objective may then be to find the "dividend policy" which maximizes the expected discounted sum of all future dividend payments. To tackle this problem we must make some assumptions about business in the future. The simplest is to assume that the profit distribution $F(x)$ will be the same in all future periods. It is convenient to assume that a density $f(x) = F'(x)$ exists.

Let $V(S)$ be the expected discounted sum, if the optimal policy is used. It is easy to see that $V(S)$ must satisfy the functional equation:

$$V(S) = \max_{0 \leqslant s \leqslant S} \left\{ s + v \int_{-\infty}^{+\infty} V(S - s + x) f(x)\, dx \right\}$$

where v is the discount factor.

Differentiating the expression in braces with respect to s, we obtain a first-order condition for a maximum

$$1 - v \int_{-\infty}^{\infty} V'(S - s + x)f(x)\, dx = 0$$

This is an equation in $S - s$. If it has a root $S - s = Z \geqslant 0$, the optimal dividend payment is

$$s = S - Z \qquad \text{if } S > Z$$

$$s = 0 \qquad \text{if } S \leqslant Z$$

A dividend policy of this form is called a "barrier policy" by Morrill [3], who has studied the conditions under which it is optimal.

3.2. Let us now write $V(S, Z)$ for the expected discounted sum of the dividend payments under an arbitrary barrier policy, i.e., with a value of Z not necessarily optimal. It follows from the definition that we have

$$V(S, Z) = S - Z + V(Z, Z) \qquad \text{for } S > Z$$

For $S < Z$ the function $V(S, Z)$ must satisfy the integral equation

$$V(S, Z) = v \int_{-\infty}^{+\infty} V(S + x, Z)f(x)\, dx = v \int_{-\infty}^{+\infty} V(x, Z)f(x - S)\, dx \qquad (1)$$

It is natural to assume that the company must liquidate if the capital is negative at the end of an operating period. It then follows that

$$V(S, Z) = 0 \qquad \text{for } S < 0$$

The integral equation can now be written:

$$V(S, Z) = v \int_{0}^{Z} V(x, Z)f(x - S)\, dx + v \int_{Z}^{\infty} \left\{ x - Z + V(Z, Z) \right\} f(x - S)\, dx$$

This is an equation of Fredholm's type, and the solution is given by the Neumann expansion

$$V(S, Z) = \sum_{n=1}^{\infty} v^n \int_{Z}^{\infty} \left\{ x - Z + V(Z, Z) \right\} f^{(n)}(x - S)\, dx$$

Here

$$f^{(1)}(x - S) = f(x - S)$$

$$f^{(n)}(x - S) = \int_{0}^{Z} f^{(n-1)}(x - t)f(t - S)\, dt$$

3.3. We want to study the properties of the function $V(S, Z)$, and the Neumann expansion is not a convenient starting point for this purpose. We shall, therefore, consider a special case, which gives a particularly simple solution

Let

$$f(x) = \frac{ab}{a+b} \, e^{ax} \quad \text{for } x < 0$$

$$f(x) = \frac{ab}{a+b} \, e^{-bx} \quad \text{for } x > 0$$

The integral equation then becomes

$$V(S) = \frac{vab}{a+b} \left\{ e^{-aS} \int_0^S V(x)e^{ax} \, dx + e^{bS} \int_S^Z V(x)e^{-bx} \, dx \right.$$

$$\left. + e^{bS} \int_Z^\infty \left\{ x - Z + V(Z) \right\} e^{-bx} \, dx \right\}$$

Here we have for the sake of simplicity written $V(S)$ instead of $V(S, Z)$.
Differentiating the equation twice, and eliminating the integrals, we obtain the differential equation

$$V''(S) + (a - b)V'(S) - (1 - v)ab\,V(S) = 0$$

The general solution of this equation is

$$V(S) = C_1 e^{r_1 S} + C_2 e^{r_2 S}$$

Here r_1 and r_2 are the roots of the equation

$$r^2 + (a - b)r - (1 - v)ab = 0$$

C_1 and C_2 are constants which must be determined so that the integral equation is satisfied. We find, for $S \leqslant Z$:

$$V(S, Z) = \frac{4va \left\{ (r_1 + a)e^{r_1 S} - (r_2 + a)e^{r_2 S} \right\}}{r_1(r_1 + a)^2 e^{r_1 Z} - r_2(r_2 + a)^2 e^{r_2 Z}}$$

3.4. We can now return to the second problem considered in para. 2.3. The company is offered an amount Q if it will cover—for one period—a portfolio with claim distribution $G(y)$. The company's overall objective is to maximize the expected discounted sum of the dividend payments, and the offer must be analyzed in terms of this objective. As in para. 2.3 it then follows that the offer is accepted if

$$V(S, Z) < \int_0^\infty V(S + Q - y, Z)\, dG(y)$$

Let us now assume that the company considers a permanent reinsurance arrangement, under which it will retain only a quota k of the portfolio in each period. This means that the company chooses to operate on a smaller scale. The integral equation (1) then becomes

$$V_k(S, Z) = v \int_{-\infty}^{+\infty} V_k(S + kx, Z) f(x)\, dx \qquad (2)$$

In our example the change of scale means that a, b and r are divided by k. It then follows that

$$V_k(S, Z) = kV\left(\frac{1}{k} S, Z\right)$$

and it is easy to see that $V_k(S, Z)$ is maximized for $k = 1$. Hence the company will not make any fixed permanent reinsurance arrangement. This result is, however, valid only in our special case, and not for an arbitrary profit distribution.

A one-period reinsurance arrangement, reducing the retention to k, will be advantageous to the company if

$$\int_{-\infty}^{+\infty} V(S + kx, Z) f(x)\, dx - V(S, Z) > 0$$

The optimal quota k must be determined so that this difference is maximized.

To stress the difference between the permanent and the one-period reinsurance arrangement, it is useful to point out that $V(S, Z)$ is the solution of the integral equation (1), and $V_k(S, Z)$ of the modified equation (2).

3.5. If the company can make short-term reinsurance arrangements whenever this is desirable, the problem will change drastically. The company will then, at the beginning of each operating period, select a vector (s, k), i.e., a dividend payment, and a retention quota for the next period. The functional equation of para. 3.1 will then be replaced by

$$V(S) = \max_{\substack{0 \leqslant s \leqslant S \\ 0 \leqslant k \leqslant 1}} \left\{ s + v \int_{-\infty}^{+\infty} V(S - s + kx) f(x)\, dx \right\}$$

This equation can be solved by the techniques of dynamic programming.

The problem is, however, not easy, and it appears difficult to make any general statement about the shape of the optimal policy.

4. Conclusion

4.1. The observations made in this paper are almost trivial. We have shown that a well defined long-term objective will contain the decision rule which should be applied in any period, and in any possible situation. For the purpose of illustration we have assumed that the long-term objective is to maximize the expected discounted sum of the dividend payments. This appears reasonable at first glance, but it leads to a dividend policy which seems different from those we observe in real life. It is possible to define other, and presumably more realistic long-term objectives, a question which has been discussed briefly in other papers, e.g., [1]. The question is obviously important. We can hardly discuss actuarial treatment of risk, without knowing what we want to achieve, i.e., what the long-term objectives of the company are.

References

1.   Borch, K. "The Theory of Risk," *Journal of the Royal Statistical Society,* Series B (1967): 432–467.
2.   Finetti, B. de. "Su una impostazione alternativa della teoria collettiva del rischio," *Transactions of the XV International Congress of Actuaries 2* (1957): 433–443.
3.   Morrill, J. "One-person Games of Economic Survival," *Naval Research Logistics Quarterly,* 1966, pp. 49–69.

20

The Rescue of an Insurance Company
After Ruin

1. Introduction

1.1. In the different versions of the "Theory of Risk" it is almost universally assumed that ruin or bankruptcy marks the end of the game. The earlier versions of the theory tried to estimate the probability of this event, and studied the steps which an insurance company could take to bring probability of ruin down to an acceptable level. The more modern versions of the theory of risk tend to formulate the problem in economic terms, and study the cost of postponing or avoiding ruin.

In a recent discussion of a paper [4] surveying the development of the theory of risk, Professor Bather suggested that ruin may not necessarily be the end. If an otherwise sound insurance company gets into difficulties, so that ruin looms large, it is very likely that steps will be taken to rescue the company, for instance by refinancing, or in more extreme cases, by a merger.

1.2. To practical insurance men the simple suggestion of Professor Bather may seem next to trivial. Insurance companies get into difficulties fairly regularly, and rescue operations are considered in the insurance world, if not daily, at least annually. The suggestion has, however, far-reaching implications for the theory of risk, and these do not seem to have been fully realized. If ruin does not mean the end of the game, but only the necessity of raising additional money, the current theories of risk may have to be radically revised. In this paper we shall discuss some of these implications.

2. The Basic Model

2.1. As our starting point we shall take a model due to de Finetti [5]. The model, which can be taken as the foundation of the modern theory of risk, can be defined as follows:

(i) The company has an initial capital S.
(ii) In each operating period the company underwrites identical portfolios of insurance contracts. The profit of these portfolios is a stochastic variable with positive expectation, and with the distribution $F(x)$.

313

(iii) If at the end of an operating period the capital is negative, the company is ruined, and has to go out of business.

(iv) If at the end of an operating period the company's capital exceeds Z, the excess is paid out—as dividend or taxes, as the case may be.

In this model the company's capital performs a *random walk*. There is an absorbing barrier at $S = 0$, and a reflecting barrier at $S = Z$. The amount Z can be interpreted as the *required reserve*, i.e., as the reserve capital which the company considers necessary before any dividend can be paid.

2.2. The choice of a value Z will determine a sequence of dividend payments: $s_0, s_1, \ldots, s_t, \ldots$, where $s_t \geq 0$ is the dividend paid at the end of the underwriting period t. For the expected discounted sum of these payments, we shall write:

$$V(S, Z) = \sum_{t=0}^{\infty} v^t E(s_t)$$

If the company is quite free in choosing Z, it is natural to assume that it will select the value of Z, which maximizes $V(S, Z)$. The assumption may, however, be unrealistic. It implies that neither government regulations nor pressure from the public will force the company to maintain larger reserves in order to provide more security to its customers. If we ignore these objections, we are led to a well defined mathematical problem, which as we shall see, has a considerable interest.

Before we attack this problem, a word of caution may, however, be useful. If the real objective of the company is to maximize the expected discounted value of its dividend payments, the real problem is to find the *dividend policy*, which will achieve this objective. A general dividend policy must specify the amount to be paid at the end of period t in all conceivable circumstances. This means that the amount may depend on previous dividend payments $s_0, s_1, \ldots, s_{t-1}$, and on the company's past history, which in our model can be described by the sequence $S_0, S_1, \ldots, S_t$, the company's capital at the end of each previous underwriting period. The dividend policy is then defined by a function

$$s_t = s(s_0, \ldots, s_{t-1}, S_0, \ldots, S_t, t)$$

The general problem consists in finding the best, or optimal dividend policy, when the objectives of the company are known. These objectives may be complex, they may for instance include a desire for a stable series of dividend payments, and for a steady growth of the company's capital.

2.3. If the company has the simple objective of maximizing the expected discounted value of the dividend payments, the optimal policy will be of a much simpler form. The payment at the end of period t will then depend only on the actual state of the company at that time, i.e., the policy is defined by a function of the form

$$s_t = s(S_t)$$

This result appears reasonable on intuitive reasons, and it has been proved rigorously by several authors, e.g., by Blackwell [1].

The dividend policy determined by a fixed reserve requirement Z will be defined by a function

$$s(S) = 0 \qquad \text{for } S < Z$$

$$s(S) = S - Z \qquad \text{for } Z < S$$

This policy may, however, not be optimal. Morrill [6] has proved that when the distribution $F(x)$ is discrete and finite, the function defining the optimal policy is of the form

$$s(S) = 0 \qquad \text{for } S < Z_0$$

$$s(S) = S - Z_0 \qquad \text{for } Z_0 < S < Z_1$$

. . . .

$$s(S) = 0 \qquad \text{for } Z_{2n-1} < S < Z_{2n}$$

$$s(S) = S - Z_{2n} \qquad \text{for } Z_{2n} < S$$

This means that the function which defines the optimal policy is determined by a finite set of numbers $Z_0, Z_1, \ldots, Z_{2n}$. Only if $n = 0$, will this policy correspond to a fixed reserve requirement.

2.4. Let us now put aside the difficulties indicated above, and determine the function $V(S, Z)$ defined at the beginning of para. 2.2. It follows from the definition that we have

$$V(S, Z) = 0 \qquad \qquad \text{for } S < 0$$

$$V(S, Z) = S - Z + V(Z, Z) \qquad \text{for } Z < S$$

For $0 \leqslant S \leqslant Z$ we see that $V(S, Z)$ must satisfy the integral equation

$$V(S, Z) = v \int_{-S}^{\infty} V(S + x)\, dF(x)$$

or $V(S, Z) = v \int_{z-S}^{\infty} \left\{ x + S - Z + V(Z, Z) \right\} dF(x) + \int_{-S}^{Z-S} V(S + x)\, dF(x)$

If the distribution $F(x)$ is discrete, this equation reduces to a difference equation. This case, which has been discussed by de Finetti [5] and Morrill [6], leads to some complications. It has been shown in another paper [3] that $V(S, Z)$ as function of Z is discontinuous, and that as function of S it does not have a continuous derivative.

If $F(x)$ is continuous, and a density function $f(x) = F'(x)$ exists, the basic equation can be written

$$V(S, Z) = v \int_0^{\infty} \left\{ x + V(Z, Z) \right\} f(x - S + Z)\, dx + \int_0^z V(x) f(x - S)\, dx$$

This is an integral equation of Fredholm's type. It has a unique continuous solution given by the Neumann expansion

$$V(S, Z) = \sum_{n=1}^{\infty} v^n \int_0^{\infty} \left\{ x + V(Z, Z) \right\} f^{(n)}(x + Z - S)\, dx$$

Here

$$f^{(1)}(x - S) = f(x - S)$$

$$f^{(n)}(x - S) = \int_0^z f^{(n-1)}(x - t) f(t - S)\, dt \quad n > 1$$

This result can be verified by a direct probabilistic argument $f^{(n)}(x + Z - S)\, dx$ is the probability that the company shall have a capital $x + Z$ at the end of period n, provided that the company was neither ruined nor paid any dividend at the end of $n - 1$ preceding periods. If the event $x > 0$ occurs, the company will pay a dividend x, and the value of future dividend payments will be equal to $V(Z, Z)$. Since the event occurs at the end of period n, the expected discounted value of the payment is obtained by multiplying with v^n and integrating over all non-negative x.

3. Ruin and Rescue

3.1.   In the model we have outlined, we shall assume that the optimal dividend policy is determined by a single number Z, which we can interpret as the optimal reserve requirement. If the company's capital at the end of an underwriting period is $S < Z$, the expected discounted value of the future dividend payments is $V(S, Z)$. It is clear that $V(0, Z)$ is positive. Even if the company has no capital (free reserves), there is a positive probability that a dividend will be paid before ruin. If $S < 0$, we have, however, by definition $V(S, Z) = 0$, because the company is not allowed to do any underwriting if its capital is negative. This means that if the company's capital falls from ϵ to $-\epsilon$, there will be a fall in dividend expectation from $V(\epsilon, Z)$ to 0; a fall which may seem out of proportion to the actual loss of capital.

3.2.   Let us now assume that the company at the end of an underwriting period is unable to pay the claims made against it, and let us assume that the deficit is T. The value of the company to the shareholders is then

$$V(-T, Z) = 0$$

since the company is not allowed to operate.

If the shareholders put up the money necessary to settle the claim, the company can continue its operations and its value to the shareholders will be $V(0, Z)$. It will then be a good investment to rescue the company if

$$V(0, Z) - T > 0$$

If the shareholders put up an amount of money S, in addition to the amount T which is strictly necessary, their gain will be

$$V(S, Z) - (S + T)$$

They may then try to determine the value of S, which maximizes this difference, i.e., to find the optimal scheme for re-financing the company. If $V(S, Z)$ is differentiable with respect to S, this value is given by the condition

$$\frac{\partial V(S, Z)}{\partial S} = 1$$

It is fairly obvious that $S = Z$ will be a solution of this equation. Heuristically this result is obtained by the following argument:

If

$$\frac{\partial V(S, Z)}{\partial S} > 1$$

an additional amount of capital will increase the dividend expectations more if it is added to the reserves, than if it is paid out as dividend immediately. As Z is the optimal reserve, it follows that the inequality must hold for all $S < Z$.

3.3. From the considerations in the preceding paragraph it follows that it is a good investment to rescue an insolvent insurance company, provided that its deficit is not too great. It is easy to see that the upper limit of the deficit is given by

$$T < V(Z, Z) - Z$$

If the deficit exceeds this limit, the shareholders should accept ruin, and let the company go into liquidation.

This result is not generally valid. There are a number of complications, particularly if the distribution $F(x)$ is discrete. These complicatons are, however, of a fairly trivial nature, and can best be illustrated by numerical examples, as we shall do in the following Section. The complications are due to the discontinuities of $V(S, Z)$ and its derivatives, and it is a tedious, but not very difficult task to sort them out.

3.4. We have so far taken an *ad hoc* approach to the rescue problem. We assumed that if the company had already become insolvent, and we asked if it would be profitable for the shareholders to rescue the company. We based our analysis on the function $V(S, Z)$, and this is appropriate only if the company will have to go into liquidation the next time it becomes insolvent. If it is possible to rescue the company, also at the next crisis, $V(S, Z)$ will no longer represent the value of future dividend payments.

If the shareholders always are prepared to rescue the company, it is not necessary to keep any capital in the company. At the end of each operating period the owners will either divide the profits among themselves, or make a payment to cover the deficit. The expected profit in an arbitrary operating period is $E(x)$, and the discounted sum of these expected payments is

$$W = \frac{v}{1-v} \int_{-\infty}^{+\infty} x \, dF(x)$$

It is obvious that $W \geqslant V(0, Z)$, since the obligation to cease operations after ruin cannot possibly increase the expected dividend payments. It is equally obvious that it does not pay to rescue the company if the deficit $T > W$. These considerations may lead the shareholders to seek some rule as to when they should cut their losses, and let the company go into liquidation. They may for instance decide that they will liquidate the company when the deficit becomes greater than Y. Let $W(Y)$ be the expected discounted value of the dividend payments (positive or negative), which will be made under this policy.

It is easy to see that $W(Y)$ must satisfy the equation:

$$W(Y) = v \int_{-Y}^{\infty} \{x + W(Y)\}\, dF(x)$$

From this we find

$$W(Y) = \frac{v}{1 - v + vF(-Y)} \int_{-Y}^{\infty} x\, dF(x)$$

We can then determine the value of Y which maximizes $W(Y)$. If a density function $f(x) = F'(x)$ exists, this value is determined by the equation

$$W'(Y) = 0$$

or $\quad Y = \dfrac{v}{1 - v + vF(-Y)} \int_{-Y}^{\infty} x\, dF(x)$

This expresses the obvious. The company should be rescued only if the deficit is smaller than the expected profits from the rescue operation.

4. Some Numerical Examples

4.1. As our first example we shall take the simple case where x can take only the values -1 and $+1$. We shall assume

$$\Pr(x = \ \ 1) = p = 0.565$$

$$\Pr(x = -1) \ = q = 0.435$$

The basic equation of para. 2.4 is then reduced to the difference equation

$$V(S, Z) = vp\,V(S + 1, Z) + vq\,V(S - 1, Z)$$

This equation has been discussed in a number of other papers, e.g., [2] and [3]. It has the solution:

$$V(S, Z) = \frac{r_1^{S+1} - r_2^{S+1}}{r_1^{Z+2} - r_2^{Z+2} - r_1^{Z+1} + r_2^{Z+2}}$$

where r_1 and r_2 are the roots of the characteristic equation

$$r = vp\,r^2 + vq$$

Table 20-1

$V(S, Z) = $ **Expected discounted value of dividend payments**

$2 = $ Initial Capital	\multicolumn{7}{c}{$Z = $ Capital required before dividends can be paid}
	0	1	2	3	4	5	6
0	1.25	1.49	1.70	1.83	1.89	1.88	1.82
1	2.25	2.69	3.05	3.30	3.41	3.39	3.28
2	3.25	3.69	4.19	4.52	4.67	4.66	4.50
3	4.25	4.69	5.19	5.56	5.79	5.76	5.57
4	5.25	5.69	6.19	6.56	6.82	6.79	6.56
5	6.25	6.69	7.19	7.56	7.82	7.78	7.51

It is easy to verify that both roots are positive, and that $r_1 > 1, r_2 < 1$. It then follows that $V(S, Z)$ will increase with S as we would expect. It also follows that $V(S, Z)$ will go to zero as Z goes to infinity—i.e., if dividend payments are postponed indefinitely. If there is a value of $Z > 0$, which maximizes $V(S, Z)$, this value will be independent of S, and can be taken as the "optimal" reserve.

If we take $v = 0.983$, we find $r_1 = 1.1$ and $r_2 = 0.7$, and we can construct Table 20-1, which gives $V(S, Z)$ for some selected values of S and Z.

We see that in this example the optimal reserve is given by $Z = 4$, at least as long as we only admit integral values of Z. To complete the analysis, we should of course investigate the meaning of non-integral values of Z, but this is not necessary for our purpose.

In this simple discrete example, the only possible deficit is $T = 1$. If the capital of the company should be -1 at the end of an underwriting period, the value of the company to the shareholders is zero. If, however, the shareholders put in new capital $T + Z = 1 + 4 = 5$, they get a refinanced company with the value $V(4, 4) = 6.82$, i.e., they make a gain of 1.82. This means that the *ad hoc* decision will be to raise money to refinance the company.

In this example the expected profit in an arbitrary operating period is $p - q = 0.13$. If the shareholders always are ready to rescue the company from insolvency, the expected discounted value of the profit is

$$W = \frac{v}{1 - v} (p - q) = 6.15$$

4.2.   As our second example, we shall take another discrete case, which has been discussed in detail by Morrill [6]. We shall assume that:

$$\Pr(x = 1) = 12/13 \qquad \Pr(x = -2) = 1/13 \qquad v = 5/6$$

Table 20-2 gives some values of $V(S, Z)$ for this example:

Here the optimal reserve seems to be $Z = 2$. If the company holds a capital

Table 20-2
$V(S, Z)$ = Expected discounted value of dividend payments

S = Initial Capital	Z = Capital required before dividends can be paid			
	0	1	2	3
0	5	4.17	4.89	4.23
1	6	5	5.87	5.24
2	7	6	7.04	6.30
3	8	7	8.04	7.21

$S > 2$, the expected discounted value of the dividend payments is maximized if the reserve requirement is set at $Z = 2$, and the excess $S - Z$ is paid out. If, however, the company's capital should fall below this level, the company may set its reserve requirements lower. If the capital falls to $S = 1$, expected dividend payments will be $V(1, 2) = 5.87$, if the company maintains the reserve requirement $Z = 2$. The company can, however, pay out a dividend of 1, and continue its operations without any reserve capital. The expected dividend payments will then be $V(1, 0) = 6$. Hence it will be profitable for the shareholders to lower the reserve requirement after an unfavorable operating period. It will, however, be even more profitable to refinance the company and bring its capital up to $S = 2$.

In this example the greatest possible deficit is $T = 2$. Should this occur, it will be a good investment for the shareholders to cover the deficit, and in addition bring the company's reserves up to the optimal level. The total outlay to the shareholders will be 4, and in return they will get dividends with an expected discounted value $V(2, 2) = 7.04$.

4.3. As an example of a continuous distribution, let us assume that the density function has the following form:

$$f(x) = k\alpha e^{-\alpha x} \qquad \text{for } x > 0$$

$$f(x) = (1 - k)\alpha e^{\alpha x} \qquad \text{for } x < 0$$

In this case there is no upper limit to the company's gain, so the example may be a little unrealistic—at least in non-life insurance.

Suppressing the argument Z, we can write the integral equation of para. 2.4 as follows:

$$V(S) = v(1 - k) \, \alpha e^{-\alpha S} \int_0^S V(x) e^{\alpha x} \, dx$$

$$+ vk\alpha e^{\alpha S} \int_S^Z V(x) e^{-\alpha x} \, dx$$

$$+ vk V(Z) e^{\alpha(S-Z)} + \frac{vk}{\alpha} e^{\alpha(S-Z)}$$

Differentiating twice, we find that the integral equation can be reduced to the differential equation

$$(1 - v) \alpha^2 V(S) + v(1 - 2k) \alpha V'(S) - V''(S) - V''(S) = 0$$

which has the general solution:

$$V(S) = C_1 e^{r_1 S} + C_2 e^{r_2 S}$$

Here r_1 and r_2 are the roots of the characteristic equation

$$r^2 - v(1 - 2k)\alpha r - (1 - v)\alpha^2 = 0$$

and the constants C_1 and C_2 must be determined so that the general solution of the differential equation also is a solution of the integral equation.

Taking $\alpha = 1$, $v = 0.97$, and $k = 0.603$, we find:

$$V(S, Z) = \frac{143 \, e^{0.1S} - 91 \, e^{-0.3S}}{16 \, e^{0.1Z} + 21 \, e^{-0.3Z}}$$

Table 20-3 gives the value of $V(S, Z)$ for some selected values of S and Z.

It is easy to verify that $V(S, Z)$ has a maximum for $Z = 3.45$, and that $V(3.45, 3.45) = 5.67$. In this example there is no limit to the deficit T, which can occur at the end of an operating period. From the result in para. 3.3 it follows that it will be a good investment to rescue the company if

$$T < V(Z, Z) - Z = 5.67 - 3.45 = 2.22$$

The argument in para. 3.4 implies, however, that it will be profitable to rescue the company as long as the deficit $Y < 6.65$.

4.4. It may be interesting to consider the probability of ruin in connection

Table 20-3
$V(S, Z)$ = Expected discounted value of dividend payments

S^Z	0	1	2	3	4	5	6
0	1.41	1.57	1.68	1.74	1.73	1.68	1.60
1	2.41	2.74	2.93	3.02	3.02	2.94	2.70
2	3.41	3.74	4.03	4.16	4.16	4.04	3.84
3	4.41	4.74	4.03	5.21	5.20	5.14	4.88
4	5.41	5.74	6.03	6.21	6.19	6.02	5.70
5	6.41	6.74	7.03	7.21	7.19	6.98	6.60
6	7.41	7.74	8.03	8.21	8.19	7.98	7.53

with the last example. If the company's capital is equal to the optimal reserve, i.e., $S = Z = 3.45$, the probability that the company shall be ruined at the end of the next underwriting period, is

$$F(-Z) = (1 - k)\, e^{-Z} = 0.01$$

For the sake of argument we shall assume that this is accepted as adequate security for the policy holders. If the company's capital should fall to $S = 1$, the probability of ruin at the end of next period is

$$F(-S) = (1 - k)\, e^{-S} = 0.1$$

which is far less acceptable. According to the orthodox theory of risk, the company should now seek a reinsurance arrangement, which will bring the probability of ruin down to an acceptable level. This probability is, however, irrelevant. The security of the policy holders does not depend on the probability that the company shall become insolvent, but on the probability that the company shall become so insolvent that it is not worth rescuing. With the argument of para. 3.3 this probability is

$$F(-S - T) = (1 - k)e^{-S-T} = 0.01$$

which may be quite acceptable.

With the argument of para. 3.4 this probability is

$$F(-Y) = (1 - k)e^{-Y} = 0.0005$$

which is even more acceptable.

5. Concluding Remarks

5.1.   The more orthodox theories of risk have been criticized for many reasons. The criticism has not always been very articulate, and neither have the replies. The subject has been discussed by actuaries for decades, but practical insurance people seem to have taken little part in this discussion. They seem in general to have considered both the theory of risk and the discussion around it as irrelevant to the problems which have to be solved by an insurance company in the real world.

The point we have tried to make in this paper, is that most studies in the actuarial theory of risk ignore the economic facts of life. The real weakness of the theory seems to be Assumption (ii) in para. 2.1. This assumption implies that the company will attract business of the same quality, regardless of its financial situation. This is a most unrealistic assumption, but it does not seem easy to modify it without constructing a general theory for the insurance market. Practical insurance men seem well aware that the assumption is unrealistic. Insurance companies usually advertise that they hold large reserves, presumably to attract business. If an insurance company goes into liquidation, it is usually because it has lost the power to attract good business, and not that random fluctuations have brought it to insolvency.

5.2.   It may be appropriate to conclude with a quotation from Adam Smith: ". . . every individual is . . . led by an invisible hand to promote an end which was no part of this intention. By pursuing his own interest, he frequently promotes that of the society more effectually than when he really intends to promote it." ([7], Book IV, Chapter 2).

When an actuary tries to apply the theory of risk, he usually intends to see that the customers of the insurance company obtain adequate security. Our examples indicate that the "invisible hand" may lead the actuary to do a better job of this, if he looked after the profits of his employers—the owners of the company.

References

1.   Blackwell, D. "Discrete Dynamic Programming," *The Annals of Mathematical Statistics* 33 (1962): 719–726.
2.   Borch, K. "Control of a Portfolio of Insurance Contracts," *The ASTIN Bulletin* 4 (1966): 59–71.
3.   ——. "A Utility Function Derived from a Survival Game," *Management Science, Series B,* 12 (1966): 287–295.
4.   ——. "The Theory of Risk" (with discussion), *Journal of the Royal Statistical Society, Series B,* 29 (1967): 423–467.
5.   Finetti, B. de. "Su una Impostazione Alternativa della Theoria Collettiva del Rischio," *Transactions of the XV International Congress of Actuaries* (1957): 433–443.
6.   Morrill, J. "One-Person Games of Economic Survival," *Naval Research Logistics Quarterly* 13 (1966): pp. 49–69.
7.   Smith, A. *The Wealth of Nations* (Edinburgh, 1776).

Part V
Insurance and Capital Markets

The decisions made by the investment department of an insurance company are in their structure very similar to those made in the company's underwriting and reinsurance departments. The investment manager presumably seeks to obtain the highest possible return on the company's funds, without running unacceptable risks. Similarly those in charge of underwriting and reinsurance will seek high underwriting profit but will sacrifice some of this expected profit in order to avoid risk.

It is not possible to say much about how these two sides of the company's activity are coordinated in practice. In the literature the two activities are, however, almost invariably treated in separate, watertight compartments. If a separation of this kind should occur in practice, it may be due to the basic attitude of the governmental supervision of private insurance companies. The ideas behind this supervision have rarely been spelled out in an operational manner, but in general they run as follows.

Let $F(x)$ be the claim distribution of the portfolio of insurance contracts held by the company, and let S be the reserve funds of the company. If claim payments exceed S, the company will be ruined, i.e., it will be unable to meet its obligations under the insurance contracts it has underwritten. The probability of this event is

$$\Pr(x > S) = 1 - F(S) = 1 - \alpha \qquad (1)$$

The supervisory authorities will usually require that the reserve fund S be so large that the ruin probability is very small. How small the probability should be in order to be acceptable, is usually an open question.

The value of the company's reserves at the time when claims are paid will in general also be a stochastic variable, say y, with the distribution $G(y)$. In its supervision of the company's investments the government will require that the probability

$$\Pr(y \geqslant S) = \beta \qquad (2)$$

be close to unity. This is achieved by requiring that the company's investments and the evaluation of the assets be "conservative." In theory $\beta = 1$ can be achieved if the company holds a reserve in cash equal to S, but in practice this will usually be impossible.

The traditional separation of the supervision of the company's investment and underwriting activities is not really necessary. If all the government wants is to secure that an insurance company be able to meet its obligations with a probability close to one, the relevant probability is

$$\Pr(y \geqslant x) = \Pr(y - x \geqslant 0)$$

If x and y are stochastically independent, we have

$$\Pr(y \geqslant x) = \int_0^\infty \left\{ \int_x^\infty dG(y) \right\} dF(x) = 1 - \int_0^\infty G(x) \, dF(x) \qquad (3)$$

If $\Pr(y = S) = 1$, the last expression reduces to $F(S)$.

The governmental supervision can achieve its objectives by requiring that (3) should be above a certain value, say γ, close to one, i.e.,

$$\Pr(y \geqslant x) > \gamma$$

This should be simpler than the current practice which seems to require

$$\Pr(x \leqslant S) > \alpha$$

$$\Pr(y \geqslant S) > \beta$$

and presumably that $\alpha\beta > \gamma$, where γ represents the standard set by the government.

Practical insurance people seem to be well aware that the company's investment and underwriting reinsurance activities ought to be coordinated, and there are good reasons to assume that such coordination takes place in practice. The only evidence available in the literature is, however, the all too few papers developing the "matching principle" of Redington, and this work does not consider risk, i.e., the possibility of deviations from the expected values.

Redington suggested that a life insurance company could place its reserves in bonds of different maturities, so that total receipts (interest + redeemed principals) in each period are equal to the company's expected payments under the insurance contracts in its portfolio. When receipts and payments are matched in this way, it is not necessary to compute the values of the two cash flows discounted at some rate of interest. The solvency of the company will be independent of fluctuations of interest rates and bond prices, provided of course that actual payments are equal to the expected.

This last assumption may be important, in both theory and practice. A life insurance company that applies the matching principle will usually have to hold a substantial part of its portfolio in very long-dated bonds. In practice most life insurance companies seem to hold less long-dated bonds than they should, according to the matching principle. Wehrle has suggested that the explanation may be that there are not enough long-term bonds in the market. Other authors, particularly in the 1950s, have suggested that insurance companies expected interest rates to increase, and therefore preferred to hold bonds of relatively short maturity. The simplest explanation may, however, be that the companies want to maintain a reasonably liquid position, because there is a risk that claim payments may exceed the expected values.

Chapter 21 takes up the ideas of Redington and indicates how they can be applied also when one allows for deviations from the expected values.

Chapter 22 deals with some aspects of government supervision of private insurance companies. The basic idea behind the paper is very simple. If the insurance contracts (policies) sold by an insurance company shall offer adequate security, the company must be able to call on a considerable reserve capital if large claims should occur. Normally these reserves will be equity capital, which the insurance company must obtain from the capital market. The market will be prepared to provide this capital only if the prospective profits in insurance compare favorably with other investment opportunities. Profits in insurance obviously depend on the premium level. If the government insists that premiums should be kept at a low and "reasonable" level, profits may become so low that the insurance company is unable to attract the necessary reserve capital in a free competitive market. This leads to the rather trivial conclusion that government supervision and regulation cannot secure the public good quality insurance at low premiums—unless, of course, the government itself is prepared to provide the reserve capital, or a guarantee that insurance contracts will be fulfilled. This should be well known, but it may be of interest to develop simple mathematical models, which explain the connection between the capital market, and the security which private insurance companies can offer at a given premium level.

The model may have some relevance in other regulated industries, such as telephone service and electricity supply. The quality of the service offered by such industries can to some extent be measured by the probability that services will break down. This probability can obviously be reduced if the companies invest more in reserve capacity. The capital for such investments can, however, be obtained from the market only if prospective profits of the industries are considered as satisfactory, i.e., if the industries are allowed to charge a sufficiently high price for their services.

In the models presented in Chapters 21 and 22, only the total premium receipts of the insurance company is relevant. This total is the sum of the premiums for a large number of insurance contracts, which usually fall in groups of different nature. To the company it is not a pressing problem to make sure that the premium paid for each contract, or each group of contracts is "fair" or "correct," but it is vital that the total amount should be sufficient. It is, of course, not desirable that some groups of insurance buyers consistently subsidize others. In most countries the supervisory authorities have tried to prevent such subsidization, at least in life insurance. In non-life insurance it seems to be assumed, fairly generally, that competition between insurance companies will make grossly "unfair" subsidization impossible. It should, however, be noted that in principle it may be impossible to determine when a premium is unfair, or whether subsidization takes place. In any industry the allocation of overhead costs to different products must to some extent be arbitrary. This is well known, but in insurance there are additional complications which may be less well known and understood. The "direct cost" of an insurance contract is the claim payment, which must be represented by a stochastic variable. The distribution of this variable may change from one period to another, and such changes may require adjustment of the premium. It is, however, usually difficult to decide if such structural changes really have taken place. Only if claims have been consistently above (or below) the expected value for some time, will it be possible to decide that the deviations cannot be due to random fluctuations. Experienced insurance men may often suspect for some time, that one class of insurance contracts subsidizes another, before sufficient experience has accumulated so that a significant statistical test can be carried out.

Chapter 23 indicates how game theory can be used to determine premiums for different classes of insurance, when the required total premium for all classes is given. The paper suggests that the Shapley value will give reasonable premium for all classes of risk groups. When the paper was written, the game theoretical concept "core" had not found a central place in economic theory. Today it would be natural to use, not the Shapley value, but the core in the analysis. This would give intervals, and not unique values, for the premiums of different risk classes. The intervals will, however, be narrow if the number of contracts in all classes is large.

Problems of this kind are discussed in detail in a recent book by Telser, *Competition, Collusion and Game Theory* (Macmillan, 1972), although without references to insurance.

21

The Optimal Portfolio of Assets in an Insurance Company

1. An Introductory Example

1.1. The liabilities of an insurance company will generally consist of a portfolio of insurance contracts. This portfolio can be changed by reinsurance arrangements, and the problem of the company is to find the arrangement which gives the best possible, i.e., the optimal portfolio. This is a familiar problem, which has been discussed at great length in the literature on reinsurance.

The company's liabilities must be balanced by assets, which usually will consist of a portfolio of investments. It is a problem of obvious interest, and possible importance, to determine the optimal portfolio, also on the asset side of the company's balance sheet. This problem has so far received little attention in actuarial literature, although it has been studied intensively by economists, e.g., by Markowitz [6].

In this paper we shall try to apply these ideas from economic theory to the problems of insurance companies. Since the ideas may be unfamiliar, we shall begin by studying an extremely simple example. This example may, in spite of its simplicity, bring out some of the essential features of the more general problems, which we really want to study.

1.2. Let us consider an insurance company in the following situation:

(i)   The company's liabilities consist of a portfolio of insurance contracts, with the claim distribution $F(x)$, i.e., the probability that total claim payments shall not exceed x is $F(x)$. For the sake of simplicity we shall assume that a density function $f(x) = F'(x)$ exists.

(ii) The company's assets consist of a capital Y. We shall assume that the company is solvent in the usual actuarial sense, so that Y is greater than the expected value of claim payments, i.e.,

$$Y > \int_0^\infty xf(x)\,dx$$

The probability that this company shall be ruined is $1 - F(Y)$. In the following we shall usually assume that Y is so great that this possibility can be ignored for practical purposes.

1.3. Let us next assume that the company can invest its capital so that it

329

earns a rate of return r. If, however, it should be necessary to liquidate a part of the investment to pay claims, it will cost the company an amount C.

If the company invests an amount $Y - y$, and retains a cash balance of y, expected return from the investment will be

$$P(y) = r(Y - y) - C \left\{1 - F(y)\right\}$$

It is natural to assume that the company will seek the value of y which maximizes $P(y)$, and consider this the *optimal cash balance*. If such a value of y exists in the interval $0 < y < Y$, it must be a root of the equation

$$P'(y) = -r + Cf(y) = 0$$

or $f(y) = \dfrac{r}{C}$

If this equation has no roots in the relevant interval, expected returns is maximized either for $y = 0$ or $y = Y$. If the equation has two or more roots, a more detailed discussion is required in order to determine the optimal investment.

1.4. As a concrete example, let us take $f(x) = e^{-x}$, $Y = 3, r = 1$, and $C = 2$. The equation then becomes

$$e^{-y} = \tfrac{1}{2}$$

and the solution is $y = 0.7$.

This means that the optimal policy for the company is to invest an amount 2.3, and keep an amount of cash equal to 0.7.

In our example expected claim payment is

$$\int_0^\infty xe^{-x}\, dx = 1$$

It may seem a little surprising that the company shall keep a cash balance smaller than the expected claim payment. The intuitive explanation is, that the claim distribution is so skew that it is worthwhile keeping a smaller cash balance, and taking the risk that it shall not become necessary to liquidate the investment. This is illustrated by Table 21-1, which gives expected investment income for different cash balances.

1.5. Our simple example can by no means be considered as realistic in the sense that it represents the investment problems, which an insurance company

Table 21-1

y = amount kept in cash	0	0.5	0.7	1.0	1.5	2.0	2.5
$P(y)$ = Expected investment income	1	1.28	1.41	1.36	1.15	0.83	0.43

has to deal with in real life. The model does, however, bring out two points of general validity:

The optimal investment depends on:

(i) The nature of the available investment opportunities—in our example the ratio r/C.
(ii) The commitments of the investor—in our case the claim distribution $F(x)$.

The claim distribution can, as we have noted, be changed by reinsurance arrangements. This means that the investment and reinsurance decisions should be analyzed together, and that the ultimate aim should be to find decisions which are jointly optimal.

Practical insurance people will probably find this a trivial and obvious conclusion, but theory has tended to separate the two problems. Actuaries have discussed reinsurance arrangements for generations, often with the explicit purpose of reducing the fluctuations in the company's underwriting results, but have only occasionally indicated that these fluctuations may be cancelled, or accentuated by fluctuations in the company's investment results. On the other hand, economists have produced an extensive literature on investment problems, not usually referred to by actuaries. The key word in this literature has, during the last years, been "portfolio selection," a term created by Markowitz [5, 6], and the problem is to determine the optimal portfolio of assets—or securities—when the amount available for investment is given. In the search for the optimal portfolio, little attention has been paid to the contingent commitments of the investor, a problem which should be relevant, also if the investor is not an insurance company.

2. Generalization of the Simple Example

2.1. Let us first, as a natural generalization, assume that n different investment opportunities are available to the company. Let investment opportunity i be characterized by

r_i = rate of return

C_i = cost of liquidation

If the company invests an amount y_i in opportunity i ($i = 1, 2, \ldots, n$), and retains an amount of cash equal to y_0, the company's portfolio can then be described by a vector $y = \{y_0, y_1, \ldots, y_n\}$, where the elements satisfy the condition

$$y_0 + y_1 + \ldots + y_n = Y \tag{1}$$

If the company has to liquidate some of its investments, it is obvious that it will first sell the assets for which liquidation costs are lowest. It is convenient to arrange the investment opportunities so that

$$C_1 < C_2 < \ldots < C_n$$

It is also convenient to introduce the symbols

$$Y_j = \sum_{i=0}^{j} y_i$$

The expected return from the portfolio, described by y, is then

$$P(y) = \sum_{i=1}^{n} r_i y_i - \sum_{i=1}^{n} C_i \left\{ 1 - F(Y_{i-1}) \right\}$$

where the sums include only the values of i for which $y_i > 0$.

The problem of the company is now to maximize $P(y)$, subject to the condition (1), and $y_i \geqslant 0$ ($i = 1, 2, \ldots, n$).

2.2.   In the preceding paragraph we have arrived at a programming problem, which is rather intricate—because $P(y)$ has discontinuities for $y_i = 0$.

The simplest approach to the problem seems to be to write

$$P = \sum_{i=1}^{n} r_i(Y_i - Y_{i-1}) - \sum_{i=1}^{n} C_i \left\{ 1 - F(Y_{i-1}) \right\}$$

and as a first step maximize this function without restrictions. Partial differentiation will then give the first-order conditions

$$\frac{\partial P}{\partial Y_{i-1}} = r_{i-1} - r_i + C_i f(Y_{i-1}) = 0$$

or $f(Y_{i-1}) = \dfrac{r_i - r_{i-1}}{C_i}$ $i = 1, 2, \ldots, n$

where $r_0 = 0$.

We must then investigate the solution indicated by these conditions, and check if it is meaningful (i.e., that $y_i \geqslant 0$), and if it really maximizes P.

2.3.   In an attempt to make these points clear, we shall study two numerical examples. We shall as in para. 1.4 take $f(x) = e^{-x}$, and

$r_1 = 1$ $C_1 = 2$

$r_2 = 2$ $C_2 = 10$

The conditions in the preceding paragraph indicate the solution

$Y_0 = y_0 = 0.7$

$Y_1 = y_0 + y_1 = 2.3$

For $Y = y_0 + y_1 + y_2 = 4$, the indicated optimal portfolio is $y = \{0.7, 1.6, 1.7\}$. It is easy to verify that this portfolio will give an expected investment income $P(0.7, 1.6, 1.7) = 3.00$, and that this actually is a maximum.

Table 21-2 gives $P(y_0, y_1, y_2)$ for some portfolios.

2.4.   If in the example above $Y = 3$, the first-order conditions are the same, and they suggest that the optimal portfolio is $y \{0.7, 1.6, 0.7\}$. We find $P(0.7, 1.6, 0.7) = 1.00$, and it is easy to see from Table 21-3 that this is not a maximum. The actual maximum is given by $P(0.7, 2.3, 0) = 1.30$.

Table 21-2
Expected investment income. Assets: $Y = 4$

$y_1 \backslash y_2$	0	1.0	1.5	2.0	2.5	3.0
0	0	1.50	2.18	2.65	2.77	2.32
1.0	0.90	2.23	2.74	2.92	2.56	1.33
1.5	1.34	2.56	2.95	2.94	2.27	—
2.0	1.73	2.77	2.97	2.65	—	—
2.5	2.05	2.79	2.68	—	—	—
3.0	2.27	2.50	—	—	—	—
4.0	2.00	—	—	—	—	—

Table 21–3

Expected investment income. Assets: $Y = 3$

$y_1 \backslash y_2$	0	0.5	1.0	1.5	2.0
0	0	0.12	0.65	0.77	0.32
1.0	0.73	0.73	0.92	0.56	0.68
1.5	1.05	0.95	0.96	0.27	–
2.0	1.27	0.95	0.65	–	–
2.5	1.29	0.68	–	–	–
3.0	1.00	–	–	–	–

The interpretation of this example is that the second investment opportunity is attractive to a rich company, but that it is not sufficiently liquid for a
company with small free reserves.

2.5.   In our example we have so far assumed that liquidation costs C_i are
independent of the size of the investment, and of the part of the investment
which must be liquidated in order to pay claims. These assumptions may be
realistic in some cases, for instance by investment in real estate and other indivisible assets. They did, however, lead to discontinuities in the return function
$P(y)$, and this made the programming problem difficult. It is, therefore, desirable
to investigate some alternative assumptions.

Let us assume that our company has total assets equal to Y, and keeps a
cash balance y. If claim payments amount to $x > y$, the company will have to
pay a penalty $c(x - y)$. We can interpret c as the expected loss per unit, if an
investment has to be liquidated at an inconvenient time. We can also take c as
the interest rate, which the company has to pay, if it borrows in the market,
rather than selling assets in order to settle unexpected claims.

Under our assumptions, the expected investment income of the company
will be

$$P(y) = r(Y - y) - c \int_y^\infty (x - y)f(x)\, dx$$

The first-order condition for a maximum is

$$\frac{dP}{dy} = -r + c \int_y^\infty f(x)\, dx = 0$$

or $F(y) = 1 - \dfrac{r}{c}$

2.6.   The formulas above correspond to those found in para. 1.3 for the
other model. They can be generalized in the same way as in para. 2.1. If the company holds a portfolio $\{y_0, y_1, \ldots, y_n\}$, expected investment income is

$$P(y) = \sum_{i=1}^{n} r_i y_i - \sum_{i=1}^{n} c_i \int_{Y_{i-1}}^{Y_i} (x - Y_{i-1}) f(x)\, dx$$

Here r_i is the rate of return, and c_i the unit cost of liquidation for investment i. As before we have $c_1 < c_2 \ldots < c_n$.

Writing

$$P = \sum_{i=1}^{n} r_i(Y_i - Y_{i-1}) - \sum_{i=1}^{n} c_i \int_{Y_{i-1}}^{Y_i} (x - Y_{i-1}) f(x)\, dx$$

we find the first-order conditions for a maximum

$$\frac{\partial P}{\partial Y_i} = r_i - r_{i+1} - (c_{i+1} - c_i) F(Y_i) + c_{i+1} - c_i = 0$$

or $\quad F(Y_i) = 1 - \dfrac{r_{i+1} - r_i}{c_{i+1} - c_i} \qquad i = 0, 1, \ldots, n-1$

where $c_0 = r_0 = 0$.

These conditions will only *indicate* a solution, and some care is required to determine the portfolio, which actually is optimal. There are, however, no real difficulties involved. It is easy to see that if the conditions should give, for instance, $Y_{i-1} > Y_i$, there will be no investment in opportunity i, i.e., we must have $y_i = 0$.

2.7. Another assumption, which also may be realistic in some cases, is that liquidation costs are proportional to the size of the investment, i.e., the cost of liquidating investment i is $c_i y_i$. Expected investment income will then be

$$P(y) = \sum_{i=1}^{n} r_i y_i - \sum_{i=1}^{n} c_i y_i \left\{ 1 - F(Y_{i-1}) \right\}$$

We shall not discuss this model in any detail, since it does not contain any significant new elements. It is easy to see that the model will give the optimal portfolio as a continuous function of $y = \{y_0, y_1, \ldots, y_n\}$, but that the expressions will be more complicated than in the two other examples.

It is evident that all the models we have are of the same structure as those studied in the *Inventory Theory*, created by Arrow, Harris and Marschak [1] and developed by others, particularly by Bellman [2]. In this theory one seeks to determine the optimal inventory, which a firm should keep when its sales are known only in a stochastic sense. The firm must then balance storage costs against the losses it will suffer if it should be unable to meet demand from its customers. There is a vast literature on such inventory problems, and this literature suggests a number of ways in which our simple models can be generalized.

It also seems that our models represent a generalization of the collective risk theory, as has been suggested in another paper [3]. In this theory one usually considers the "probability of ruin," or the probability that the company's reserves shall fall below a certain inconveniently low level. This is not a complete theory, since it does not tell us what probabilities should be considered as acceptable, and how much the company should be willing to pay for a reduction in the probability of such unpleasant events. The models we have studied indicate that we can obtain the missing elements by considering the costs incurred if a fall in the reserves should make it necessary to liquidate investments.

3. The Time Element

3.1. In the examples we have discussed so far, we have considered only the total amount paid to settle claims under the insurance contracts in the portfolio of the company. We have not taken into account the distribution of these payments over time. This means of course that our models are applicable only to insurance companies, which hold exclusively contracts of short duration in their portfolios, i.e., essentially to nonlife companies.

In life insurance, contracts are usually of long duration, and a portfolio of such contracts cannot be represented by a simple claim distribution $F(x)$, as in our examples. If the contracts last for n periods, it is natural to represent the portfolio by a stochastic vector $x = \{x_1, \ldots, x_t, \ldots, x_n\}$, where x_t is the amount paid to settle claims in period t. The portfolio is then completely described by a joint probability distribution $F(x_1, \ldots, x_n)$. This distribution is really the foundation of all actuarial mathematics. The expected discounted value

$$V = \int_0^\infty \cdots \int_0^\infty \left\{ \sum_{t=1}^n v^t x_t \right\} dF(x_1, \ldots, x_n)$$

is the technical reserve of the company. This amount appears on the liability side of the company's balance sheet, and there must be an entry of at least the same value on the asset side.

3.2. Let us now assume that the company's assets consist of a sequence of receipts $y = \{y_1, \ldots, y_t, \ldots, y_n\}$. y_t is the amount which the company receives in period t. We can think of y_t as the sum of interests payable and principals of bonds, which mature in the period. If the company shall be solvent in the classical actuarial sense, we must have

$$\sum_{t=1}^{n} v^t y_t > V$$

This solvency condition can be written

$$\sum_{t=1}^{n} v^t \left\{ y_t - E\left\{x_t\right\} \right\} \geqslant 0$$

It is clearly possible to find values of $y_1, \ldots, y_n$ so that all terms in the sum on the left-hand side are nonnegative. If we choose such a set of values, and if claim payments in each period are equal to expectation, there will be no liquidation costs. The company's receipts in each period will be equal to, or greater than claim payments in the period. This means in a sense that the company is "immune" to changes in the interest rate, as observed by Redington [7]. Fluctuations in the market rate of interest does not affect the company, simply because the company does not expect to buy or sell bonds in the market.

This result has an obvious theoretical interest, but its practical value is limited for two reasons:

(i) One cannot ignore the possibility that claim payments deviate from their expected value.
(ii) It may not be possible to find a portfolio of investments, which gives a sequence of receipts with the desired properties. It has been observed by Wehrle [8] that there are not long-term bonds enough in the American market to make immunization possible for life insurance companies.

3.3. In general we can assume that an investment, which ties up capital for a long time, will give a higher return than a short-term investment. We can bring this element into our model by assuming that

$$y_t = (1 + r_t)^t \, \bar{y}_t$$

where

$$r_1 < r_2 \ldots < r_t < r_n$$

and $\bar{y}_1 + \bar{y}_2 + \ldots + \bar{y}_n = Y$

Here Y can be interpreted as the capital available for investment.
The total receipts of the company is then

$$\sum_{t=1}^{n} (1 + r_t)^t \bar{y}_t = W(y)$$

an expression which obviously is maximized for $\bar{y}_n = Y$ and $\bar{y}_1 = \ldots = \bar{y}_t$
$= \ldots \bar{y}_{n-1} = 0$.

If, however, the company places all its assets in a long-term investment,
which pays a return only on maturity, it is practically certain that the investment
will have to be liquidated to pay claims. The problem is to strike the optimal
balance between high return from long-term investment, and the expected cost
of premature liquidation. We shall not speculate on the nature of these costs, but
we shall simply assume that it will cost the company an amount K_s to liquidate
an investment s periods before maturity.

The investment maturing in period t is $y_t = (1 + r_t)^t \bar{y}_t$. It will be necessary
to liquidate this investment s periods earlier if

$$X_{t-s} = x_1 + x_2 + \ldots + x_{t-s} > Y_{t-1} = y_1 + \ldots + y_{t-1}$$

and $X_{t-s-1} < Y_{t-1}$

Hence the expected cost associated with this liquidation is

$$K_s \Pr \left\{ X_{t-s} > Y_{t-1} > X_{t-s-1} \right\}$$

From these considerations we can formulate the general programming problems, and we can introduce different varieties corresponding to those considered
in Section 2.

4. Formulation of the General Problem

4.1. At a given point of time an insurance company will be in a situation
which can be described by two discrete stochastic processes:

(i)   The *payment process*

$$x_1, x_2, \ldots, x_t, \ldots$$

where x_t is the amount which the company pays in period t to settle claims, made under the insurance contracts in the company's portfolio.

(ii)   The *receipt process*

$$y_1, y_2, \ldots, y_t, \ldots$$

where y_t is the total amount which the company receives in period t. These receipts consist of:

$y_t^{(1)}$ = dividends and interest from the company's investments

$y_t^{(2)}$ = repayment of loans which mature

$y_t^{(3)}$ = premiums payable under the insurance contracts in the portfolio, and possibly other receipts

The periods can be chosen as short as we wish, so it is possible to give a *complete description* of the company's situation by two stochastic processes of this kind.

In practice one settles for a less complete description, and replaces the two stochastic processes by two numbers, representing *assets* and *liabilities*. The difference between these two numbers, is the company's *surplus,* and is often taken as a course measure of how good the situation is. A conscientious analyst will look, not only at the surplus, but at all entries in the balance sheet, in order to evaluate the situation of the company. In reality, this analyst will try to estimate the future development of the company, i.e., he will try to retrieve some of the information contained in the two stochastic processes.

4.2.   The liabilities in the balance sheet are usually computed as the expected discounted value of the payment process, i.e.,

$$V = \sum_{t=1}^{\infty} v^t E\{x_t\}$$

This computation is the responsibility of the actuary.

The assets are in principle computed in the same manner:

$$W = \sum_{t=1}^{\infty} v^t E\{y_t\}$$

This job is, however, not done by the actuary alone. He will usually be responsible for computing the expected discounted value of the premium receipts, i.e.,

$$W_2 = \sum_{t=1}^{\infty} v^t E\left\{y^{(3)}_t\right\}$$

This amount is deducted from V, and the difference $V - W_2$ is usually entered on the liability side of the balance sheet as the *premium reserve.*

The receipt from the company's investment could in principle be computed in the same way:

$$W_1 = \sum_{t=1}^{\infty} v^t E\left\{y^{(1)}_t + y^{(2)}_t\right\}$$

will then be the discounted expected value of the company's investments. This computation is, however, not done by the actuary, but by the "market," which presumably carries out an operation of this kind, although possibly with a discount factor and with probabilities different from those which the actuary will use.

This leads to the familiar balance sheet:

Assets: W_1 = investments at market value
Liabilities: $V - W_2$ = premium reserve

The usual solvency condition is that there is a nonnegative surplus, i.e.,

$$W_1 - (V - W_2) = W - V \geqslant 0$$

4.3.   It may be interesting to note that there are no obvious reasons for preferring the market's evaluation of the assets to an evaluation by the actuary. It is quite possible that the actuary is in a better position to judge the real value of the investment, than the market. The only justification for preferring the evaluation by the market is, that if the company should be forced to liquidate, it will be the market and not the actuary who buys the assets of the company.

It seems, however, that in practice, common sense takes precedence over principles. It is quite possible that a sudden drop of the stock market may make an insurance company technically involvent. This will, however, usually not force the company to liquidate. The actuary and other men of experience are likely to put their own opinion above that of the market. They can find a

theoretical justification for this attitude in the immunity principle of Redington
[7]. Whatever value the market gives a bond is completely irrelevant for an
insurance company, which will hold the bond to maturity—provided that default
can be ruled out.

4.4.   The two stochastic processes, which describe the situation of the
company, can be changed by action taken by the management. The objective of
the management will then be to find the actions which give the best attainable
pair of processes. This means that in order to act really intelligently, the management should have a *preference ordering* over pairs of stochastic processes—i.e.,
the management should be able to decide whether a possible change in the situation represents an improvement or not.

At first sight this may appear a very reasonable requirement, but some
reflection will show that it is not so. It is in general not easy to establish an
ordering over a set of stochastic processes, and the simpler orderings do not
seem to give a realistic representation of the objectives of an insurance company.
These problems have been discussed in other papers [3] and [4], where some
examples are given. The simplest example is provided by the collective risk
theory. The basic idea of this theory is to consider the process

$$z_t = y_t - x_t$$

and establish the ordering by the probability that

$$Z_t = \sum_{j=1}^{t} z_j$$

shall be nonnegative for all values of t. The greater this probability is, the higher
will the process pair rank in the preference ordering.

This leads to a rather unrealistic theory, since the implication of the preference ordering suggested is, that the company really would like to quit the insurance business altogether. It is, however, possible to modify the assumptions and
establish objectives, which make more sense.

4.5.   The very general formulation, which we have suggested, may not be
immediately useful in practice. It shows, however, that all actions which affect
the two processes—be it in the fields of investment, reinsurance or sales promotion—should be analyzed together. If decisions in these fields are made in
separate, watertight compartments, the joint outcome may well be suboptimal.
This may be a trivial remark, but it is not inconceivable that a company, which
is extremely prudent in its underwriting, takes considerable risks in its investments, and vice versa.

References

1. Arrow, K. J., T. Harris, and J. Marschak. "Optimal Inventory Policy," *Econometrica* 1951, pp. 250–272.
2. Bellman, R. *Dynamic Programming* (Princeton, 1957).
3. Borch, K. "Una Generalizacion de la Teoria del Riesgo Colectivo," *Anales del Instituto de Actuarios Españoles,* Vol. 5, pp. 13–30.
4. ———. "Dynamic Decision Problems in an Insurance Company," *The ASTIN Bulletin,* vol. 5.
5. Markowitz, H.M. "Portfolio Selection," *The Journal of Finance,* 1952, pp. 77–91.
6. Markowitz, H.M. *Portfolio Selection: Efficient Diversification of Investments* (Wiley, 1959).
7. Redington, F.M. "Review of the Principles of Life-Office Valuation," *Journal of the Institute of Actuaries* 78 (1952): pp. 14–73.
8. Wehrle, L. S. "A Theory of Life Insurance Company Portfolio Selection," *Yale Economic Essays* vol. 1, 1961.

22

Insurance and the Theory of Financial Markets

1. Introduction

1.1 A market is a place where buyers and sellers meet. A financial market is the meeting place for investors who have capital to offer, and for entrepreneurs who want to obtain capital for different purposes. An insurance company will usually have substantial funds available for investment, and will generally come to the market as an investor. The company will then buy a portfolio in the market, and the problem is to find the portfolio which best suits the company's particular investment objectives.

In general insurance companies do not seem to have investment objectives which differ significantly from those of some other investors, such as conservative mutual funds, and little has been done to develop a special theory for the investments of insurance companies. The reason may be that the company's investment activitity usually is carried out independently of its underwriting operations. If the two activities are seen together and coordinated, it may be desirable to develop a specific theory of investment for insurance companies. The first step towards a theory of this kind is made in the work by Redington [6] on the "matching" of assets and liabilities. These problems have been taken up in a few other studies, e.g., [2] and [8], but have hardly received the attention they deserve. In this paper we shall, however, not discuss the insurance company's role as an investor in the capital market. We shall instead study the company as an entrepreneur.

1.2. It may be an unfamiliar idea to consider an insurance company as an entrepreneur coming to the market in search of capital to finance its operations. An insurance company does not need large amounts of capital for plant and equipment, and in most countries an insurance company is not allowed to borrow money to finance current operations.

The main problem in business finance is to obtain the necessary capital from the market at the lowest possible cost. For most firms this is a complicated problem, because the range of choices is wide. The firm may obtain capital by borrowing in the bank on short term, by selling long term bonds in the market, or by selling other kinds of securities, such as ordinary shares, preference shares, debentures and convertible bonds. Usually an insurance company will have no choice in this respect, and the problem is of little importance. Some authors, e.g.,

343

Launie [3] have argued that the concept "cost of capital," which plays a central part in the theory of business finance, can be adapted and applied in insurance. We shall, however, not find this concept useful in the following.

An insurance company does, however, need equity capital, and this capital must, in general, be obtained from the financial markets. In the following we shall study the conditions under which these markets are willing to supply such capital.

2. A Simple Model

2.1. In this section we shall discuss a simple model, which contains most of the essential elements in the situation from real life, which we want to study. Our basic concept is the *insurance contract* which is defined by the following two elements:

p = the premium which the company receives under the contract

x = a stochastic variable which represents the amount the company pays to settle insurance claims made under the contract.

It is obviously possible to define a more general insurance contract, by bringing in the time-element explicitly, and by letting both p and x be stochastic processes. Such generalizations are, however, not necessary for our present purposes.

2.2. We shall now assume that the company has acquired a portfolio of insurance contracts.

Let $P = \Sigma p_i$ be the total amount of premiums received, and let the stochastic variable $X = \Sigma x_i$ represent the amount paid to settle claims. Let further $F(x)$ be the distribution of X. If claim payments exceed the premium received, i.e., $X > P$, the underwriting of the portfolio will bring the company a loss. The probability of this event is:

$$\Pr(X > P) = 1 - F(P)$$

If the company has no reserves, it will be unable to meet its obligations if an underwriting loss should occur. This means that if the probability above is significantly different from zero, the insurance contracts sold by the company will not give adequate protection. It is, therefore, usual to require that an insurance company must hold reserve funds, or equity capital, which can be drawn upon to cover underwriting losses. If these funds amount to S, the probability that the company shall be unable to meet its obligations will be:

$$\Pr(X > S + P) = 1 - F(S + P)$$

2.3.   The concepts introduced above are familiar, and they lead us to ask how much equity capital the insurance company will need in order to operate. The obvious answer seems to be that the capital must be so large that the public has confidence in the company, and is willing to buy the insurance contracts which it offers to sell. In practice this answer is not very useful. The public complains, only too often, about difficulties in understanding and interpreting the fine print in the insurance contract. If in addition the public should be asked to read the company's balance sheet and evaluate the company's ability to fulfill the promises made in big print, the public may well revolt and ask for government protection. The revolt has not taken place, but in most countries the government has stepped in to protect the insurance-buying public. Often the government supervision has been established at the explicit request of the insurance companies, simply because they found it difficult to do business without some official stamp of approval. *Caveat emptor* is not a good foundation for a business which depends on a high degree of mutual confidence.

2.4.   The general objective of government supervision of insurance has been formulated as follows: "To safeguard proposers, policy holders, beneficiaries and any other third party interested in the due performance of the contract" [5, page 10]. This leads straight to minimum requirements for the company's equity capital. The government wants to make sure that the company fulfills the insurance contract, and this means that it must see that the company is able to do so, which finally means that the government must make sure that the insurance company has a sufficient equity capital.

In most cases it will be impossible to set the capital requirement so high that it is absolutely certain that the insurance company will be able to fulfill the contracts. In real life one must settle for practical certainty, i.e., a probability very close to one. The objectives of the supervision can then be achieved by requiring that an inequality of the following form shall be satisfied:

$$\Pr(X > S + P) = 1 - F(S + P) \leqslant \alpha \qquad (1)$$

and take $1 - \alpha$ as a measure of the minimum *quality* of the insurance contracts which the government allows the company to offer to the public.

2.5.   Let us now consider a new insurance company, which proposes to do underwriting that will give it a portfolio of insurance contracts described by P and $F(x)$. If the company shall be allowed to operate, it must obtain an equity capital S, so that the condition (1) is satisfied. This capital must be obtained from the financial market, and we must discuss how a potential investor will evaluate the proposed insurance company. If he provides the required capital S, his net profit will be the stochastic variable y, defined by

$$y = P - X \quad \text{if } X < S + P$$

$$y = -S \quad \text{if } X > S + P$$

It is easy to see that this investment will become more attractive with increasing P, and less attractive with increasing S. If $S + P = Z$ is determined by the condition $F(S + P) = 1 - \alpha$, imposed by the government, the problem is to determine the value of P which will make the investment acceptable to the investor, or to the market as a whole.

As a first step in our approach to this problem, we compute expected profit

$$E\{y\} = \int_0^{S+P} (P - x)\, dF(x) - S \int_{S+P}^{\infty} dF(x) = P + \int_0^Z (Z - x)\, dF(x) - Z$$

and the second moment

$$E\{y^2\} = \int_0^{S+P} (P - x)^2\, dF(x) + S^2 \int_{S+P}^{\infty} dF(x)$$

$$= (Z - P)^2 - \int_0^Z (Z^2 - x^2)\, dF(x) + 2P \int_0^Z (Z - x)\, dF(x)$$

The variance of the profit is

$$V(y) = E\{y^2\} - (E\{y\})^2 = \int_0^Z (Z - x)^2\, dF(x) - \left(\int_0^Z (Z - x)\, dF(x) \right)^2$$

We see that the variance depends on P only through $Z = S + P$.

These expressions bring out more clearly the observations made earlier:

(i) An increase in the premium P, with Z held constant, will increase the expected profit, and leave unchanged the risk, measured by the variance.
(ii) An increase in Z, i.e., in the government's quality requirements, will reduce the expected profit, and increase the risk.

2.6. The investor we have considered will naturally compare the proposed insurance company with investments offered by other entrepreneurs in the market. In order to make such comparisons, he must have some rule which enables him to decide when one investment should be preferred to another. If this rule is consistent, it can be represented by a utility function $u(x)$, in the sense that the investment which is most attractive, also has the greatest "expected utility."

Let us assume that the most attractive alternative to investing the amount S in the new insurance company, is to lend the money out, without risk, at a rate of interest r. The investment in the insurance company will then be preferred if

$$\int_0^{S+P} u(P-x)\,dF(x) + u(-S)\int_0^{S+P} dF(x) > u(rS)$$

This inequality says that the expected utility of the profits obtained by investing in the insurance company, is greater than the utility of the certain profit rS.

Replacing the inequality sign by that of equality, we obtain the equation

$$\int_0^Z u(P-x)\,dF(x) + (1-\alpha)u(-S) = u(rS) \qquad (2)$$

where $\alpha = 1 - F(S+P) = 1 - F(Z)$.

This equation will determine the lowest premium P, which will make the new insurance company an acceptable investment. The two given elements are:

(i) r = the risk-free rate of interest in the market,
(ii) $1 - \alpha$ = probability that the company will be able to meet its obligation, a standard set by the government.

In our model these two elements will determine the minimum premium. Should the government insist on a lower and "more reasonable" premium, the company cannot go to the market and obtain the equity capital necessary to satisfy the quality standard set by the government.

2.7.   The model we have discussed is extremely simple, but it brings out an essential relationship between premium levels and conditions in the capital market. This relationship must have some significance for any insurance company which operates in a free economy, and it may be useful to give a simple numerical example as an illustration. Let

$$F(x) = 1 - e^{-x}$$

$$u(x) = x - cx^2$$

Equation (2) then becomes

$$\int_0^Z (P - x - c(P-x)^2)e^{-x}\,dx + (S + cS^2)e^{-Z} = rS - cr^2S^2$$

From this we obtain a quadratic equation in P:

$$c(1-r^2)P^2 - \left\{1 + r - 2cr^2Z + 2c(1 - e^{-z})\right\}P$$

$$+ \left\{1 + 2c + rZ - cr^2Z^2\right\} - \left\{1 + 2c + 2cZ\right\}e^{-z} = 0$$

Here we take $c = 0.1$ and solve for some selected values of r and Z. The results are given in Table 22-1.

Table 22-1

Minimum Premium when the Interest Rate and the Acceptable Probability of Ruin are given

Acceptable probability of ruin	Rate of Interest		
	0.04	0.05	0.06
10^{-3}	1.70	1.78	1.85
10^{-4}	1.82	1.92	2.03
10^{-5}	1.98	2.13	2.28
10^{-6}	2.13	2.38	2.53

As an illustration, let us assume that the highest probability of ruin which the government will allow, is $\alpha = 10^{-6}$. From $e^{-S-P} = 10^{-6}$ we find $S + P = 14$. If the rate of interest is 0.04, the premium can be set at $P = 2.13$. This will make the company so attractive as an investment opportunity, that it can obtain the necessary capital $S = 11.87$ from the market. Should the interest rate be 0.05, the premium must be set at $P = 2.38$ in order to attract an equity capital of $S = 11.62$.

If on the other hand the government allows a maximum premium of, say $P = 2.0$, the company will not be able to raise a sufficient equity capital. A simple calculation shows:

For an interest rate $r = 0.04$, the company will be able to obtain a capital $S = 10$, which will give a probability of ruin $\alpha = e^{-12} \approx 6.10^{-6}$.

For an interest rate $r = 0.05$, the company can obtain a capital $S = 8$, and the probability of ruin will be $\alpha = e^{-10} \approx 5.10^{-5}$.

3. Discussion of the Simple Model

3.1. Our model brings out a fact which should be well known. Supervision and legislation cannot alone provide insurance of good quality at low premiums. Substantial reserve capital is required, and unless the government itself is prepared to supply this capital, for instance in the form of guarantees of some kind, the capital must be obtained from the market. The amount of capital which can be raised in this way, will clearly depend on the profitability of the insurance business, compared to other investment opportunities in the market.

This argument appears almost self-evident, but it may be unfamiliar. In practice, in their day to day operations, insurance companies do not seem to be particularly concerned about the sufficiency of the equity capital. The reason is clearly that reinsurance arrangements can compensate a lack of equity capital.

3.2. To illustrate the last point, let us return to condition (1) in para. 2.4. An insurance company may be unable to satisfy the government requirement, either because some of the equity capital has been lost, or because the volume of its underwriting is greater than anticipated. The company can then reinsure a quota $1 - k$ of its portfolio, i.e., retain only a quota k. If the reinsurance is obtained on original terms, the company will retain only an amount kP of the premium, and pay only the amount kx if total claims are x. The probability of ruin then becomes

$$\Pr\{kx > S + kP\} = \Pr\left\{x > \frac{1}{k}S + P\right\} = 1 - F\left(\frac{1}{k}S + P\right).$$

By choosing k sufficiently small, the company can bring this probability under the maximum acceptable to the government.

The crucial assumption in this example is that reinsurance on original terms is available. The reinsurer will usually be another insurance company, which may or may not, be subject to the same kind of government supervision as the first company. In any case the reinsurer will also have to watch his equity capital to remain able to meet his obligations with a sufficiently high probability. From these considerations a general picture emerges:

By reinsurance arrangements the companies reduce the probabilities that they shall be unable to meet their obligations. If the reductions which can be obtained this way are unsatisfactory, there will be complaints that the reinsurance market has insufficient capacity. This can only mean that the insurance sector as a whole does not have enough equity capital. The obvious remedy is to increase the premiums, so that more capital can be attracted from other sectors of the economy. This is in fact the only remedy in a world with free competitive capital markets.

3.3. The function of the equity capital of an insurance company is to cover losses in the underwriting. If the premiums are adequate, such losses should not occur too often. The capital can, therefore, be invested in the market and yield a return. It must, however, be invested in assets which are fairly liquid, since the capital at any time can be called in to meet emergencies. The interest rate, r, in our simple model should, therefore, not be taken as the market rate for risk-free loans—of long or short duration. It should rather be taken as the additional return which the investor could obtain if the capital did not have to be kept in a liquid form. Often the government will lay down rules as to how the companies should invest their reserve funds. The stricter these rules are, the greater will the potential loss in earnings be, and hence the higher will be the premiums necessary to attract the capital.

3.4. Our model may throw some light on the discussion about how far an insurance company's investment income should be considered when premium rates are determined. The premiums are usually paid to the company in advance, and some time will pass before they are paid out to settle claims. If the premiums earn some interest during the period they are kept by the company, this income should as every actuary knows, be brought into the calculations.

In the model P will represent the usual premium reserve at the beginning of the underwriting period, and the investment income derived from P should be included in the company's actuarial calculations. The S in the model represents the "free reserves," or the contingency funds of the company. This capital will, in general, have been supplied by investors, who expect a return comparable to that which they could have obtained from alternative investments in the market. In the company's hands the capital S must be kept in a fairly liquid form, and will presumably earn a lower return than if it could be invested without restrictions.

The investors who make capital available to insurance companies, run a risk of total loss, and their capital is likely to earn the modest return usually associated with conservative management. As compensation they will require a share of the company's underwriting profits, and they will not supply the capital unless premiums are set at a level which will give a positive expected profit on the underwriting.

The discussion of this question has on occasions been heated, and this is surprising, since the basic relations involved are clear and simple. The reason may be that the discussion originated in mutual insurance companies, where the questions of ownership may be confused. A mutual company can, when necessary, make an assessment on its members to cover underwriting losses, and does not really need large contingency reserves. It has been argued in another paper [1] that considerations of administrative convenience should determine the size of the reserve funds kept by such companies. To make an assessment is likely to be a costly operation, and reserves should be so high that the probability of this event is very small.

Things are clearer at the other end of the line of insurers. A member of Lloyds must have a personal fortune, which he presumably has invested so that it gives a good return. It has never been suggested that a member with an unusually high investment income should do his underwriting cheaper than other members.

4. Generalization of the Simple Model

4.1.   In this section we shall give some brief indications as to how the simple model of Section 2 can be generalized in different directions.

In para. 2.6. we assumed that all relevant information about the situation in the capital market was contained in one single parameter r, which could be interpreted as the risk-free market rate of interest. This is an obvious oversimplification, and we shall sketch a more general model, often referred to as the *Sharpe-Mossin asset price model* [7, 4].

The model consists of two groups of elements.

(i) m investors. Investor i has an initial capital w_i, and his preferences are represented by the utility function $x - a_i x^2$.
(ii) n asssets or "firms." Firm j will give a profit x_j, a stochastic variable, such that

$$E\left\{x_j\right\} = E_j$$

$$E\left\{(x_j - E_j)(x_k - E_k)\right\} = C_{jk}$$

To this model we add an insurance company, which will give a profit with expectation E and variance V. We shall assume that the profit of the insurance company is stochastically independent of the profits of all firms.

Let further p_j be the market value of firm j, and p the value of the insurance company.

4.2.   We shall now assume that investor i buys ordinary shares in the n firms and the insurance company, so that he obtains a fraction z_{ij} of firm j, and a fraction z_i of the insurance company. This will give him a portfolio with expected profits

$$E^{(i)} = z_i E + \sum_{j=1}^{n} z_{ij} E_j$$

The variance of the profit will be

$$V^{(i)} = z_i^2 V + \sum_{j=1}^{n} \sum_{k=1}^{n} z_{ij} z_{ik} C_{jk}$$

To this portfolio the investor will assign the expected utility

$$U^{(i)} = E^{(i)} - a_i (E^{(i)})^2 - a_i V^{(i)}$$

His problem is now to determine the portfolio which will maximize this expression, subject to the condition

$$pz_i + \sum_{j=1}^{n} p_j z_{ij} = w_i$$

i.e., that he cannot spend more than his initial capital. The problem is easy to solve, and the solution will give us the optimal portfolio $\{z_i z_{i1}, \ldots, z_{in}\}$. The elements of this vector will be the functions of the—so far unknown—market values $p, p_1, \ldots, p_n$. These can be determined by requiring that the market shall be cleared, i.e., that all shares must be held by some investor. This gives the conditions

$$\sum_{i=1}^{m} z_i = 1 \quad \text{and} \quad \sum_{i=1}^{m} z_{ij} = 1 \quad j = 1, 2, \ldots, n$$

4.3.   By making use of these conditions, it can be shown that the value of the insurance company is

$$p = \frac{B_1}{B_1 + B_2} \sum_{i=1}^{m} w_i$$

where

$$B_1 = E\left\{A - \sum_{j=1}^{n} E_j\right\} - E^2 - V$$

$$B_2 = \sum_{j=1}^{n} E_j \left\{A - \sum_{j=1}^{n} E_j\right\} - \sum_{j=1}^{n} \sum_{k=1}^{n} C_{jk}$$

$$A = \sum_{i=1}^{m} \frac{1}{2a_i}$$

This formula shows how p, the amount which investors will pay for the insurance company, depends on:

(i)   The capital available for investment: Σw_i
(ii) Other investment opportunities in the market, represented by E_j and C_{jk}
(iii) The investors' attitude to risk, represented by a_i.

If we now require that $p = S =$ the amount of equity capital the insurance company must obtain in order to satisfy the government condition, we get an equation which will determine the premium P.

4.4. The Mossin-Sharpe model which we have outlined, obviously gives a grossly over-simplified representation of the financial markets in the real world. The model is static in the sense that an investment is assumed to be completely described by a single probability distribution. Further the model rests on the assumption that only the first two moments of this distribution are considered when alternative investments are compared.

In spite of such objections, the model seems to capture some of the essential elements in the real situations we want to study. The model brings out some of the aspects which have to be taken into account when an insurance company considers raising additional equity capital, for instance, to become less dependent on reinsurance.

References

1. Borch, K. "The Objectives of an Insurance Company," *Skandinavisk Aktuarietidskrift*, 1962, pp. 162–175.
2. ——. "The Optimal Portfolio of Assets in an Insurance Company," *Transactions of the 18th International Congress of Actuaries*, vol. 2, pp. 21–31, Munich 1968.
3. Launie, J. J. "The Cost of Capital Insurance Companies," *The Journal of Risk and Insurance* 38 (1971): 263–268.
4. Mossin, J. "Equilibrium in a Capital Asset Market," *Econometrica* 34 (1966): 768–783.
5. OECD: Supervision of Private Insurance, OECD, Paris 1963.
6. Redington, F. M.: "Review of the Principles of Life-Office Valuation." *Journal of the Institute of Actuaries,* Vol. 78 (1952), pp. 14–73.
7. Sharpe, W. F.: "Capital Asset Prices: A Theory of Market Equilibrium under Conditions of Risk," *Journal of Finance* 19 (1964): 425–442.
8. Wehrle, L.S.: "Life Insurance Investment: The Experience of Four Companies," *Yale Economic Essays* 1 (1961): pp. 70–136. A revised version is included in Cowles Foundation Monograph No. 20 (John Wiley & Sons, 1967).

23

Application of Game Theory to some
Problems in Automobile Insurance

Introduction

In this paper we shall study the problem of determining "correct" premium rates for sub-groups of an insurance collective. This problem obviously occurs in all branches of insurance. However, it seems at present to be a really burning issue in automobile insurance. We shall show that the problem can be formulated as a conflict between groups which can gain by cooperating, although their interests are opposed. When formulated in this way, the problem evidently can be analyzed and solved by the help of the "game theory" of von Neumann and Morgenstern [5].

1. Discussion of a Numerical Example

1.1. We shall first illustrate the problem by a simple example. We consider a group of $n_1 = 100$ persons, each of whom may suffer a loss of 1, with probability $p_1 = 0.1$. We assume that these persons consider forming an insurance company to cover themselves against this risk. We further assume that for some reason, government regulations or prejudices of managers, an insurance company must be organized so that the probability of ruin is less than 0.001.

If such a company is formed, expected claim payment will be

$$m = n_1 p_1 = 10$$

and the standard deviation of the claim payments will be

$$\sigma = \sqrt{n_1 p_1 (1 - p_1)} = 3$$

If the government inspection (or the company's actuary) agrees that the ruin probability can be calculated with sufficient approximation by assuming that the claim payments have a normal distribution, the company must have funds amounting to

$$m + 3\sigma = 10 + 9 = 19$$

This means that the company must collect the following amount from the 100 persons:

A net premium   10
+ a safety loading   9
= Total premium   19

Hence each person in this group, which we shall call *group* 1, must pay a premium of 0.19.

1.2.   We then consider group 2, which consists of n_2 = 100 persons for whom the probability of a one unit loss is p_2 = 0.2. If these persons form an insurance company, they will have to pay:

Net premium   20
+ Safety loading   12
= Total premium   32

in order to reach the security level required, i.e., each person will have to pay a premium of 0.32.

Assume now that the two groups join, and form one single company. In order to ensure that the ruin probability shall be less than 0.001, this company must have funds amounting to

$$n_1 p_1 + n_2 p_2 + 3\sqrt{n_1 p_1 (1 - p_1) + n_2 p_2 (1 - p_2)} = 10 + 20 + 15 = 45$$

1.3.   We see from this example that it is to the advantage of the two groups to form one single company. Total payment of premium will then be 45, while it will be 19 + 32 = 51 if each group forms its own company.

The open question is how this advantage shall be divided between the two groups. The classical actuarial argument is that each group shall be charged its "fair" premium. However, this principle has meaning only as far as the net premium is concerned, it does not say anything about how the safety loading should be divided between the two groups. The orthodox method would be to divide the safety loading *pro rata* between the two groups, i.e., to let them pay total premium of 15 and 30, respectively. The "fairness" of this rule is certainly open to question, since it gives group 1 most of the gain accruing from the formation of one single company. In any case the rule is completely arbitrary.

The theory of games has as its purpose just to analyze such situations of conflicting interests. In some cases the theory will enable us to find a solution without resorting to arbitrary rules. In other cases the theory will make it clear that the problem in its very nature is indeterminate, and that some "additional assumption" or "arbitrary rule" is indeed required.

1.4.   In the example we have analyzed, most actuaries will reject as "unfair" the suggestion that both groups should pay the same premium of 22.5, i.e., that each person should pay 0.225. The game theory also rejects this suggestion, but not on the basis of some arbitrary rule of fairness. In game theory one notes that group 1 by forming its own company will have to pay a premium of 19. If the joint company demands a premium of 22.5, group 1 will then break out and form its own company. This will increase the premium for group 2 from 22.5 to 32. Hence it will be to the advantage of this group to offer some concession in order to keep group 1 in the company. For instance if group 1 is charged a premium of 18, it will lose if it breaks out and forms its own company. Group 2 will in this case have to pay a premium of 27, which is considerably less than 32, the premium group 2 will have to pay if it cannot persuade group 1 to stay in the joint company.

1.5. The considerations in the preceding paragraph do not give a determinate solution to our problem.

Let P_1 and P_2 be the amount of premium paid by the two groups. If the groups act "rationally" and form a joint insurance company, we have

$$P_1 + P_2 = 45$$

The groups will stay in this company only if $P_1 \leqslant 19$ and $P_2 \leqslant 32$, hence we must have

$$13 \leqslant P_1 \leqslant 19$$

$$26 \leqslant P_2 \leqslant 32$$

Any pair of premiums which satisfy the equation and the inequalities in this paragraph, will constitute an acceptable solution to our problem.

1.6. We now assume that a group 3 enters the picture. Let $n_3 = 120$ and $p_3 = 0.3$. It is easy to see that if this group forms its own insurance company, the group will have to pay a total premium of

$$n_3 p_3 + 3 \sqrt{n_3 p_3 (1 - p_3)} = 36 + 15 = 51$$

in order to keep the ruin probability under 0.001. If the three groups join to form one company, the total amount premium will be

$$10 + 20 + 36 + 21 = 87$$

As in the preceding paragraph we find the indeterminate solution, given by

$$P_1 + P_2 + P_3 = 87$$

$$4 \leqslant P_1 \leqslant 19$$

$$17 \leqslant P_2 \leqslant 32$$

$$36 \leqslant P_3 \leqslant 51$$

It may seem surprising that one of the two first groups actually may be charged an amount less than the net premium. However, this is not complete nonsense. If for instance group 1 pays only 7, the two other groups together will have to pay 80, which is less than $32 + 51 = 83$ which they would have to pay if *each* of them had to form its own company.

1.7. The rather surprising result in the preceding paragraph cannot materialize if groups 2 and 3 can form an insurance company without group 1. If they form such a company, the amount of premium to be paid will be

$$n_2 p_2 + n_3 p_3 + 3\sqrt{n_2 p_2 (1 - p_2) + n_3 p_3 (1 - p_3)} = 20 + 36 + 19.2 = 75.2$$

It is then clear that the two groups will admit group 1 into their company only if this will reduce their own premium, i.e., lead to a solution where $P_2 + P_3 < 75.2$. This means that group 1 will have to pay a premium $P_1 > 11.8$. However, it will be to the advantage of group 1 to accept this, as long as $P_1 < 19$, the premium the group must pay if it forms its own insurance company.

Similar considerations of the companies which can be formed by groups 1 and 2 and by groups 1 and 3 gives

$$P_1 + P_2 < 45$$

$$P_1 + P_3 < 63.4$$

Hence we get the final solution

$$P_1 + P_2 + P_3 = 87$$

where

$$11.8 \leqslant P_1 \leqslant 19$$

$$23.6 \leqslant P_2 \leqslant 32$$

$$42 \leqslant P_3 \leqslant 51$$

1.8. This simple example should be sufficient to illustrate the power of game theory when it comes to analyzing some of the essential problems in insurance. The basic idea is that a group will have to pay a premium which depends on the alternative actions available, if the group should decide to reject an offer from other groups, i.e., from an insurance company. In other words, the *bargaining strength* of the group will determine the premium. There can be little doubt that this is a more realistic approach to the problem than one based on more orthodox actuarial considerations of "fairness."

During the last decade we have seen that a number of groups, civil servants, physicians, teetotallers etc. have felt strong enough to form their own, usually mutual, automobile insurance companies. A number of authors deplore this development, which they consider a danger to the whole insurance industry. For instance Thépaut [7] states:

> Ces groupements ou mutuelles qui bouleverseraient complètement la distribution de l'assurance automobile et partout de l'assurance tout court, paraissent de nature à mettre en question l'existence même des réseaux d'Agents Généraux des Sociétés.

It is possible to find even stronger statements. It seems, however, that these authors, as long as they argue in the terms of more orthodox actuarial concepts, have difficulties, both in explaining the development, and in proposing remedies.

2. A More General Case

2.1.   In this section we shall try to build a more general theory on the basis of our discussion of the example above.

We shall now consider m groups. Group i ($i = 1, \ldots, m$) consists of n_i persons who are exposed to risk of a unit loss with probability p_i. We shall refer to this set of groups as M. Let S be an arbitrary subset of M.

We assume that the groups in any subset can form an insurance company to protect the members of the groups against the losses, and we assume further that the safety requirements are the same as in the example of the preceding section (i.e., probability of ruin < 0.001).

If the groups in the subset S form an insurance company, the amount of premium they have to pay will be

$$v(S) = \sum_S n_i p_i + 3(\sum_S n_i p_i (1 - p_i))^{1/2}$$

where summation is over all members of S.

Our problem can then be formulated as follows:

Which of the $2^m - 1$ possible subsets will form their own insurance companies, and what premium will then be paid by each of the groups which belong to these sets?

2.2. Let us consider a set S consisting of s groups, and let $\bar{S}$ be the set consisting of the $m - s$ groups which are not members of S.

It is easy to prove by elementary arithmetics that for any S we have

$$v(S) + v(\bar{S}) > v(M)$$

This inequality states the rather obvious, namely that the total amount of premium will be lowest, if all groups join to form one single insurance company.

Hence, if the groups act rationally, we should expect this company to be formed. We have thus found the answer to the first question in the preceding paragraph. The second question can only be answered in part, all we can conclude so far is that we must have:

$$\sum_{i=1}^{m} P_i = v(M) \tag{1}$$

where P_i is the premium to be paid by Group i.

If group i refuses to cooperate with any other group, it will have to pay a premium

$$v(i) = n_i p_i + 3\sqrt{n_i p_i \ (1 - p_i)}$$

If the group acts rationally, it will not cooperate with other groups, if such cooperation gives a higher premium than it can obtain by forming its own insurance company. Hence we must have

$$P_i \leqslant v(i) \qquad \text{for all } i \tag{2}$$

2.3. Any set of values $P_1, \ldots, P_m$ which satisfy the two conditions (1) and (2) constitute in the terminology of von Neumann and Morgenstern an imputation of the n-person game. The conditions are obviously a generalization of those found in para. 1.5.

The solution is indeterminate, in the sense that it gives only an interval in which the premium for each group must lie.

We see this if we write

$$P_i = v(i) - t_i$$

where t_i is nonnegative and satisfies the condition

$$\sum_{i=1}^{m} t_i = \sum_{i=1}^{m} v(i) - v(M)$$

$\Sigma_{i=1}^{m}\ t_i$ represents the gain obtained collectively by the groups if they cooperate and form one single insurance company. How this gain should be divided among the groups is left undetermined.

2.4.   The solution concept of von Neumann and Morgenstern is obviously not entirely satisfactory. A number of devices or additional assumptions have been proposed in order to make the solution completely, or at least more deter-minate.

A fairly innocent looking assumption is that for any set S contained in M we shall have

$$\sum_S P_j \leqslant v(S) \tag{3}$$

This is the same assumption which we made in para. 1.7. It implies that no set of groups will stay in the joint company, if the total amount of premiums to be paid by these groups will be lower if they form their own company. All sets of values $P_1, \ldots, P_m$ which satisfy the conditions (1), (2), and (3) is referred to as the *core* of the game. This term is due to Gillies (see [3, page 194]).

2.5.   As we did for a special case in para. 1.7, we shall use the core to obtain narrower limits for P_i.

Let $M - i$ stand for the set consisting of all groups except group i. Under our assumptions we have

$$\sum_{j=1}^{m} P_j = v(M)$$

$$\sum_{j \neq k} P_j \leqslant v(M - k)$$

By subtracting the inequality from the equation, we obtain

$$P_k \geqslant v(M) - v(M - k)$$

Hence we get the following interval for P_i:

$$v(M) - v(M - i) \leqslant P_i \leqslant v(i)$$

2.6.   We now introduce the symbols

$$\pi_j = n_j p_j$$

$$\pi = \sum_{j=1}^{m} \pi_j$$

$$u_j = n_j p_j (1 - p_j)$$

$$u = \sum_{j=1}^{m} u_j$$

i.e., π_j and u_j are the mean and variance of the losses in group j. With this notation we have

$$\sum_{j=1}^{m} P_j = \pi + 3\sqrt{u}$$

It is easy to see that if u_j is small in relation to u, the inequality in the preceding paragraph can approximately be written in the following form:

$$\pi_i + 3 \frac{u_i}{2\sqrt{u}} \leqslant P_i \leqslant \pi_i + 3\sqrt{u_i}$$

We see from this that a P_i which belongs to the core cannot be smaller than the net premium π_i. The inequality when written in this form, indicates that it will not be possible to obtain a determinate solution by some limiting process.

If $n = \sum_{j=1}^{m} n_j$ increases towards infinity, it is of course trivial that each *person* will have to pay a premium approximately equal to the net premium. However, the group to which he belongs will still have to pay a nonzero safety loading.

2.7. It is clear that in order to get a determinate solution we need stronger assumptions than the three conditions which define the core. These assumptions must state something about how the groups negotiate their way to a final arrangement, how they make offers and counter-offers, and how they compromise or break off negotiations.

Let us first assume that group 1 forms its own company, i.e., that

$$P_1 = v(1)$$

Let us then assume that the manager of this company wants his company to grow at all costs, and that he persuades group 2 to join the company on the condition that the group is charged the lowest possible premium, i.e., that group

1 shall get no reduction in premium owing to group 2 joining the company. This means that group 2 will pay

$$P_2 = v(1, 2) - v(1)$$

If similarly group 3 joins the company on the same conditions, we get

$$P_3 = v(1, 2, 3) - v(1, 2)$$

If group m is the last to join the company, it will be charged a premium

$$P_m = v(M) - v(M - (m - 1))$$

2.8. The premiums $P_1, \ldots, P_m$ which we determined above satisfy the conditions (1), (2), and (3), and hence constitute an acceptable solution. However, we cannot accept this as the final unique solution to our problem, unless we know that the m groups can join the company only in the particular order we assumed.

Altogether the groups can join the company in $m!$ orders. If we consider all these orderings as equally acceptable, it is reasonable that group i shall pay the average of the premium it will be charged in these orderings. Hence we get

$$P_i = \sum_s \frac{(s - 1)! \, (m - s)!}{m!} \left\{ v(S) - v(S - i) \right\}$$

where summation is over all subsets S in M, and where s stands for the number of groups in S.

This solution is due to Shapley [6]. It certainly appears reasonable, although one may hesitate in accepting it as the final correct solution to the rating problem in automobile insurance. One may for instance accept that the differences $v(S) - v(S - i)$ are the essential strategic elements which must determine the premium of group i, but one may suggest a different set of weights, for instance a set giving less weights to the extremes $v(M) - v(M - i)$ and $v(i)$.

It is hard to argue against such suggestions from the rather arbitrary way in which we have derived the solution. However, the Shapley solution can be derived in a number of different ways which may be more convincing than the one we have followed.

2.9. In his original proof Shapley [6] took a quite different approach. He first proved that the set function $v(S)$, usually referred to as the *characteristic function* of the game, can be written as a linear combination

$$v(S) = \sum_R c_R v_R(S)$$

Here summation is over all subsets R of M, c_R are constants and v_R (S) are characteristic functions of symmetric games.

His basic assumptions are, in our symbols:

(i)   The premium of each group is determined by the characteristic function, i.e., $P_i = P_i(v)$.
(ii) In a symmetric game, the participants will divide the gain equally among themselves.
(iii) $P(v)$ is additive, i.e., $P_i(v + w) = P_i(v) + P_i(w)$.

From these assumptions it follows that

$$P_i(v) = \sum_R c_R \frac{v_R}{r}$$

where r are the number of players, or groups in the subset R. It is then easy to show that this reduces to the expression which we found in para. 2.8.

2.10. Harsanyi [2] has obtained the Shapley solution as a special case of a far more general game. In the game studied by Harsanyi each player attaches a *utility* to the gain, and this utility may be different from the monetary value of the gain. The starting point is the Nash [4] solution to the two-person game, according to which two rational players will agree on the solution which maximizes the *product* of the gains in utility. Harsanyi generalizes this to n-person games, and finds that his solution reduces to the Shapley solution if utility is equal to monetary value.

2.11. If the Shapley solution is applied to the two numerical examples in Section 1, we find:

For the two-group example:

$$P_1 = 16 \quad \text{and} \quad P_2 = 29$$

and for the three-group example:

$$P_1 = 14.5 \quad P_2 = 26.9 \quad P_3 = 45.6$$

Whether these premiums are more "reasonable" than those found by more intuitive arguments, is of course open to discussion. However, our premiums have been derived from a few simple assumptions about rational behavior, which seem to have a fairly general validity. This should at least mean that these premiums ought not to be rejected outright in favor of other premiums derived from necessarily arbitrary considerations as to what constitutes actuarial fairness.

2.12. In our model we have assumed that each group of persons behaves as one "rational player" in the sense given to this term in game theory. With our present knowledge of group behavior it is difficult to say much either for or against this assumption.

Our assumption implies, however, that each group attaches the same utility to a given gain, i.e., to a given reduction in the total amount of premium payable by the group. It may be more natural to assume that the utility which the group attaches to a certain reduction in total premium is equal to the reduction obtained for *each member* of the group. Under this assumption the gain t_i of group i will have the utility

$$u_i(t_i) = \frac{t_i}{n_i}$$

If groups in fact behave in this way, the Shapley solution will no longer be valid. We will then have to analyze the problem either with the more general method of Harsanyi, or use Shapley's approach to a game between n persons instead of a game between m groups. This will require some very heavy arithmetics, and we shall not in the present paper pursue the matter any further.

3. Another Numerical Example

3.1. The difference between the traditional approach of fairness and the game theory solution is brought out most clearly if the groups are of very unequal size.

If in the example studied in Section 1, we assume

$$n_1 = n_2 = 10 \quad \text{and} \quad n_3 = 300$$

we find

$$P_1 = 2.20 \quad P_2 = 3.70 \quad P_3 = 111.39$$

Hence the Shapley solution gives the following premiums per person in the three groups:

$$q_1 = 0.220 \quad q_2 = 0.369 \quad q_3 = 0.371$$

The traditional method of making the safety loading proportional to the net premium would give

$$q_1' = 0.126 \quad q_2' = 0.252 \quad q_3' = 0.378$$

3.2. Groups 1 and 2 do not get "fair" treatment if we accept the Shapley solution. However, they can do little about this. If the two groups each form their own company, they will have to pay the following premiums:

$$q_1'' = 0.385 \quad \text{and} \quad q_2'' = 0.572$$

If the two minority groups join and form one company, they do better. If the gain resulting from this cooperation is divided equally, the premiums per person become

$$q_1''' = 0.294 \quad \text{and} \quad q_2''' = 0.481$$

To group 3 it does not matter much whether the two other groups cooperate or not. If group 3 has to form a company alone, the premium per member of the group will be

$$q_3''' = 0.379$$

Hence group 3 can afford to refuse the demand for actuarial fairness from the other groups.

3.3. If all three groups form one company, and if this company charges the same premium to all members, this common premium will be $q = 0.367$.

This means in practical terms that if the Shapley solution is accepted, group 2 will not be able to obtain its own rating, since q_2 and q_3 above are practically equal.

Group 1 will, on the other hand, be recognized as a group of particularly good risks, and will get its own rating. However, the group will have to pay a premium which probably will be considered as "unfair" by any actuary the group may consult.

4. Conclusion

4.1. The particular results which we have arrived at in the preceding sections obviously depend on our very arbitrary assumptions about the safety requirements of insurance companies. It is, however, clear that the whole argument could be carried through with safety requirements or equivalent restrictions in a different form.

It might have been more realistic if we had considered administrative costs instead of safety loading. We can for instance assume that these costs in an insurance company depend on the number of policies n, and on the number of claim payments m.

If we assume that the cost function is of the form

$$a \sqrt{n} + b \sqrt{m}$$

the expected cost of an insurance company formed by group 1 will be

$$C_1 = n_1 p_1 + a \sqrt{n_1} + b \sqrt{n_1 p_1}$$

If this group forms a company together with group 2, expected cost will be

$$C_{12} = n_1 p_1 + n_2 p_2 + a \sqrt{n_1 + n_2} + b \sqrt{n_1 p_1 + n_2 p_2}$$

It is easy to see that

$$C_{12} < C_1 + C_2$$

Hence this model is substantially the same as the one we have studied in the preceding sections. The gain will in this case be a saving in administrative cost.

4.2. In a general analysis we would have to consider the *utility* of the different groups. It has been argued in a previous paper [1] that a utility concept is essential to deeper studies in the theory of insurance. However, the concept is not strictly necessary for our present purpose which is to illustrate how the theory of *n*-person games can be applied to some of the central and most controversial problems in insurance.

4.3. The problem we have studied seems at present to have particular importance in automobile insurance. However, the problem obviously exists in all branches of insurance.

For instance, a number of fires are caused by careless smokers and children playing with matches. Hence nonsmoking and childless home owners could with some right demand lower fire insurance premiums. When they have neither obtained, nor even claimed this, the reason may be that as a group they are not strong enough to form their own insurance company. If they were sufficiently strong, it is likely that the existing companies would offer this group concessions which would balance any advantages the group could gain by forming its own company.

4.4. Our problem may have some real importance in life insurance. During the last decades most companies have become more and more "liberal" in accepting at normal premium, risks which previously were considered as "substandard." The game theory indicates that there may be limits to how liberal a company can be if it wants to avoid a revolt among the "standard" risks, who in the end pay for the company's liberal policy.

References

1. Borch, Karl. "The Utility Concept Applied to the Theory of Insurance," *The ASTIN Bulletin* 1 (1961): 245–255.
2. Harsanyi, John C. "A Bargaining Model for the Cooperative *n*-person Game," *Annals of Mathematical Studies,* no. 40, pp. 325–355, Princeton, 1959.
3. Luce, R. Duncan, and Howard Raiffa. *Games and Decisions* (John Wiley & Sons, 1957).
4. Nash, John F. "The bargaining problem," *Econometrica,* 1950, pp. 155–162.
5. Neumann, John von, and Oskar Morgenstern. *Theory of Games and Economic Behavior* (Princeton, 1944).
6. Shapley, Lloyds S. "A Value for *n*-person Games," *Annals of Mathematical Studies,* no. 28, pp. 307–317, Princeton, 1953.
7. Thepaut, A. "Quelques réflexions sur la réforme du tarif français d'assurance automobile," *The ASTIN Bulletin* 2 (1962): 109–119.

Index of Names

370

Index of Subjects

About the Author

Karl Borch is Professor of Insurance at the Norwegian School of Economics and Business Administration in Bergen. He obtained the M.A. in actuarial science from Oslo University in 1947. The following seven years he spent in different offices of the United Nations in Africa and Asia. In the years 1955–1959 he served as head of the Section for Productivity Measurement and Statistics in the Organization for European Economic Cooperation in Paris. He then returned to Norway, and obtained the Ph.D. in mathematics at Oslo University in 1962. The following year he was appointed to the new chair in insurance in Bergen. He is the author of *The Economics of Uncertainty* (1968) and about 100 papers on insurance and related subjects.